Ice, Fire, and Nutcrackers

T0321402

Ice, Fire, and Nutcrackers

A ROCKY MOUNTAIN ECOLOGY

George Constantz

THE UNIVERSITY OF UTAH PRESS
Salt Lake City

The Defiance House Man colophon is a registered trademark
of the University of Utah Press. It is based on a four-foot-tall
Ancient Puebloan pictograph (late PIII) near Glen Canyon, Utah.

LIBRARY OF CONGRESS CATALOGING-IN-PUBLICATION DATA

Constantz, George, 1947-
 Ice, fire, and nutcrackers : a Rocky Mountain ecology / George
Constantz.
  pages cm
 Includes bibliographical references and index.
 ISBN 978-1-60781-362-0 (pbk. : alk. paper) — ISBN 978-1-60781-363-7
(ebook)
 1. Natural history—Rocky Mountains. 2. Mountain
animals—Adaptation—Rocky Mountains. 3. Mountain
plants—Adaptation—Rocky Mountains. 4. Mountain ecology—Rocky
Mountains. I. Title.
 QH104.5.R6C66 2014
 508.78—dc23
                                                    2014014484

Dedicated to the men and women
who have invested their lives protecting
Rocky Mountain ecosystems;

to the folks who plan, build, and maintain
the trails that gave us access to the heights; and

to the cairn builders,
for they helped us stay on-trail
during the whiteouts.

Contents

Introduction

A Writer's Path

*I had better admit right away
that walking can in the end become an addiction.*

Colin Fletcher, *The New Complete Walker*

I FIND MYSELF DRAWN to wild places that feed certain needs—they nurture my spirit, challenge me physically, and offer lessons about how evolution has shaped living things. One of my favorite regions for satisfying these cravings has been the Rocky Mountains of western North America. This chain of high, windy, cold places not only draws landscape artists and athletic mountaineers, it also hosts a marvelous collection of plants and animals. And each of these montane species features its own suite of remarkable adaptations: the scarlet gilia, a showy member of the phlox family, sports brilliant red trumpet-shaped flowers and actually benefits from being chewed by elk; a jay called the Clark's nutcracker can remember—after several months—exactly where it buried tens of thousands of food caches; and the little hamster-like pika survives the long winter by gathering plant clippings into a haystack and then eating the different kinds of plants in a sequence that promotes their chemical preservation—a neat trick that extends the nutrient value of its stash.

I write about these remarkable slices of mountain life for several reasons. First, I want to share my enthusiasm for viewing Rocky Mountain organisms from an evolutionary perspective. As I encounter folks both at home and along the trail, the conversation often turns to "why" questions. They wonder why the plants and animals they bump into have certain features. Rather than being scattered across the landscape, why do quaking aspen grow in prominent clumps? Why does a rufous hummingbird drop its metabolism to one one-hundredth of its normal rate when it's sleeping? Why do bull elk grow such humongous antlers? The human mind seems to inherently gravitate to questions of ultimate causes.

My second motive stems from my seasoning as a teacher. I want to see people do more backyard biology. Even though the intimate mutualism between Amazonia's bees and orchids and the annual migration of the Antarctic's penguins can offer vital lessons, biology students in the Rocky Mountain provinces and states cannot readily experience these phenomena firsthand. Teachers and their pupils can, however, visit a local mountain park and directly study cloning in aspens by mapping the trees and recording the timing and color of leaf change, or the thermal biology of basking butterflies by measuring the angle between the sun and their wings.

My final motive is to stimulate conservation through appreciation. Over the course of 40 years I have worked as a camp counselor and park naturalist; high school and college teacher of biology, population ecology, and environmental ethics; research ecologist; and manager of watershed education and research programs. I discovered that I could stir a person's curiosity by sharing a quirky nature story, such as how a rattlesnake hunts in total darkness by detecting the infrared radiation emitted by a mouse; how white-tailed ptarmigan thrive in the high, treeless alpine—through the winter!—or how the alpha bitch gray wolf cowers her packmates into tolerating celibacy. Such a story, often driven home by a counterintuitive twist, frequently leads to other connections and broadens the listener's perspective. Sometimes he or she comes to a new understanding—and thence to enhanced vigilance—of a favorite place, like a mountain range or a stream. In essence, I learned how to nurture environmental stewardship by exploiting provocative nature stories.

I responded to these personal needs and intellectual motives by immersing myself in the mountains. Over 13 years I explored the wilderness between the Maligne Range (Jasper, southwestern Alberta) and the Sangre de Cristo Mountains (Santa Fe, north-central New Mexico). Most of my backpacking treks are mentioned in the Thank Yous. About 1,200 miles (1920 km) long and up to 450 miles (720 km) wide, this region includes eastern British Columbia and western Alberta; all of Idaho; the western parts of Montana, Wyoming, and Colorado; and north-central New Mexico.

For convenience, let's break this vast montane landscape into manageable parts. From north to south my eye sorts this lofty realm into four sections, which I'll be referring to throughout the book:

1. Canadian Rockies—extends from Jasper southward to the Canada–United States international border
2. Northern Rocky Mountains—extends from the international border southward through the northern two-thirds of Idaho and all of western Montana
3. Central Rockies—consists of a polygon including the area from Yellowstone eastward to Sheridan, southward through Casper to Laramie, westward through Kemmerer to Pocatello, then back to Yellowstone
4. Southern Rockies—encompasses western Colorado and north-central New Mexico

By hiking through the mountains, I was able to camp among the native plants and animals, observe their habits, and scent their sourness—I bonded with them. At the end of each hiking day, while flat on my pad—coaxing pain from my lumbar muscles—I scrawled a paragraph or two about the day's highlights: my first sighting of a monkeyflower, a falcon's bizarre behavior, an inconsistency between what I had read in the scientific literature and what I observed along the trail. I also jotted questions for later homework.

Once back home I pursued a second kind of relationship with my subjects—a scholarly connection. I retreated to my library and auditioned some of the characters I had met along the trail. The tryout started with a survey of the scientific literature. If I detected an interesting story I assembled the data and recast the account in less technical language.

My process—from hiking to homework to writing—did not deliver a comprehensive ecology of the Rockies. Rather, you hold a series of vignettes on the fascinating, often surprising, adaptations of some of the plants and animals I encountered along the trail. I also picked these topics for their value in illuminating diverse ecological and evolutionary processes.

After reviewing just enough evolutionary biology to make sense of the stories, we'll leave the trailhead and meet a prominent montane bird, the Clark's nutcracker. Its remarkable adaptations introduce us to life in the mountains (chapter 1). The core of the book (chapters 2–21) explores the equally fascinating adaptations of a wide variety of plants and animals. After taking a stab at inferring the general ecological and evolutionary trends in the Rockies (chapter 22), I close by offering my personal view of the region's biggest conservation priority (chapter 23).

Moving to a practical concern, I'd like to say a word about how we will handle jargon. Like other academic disciplines, the fields of ecology, animal behavior, and evolutionary biology are facilitated by technical words. I'll define such words or concepts at their first mention; thereafter I'll assume you'll remember what they mean or will use the glossary.

And finally, I want to introduce you to my backpacking partner—my wife, Nancy. We walked most of these trails together. Without her keen powers of observation and unwavering positive attitude I could not have come to know these inspiring places and their fascinating residents.

A Red Squirrel Sticks Its Landing

A gene is selected on one basis only,
its average effectiveness in producing individuals able to
maximize the gene's representation in future generations.

George C. Williams, *Adaptation and Natural Selection:*
A Critique of Some Current Evolutionary Thought

It's a common scene: late afternoon, the end of a grueling day of backpacking—I'm sweaty and sticky, thirsty and hungry. I pull into the campsite, prop my pack against a tree.

"Chir-r-r-r!" A red squirrel, huddled under its bushy tail, chews me out with its rattle call. This vocalization functions as a "keep out" signal, an advertisement of territory (Lair 1990). The squeaky outburst seems to lift it off its feet. Noisy and energetic, it's quick and jerky, busy.

"I hear you, I hear you, you little bugger," I mumble.

Occasionally, when we were lucky it would put on an acrobatics show—spinning around a tree trunk, jumping from limb to limb, vaulting from one tree to another. At first I dismissed these jumps as simple maneuvers, but when I looked more closely, the squirrel's carefully calibrated leaps, subtle midair adjustments, and precise landings rivaled the performance of an Olympic gymnast that "sticks her landing."

How did my red squirrel come to behave in this way? That is, what evolutionary processes have delivered the modern red squirrel species— and, by extension, all other Rocky Mountain organisms?

To answer these questions I'm asking you to do a bit of homework— just as Nancy and I had to prepare in order to better the odds of a successful backpacking trek. In this introduction I present the basic concepts embodied in what biologists call "the theory of evolution by natural selection" (Darwin 1859; Dawkins 1976; Reznick 2010). The scientific theory will help you appreciate the stories in this book.

The thread that runs through these stories is the power of the theory of natural selection to illuminate why the Rockies' plants and animals—such as my scolding, jumping red squirrel—are the way they are. This approach reflects a particular scientific view of life: the traits of my red squirrel are there because they contributed to the reproductive success of its ancestors. I can make the same point in the present tense: the function of a particular feature of a living squirrel is to maximize the number of its pups that, in turn, survive to have their own young (G. Williams 1966). In this view of life, the population's sustainability—or the "survival of the species"—is merely an incidental by-product of thousands of individual squirrels selfishly pursuing their own reproductive success. In essence, the main creative force that has shaped my red squirrel—and all of Earth's living things—is reproductive competition among individuals (Pianka 1994).

 The Red Squirrel

Red squirrels average 13 inches (33 cm) long and weigh 7 ounces (190 g) (Whitaker 1980; Clark and Stromberg 1987; Streubel 1989). Brownish-red on the upper half, they sport a dark lateral stripe, a light-colored eye ring, and a bushy tail. They are also called pine squirrels and chickarees. According to my informal trailside sampling, the red squirrel is the most frequently seen mammal in the Rockies. Red squirrels can be found from the foothills up to 12,000 feet (3660 m) in elevation. Spruce seeds seem to be a favorite food and spruce-fir forests their optimal habitat, but they can also be found in stands of lodgepole pine, other conifer forests, and even deciduous woods (Ryden 1991).

Red squirrels are solitary. Each individual amasses its own food cache, a midden built of thousands of cones (Hurly and Robertson 1987; Johnson and Crabtree 1999). The cones hold pine nuts. Often assembled at the base of a tree, a midden can be up to 30 feet (9.1 m) across and 1.5 feet (0.5 m) deep (Streubel 1989). A large midden can be several decades old and represent the labor of many squirrel generations. Inside the midden's mound the squirrel excavates a network of tunnels leading to various storage chambers. In winter, while their middens are buried by snow, red squirrels crawl through the burrows. A cost of this food-storing strategy is that martens, weasel-like predators, sometimes tunnel through middens in pursuit of their resident squirrels.

For four to six weeks in the autumn, spruce, fir, and pine cones are fully developed and their seeds are mature. A red squirrel will harvest these cones from outer branches while they are still sealed shut. It will cut cones near the top of a tree for five minutes and then descend and carry them one at a time to its midden.

Red squirrels mate in March and April. On the one day she is in heat, the female suspends aggression and several males congregate in her territory (Clark and Stromberg 1987). One male becomes dominant and defends the female from the other males by chasing and calling (C. Smith 1968). These mating chases are high-energy twirling and jumping affairs. To my eye it looks like the female is weeding out inferior suitors by testing their climbing and scampering skills.

Several predators, including the red-tailed hawk, northern goshawk, bobcat, coyote, and grizzly bear, kill and eat red squirrels (Ryden 1991). When it detects a potential predator a red squirrel emits an alarm call. Escape actions can also include ducking around to the backside of a tree trunk, scampering up a trunk, and jumping from one limb to another.

Modern biologists call this idea the neo-Darwinian paradigm, literally "new Darwin," since it has been built on Charles Darwin's original ideas. The theory holds that evolution by natural selection is the primary cause of change in living things over the long term (Reznick 2010). For natural selection to occur, though, populations of red squirrels—or of any living thing—have to meet three conditions (Alcock 1984):

- There is variation among individuals. Imagine a red squirrel population that includes some individuals with black hair and others furred in brown.
- The variation has a genetic basis. Whether individual squirrels sport black or brown fur is determined by differences in their genes.
- The variation has survival and/or reproductive consequences. Squirrels with brown fur are harder to detect, so they get killed by hawks less frequently than black ones. So, over several generations, and on average, brown squirrels survive longer than black squirrels and thus have more brown babies that, in turn, live long enough to reproduce.

If a lineage satisfies all three criteria, a trait that helps a single individual reproduce more successfully—such as brown fur—can eventually spread through the whole population. A feature that has been shaped by this process and that is expected to continue maximizing individual reproductive success, like brown fur, can be called an adaptation (Ricklefs 1990).

So how does this neo-Darwinian theory explain my red squirrel's aerial acrobatics? Let's start by thinking about the act of jumping. Squirrels jump for a variety of reasons, such as collecting pine cones from outer twigs, dodging a swift Cooper's hawk, or chasing a potential mate during their frenzied courtship ritual. A suite of remarkable adaptations helps the squirrel execute its jumps: the fast-twitch muscles of the hind legs flick the animal forward and upward; the middle ear detects body position and issues continuous signals to the brain; and the tail offers a counterbalance for making midair adjustments in the body's position.

The riskiest part of a squirrel's jump, though, is the landing. And it turns out that a safe landing depends on well-tuned depth perception—the squirrel's ability to precisely discern the distance between itself and another object. And depth perception, in turn, is a function of the distance between its eyes. If the eyes are too close together, a squirrel's depth perception is less discriminating than if its eyes are farther apart.

So how did my squirrel's eyes end up where they are today? For one possible answer let's travel back in time and visit a hypothetical population of red squirrels. They live in a spruce-fir forest on a mountainside, isolated from other squirrel populations. Let's see whether this population meets the three criteria for evolution by natural selection.

First, we assess criterion #1: Does intereye distance vary among the squirrels? To find out, we catch a random sample of 1,000 squirrels and put a caliper between their eyes. We discover that the distance between their eyes, specifically the postorbital breadth measured across the frontal bones at the notch behind the postorbital processes, ranges between 0.51 and 0.57 inch (13.0–14.5 mm), a difference of 12 percent. After graphing our data, we realize that intereye distance falls into three general groups:

- Average-eyed squirrels—About half of the squirrels have eyes that cluster around 0.54 inch (13.6 mm) apart.
- Narrow-eyed squirrels—About one-quarter of the squirrels have eyes closer together than average, about 0.52 inch (13.2 mm) apart.
- Wide-eyed squirrels—The remaining quarter of the sample have eyes farther apart than average, about 0.56 inch (14.2 mm) apart.

With this demonstration of variation in intereye distance, we move on to the second criterion: Does the variation in intereye distance have an underlying genetic basis? After we release most of the squirrels, we perform a simple experiment with a few detainees. In cages we pair males and females with similar eye widths. When narrow-eyed squirrels mate with each other, they produce narrow-eyed babies; wide-eyed parents yield wide-eyed offspring. We conclude that the trait of intereye distance breeds true, that it is genetically controlled.

This takes us to criterion #3: Does the variation in intereye distance have any effect on survival and reproduction? To find out, we monitor our squirrel population for accidental falls. Every day for 10 years we walk the same network of trails, scanning the ground for squirrels. We assume that any dead and injured squirrels that we find below trees have fallen. When we tally our data we discover that, on average, the wide-eyed squirrels are significantly less likely to get maimed or killed in a crash landing than closer-eyed individuals.

To see the outcome of this difference in survival and reproduction, we sit back and watch…for a thousand years. At one squirrel generation per year that's a thousand generations. Slowly but surely we see that the wide-eyed squirrels fall less often, live longer, and produce more pups per lifetime, and that those pups in turn also live long and reproduce bountifully. Thus, wide-eyed squirrels have greater reproductive success than the other squirrels. This slow process, inching along one generation at a time, eventually yields a squirrel population that has, on average, wider eyes than the one we started with. This kind of evolutionary trend is an example of directional selection (Strickberger 1968).

Obviously, however, intereye distance did not continue increasing forever. Why not? It turns out that even while our red squirrels were leaping through trees they were also negotiating tight places, like the tunnels through their middens. But the squirrels weren't alone inside their middens. Martens were also slipping into midden tunnels, tracking down squirrels, and killing and eating them. Thus, because squirrels with big heads and very wide eyes negotiated their tunnels less efficiently, they were at a disadvantage in escaping martens. So, two kinds of selection were happening at the same time: selection for wide eyes, advantageous for landing, was opposed by selection for narrow heads, which was good for escaping martens. In this example, a counteracting selection force helped to limit the eye-widening trend. This is an example of stabilizing selection (Strickberger 1968). Compared to narrow and wide eyes, the trait "average intereye distance" contributed the most over the long term to the squirrels' survival and mating—their ultimate reproductive success—and thus can be interpreted as an adaptation.

In addition to the basic process of natural selection as sketched above, four specialized forms of natural selection may have contributed to shaping the red squirrel's adaptations. The first, called kin selection, occurs in organisms in which individuals are physically close enough to each other that they can influence each other's behavior (Wilson 1975). Kin selection favors traits that increase the survival and reproduction of genetic relatives other than one's own children—such as siblings, nephews, and cousins. So, for example, a red squirrel is more likely to shout an alarm call, and risk announcing its position to a marten, by scolding me and other potential predators, if a niece or nephew lives nearby. Thus, in kin selection the reproductive competition occurs between lineages of genetically related individuals. The theory of kin selection is used to explain some behaviors that may seem inconsistent with reproductive selfishness, like sharing food, cooperatively defending offspring, and even forgoing reproduction. In each case the behavior may not benefit the individual, but it may benefit kin that share the same genes.

The second specialized type of natural selection is called sexual selection, which is competition among the members of one sex for access to individuals of the other sex (Wilson 1975). During the mating season males compete for females, or females choose among males, or both. The theory of sexual selection helps explain why red squirrels do all that chasing: males chase each other in a female's territory (male-male competition) presumably because in the past females have chosen to mate with the most persistently chasing males (female choice). As you will see in later chapters, the theories of kin and sexual selection will help explain other behaviors, like adoption in grizzly bears, as well as a variety of body traits, like the architecture of the bull elk's antlers.

Third, reciprocal altruism may contribute to the evolution of selfless behavior (Trivers 1971, 1985). However, it can be maintained only under a couple of narrowly specific situations: long-term interactions between potential cooperators and minimal cheating. Then individuals can gain more fitness by cooperating than by acting selfishly. Selfless acts can evolve if the animal can count on deferred gain from the favored individual. Two individuals trade altruistic acts. Selection for selfless behavior may occur as long as it's returned in kind. Individuals must discriminate against cheaters, those who accept altruistic benefits without returning the favor. In the Rockies, reciprocal altruism may partly explain food finding in Clark's nutcrackers and alarm calling in marmots.

Finally, the fourth extension of natural selection is called group selection. Although rejected by most biologists for decades, the hypothesis is receiving renewed support. It has been granted new predictive power, especially in hypotheses that attempt to explain the evolution of social behavior (Nowak et al. 2010; Wilson 2012). Several traits, specifically multiple generations living together, cooperating in home defense and parental care, and dividing labor, are seen as prerequisites for the evolution of reproduction by only some individuals. It is important to note that, as I write, the revival of group selection has not achieved a consensus among evolutionary ecologists (Abbot et al. 2011; Boomsma et al. 2011; Strassmann et al. 2011; Ferriere and Michod 2011; Herre and Wcislo 2011). Nevertheless, I believe that a fresh look at group selection is relevant to this book because it may have contributed to the evolution of eusocial behavior in several species of Rocky Mountain organisms, like bumblebees, Clark's nutcrackers, marmots, gray wolves, and Native Americans.

Ultimately, I suspect that all five forms of natural selection will be shown to be relevant. More specifically, I expect that the adaptations of each species, in fact each adaptation of each population, will be found to reflect the action of a unique mix of the five forms of natural selection. That is, each feature will be found to result from an idiosyncratic multilevel selection regime. The challenge I see for the next generation of evolutionary ecologists is to tease apart the relative contributions of each form of selection to the origin and maintenance of any particular adaptation.

With this review of basic evolutionary biology under our belts, we're in a stronger position to explore the adaptations that enable life in the Rockies. So let's tie our bootlaces, heft our packs, and see what lies around the bend.

CHAPTER 1

Nutcracker's Brain

Some trees and birds are made for each other.

Ronald Lanner, *Made for Each Other:*
A Symbiosis of Birds and Pines

BEFORE I KNEW IT we had developed a ritual. It would express itself at the launch of each mountain trek: Nancy and I would drive to the trailhead, recheck our gear, and stress over a missing item. We'd review the trail map, glance skyward, conjecture a short-term forecast, and with great expectations set off down the trail. The first few miles were simple—the clear air invited grand views, the rhythm of boot crunch and staff swing comforted me, a pungent smell begged interpretation. But all the while a vague hunger grew. It didn't resolve until I was stopped in my tracks by the approaching clamor: "Kraaaw kraaaw kraaaw." Seeing a boisterous gang of gray, pigeon-sized birds, I'd whisper to myself, "Hello friends. Yeah, I'm back now."

Intercepting a gang of Clark's nutcrackers reinjected me into the lives of montane organisms, flooding my mind with hypotheses about food storage, hibernation, and social behavior. It's in that first category, specifically how the nutcracker stores and retrieves food, that this fascinating bird has taught me a lot about mountain life. I'm especially amazed by its ability to hide tens of thousands of pine nuts in soil at high elevation—and then find them again many months later. And in one of science's serendipitous outcomes, by learning how this montane bird performs its memory feat, neurologists have gained new insights into how they might mend our own broken brains.

To set the stage for appreciating this bird's remarkable features, let's first review its natural history (Tomback 1998). Although surely known to

Blackfoot, Ute, and other mountain peoples, the Clark's nutcracker was first described for western science by the coleader of the Corps of Discovery, William Clark (yes, he of the Lewis and Clark expedition), and the bird was later named for him. He first saw this mountain bird on the expedition's westward leg at Lemhi Pass in the Bitterroot Range (near Tendoy, east-central Idaho).

On August 22, 1805, Clark wrote, "I Saw to day Bird of the wood pecker kind which fed on Pine burs its Bill and tale white the wings black every other part of a light brown, and about the Size of a robin" (W. Clark 1805). Later, in May 1806, Lewis got closer to its current classification when he associated it with *Corvus*, the crow's genus, and called it a "Jaybird."

Indeed, modern bird taxonomists assign the Clark's nutcracker to the family Corvidae, which includes the common raven, Steller's jay, and black-billed magpie. About the size of a northern flicker and shaped like an American crow, the Clark's nutcracker features a long, sharp beak; black wings, tail, and bill; and obvious white patches on the wings and along the tail. Like woodpeckers, nutcrackers fly with slow wing beats and deep undulations.

The Clark's nutcracker is a creature of the highest montane forests, although the birds occasionally visit the lower pinyon-juniper woodlands (Tomback 1998). In some places they share the subalpine zone with mountain goats—and may even ride the goats' rumps, picking off ticks and warning of approaching predators.

Not just one, but a complex set of adaptations allows the nutcracker to succeed in this extreme environment. For example, it breeds earlier in the year than any other songbird—in late winter. From early February to mid-April the mated pair cooperates in building large, bulky nests on branches 6 to 73 feet (2–24 m) up (Tomback 1998). It may astonish you that a mountain bird would breed in the winter, but nesting this early provides young nutcrackers with enough time to gain weight and practice specialized foraging skills, described in a bit, before the onset of their first winter (Vander Wall and Balda 1983).

The timing of their breeding season, however, means that nutcrackers must be able to incubate their two to five brown- and purple-specked eggs through subfreezing storms (Tomback 1998). To keep the eggs from freezing, both the male and female parents develop an incubation patch. The mates use this featherless swollen area on their belly, which is perfused with a high density of blood vessels, to warm their eggs and brood their young. In other songbirds, where the female is the primary egg incubator, only she develops this hot patch. But in nutcrackers, the male's incubation relieves the female so she can retrieve seeds from her own food cache.

The chicks typically hatch in March, after 18 days of incubation. In the snowscape of late winter and early spring, the only food available to the nestlings is the pine nuts their parents stored the previous fall. In a behavior unique among birds, parents feed young nutcrackers these shelled pine nuts almost exclusively (Vander Wall and Hutchins 1983).

After the juveniles fledge, parent nutcrackers continue to feed them for 13 or 14 weeks (Tomback 1998). During this long dependency, fledglings learn the precise skills needed to extract seeds from pine cones. At first the young birds are awkward, losing their footing on swaying branches and missing the target with their stabbing bill. By late July or early August, though, juvenile nutcrackers can feed themselves (Vander Wall and Balda 1983; Vander Wall and Hutchins 1983). And by September, the semi-independent chicks begin stashing their own seeds.

In many subalpine areas, Clark's nutcrackers harvest mainly the nuts of whitebark pine (Tomback 1998). At 0.06 ounce (175 mg) each, whitebark pine seeds are the largest nuts produced by any of the subalpine conifer species in the bird's range (Vander Wall and Balda 1983). From photographs I took between North Fork and Raid Lakes in the Wind River Range (Old Highline Trail, Bridger Wilderness, Bridger-Teton National Forest, west-central Wyoming), I estimated whitebark nuts to be about half an inch (1.3 cm) long. By weight the seeds contain 21 percent carbohydrates, 21 percent protein, and 52 percent fat (Lanner and Gilbert 1994). It is these large, nutritious, energy-laden pine seeds that power the nutcracker's remarkable wintertime reproduction.

Exploiting whitebark pine nuts, however, requires yet another suite of nuanced adaptations—including a remarkable "sound test" of each nut and a unique cargo pouch for carrying heavy loads. The nut harvest typically starts in mid-August (Tomback 1998). At first the birds shred the immature, tightly closed purple cones. (Our pioneer ornithologists would have served us better by naming it the Clark's "coneshredder" or "nutcacher.") Later, in September, the cones are dry and brown and their loose scales break off easily. But even as the scales are shed and fall to the ground, the seeds remain firmly attached to the cone's core.

After a nutcracker uses its chisel-like bill to extract a seed from its cone, the bird rattles the nut in its bill (Vander Wall and Balda 1983; Tomback 1998). The clicking sound and the seed's mass hint at the kernel's value. A lightweight, hollow-sounding nut, like one that has been mined by an insect larva, is discarded. When a seed is judged to be worthy, though, the nutcracker brings it into its mouth and often drops it into its throat pouch—usually with a backward toss of its head and an upward thrust of its bill. Called the sublingual pouch, this thin-walled elastic storage sack is located under the tongue (Bock et al. 1973). The pouch can hold up to 150 whitebark pine seeds and when fully stretched creates an obvious throat bulge nearly the size of a walnut.

The Clark's nutcracker is the only bird in North America with a sublingual pouch—and it is critical to the bird's ability to store seeds. That's because nutcrackers usually forage in the lowlands and then fly fully loaded to bury their nuts in higher sites. In some places birds complete up to three 28-mile (45 km) round-trip caching flights per day—a daily commute of over 80 miles (128 km) (Vander Wall and Balda 1983). And a sublingual pouch full of seeds can hold quite a load: the cargo can weigh up to 20 percent of the bird's total mass (Tomback 1998). Hauling this weight uphill over these distances may seem energetically prohibitive, but the birds sometimes save energy by exploiting updrafts.

After arriving at its cache site with a pouch full of seeds, a nutcracker will often perch in a tree, cry loudly several times, and look around before flying to the ground (Lanner 1996). If a Steller's jay arrives, the nutcracker may fly off or wait for the jay to leave. Such cautious behavior hints that the bird has learned to thwart thievery by waiting to store seeds until it is not being watched. Once into the routine of caching, though, a nutcracker is quiet and purposeful, working alone, even though other nutcrackers may be coming and going throughout the communal storage area.

To find a burial spot, the engorged bird lands in its group's caching zone, hops along the ground, and turns its head from side to side examining the terrain (Tomback 1978). Most nuts are placed in soil within two inches (5.1 cm) of several conspicuous surface objects. The nutcracker then jabs its bill into the ground, loosens the soil, and removes a seed from its sublingual pouch by tossing its head back slightly. Then, while holding the seed in its bill tip, the bird jabs it into the hole. In another burying style it may sweep its bill sideways to dig a shallow trench in which it plants a tight row of several nuts. I've also seen them trailside forcing seeds into the cracks of boulders and downed trees.

Once its seeds are in a hole the nutcracker swishes its bill sideways to rake soil and grass over the spot (Tomback 1998). It also puts an object such as a pebble, twig, or pine cone on top. The item presumably camouflages the site until wind erases the cues left by burial. At the end of the planting sequence the bird shifts its body orientation, turning one way and then another (Kamil et al. 1999). Changing directions seems to allow the bird to memorize landmarks—a twig here, a stone there (Vander Wall 1982). A caching bird repeats this sequence at several spots until its pouch is empty.

Once cached, interred seeds are at risk of being pilfered by rodents— and by snooping nutcrackers. If a bird knows that it has been observed making a cache it may engage in various cache-protection behaviors (Clary and Kelly 2011). For example, it may create more caches or prematurely eat some of its seeds. It could even recache the lot in a different spot.

How many seeds does a nutcracker cache? And in how many spots? In the San Francisco Peaks (north-central Arizona), individual birds stored 22,000 to 33,000 nuts per season (Vander Wall and Balda 1977), equivalent to 2.2 to 3.3 times the amount of food a bird needs to survive through the winter (Tomback 1998). On Mammoth Mountain in the Sierra Nevada (east-central California), each individual deposited an average of 35,000 seeds in 9,500 caches (Tomback 1982), three to five times as many as needed; in another Sierra locality adult and juvenile birds each stored 89,000 and 34,000 seeds, respectively (Dimmick 1993). In Squaw Basin in the Central Rockies (19 miles [30 km] east of Moran Junction, Bridger-Teton National Forest, northwestern Wyoming), nutcrackers flew an average of 1,053 trips to cache 98,000 nuts (30,600 caches, each with 3.2 seeds) (Hutchins and Lanner 1982). So the impressive answer is that each year an individual nutcracker buries 22,000 to 98,000 seeds in 6,500 to 31,000 caches.

Through the winter, each nutcracker returns to its own individual reserve to retrieve seeds (Vander Wall and Balda 1983). To locate one of its caches a bird either perches in a branch and flies down to the site or hops along the ground looking for the spot. It thrusts its bill down through the forest litter, soil, or shallow snow, probing for seeds (Tomback 1998). A nutcracker will even punch through the ice along the edge of a snowbank. Successful birds leave a record—discarded pine seed coats next to holes (Tomback 1980). If the bird miscalculates, it changes position and probes again. Based on the proportion of seed coats that are left behind, about two-thirds of the probes are successful, a simple observation that demonstrates that nutcrackers do not retrieve seeds merely by random trial and error (Kamil and Balda 1985).

Nutcrackers also remember the size of the seeds they have cached (Moller et al. 2001). As they retrieve seeds from the ground, they gape wider to recover larger seeds than they do for smaller ones. The ability to remember the size of seeds in a cache would improve the efficiency of their recovery movements. So nutcrackers know where to dig. But how—by what sensory mechanism—does a nutcracker find the exact spot overlying a buried seed? A series of experiments ruled out specific kinds of sites and surface marks, the seeds' odor, use of specific routes, and random searching (Balda 1980; Vander Wall 1982; Kamil and Balda 1985; Balda and Kamil 1989, 1992). It turns out that Clark's nutcrackers cue on landmarks like soil microtopography and small surface objects, structural features they memorize during the act of caching (Vander Wall 1982; Vander Wall and Balda 1983; Gould-Beierle and Kamil 1996, 1998, 1999; Tomback 1998). Even with light snow covering the burial sites, these little surface items still reveal themselves as bumps in the snow.

To remember specific points sprinkled through space, nutcrackers appear to use two types of mental mapping. Think of a mental map as the information maintained in the brain by which an animal finds a previously visited spot. According to an early study of nutcrackers in the subalpine zone of Yellowstone National Park in northwestern Wyoming, one type of mental map is the ability to recall a point halfway between two surface landmarks. This may seem simple, but this mechanism of orientation requires two steps: using directional bearings to find the line connecting two points and then finding the correct halfway spot along the line (Kamil and Jones 1997). It's even more impressive that the birds can ignore absolute distance (Kamil and Jones 2000). That is, they're able to determine halfway points even though the absolute distance between the points varies (Jones et al. 2002).

Other experiments have demonstrated that nutcrackers also use a more complex type of spatial memory, specifically remembering the angles between a cache and two nearby landmarks, like boulders, trees, and logs (Kamil and Jones 2000; Gibson and Kamil 2001). That is, they triangulate—as Nancy and I did when we were confused out on the trail.

More recently, a series of experiments has revealed that nutcrackers show considerable flexibility in how they integrate spatial information (Gibson and Kamil 2001; Kelly et al. 2010), like using both absolute and relative information about spatial relationships (Goodyear and Kamil 2004). In some cases they weigh directional information more heavily than distance information (Kamil and Jones 2000). The proximity of the visual cues is more important than other spatial information (Gould-Beierle and Kamil 1999). Taken together, these findings suggest that nutcrackers remember various forms of abstract geometric relationships. In psychological terms, they develop a cognitive map (Gibson and Kamil 2001; Kelly et al. 2010), a memory of three-dimensional space.

A nutcracker can remember where it buried seeds for at least nine months. In one experiment 25 birds were tested for their ability to remember cache sites for 11, 82, 183, and 285 days after burial (Balda and Kamil 1992). Although the birds made more errors as the time lengthened (Bednekoff and Balda 1997; Tomback 1998), by the end of the trial they still retrieved more caches than they would have if their searches had been random. Two competing hypotheses may explain the birds' dwindling recall. First, a bird may simply recover its best-remembered caches first (van der Vaart et al. 2011). Or second, a caching bird may acquire extraneous information when it memorizes spatial information, creating so-called interference effects (Lewis and Kamil 2006). My guess is that both methods apply and that further research will resolve their relative contributions.

I'll pause now to emphasize the enormity of the Clark's nutcracker's skill: each year a nutcracker remembers for several months the locations of up to 31,000 spots overlying buried seeds. Here we have nothing less than one of the animal kingdom's most remarkable displays of spatial memory.

To put this in context, imagine yourself as the seed cacher. How many surface spots could you, a prime specimen of *Homo sapiens* (which translates as the "knowing ape"), remember throughout your neighborhood after nine months? Here's an analogy built roughly to human scale: Imagine crawling over an acre (0.41 ha)—a square measuring 209 feet on each side (64 m × 64 m), roughly a fifth of a city block—while probing the ground with tweezers. You retrieve 60,000 seeds from 20,000 unique spots nine months after burial, all the while scoring on 8 of 10 probes. There's no way you would come close; at best, my brain might retain a couple of dozen locations.

Extending this story begs another question: How many sites can a nutcracker's brain hold? What is a bird's limit? The simple answer is that nobody knows.

One thing we do know, though, is that the birds do not fight over seeds. Within the flock's larger communal caching area each individual nutcracker has its own small reserve, which it does not defend against its flockmates (Tomback 1998). In one study, for instance, a flock of 10 to 15 nutcrackers showed no aggression as they cached at the same time, often working within three feet (0.9 m) of each other in the group's patch of 120 square yards (96 m²). This tolerance squares with my trailside observations as they forage in pine trees and on the ground as they bury seeds. The existence of such a peaceful society provokes an evolutionary question: What is the genetic relationship among the group's members? Based on anecdotal reports and the calm I have seen within nutcracker gangs, I suspect that each flock consists of genetic relatives, like parents and their offspring, and maybe even aunts, uncles, and cousins. Although the familial composition of nutcracker flocks is unknown, I suspect that kin selection has been at work here. Yet another research question.

For a final unexpected twist, here's an exciting example of how basic research—doing science just to satisfy curiosity—can lead to a practical use: the study of seed-caching birds is contributing to a revolution in how we view our own brains.

Researchers discovered that during the autumnal seed-storing period, chickadees grow new neurons in their brain's hippocampus, the seat of spatial memory (Sherry 1989; Smulders et al. 1995). The hypothesis is that the birds grow new brain cells that store the locations of their food caches, and then, once the items have been retrieved and the bird no longer needs the spatial data, these brain cells die and are replaced by other neurons with different functions (Clayton 1998). If you need a light brain that carries critical information only when it is useful, growing and shedding specialized neurons on an annual cycle sounds pretty efficient.

Experiments also support a hippocampal role in the Clark's nutcracker's caching behavior. In the 1960s a researcher in the Soviet Union surgically removed the hyperstriatum—the part of the brain that includes the hippocampus—from Eurasian nutcrackers, a closely related species (Krushinskaya 1966). The nutcrackers lacking a hippocampus found only 13 percent of seed caches, compared to the 78 to 91 percent success rate of full-brained birds.

More broadly, several avian anatomists have detected that among birds in general, caching species have larger hippocampi than nonstorers (Krebs 1990; Healy and Krebs 1992, 1993; Lucas et al. 2004). This may be an intuitively attractive conclusion but we need to be cautious—another paper concluded that no correlation exists between food-hoarding specialization and hippocampal volume (Brodin and Lundborg 2003). Let's stay tuned to this lively debate.

The discovery of seasonal neurogenesis, that is, the making of new nerve cells during specific seasons, in the brains of adult birds has huge implications (Clayton and Lee 1998). It hints that we might be able to stimulate the brains of other adult vertebrates to grow new neurons. Imagine the medical implications! How sweetly ironic would it be for seed-storing birds like the nutcracker to teach human neurologists how to reverse the ravages of your mother's stroke? The newly recognized phenomenon of neuroplasticity, literally "changeable nerves," includes the development of new neurons as well as the reassignment of functions to preexisting neurons. Neuroplasticity may allow our damaged adult brains to relearn essential tasks. Someday, your grandfather's failing brain may be stimulated into growing neurons to alleviate its Alzheimer's dysfunctions. Will the Clark's nutcracker help us fix our broken brains?

Nutcracker-Dependent Landscapes

 The western landscape owes much to the mutualism that has coevolved between the Clark's nutcracker and whitebark pine (Lanner 1996; Vander Wall and Hutchins 1983). A whitebark pine germinates where a bird plants it, not just in any random place (Vander Wall and Balda 1983). Birds often bury the seeds on steep and bare south-facing slopes, where strong winds keep the ground free of snow through the winter. They also plant pine nuts in recently burned forests. The nutcracker's seed caching is crucial to the whitebark pine for two reasons: If the nuts were to just fall onto the ground they would perish from the desiccating sun or be lost to predatory birds and rodents. Further, birds plant the seeds one inch (2.5 cm) deep in bare ground, which promotes the nuts' germination (Tomback 1998).

In the Rockies, as well as in the Cascades, Sierra Nevada, and many ranges throughout the Great Basin, ecologically sensitive high-elevation sites are protected by whitebark and limber pines, both of which are nutcracker-dependent species (Vander Wall and Balda 1983; Lanner 1996; Lantz 2002). By planting pines, the nutcrackers are creating future spruce habitat. In this way, 100 Clark's nutcrackers, with a total mass of a mere 35 pounds (15.8 kg), can determine the kinds and numbers of plants, and thereby those of resident animals, of an entire mountain range for centuries.

Out on the trail I puzzled over why I crave to connect with a flock of Clark's nutcrackers. I now see that my hike-launching ritual developed unconsciously at several levels. From a superficial, fun point of view, because the bird is not shy I looked forward to being entertained by its tight, raucous gangs. Intellectually, knowing something about its ecological niche helped me predict environmental nuances around the bend. And to watch a flock of nutcrackers moving among the trees, peacefully sampling and feeding on pine cones, efficiently evaluating and storing seeds—reminders all of the birds' remarkable memory—helped me appreciate some of the awesome adaptations that enable life to succeed in the extreme environment of the Rockies.

CHAPTER 2

Lupine's Defense

*Each plant and plant population produces a relatively
distinct set of defensive chemicals...and these chemicals
affect different animals in different ways.*

W. J. Freeland and Daniel H. Janzen, "Strategies in Herbivory
by Mammals: The Role of Plant Secondary Compounds"

FROM MY FIELD NOTES: "Frustrating, grueling, and scary." After
pointed debate, repeated compass sightings, and several fresh looks at the
trail map, Nancy and I took the left fork. But that just led to a horse-
packer camp with no exit trail—a dead end. Working to get back on-trail
we spent most of the day slipping on steep scree and bushwhacking our
way through a thicket-choked ravine. By then we had lost two days of
time and rations. So we aborted this leg of the hike, retraced our path to
the trailhead, and redeployed via bushplane to our next cache.

Although this vast and magnificent place would eventually show us
sego lily, mule-ears, white phlox, and shooting star, the retreat took us
through a dry landscape that offered few colors to soften my disappoint-
ment. So I felt a spike of hope when I came across a single vigorous lupine
in full bloom growing on the dry, bare, overgrazed ground of the unnamed pass between South Fork and Cottonwood Creek in the Salmon
River Mountains (Rat Creek Trail, Frank Church–River of No Return
Wilderness, Challis National Forest, central Idaho). Those blossoms
brought optimism to the day, new bounce to my legs, and some reas-
surance that I would meet new plants and animals. A cheery bit of blue
purple lifted a dejected mind above an earth-toned landscape.

But whoa, wait a minute. What was that lone happy lupine doing on
that arid ridge, thriving amid clipped brown plants? How had this single
plant escaped being eaten—it sported intact, healthy green leaves and

thick, robust flowers—while its neighboring plants had been reduced to stubs? Its tenacity hinted at interesting adaptations.

Before we explore the traits that underlie the lupine's success, let's dip into a little background. Of the roughly 300 species of lupines found on Earth, about 50 occur in the Rockies (Craighead et al. 1963). Our lupine wealth may have arisen through the same kind of explosive radiation that was suggested for the lupines of the Andes, namely, that many species arose in diverse habitats on the newly created island-like mountaintops when the range was uplifted (Hughes and Eastwood 2006). In the case of the Rockies' perennial lupines, the rate of speciation has been estimated at 2.0 to 5.9 species per million years, from 0.7 to 2.1 million years ago (Drummond 2008). Another consequence of insular habitats has been that some small populations and at least one lupine species have been inbreeding to the point where they are suffering a drop in fitness (Michaels et al. 2007).

In many places throughout the Rockies, though, lupine does well and can be overwhelmingly abundant. Nancy and I have trekked across several mountainsides that were smothered with lupine blooms, especially in July and August. In the Greater Yellowstone Ecosystem (Yellowstone National Park, northwestern Wyoming), for example, the showy blue, purple, and cream flowers of four lupine species, including silvery and silky lupines, are among the most plentiful wildflowers (Rosing 1998).

Such an observation of a dominant plant—where an area is literally covered by one plant species or a few closely related species—ushers us to one of ecology's classic questions: How is it possible for a plant to beget a green landscape even though it cohabits with hordes of plant-eating animals (Hairston et al. 1960)? Plants in general would seem to be at a disadvantage in their relationship with herbivorous insects: individual plants are large, long lived, and rooted in one spot, whereas the attacking insects are short lived, highly mobile, and rapidly evolving.

One reason lupine dominates in some places is that it revegetates well after fire. For instance, in the oak savannas of the Oak Openings Region in the Lake Plains Physiographic Region (northwestern Ohio), sundial lupine responded favorably to burning (Grigore and Tramer 1996). Compared to plants in unburned plots, even though fire killed most seeds and seedlings on the surface, adult lupines in burned plots held more nitrogen, grew more biomass, allocated more biomass to leaves and stems, developed more flowering stems that set seed, and grew a higher density of pods.

Herbivorous insects attack lupine seedlings and all parts of mature lupine plants, even their roots and seeds (Maron 1997, 2001; Maron and Simms 1997). The combined effects of herbivory both above and below the ground can demolish a plant (Maron 1998). For example, bush lupine attacked by tussock moth larvae resprouted smaller leaves, which reduced energy capture, and produced up to 80 percent fewer seeds, which lowered individual reproductive potential (Harrison and Maron 1995). Research on lupine and its insect herbivores has helped us understand how plants resist—and even thrive—in a world pulsing with ravenous herbivores.

The generic name *Lupinus* comes from *lupus*, Latin for "wolf," as early naturalists mistakenly believed that the plant stole nutrients from the soil (Craighead et al. 1963). But the plant actually has the opposite effect. As members of the pea family, all lupine species assimilate nitrogen from the atmosphere and store it in root nodules (Rumbaugh and Johnson 1991; Ayisi et al. 1992; Maron and Jefferies 1999; Canals et al. 2005). In the sterile volcanic soil on Mount St. Helens (Mount St. Helens National Volcanic Monument, Gifford Pinchot National Forest, 96 [154 km] miles south of Seattle, Washington), prairie lupine has been facilitating the establishment of pioneering microbial communities, thereby improving the soil for succeeding plants (Halvorson et al. 1991; Ibekwe et al. 2007). Lupine can improve the soil so much that it facilitates the invasion of exotic annual plants, to the detriment of the native plant community (Maron and Connors 1996; Maron and Jefferies 1999).

Because the various lupine species conform to a fairly common body plan, I'll use one of the West's widespread species to sketch a generic lupine portrait. Lodgepole lupine is distributed throughout the Intermountain West at high elevations up to the treeline. It is an example of a perennial forb, an herbaceous plant other than grass that lives for more than two years. Lodgepole lupine grows in moist spots within pine and aspen forests, on open hillsides, and in meadows (Craighead et al. 1963). Individual plants are one to two feet (0.3–0.7 m) tall and present palmately compound leaves, that is, the leaflets on each leaf spread out like fingers from the palm of your hand. Lodgepole lupine is toxic to herbivorous mammals in the spring. It has one to five dozen blue, pealike flowers, each less than a quarter inch (0.6 cm) long, that are packed into showy clusters on long, erect spikes. After blooming from late June to early August, it produces fuzzy pods that hold several seeds each.

Let's start the story of lupine's relationship with its insect herbivores by returning to the 1950s, with two entomologists traveling throughout the West as they collected specimens of the icarioid blue butterfly (Downey and Fuller 1961). This pretty little insect, with a wingspan of only 1.2 inches (32 mm), features iridescent icy blue on the upper sides of its wings and black-spotted light gray on the undersides. Our roving lepidopterists noticed that they found icarioid blues only in certain places, specifically at sites with lupine. With further study they realized that this co-occurrence was even more specific: this butterfly was never more than 50 yards (45 m) from a lupine plant.

Further, even though they found the icarioid blues living among several species of lupine, their caterpillars fed on the plants of only one lupine species (Downey and Fuller 1961). These wild larvae were monophagous, meaning that they ate just one thing. In captivity, though, the caterpillars readily ate any species of lupine. These observations suggested that wild females laid their eggs on, and thus their caterpillars ate, only one of several available lupine species.

This pattern of host-plant specialization seems to be a common contract between butterflies and lupine. In the remnant upland prairies of the Willamette Valley (western Oregon), the larvae of the Fender's blue butterfly, a subspecies of the icarioid blue, is also a host-plant specialist, as it oviposits primarily on the rare Kincaid's lupine (Kaye 1999). In the Great Lakes region (Indiana Dunes National Lakeshore, northwestern Indiana), the Karner blue, a closely related species, oviposits only on sundial lupine (Grundel et al. 1998).

To understand why an insect would discriminate among several food plants, we need to look holistically at the various ways that plants thwart their enemies (Janzen 1985; Marquis 1991). A handy way to understand this is by sorting the antiherbivory adaptations of plants according to how obvious they are. For instance, biologists have traditionally interpreted several gross plant structures, like the sharp thorns of cactus and the tough, leathery leaves of Gambel oak, as adaptations that discourage herbivores.

Other, less apparent antiherbivore adaptations can be detected only by studying the plant for a longer time. It can take several days, for instance, to understand the defensive functions of an enhanced resinous sap flow from a lodgepole pine (Nebeker et al. 1995), or the ability of the silica-enriched leaves of some grasses to render them more abrasive and less digestible (Karban and Baldwin 1997). Some plants protect themselves by presenting foliage of poor nutritional quality (Moran and Hamilton 1980). And here's yet another example. The attacks of gall aphids can induce narrowleaf and Fremont cottonwoods to drop their leaves prematurely (Williams and Whitham 1986). Premature leaf abscission has been interpreted as an antiherbivore adaptation because it degrades the aphids' survival.

Even less observable are various life-history traits of plants that function to thwart herbivorous insects. Understanding such nuanced adaptations may require yearlong study. For example, in the Elk Mountains, a range along the western slope of the Southern Rockies (25 miles [40 km] northwest of Crested Butte, west-central Colorado), female silvery blue butterflies laid their eggs on the immature flower parts of Baker's lupine (Breedlove and Ehrlich 1968). If some flowers of a cluster were already open, the butterfly would not oviposit there. When the larvae hatched they fed on the flower's corolla and developing stamens, which are the ring of petals and the male pollen-producing organs, respectively. Attacked flowers did not reach maturity, so they yielded neither pollen nor seeds. All told, at this site the caterpillars destroyed nearly 50 percent of the plants' potential seed production.

In response to such intense herbivory, you might expect Baker's lupine to have evolved counteradaptations. And in fact, it has: compared to lupine in nearby areas, the Elk Mountain lupine was found to flower earlier. Flowers that matured early in the flight season, before the adult silvery blues emerged, incurred the least damage. These early-blooming plants developed seeds when more than a month of the growing season remained, so a "temporal escape" from the butterfly was the most logical reason for flowering this early. In fact, many flowers bloomed so early they were killed by spring freezes, suggesting that directional selection exerted by its insect herbivore had pushed the lupine to the site's earliest possible frost-free blooming date (Emmel 1976).

This brings us to one of the least obvious of all antiherbivore adaptations, poisonous chemicals. Botanists now believe that much of an insect's food choice, like the plant hosts of those choosy icarioid blue butterflies, is determined by poisonous chemicals that are synthesized by the plant's own cells (Ehrlich and Raven 1964). Pioneer chemical ecologists called these molecules "secondary compounds" because, at the time they were discovered, they seemed to play no role in the plant's basic metabolic pathways and were seen as waste by-products (Raven and Curtis 1970). These seemingly functionless molecules eventually made sense as defensive adaptations (Levin 1976b; Seigler and Price 1976).

 ### We Also Use Plant Secondary Compounds

For centuries we humans have been exploiting various plant secondary compounds as flavorings, medicines, insecticides, and recreational drugs (Verpoorte 1998; Bourgaud et al. 2001). Some of our spices and fragrances, like menthol and camphor, owe their appeal to terpenoids, a class of plant secondary compounds that includes about 3,800 molecular structures that occur in various plant families. Other secondary compounds, like the alkaloid piperidine in lupines, offer therapeutic potential (Molyneux et al. 2007). Terpenoids like azadirachtin from the neem tree serve as insecticides (Naumann et al. 1994). We've been using other alkaloids for various purposes, like atropine from deadly nightshade to accelerate heart rate; cocaine from the coca plant to stimulate the nervous system and induce euphoria; and codeine from the opium poppy to relieve cough. Tetrahydrocannabinol from cannabis offers analgesic and psychoactive effects. And still another alkaloid in the opium poppy, morphine, is celebrated by some primates for its brain-altering effects (Raven and Curtis 1970).

Here's one more example—wild chili (Borrell 2009). Chili plants accumulate a compound called capsaicin in their fruits. Its concentration increases as the fruit ripens. Capsaicin and related molecules are plant secondary compounds in the class called capsaicinoids. When you chew on a hot pepper, capsaicin stimulates the neural sensors in your tongue that normally function to detect rising temperature. Humans also use capsaicin to repel other mammals, as we did when we carried bear-deterring pepper spray with 2.0 percent capsaicin on our treks through grizzly bear country.

Why do pepper plants synthesize capsaicin? The initial, more conventional, hypothesis was that this secondary compound protects chilies from herbivorous rodents. It was consistent with the laboratory observation that pack rats and cactus mice ate mild chilies but avoided hot ones. This led investigators to conclude that natural selection had increased capsaicin in chilies because it renders the fruits and seeds less vulnerable to herbivorous animals, which chew on and kill the seeds. On closer study, though, it seemed that capsaicin also functioned as an antifungal agent, limiting the chili seeds' mortality from fungal infection. And yet, capsaicin did not deter birds from eating the chili seeds. Rather, the birds consumed but did not chew the seeds; they passed them through their guts ready to germinate and thereby helped spread the seeds. Deter mammals and fungi, which kill chili seeds, yet encourage birds to spread viable seeds—now there's an elegant evolutionary outcome!

We continue to learn a lot about plant secondary compounds through, of all things, capitalism. Bioprospectors are surveying Earth's natural environments for useful, potentially marketable, organic compounds. In many cases their search has focused on microorganisms, plants, and fungi in rain forests and hot springs. Bioprospecting typically draws on indigenous knowledge about the features and uses of native plants and animals. Most recently, bioprospecting, supported by advances in plant genomics, metabolite profiling, and cell culture, has been driving the commercial production of plant secondary compounds with medical uses (Oksman-Caldentey and Inze 2004)

Specific kinds of secondary compounds are characteristic of whole families of flowering plants (Raven and Curtis 1970; Pasteels and Rowell-Rahier 1992). In seed-bearing plants, one of the most common categories of secondary compounds is the alkaloids, bitter organic bases. Among lupines the ripening pods and seeds accumulate molecules of poisonous alkaloids. Lupanine, for example, a bitter poisonous alkaloid found in silvery lupine, causes tremors and breathing difficulty in guinea pigs and mice and convulsions and cyanosis in rats (www.LookChem.com).

Throughout the plant kingdom, alkaloids have been detected in over 7,500 species in 300 families (Li and Willaman 1972; Levin 1976a). A single plant species typically synthesizes fewer than five different kinds of alkaloid molecules. Annual plants contain roughly twice as many kinds of alkaloids as perennials. Further, there is an evident gradual latitudinal gradient in the number of different kinds of alkaloid molecules—there are more in tropical plants than in plants of colder climates. Alkaloids are synthesized mainly in the plant's roots, from which they are transported to other organs. This is how alkaloids come to be found in a plant's above-ground parts, like the shoots, flowers, and seeds.

The kinds and amounts of alkaloids can vary among the various parts of a plant. For example, in velvet lupine, the alkaloids anagyrine, lupanine, and 5,6-dehydrolupanine were highest in flowers, vegetative tissues, and stems, respectively (Lee et al. 2007).

So how in the world can we explain the presence of poisonous secondary compounds in floral nectar? Nectar is, after all, an adaptation for attracting pollinators, yet botanists have reported that the floral nectar of a wide variety of plant species and families contains toxic chemicals (Baker and Baker 1975; Rhoades and Bergdahl 1981). Phenolic and alkaloid compounds, which are especially common in nectar, have been interpreted as plant adaptations that manipulate pollinator behavior, specifically by minimizing generalist flower visitors, like lepidopterans, and thereby maximizing conspecific pollen transfer by specialists, like bees. Some nectar poisons also exclude nectar thieves.

How—by what mechanisms—do secondary compounds like alkaloids deter herbivorous insects? The toxic molecules seem to operate in two ways. The prevailing hypothesis is that they taste bitter and poison the attackers. The usual effects of such poisons are to render the leaves distasteful and to induce illness in a leaf-eating insect, but seldom do they cause the insect's death. The tannins of oak leaves, for instance, cause sloughing of midgut epidermis and consequent midgut lesions, harm symbiotic gut microorganisms, and lessen the digestion of dietary protein, all of which may inhibit an insect's growth (Bernays et al. 1989). The quinolizidine in white lupine causes one of its herbivores, the plorans grasshopper, to digest its food less efficiently, grow more slowly, lose weight, and thereby incur an increased mortality of 10 percent (El Sayed 1999).

An alternative hypothesis, one growing in acceptance, is that some secondary compounds do not poison the insects at all; rather, they protect the plant by attracting the herbivore's predators (Dicke 1999). That is, a plant may defend itself by enhancing the effectiveness of the herbivore's carnivorous enemies, a category of antiherbivore adaptations labeled indirect induced defense. Among legumes, indirect induced defenses have been detected in the lima bean, cowpea, and broad bean, and in the leaves of one species of lupine, the yellow bush lupine. In some plants species, herbivory induces individual plants to synthesize volatile compounds, like terpenoids, that attract carnivores. Terpenoids are primary constituents of the essential oils of many plants. Imagine a plant under siege by herbivores: it issues a chemical signal, the terpenoid molecules float through the air, the volatile molecules attract predatory or parasitic insects, and these carnivores, in turn, attack the insects eating the plant.

Let's step back to consider the more general, more inclusive category of induced defenses (Tollrian and Harvell 1999). This form of antiherbivore response has been detected in several Rocky Mountain tree species, including white spruce, lodgepole and ponderosa pines, red alder, paper birch, balsam poplar, and quaking aspen (Karban and Baldwin 1997; Trewhella et al. 1997). Because induced resistance has been found in many and diverse plant families and habitats, I expect that eventually it will be found in many, if not all, species of plants throughout the Rockies, especially all of the species of lupine.

The kinds and amounts of secondary compounds in plants are not static; rather, they are dynamic, changing through time and space. As I've said, a chewing insect can cause a plant to activate its production of defensive chemicals (Edwards and Wratten 1982; Schultz 1988; Karban and Myers 1989; Adler and Harvell 1990; Chessin and Zipf 1990; Karban and Baldwin 1997; Tollrian and Harvell 1999). Induced responses are diverse (Agrawal and Karban 1999), including changes in regrowth, shifts in phenology, production of spines, early leaf abscission, and resin exudation.

One of the most studied types of induced response is chemical, including secondary compounds like phenolics, alkaloids, and protein inhibitors. In white birch, after an attack by insects the tree's leaves quickly develop an enhanced resistance. After caterpillars of the velvet bean moth chewed on white lupine, the plant showed a higher concentration of quinolizidine, which lessened subsequent attacks (del Pilar Vilarino et al. 2005). Called a rapidly inducible defense because it starts immediately or within hours after damage (Jaremo et al. 1999), the birch's secondary compounds are almost equally effective at thwarting insects in both the chewed leaves and in the plant's nearby but unchewed, still-intact leaves (Edwards and Wratten 1982).

At this point I'll mention a few caveats. Don't assume that all herbivores induce resistance in plants. For example, neither the weight of female tussock moths at pupation nor the rates of early larval dispersal, called ballooning, were affected by prior foliar damage of their host plant, the bush lupine (Harrison 1995). So, although this story of induced resistance is intuitively compelling, it is almost surely just one of several factors at work.

Further, let's not slip into the easy notion that all plant secondary compounds are toxic to herbivorous insects. The bigleaf lupine's alkaloid fraction deterred feeding by sixth-instar larvae of the spruce budworm (Bentley et al. 1984). When this alkaloid fraction was separated into its various kinds of molecules, eight unique alkaloid molecules were identified. Of these eight, only two, like 13-tigloyloxylupanine, were highly deterrent; the other six, like 17-oxolupanine, were not. Thus, in this particular case there was wide variation in the insect's response to the different kinds of alkaloid molecules. I suspect that some degree of idiosyncratic herbivore-alkaloid response occurs among all combinations of herbivorous insects and their host plants.

A plant may also show induced resistance that persists for years after an attack (Haukioja and Neuvonen 1985; Neuvonen et al. 1987; Jaremo et al. 1999). Called delayed inducible resistance, it is strongest in the first two years, but the extra chemical defenses can depress the growth of caterpillars for up to four years after a defoliation event (Haukioja 1982). Thus, some plants can mobilize one kind of secondary chemical to counter an acute threat, yet activate a different type of molecular shield to thwart a chronic, multiyear insect pest. In part because of their long lives, I suspect that perennial lupines produce both rapid and delayed inducible secondary compounds.

It's also possible that a plant's secondary molecules may change with the season. In the narrowleaf lupine, higher temperatures caused higher alkaloid concentrations in the seeds (Jansen et al. 2009). It seems that the seeds' alkaloid levels were influenced by temperatures from the start of flowering until the pods opened. Perhaps selection favored individual plants that cued their alkaloid production to higher air temperature, which has been evolutionarily associated with more insects and herbivory.

The story as sketched above is not squeaky clean: there's one last caveat. Some researchers have proposed an alternative hypothesis, namely, that the induction of chemical defenses results from nutrient deficiency, and that it's not actually an active defense against herbivores (Haukioja and Neuvonen 1985; Hunter and Schultz 1995). In one oak species, added nutrients prevented induction responses among leaves within individual trees. Specifically, damaged leaves within unfertilized chestnut oak saplings showed increased foliar astringency and proanthocyanidins. Northern red oak saplings also induced astringency and the poison, but their induction was not affected by fertilization. On both oak species, herbivorous insects were repelled from the damaged leaves of unfertilized trees. These findings suggest that nutrient availability can affect the induction of chemical defenses as well as an herbivore's response. More simply, the induction of protective secondary compounds can be turned off by high soil fertility.

Like the finely tuned adaptations we see in organisms everywhere, the amounts of secondary compounds can vary spatially among the populations of a single plant species. This is because separate patches of plants can incur different kinds and intensities of herbivory. The kinds of monoterpenes in Douglas-fir trees on the coast of British Columbia differed from those of trees in the continental interior (Pureswaran et al. 2004). In a pumice region of the Pacific Northwest (Deschutes National Forest, central Oregon), chemical ecologists sampled the needles of ponderosa pine at three sites. The alkaloid pinidine was lower at two of the sites than it was at the third site (Gerson and Kelsey 1998). In lodgepole pine, trees from forests where this species was not dominant had less foliar defense compound than trees from areas where these pines were the dominant species (Wallis et al. 2010). Among 12 stands of lodgepole pine in British Columbia, trees from two biogeoclimatic zones, the Western Hemlock and Interior Cedar/Hemlock Zones, had greater levels of phenolics and terpenoids in their needles than did trees in other stands.

At a more local scale, plant ecologists measured the amount of an alkaloid, quinolizidine, in the leaves and seeds of silvery lupine living at seven different altitudes in the Elk Mountains (Carey and Wink 1994). Leaves of the lowest plants, at 9,158 feet (2775 m) above sea level, held six times greater alkaloid levels than leaves at the highest site, at 12,095 feet (3665 m). This difference makes sense, as there are usually more herbivorous insects at lower elevations. When seeds from low- and high-altitude plants were grown under identical conditions in a greenhouse, the alkaloid concentrations in low-elevation plants were still higher, demonstrating that the elevational differences in alkaloid levels were at least partly genetic.

One of the most fascinating ideas within the theory of inducible responses is the hypothesis known as "talking trees" (Fowler and Lawton 1985; Karban and Baldwin 1997; Jaremo et al. 1999). The proposal is that a secondary compound that is rapidly induced in one tree spreads through the air to its unattacked neighbors and induces a defensive response in the receiving trees (Baldwin and Schultz 1983; Chessin and Zipf 1990; Bruin et al. 1992). When some plants are attacked by insect herbivores, the plants release signal molecules called synomones that attract predatory or parasitic insects. Synomone production is induced in the attacked plants and its effects may spread to nearby unattacked plants.

The proposal of airborne, interplant communication is hotly debated (Fowler and Lawton 1985; Bruin et al. 1995), though, for two reasons. First, rather than plants actively communicating with each other, unattacked neighbors may simply be passively contaminated by airborne by-products from tissue damage that, in turn, triggers synthesis of secondary compounds. And second, it has not been clearly demonstrated that the responding plant garners a fitness benefit by responding to attacks on its neighbor. If the phenomenon of talking plants is eventually demonstrated to be adaptive, I expect kin selection will be fingered as an ultimate cause. That is, signaler and receiver will be close genetic relatives that are rooted near each other.

The adaptive significance of secondary compounds in modern plants seems established, but how did secondary compounds evolve in the first place? Through occasional genetic mutations, some species of angiosperms, the flowering plants, started producing molecules that by chance did not function in their plant's basic metabolic reactions (Whittaker and Feeny 1971). Of these new nonfunctional chemicals, some also did not hurt the plant's normal physiological processes. And a few of these novel, nonfunctional, nonharmful compounds were, by chance, toxic to insects and thereby lessened the plant's palatability. The mutant plants that synthesized molecules that were both metabolically neutral in their own tissues and yet toxic to insects presumably experienced greater survival and reproductive success than plants without the genetic variant, so the genes for the secondary compound spread through the species by natural selection.

Insect herbivores, meanwhile, have not been powerless against plants' poisons. Once an alkaloid is ingested along with plant tissue, an insect's enzymes, intestinal flora, or other assets may exclude or neutralize the toxic molecules (Levin 1976a). In some cases, biochemical variation within an insect population allows a few individuals to detoxify the poison of the now formerly protected plant group. These individual insects will then enjoy greater reproductive success and the new poison-neutralizing allele will spread through the insect population.

Like the adaptations of living things everywhere, the defenses and counterdefenses of host plants and their herbivorous attackers can be understood through cost-benefit analysis (Simms and Rausher 1987; Harvell 1990). The plant host incurs costs in defending itself against herbivory; its insect herbivore incurs costs in neutralizing the plant's defense. Through trade-offs, a plant is presumably balancing the benefits of inducible defenses with fitness costs, such as slower regrowth, less reproductive output, and impaired survival (Loehle 1988; Van der Meijden et al. 1988; Fagerstrom 1989; Berenbaum and Zangerl 1994).

On the other side of the interaction, the insect may pay a price to detoxify a plant poison. The parsnip webworm, for instance, feeds on the flowers and fruits of the wild parsnip, which produces a secondary compound called xanthotoxin (Berenbaum and Zangerl 1994). The insect is able to detoxify this poison but at the expense of its growth. The detoxication of plant poisons is generally thought to impose a metabolic price on herbivorous animals.

For such a recently resistant herbivore, like an insect that has just evolved the capability to neutralize a plant's poison, the plants would represent a rich resource with few competitors, and perhaps a basis for a whole new lifeway—a novel niche in which the plant-eating animal diversifies swiftly (Ehrlich and Raven 1964; Feeny 1975). For example, some lepidopterists have proposed that the adaptive radiation of the cabbage butterfly family, with 1,100 species in 76 genera, occurred after an ancestor spontaneously acquired the ability to mitigate the poisons of mustard plants (Raven and Curtis 1970). Whereas the caterpillars of many butterfly families ignore mustards and do not feed on them—even if starved—the larvae of the cabbage white butterfly (a subfamily of the cabbage butterfly) feed only on these plants. Through such an evolutionary process, a secondary chemical that deters the feeding of one insect species can stimulate the feeding of another herbivore.

On the broader landscape scale, the chemical defenses of many individual plants can cumulatively affect ecosystems. The first example is a personal observation. On August 22, 2006, while hiking through a recovering burned zone between North Fork and Boulder Lakes in the Wind River Range (Highline and Ruff Lake Trails, Bridger Wilderness, Bridger-Teton National Forest, west-central Wyoming), I noticed that lupine was the only uneaten green plant across vast areas. In another example, drawn from the literature, researchers reported that elk avoided tasty, nutrient-rich forage growing in the midst of a large bloom of the

unpalatable silky lupine in a charred area of Yellowstone's sagebrush grassland (Tracy and McNaughton 1997). In both of these instances, powerful
antiherbivore defenses presumably allowed lupine to persist—to outlast
other plant species—and thereby become ecologically dominant.

These landscape-level patterns reflect, in part, the susceptibility of
large-bodied herbivorous mammals to lupine's poisons. Cattle ranchers
watch for lupine-induced crooked calf disease, a congenital malady. If a
cow eats lupine with the alkaloid anagyrine during gestation, its calf may
develop a cleft palate and/or skeletal contracture malformations, which
can include a twisted back or neck and twisted or bowed legs (Rimbey
1969; Panter et al. 1998; Panter et al. 1999). The secondary compounds in
lupine that poison cattle may not have evolved in response to herbivory
by large ungulates; rather, they were probably selected by intense insect
herbivory. The poisoning of cows can be interpreted as an incidental
by-product of previous natural selection for secondary compounds that
thwarted herbivorous insects.

This pretty plant, whose bright blue flowers lifted our spirits during difficult days in the backcountry, turns out to be one tough customer. Recent
research has demonstrated that its poisons, namely various kinds of alkaloid molecules, probably evolved in response to selection pressures from
herbivorous insects. The synthesis and maintenance of alkaloids form a
dynamic adaptation—plants vary the poison in their tissues as needed
through time by the hour, day, season, and year; and through space
among organs, individuals, populations, altitudes, and regions. Now that
defensive chemicals have provided an edge for lupine's speciation, a small
set of insects may be breaking through this molecular shield. In turn, this
adaptation may allow the insects themselves to radiate. In these ways
the chemical variation within green plants and herbivorous insects has
been catalyzing an ongoing evolutionary arms race in plants and insects
throughout the Rockies.

And, as we'll see in the next chapter, a plant's secondary compounds
can exert more far-reaching effects than just deterring a leaf-chewing
animal.

CHAPTER 3

Paintbrush Parasites

These categories [mutualism and parasitism]
intergrade imperceptibly, and in many boundary cases
clear-cut distinctions cannot be made.

Paul Weisz, *The Science of Biology*

THROUGHOUT OUR Rocky Mountain treks, blooming paintbrushes served as one of my favorite photographic frames. In a small meadow along the upper Lamar River, near Little Saddle Mountain in the Absa-roka Range (Lamar River Trail, Yellowstone National Park, northwest-ern Wyoming), I belly-crawled around clusters of elephant's head and penstemon toward my target, a paintbrush plant in full bloom. The red flowers offered depth and a splash of color for what turned out to be one of my favorite Yellowstone shots, a portrait of Grant Peak. Its dense flower clusters, bright red but not overbearing, contrasted nicely with the landscape's dominant greens and browns. Nancy and I had to restrain ourselves from taking too many pictures of this pretty plant. So I was startled to learn, once back in the library, that this photogenic plant leads a nefarious life—with a series of consequences for its plant neighbors and their insect enemies.

Paintbrush acquired its common name from an Indian legend about a brave trying to paint a prairie sunset ("Flora and Fauna" 1999). When he threw down his brushes in frustration, red flowers sprouted where the brushes landed. Classified in the figwort family, paintbrush plants bear small, inconspicuous, greenish-yellow tubular flowers enclosed by and almost hidden within their obvious showy bracts (Craighead et al. 1963; Shaw and On 1979). A bract is a modified leaflike structure attached to a

35

flower's stem. Paintbrushes bloom from mid-June into early September. Native primarily in western North America, many of the more than 200 species of paintbrushes hybridize readily (Craighead et al. 1963; Anderson and Taylor 1983; Gadd 1995; Bezener and Kershaw 1999; Phillips 2001; Coffey 2004). This makes them challenging to identify at the species level (Spellenberg 1998; Phillips 1999; Mathews 2003). One reason for all of this hybridization may be weak pollinator constancy (Hersch and Roy 2007). Three species of Rocky Mountain paintbrushes, the giant red, alpine, and sulphur, commonly grow together in many places. In montane meadows of the Southern Rockies (Gunnison County, western Colorado), pollinator constancy was found to be weak in areas where the three species co-occurred, which would enable pollen flow among species, and also where plants were morphologically intermediate, which would reflect ongoing hybridization among species. In combination, the weak pollinator constancy, greater hybridization, and greater flower diversity may contribute to a self-reinforcing feedback loop that could maintain a local hot spot of hybridization (Hersch-Green and Cronn 2009).

To help you develop a general sense of the paintbrush plant, here are brief descriptions of three Rocky Mountain species, including two of those mentioned above. The giant red paintbrush is common in the Canadian and Northern Rockies (Waterton-Glacier International Peace Park, southwestern Alberta and northwestern Montana) (Shaw and On 1979; Shaw 1992; Phillips 1999; Spellenberg 1998). It grows up to three feet (0.9 m) tall, lives in moist meadows, and features bright red-orange bracts. Sulphur paintbrush, so named because its flowers are tucked within yellow bracts, occurs throughout the Rockies in moist to medium-dry soil near the treeline (Craighead et al. 1963). It blooms from May through July. From June to early August, Wyoming paintbrush displays brilliant red bracts in flowers about one inch (2.5 cm) long (Craighead et al. 1963; Shaw and On 1979; Alden et al. 1998). The official state flower of Wyoming, this species is found in dry to moist soils of the plains and mountains at elevations of up to 9,000 feet (2743 m) above sea level. With 24 species, the Southern Rockies are a center of paintbrush diversity. A quarter of the paintbrush species sport flowers that draw hummingbirds (Adler 2002).

With that bit of paintbrush natural history in mind, let's explore their outlaw life. Paintbrush plants are semiparasitic, that is, they derive part of their food from other plants (Marvier 1995; Spellenberg 1998; Whitney 1998; Beidelman et al. 2000). Sagebrush is one of their favorite victims. Parasitic plants use enzymes that degrade cell walls to penetrate their host plant and attach to the host's vessels (Lewis et al. 2010). More specifically, fingerlike projections of the paintbrush's roots, called haustoria, weave through the host's root tissue—but do not penetrate its cells—and draw water and nutrients from the host. This is why, during a drought, paintbrushes may appear healthier than their withered host (Phillips 2001; Mathews 2003).

You might notice that I called the paintbrush plant a semiparasite, not a parasite. A paintbrush plant does not need a host to survive (Matthies 1997). Because of its partial dependence it is also called a facultative parasite, whereas an obligate parasite, in contrast, needs a host plant just to survive. Still, paintbrushes definitely do better when they tap a host plant. In one experiment plant ecologists grew three paintbrush species, the wholeleaf, giant red, and early, with and without host plants. All three species were able to grow without a host. One of them, the early paintbrush, even produced flowers without a host plant. The paintbrushes growing with hosts produced 3 to 41 times more shoots by weight than those without a host.

As with any ecological relationship, we can look at semiparasitism from two points of view. Let's first examine the paintbrush's side—specifically, whether one kind of host is better than another. In one experiment, the growth of paintbrush drawing off alfalfa, a legume, was more vigorous than paintbrush tapping into ryegrass, which is not a legume. Further, the host plant can change the way the parasite allocates nutrients. Paintbrushes with a legume host, for example, needed to shunt less nutrients and energy to their roots than those parasitizing a grass, perhaps because the legume did a better job of providing its semiparasite with crucial nutrients.

Of the many potential host species available to paintbrush, lupine is one of the more effective. When a researcher compared the effect of silvery lupine on herbivory, pollination, and female plant fitness of the semiparasitic giant red paintbrush, those paintbrush plants that parasitized lupines experienced lower herbivory from the larvae of plume moths and leaf-miner flies and from deer, compared to paintbrushes parasitizing other host species (Adler 2002). Further, paintbrush plants parasitizing lupines produced twice as many seeds as paintbrushes tapping other host species. The gain in fecundity seemed to be an effect of both more nitrogen and less herbivory. In yet another experiment, Texas paintbrush parasitizing the lupine species called Texas bluebonnet produced three times as many seeds as a paintbrush that was parasitizing big bluestem, a nonalkaloid, non-nitrogen-fixing grass (Adler 2003), and it was also more attractive to pollinators.

And now we can turn to the host plant's point of view. Paintbrush was found to have strong negative effects on a host's growth, but the extent of the host's decrement depended on the particular species of paintbrush (Marvier 1995). Semiparasitism by early paintbrush, for example, affected the growth of the legume more strongly than it impacted grass, whereas giant red paintbrush depressed the growth of grass more strongly. Similarly, host grasses parasitized by giant red paintbrush allocated more biomass to their roots than nonparasitized grasses.

We've also learned that two host species can offer a better diet than one. Botanists studied the Wight's paintbrush and found that its growth and reproduction greatly improved when it was able to simultaneously attack two host species, the yellow bush lupine and lizard tail (Marvier 1998).

We can now combine the previous chapter's ideas about plant secondary compounds with the paintbrush's semiparasitism. You'll not be surprised to learn that the impacts of semiparasitism extend to the insects that eat the paintbrush. In a greenhouse, botanists examined the interactions among Wight's paintbrush, three host species, and paintbrush-eating aphids. The paintbrush's nitrogen content reflected the kinds and combinations of the host plants it was tapping (Marvier 1998). In turn, as the nitrogen level of the paintbrush plants increased, so did the number of individual aphids in the colonies feeding on the plant. Further, the number of aphids in colonies feeding on paintbrush plants that were sipping from a mixture of host species increased more slowly than the number of those eating paintbrush plants drawing off two lupine individuals. Thus, the simultaneous parasitism of different host species can lead to the improved performance of a paintbrush plant in two ways, by (1) providing a direct benefit to the paintbrush's growth and flowering and (2) indirectly depressing the effectiveness of the paintbrush's insect enemies.

These findings hint that energy and nutrients aren't the only resources that paintbrushes steal from their host plants: they also take up insect-deterring secondary compounds. For example, paintbrushes semiparasitize larkspur species of the genus *Delphinium*. All parts, including roots, stems, and leaves, of larkspur plants contain poison. The larkspur's alkaloids end up in all parts of the paintbrush, including its roots, leaves, and seeds—even in its flower nectar (Marko and Stermitz 1997). So, alkaloids synthesized by larkspur are taken up by roots of the sulphur paintbrush, from where they are translocated and deter herbivorous insects throughout the paintbrush.

Reduced herbivory isn't the only benefit paintbrush plants gain from stealing insect poisons. It can also enable them to invite more visits by pollinators (Adler 2000). In one experiment, chemical ecologists grew Texas paintbrush on bitter (high-alkaloid, less preferred) and sweet (low-alkaloid, more preferred) strains of white lupine. In the test, the researchers reduced the intensity of herbivory by applying an insecticide and then randomly subjecting the paintbrush plants to natural or reduced levels of herbivory. The paintbrush's uptake of alkaloids from its host directly reduced the parasite's damage from insects, while increasing its visitation by pollinators, which, in turn, presumably raised its lifetime seed production.

As you have seen, how host plants synthesize and retain secondary compounds, how semiparasitic plants take up and translocate these insecticides, and how herbivorous insects ingest, sequester, detoxify, and excrete plant secondary compounds are highly variable, differing among species, sites, individuals, years, and sexes. The lack of a general pattern, even within and among paintbrush species, hints at many kinds of chemical relationships. With all this variability, the members of these food chains—the host plants, semiparasites, and herbivorous insects—are surely undergoing continual evolution.

The last time I squatted to frame a picture with a bouquet of paintbrush, I could feel my concentration being siphoned off by ecological chemistry. Composing the shot, I was reminded that this photogenic plant was stealing food—and I couldn't help but scan sideways, looking for a depleted host. Along with energy and nutrients come the host's toxic secondary compounds, which are incorporated in the semiparasitic paintbrush's tissues. The poisons, in turn, are ingested by herbivorous insects. And, I expect, these acquired poisons protect paintbrush-eating insects from their own carnivorous predators. Mentally checking off the various levels of this complex sequence muddles my simple desire for a pretty picture.

Many kinds of Rocky Mountain plants—pines, shrubs, wildflowers—are known to synthesize toxic secondary compounds, but how many pass them on to another plant? Through how many links and in how many food webs do the secondary compounds originating in one host plant exert their effects? The answer awaits an integrative ecologist willing to perform a metastudy.

CHAPTER 4

Eat Me!

There is an immediate reproductive
advantage to being eaten.

—Ken Paige and Thomas Whitham, "Overcompensation in
Response to Mammalian Herbivory: The Advantage of Being Eaten"

SCARLET GILIA, a common western member of the phlox family that
also goes by the names of skyrocket, foxfire, and skunk flower, added
sparks of red to several of our treks. That last name, skunk flower, comes
from the fetor given off when its leaves are crushed. This showy perennial
herb can grow up to three feet (0.9 m) tall; is reported to contain saponin,
a poisonous, bitter glycoside allied to soap; and grows on dry slopes from
the sagebrush zone upward almost to treeline (Craighead et al. 1963).

Scarlet gilia blooms from early July through late September (Paige
and Whitham 1987). After one to eight years of vegetative growth a plant
can produce up to 250 flowers on each paniculate-racemose inflorescence,
which is a branched stem of flowers. Because its seed set is mainly a product of pollen transfer between plants, the species has traditionally been
classified as a self-incompatible, obligate outcrossing plant. A scarlet gilia
plant can feature numerous showy red, but sometimes pink, orange, or
white, trumpet-shaped flowers, each 0.75 to 1.5 inches (1.9–3.8 cm) long
(Craighead et al. 1963; Brooks 1967). It is pollinated by resident broad-
tailed hummingbirds, migrating rufous hummingbirds, and a species of
hawk moth called the white-lined sphinx (Paige and Whitham 1985).

One place it does well is on Fern Mountain, a site at 8,250 feet (2515 m)
above sea level on the western flank of the San Francisco Peaks (10 miles
[16 km] north of Flagstaff, north-central Arizona). As Fern Mountain's
flowering season advances, the corollas of scarlet gilia shift from dark
to light colors (Paige and Whitham 1985). Red flowers are common on

plants that initiate their flowering in mid-July, whereas plants starting to flower a month and a half later produce corollas of mainly a lighter hue. This color shift, which occurs both within single inflorescences and among plants, coincides with the departure of hummingbirds. Specifically, 78 percent of the flowers' color changes occur as the hummingbirds are leaving in August.

In the absence of hummers, the light-colored flowers attract one of the remaining pollinators, the white-lined sphinx. Found throughout the Rockies, this large, handsome hawk moth is also called hummingbird moth because it hovers while feeding at flowers. With a wingspan of three inches (7.6 cm), it has a narrow tan stripe on its forewings and a broad pink median band on its hindwings. At sunset hawk moths selectively visit the red flowers of scarlet gilia, but as the light fades the moths shift to lighter-colored flowers. By dark they visit white flowers almost exclusively. In this way, scarlet gilia has adapted to exploit the shifting presence and preferences of its pollinators.

In some places, scarlet gilia supports the pollination of other plant species. The term *mutualism* is reserved for symbioses that benefit two different but collaborating organisms (Rathcke 1983)—a green alga and a fungus entwined as lichen in an Appalachian forest, a wrasse exposing its gills to a cleaner goby on a Caribbean coral reef, a bat pollinating a saguaro cactus in the Sonoran Desert. A type of mutualism that may arise among several plant species sharing a particular site is the maintenance of pollinators.

How does this happen? A plant species that flowers early in the season may support an initial population of short-lived pollinators. Some of these ephemeral pollinators survive and reproduce, and their descendants then pollinate a different, later-blooming plant species (Rathcke 1983). Bumblebee queens forage early in the season and the success of their later colonies depends on the initial support they gain from early-flowering plants. Such a sequential mutualism can also maintain long-lived pollinators like hummingbirds and bats.

Several studies have shown that floral densities vary greatly and independently from one year to the next, even in seemingly stable communities of perennial plants. In areas where floral abundance varies greatly among years, a plant species that is sparse in one year and cannot provide much nectar to pollinators may benefit the next year from the past support of other flowering species. In this way, a sequential mutualism involving several species of flowering plants, including scarlet gilia, can carry over from one year to another.

I'll use an exception to illuminate the general point. In the Elk Mountains (near Crested Butte, west-central Colorado), a lack of facilitation occurred between two plant species. When early-flowering larkspur was sparse, migrating hummingbirds did not stay in the area and were subsequently not available to pollinate the later-flowering scarlet gilia (Rathcke 1983).

With that bit of background on the scarlet gilia, we can move on to the main story. Plant ecologists have long been at odds with each other over the nature of the relationship between plants and their herbivores (Owen and Wiegert 1976). On one hand, we know that some herbivores harm their food plants: they reduce the growth, survival, and reproduction of the plants they eat. But several recent studies have reported that some plants benefit from being chewed on. For example, at the community level, moderate grazing can stimulate the growth of individual plants of some grass species and thereby raise the annual production of the entire grassland.

In some cases the damage inflicted by herbivores can improve pollination within a population of plants. Experimental clipping of scarlet gilia plants, which was intended to simulate browsing by ungulates, reduced the production of flowers, fruits, and seeds, whereas emasculation, which is removing the anthers from a plant's floral buds, increased the production of these reproductive products (Juenger and Bergelson 2000a). Investigators also detected an interaction between clipping and emasculation, such that emasculation increased the fitness of unclipped plants, but not of clipped plants. Two hypotheses, which are not mutually exclusive, could explain these results: (1) damaged plants experience less self-pollination due to reductions in pollinator visitation or effectiveness, and (2) they lack the resources, or the ability to allocate resources, to benefit from emasculation. These results hint that herbivory can benefit plant fitness indirectly via its positive effects on other plant-animal interactions.

When scarlet gilia plants were clipped, plants from small populations grew more slowly and suffered higher mortality than plants from larger populations (Heschel and Paige 1995). This contrast suggests that the reductions in fitness were due partially to genetic causes, possibly via genetic drift or inbreeding depression.

Let's consider the effects of another type of herbivory, nectar robbing, defined as the sucking of nectar through a hole cut directly into a flower's nectary. Nectar robbing was traditionally dismissed as unimportant to a plant's reproductive success, but now we're not so sure. Does variation in the amount of nectar among scarlet gilia plants caused by nectar-robbing western bumblebees affect pollination by hummingbirds? And if so, does the altered feeding by hummers impact the reproductive success of the scarlet gilia hosts? In alpine meadows of the Elk Mountains hummers visited fewer plants that had incurred heavy nectar robbing, defined as plants in which more than 80 percent of flowers had been robbed (Irwin and Brody 1998). Hummers also visited fewer flowers on such plants. This avoidance decreased pollen donation and receipt, the percentage of fruit set, and total seed set (Irwin and Brody 1999). High levels of robbing cut total plant reproduction from both male and female contributions by 50 percent (Irwin and Brody 2000). These results demonstrate that avoidance by hummingbirds reduces the fitness of nectar-robbed scarlet gilia plants.

So if hummingbirds avoid nectar-robbed blossoms, what cues do the birds use to discriminate between robbed and intact flowers? How do the birds know which flowers to pass up? When hummers were presented with scarlet gilia plants with nectar-robber holes and variable volumes of nectar, the hummers visited more plants with nectar and probed more flowers on those plants, regardless of the presence of nectar-robber holes (Irwin 2000). The hummers could have been avoiding robbed plants based on their spatial memory of the location of unrewarding plants. When the experimenters removed any spatial cues by randomizing the position of the plants after each hummingbird foraging bout, the hummers still selected the plants with nectar. Thus, hummingbirds do not rely on spatial hints when discriminating among flowers.

So, what do they use? The scarlet gilia's corolla is translucent, which may allow hummingbirds to see the nectar level through the side of the flower. To test whether hummers use this visual cue, investigators painted the flowers with acrylic paint, which rendered the corollas opaque. The birds still visited more plants with nectar and probed more flowers on those plants, regardless of the corolla's opacity (Irwin 2000). Even without simple visual indicators, hummingbirds still avoid nectar-robbed, nonrewarding plants, so how the birds do it remains a mystery.

Let's move from nectar robbery to classic herbivory, like the browsing of snowshoe hares on woody stems and the grazing of bighorn sheep in mountain meadows. As I mentioned a few paragraphs back, plant ecologists sort themselves into competing camps as to how they interpret the impact of herbivores on plant fitness. The more common, traditional view has of course been that herbivores harm their food plants and over evolutionary time have selected for the plants' toxic secondary compounds.

The idea that herbivory has negative effects on plant fitness has been accepted for a long time. Experimental removal of leaves, stems, sap, inflorescences, or roots reduces photosynthetic area, decreases surface area for the absorption of water and nutrients, and/or slows the intake of nutrients and carbohydrates. Since a plant's size influences its ability to capture solar energy, nutrients, and water, an herbivore removing plant parts should decrease the plant's competitive success. Presumably, the degree to which a plant resists herbivores reflects a trade-off between the benefits of reduced herbivory and the costs of decreasing resources allocated to other functions like reproduction.

Although such a defense-reproduction trade-off hypothesis seems intuitively attractive, it has received only inconsistent empirical support. The morning glory is eaten by the potato leaf beetle and yet shows no evidence of incurring a cost of resistance. This observation, along with similar findings in other plant species, indicates that incurring costs of resistance is not universal. This leads us elsewhere: we need another framework to supplement cost-benefit theory to explain the levels of defense and resistance found in natural plant populations.

A new, minority view is that some plants benefit from being eaten; that is, they overcompensate for their losses and eventually attain greater reproductive success than they would have if they had not been chewed on (Gronemeyer et al. 1997). Opposing this upstart hypothesis, some plant ecologists assert that strong experimental evidence has not been forthcoming to demonstrate increased levels of these adaptive responses of plants to herbivory (Belsky 1986).

To avoid unnecessarily aggravating the debate, let's be clear about some terms. By compensatory growth I mean all of the various kinds of positive responses by plants to injuries. Overcompensation occurs when the weight of grazed plants is greater than the weight of uneaten controls. Undercompensation is when the weight of chewed plants is less than that of uneaten controls; exact compensation is when the mass of treated plants equals that of control plants.

In the Yellowstone grasslands (Yellowstone National Park, northwestern Wyoming), the aboveground productivity of grazed vegetation was 47 percent higher than that of ungrazed plants (Frank and McNaughton 1993). This indicates a positive grazer effect. The stimulation of plant production by ungulates may be due in part to the migrations of ungulates as they track young, high-quality forage as it shifts across the landscape. This kind of natural wandering and clipping remind me of rotational grazing, a best management practice my cattle-farming neighbors talk about.

Although few species from the tallgrass prairie show such compensation to herbivory, most of Yellowstone's montane grasses do seem to compensate. Range ecologists compared the responses to herbivory of two grass species, big bluestem from the tallgrass prairie (Oklahoma) and timothy from Yellowstone. Big bluestem showed an uptake of nitrogen only when it was left unclipped and the surrounding plants were clipped, whereas clipped timothy did show a nitrogen uptake (Wallace and Macko 1993). This contrast suggests that compensating species, though they do not grow in all grasslands, may be competitively superior after herbivory. In obligate grazophiles, that is, plants that must be grazed, growth-promoting chemicals in the mammals' saliva seem to stimulate the plants' growth (Owen and Wiegert 1981).

For these and other reasons, some ecologists have proposed that grasses and grazers have coevolved, that one group would not have arisen without the other (Owen and Wiegert 1981). Several adaptations seem consistent with this sort of mutualism: the grazer's saliva that stimulates grass growth, basal meristems that are out of reach of most grazers, highly palatable grass leaves and shoots, and vegetative reproduction. It is also consistent that grazers and grasses evolved together in the Miocene epoch, 24 to 5 million years ago. In short, grasses seem to have adaptations that encourage grazing.

Let's apply this line of inquiry to the scarlet gilia. In some places ungulate browsing can be high during the flowering season. In a study on the San Francisco Peaks, 72 percent of the scarlet gilia plants were chewed during the flowering season (Paige and Whitham 1987). Of these, 63 percent were exposed to intense herbivory, defined as the consumption of 95 percent or more of the aboveground plant. Browsed plants produced 4.1 new inflorescences per plant versus only 1 in the uneaten controls.

How can this be? The removal of an inflorescence activated the growth of several flowering stalks from buds that had been lying dormant at the base of the stem. Compared to intact plants, browsed plants sprouted multiple inflorescences and produced 2.8 times as many flowers and 3.1 times as many fruits. Because there were no differences between browsed and unbrowsed individuals in number of seeds per fruit, weight per seed, germination success, or survival, browsed scarlet gilias experienced 2.4 times the fitness of uneaten plants.

In another study, on Fern Mountain, 77 percent of the scarlet gilia plants were browsed by ungulates during the flowering season (Paige 1992). On average the removal of the single inflorescence stimulated the production of five new flowering stalks. Thirty-three percent of these new stalks were then browsed again, a repeat attack called secondary herbivory. After the initial bout of herbivory, an apparent change in plant quality, possibly the induction of secondary chemicals, deterred high levels of subsequent herbivory and restricted tissue removal to the tips of the plant. Secondary herbivory had the same effect on the compensatory outcome, namely, that secondarily browsed plants produced more flowers and fruits than uneaten plants did. Therefore, scarlet gilia on the Fern overcompensated for herbivorous damage.

But wait, not so fast. In contrast to the findings reported above, other studies of scarlet gilia have found no evidence of overcompensation (Belsky 1986; Bergelson et al. 1996; Paige and Rausher 1994; Juenger and Bergelson 1997, 2000b). Along Coyote Creek (near Kettle Falls, Okanagan National Forest, north-central Washington), plant ecologists compared scarlet gilia plants on grazed and ungrazed sides of fences, as well as artificially clipped and control plants (Bergelson and Crawley 1992). Here, where plant density was 25 times higher in the protected plots, suggesting that ungulate grazing killed many of the plants, the grazing on young bolting shoots had little influence on fruit production.

For a more holistic view of this issue, let's look across the scarlet gilia's broad geographic distribution. Among eight populations of scarlet gilia in the Southern Rockies (Colorado) and the Southwest (northern Arizona), evidence for overcompensation was found in more than half (Paige 1999). Results from this metastudy, that is, a study of studies, and other

research on another biennial herb, the field gentian, demonstrate that, despite variable responses among the populations of scarlet gilia, overcompensation is real in some places and may be widespread geographically
and taxonomically (Trumble et al. 1993).

In the spirit of balanced reporting, I'm compelled to share three confounding findings. One study showed that a single population of a scarlet
gilia relative, the Arizona firecracker, can show a continuum of compensatory responses to herbivory (Maschinski and Whitham 1989). The most
common response was equal compensation, in which grazed plants set
the same numbers of fruits and seeds as the controls. Overcompensat-
ing plants, which had been grazed and fertilized with nutrients and were
free of competition, yielded 33 to 120 percent more fruits than ungrazed
plants. Undercompensation occurred in plants growing with grasses or
without added nutrients; these plants yielded only 28 to 82 percent as
many fruits as ungrazed plants.

The second complication is that scarlet gilia's form of plasticity may
reflect differences in water availability. During an extreme drought,
scarlet gilia plants showed severe undercompensation (Levine and Paige
2004). Water availability limited compensation partly because ungulates
browsed the plants unusually severely during the drought, resulting in
severe undercompensation. In this case the overriding factor determining
the level of fitness achieved through compensation was the indirect effect
of drought-associated ungulate browsing.

And here's a third factor muddying the waters. Whether a plant is
scored as an overcompensator is in part a function of the time scale of an
investigator's study (Becklin and Kirkpatrick 2006). On the eastern slope
of the Cascade Range (Wenatchee National Forest, north-central Washington), 90 percent of plants that lost flowers to hand cutting, which
was intended to simulate herbivory, regrew multiple flowering stalks
but produced fewer fruits and seeds than intact plants did. At this stage,
these plants were scored as undercompensating. However, the plants that
regrew multiple flowering stalks were also more likely to form ancillary
rosettes, which are supplementary circular arrangements of leaves. Over
the course of the next several years of the plant's life, ancillary rosettes
actually increased compensation. Thus, herbivory depressed fecundity at
first, but the morphological changes enabled the plant to achieve greater
compensation over its lifetime.

To summarize, a plant can overcompensate via several possible mechanisms, including allowing the action of hormones in animal saliva to promote its growth, producing extra aboveground growth at the expense of its root mass, and activating dormant buds and increasing its photosynthetic rates.

From an evolutionary point of view, where herbivory has been sufficiently strong and size selective (because herbivores prefer plants of a certain size), natural selection may have favored individual plants that withhold some resources against the likelihood that their early growth will be consumed (Vail 1992). Under these conditions plant fitness may be enhanced by herbivory—and selection may even favor some plant adaptations that invite being eaten. In this way, overcompensation can be interpreted as an adaptation that hedges the plant's bets in areas where predictably intense herbivory occurs.

Little did I know when I first bonded with scarlet gilia along the trail that my follow-up homework would show it to be a key player in a lively academic debate about overcompensation. Perhaps the researchers were initially attracted to it for the same reason I was—its vibrant red flowers rising to invigorate the day. And it now seems plausible that individual scarlet gilia plants maximize their reproductive success by inviting herbivores to eat them—the browsing stimulates the growth of more flowers, which in turn discharge more seeds. In some ways this system is reminiscent of the fire-promoting adaptations of lodgepole pine, which we'll explore in the next chapter. So here's the first of several pitches to view ecological disturbances, in this case herbivory, not solely as a negative constraint but as an opportunity ripe for evolutionary exploitation.

CHAPTER 5

Lodgepole Cones

Lodgepole forests represent a fire climax, that is,
a forest destined to burn periodically that seldom,
if ever, attains the climatic climax condition.

John J. Craighead, *The Greater Yellowstone Ecosystem:*
Redefining America's Wilderness Heritage

AS WE WALKED, a starkness—those silent, eerily still-standing black boles—dulled my mind. In some places the fires of 1988 were so intense they burned even the soil's organic layer. When Nancy and I backpacked through the Cache Creek basin (Cache Creek Trail, Yellowstone National Park, northwestern Wyoming) in June of 2000, 12 years after the fires, entire mountainsides were still devoid of any hints of ecological recovery.

But other places in Yellowstone, like the Howell Creek meadow west of Eagle Pass (Mountain Creek Trail), were blanketed by thick stands of lodgepole saplings. The trails through convalescing areas supported varying densities of grasses; mixes of wildflowers like fireweed, paintbrush, and glacier lilies; saplings of lodgepole pine and quaking aspen; the castanet grasshopper; birds like the red-shafted flicker, mountain bluebird, Oregon junco, and red-tailed hawk; and a few mammals like chipmunks and elk.

The diversity in recovery and the contrast in vegetative cover can indicate differences in the fuel load, wind speed, and other factors that determined the fire's intensity. The differences can also reflect a variable time lag of seed dispersal. Some individual lodgepole pine trees release fewer seeds the year after forming them, while others jettison more seeds after they've been heated by fire.

By combining these two concepts—fire intensity and reseeding time lag—we can begin to understand what causes the variety of vegetation patches across a convalescing Rocky Mountain landscape. The patterns in which lodgepole pine burned in Yellowstone in 1988 and by which the region has been showing recovery will continue to provoke us, and thereby teach us, for years to come.

Let's set the stage with a little lodgepole pine biology. A lodgepole pine tree features two-needled clusters, yellow-green foliage, and a trunk that may reach 75 feet (23 m) tall (Shaw and On 1979). In a thick stand only the treetops have branches, which form a gently rounded crown only a few feet (e.g., 1–2 m) across. Some tribes of Native Americans framed their lodges with its long, straight boles, hence the tree's common name (Hunt 1976).

One of the most common coniferous trees throughout the Western Cordillera, lodgepole pine also has one of the largest ranges of any plant in the region, from Alaska and the Yukon southward to Baja California and the Southern Rockies (southern Colorado) (Fowells 1965).

On either side of the Rockies the species has shown somewhat different evolutionary trajectories (Parchman et al. 2011). In the central core of its range, trees on the two sides of the Continental Divide show minimal genetic differentiation, yet its isolated populations show more differences on the two sides. This suggests at least a minimal level of reproductive isolation within the species. Perhaps it is in the process of diverging into two or more species. As I write, lodgepole is also expanding northward through the central Yukon, presumably as a response to climate change (Johnstone and Chapin 2003).

As you might expect, such a geographically widespread species shows broad ecological tolerances, which have been detected in both paleoecological and contemporary times. Even though, at 9,834 feet (2980 m) in elevation, Little Windy Hill Pond in the Medicine Bow Mountains (Carbon County, southeastern Wyoming) has experienced varying climate and prominent vegetation shifts over the last 10,700 years, from sagebrush steppe to spruce-fir parkland, the lodgepole pine forests that established 8,500 years ago have not changed (Minckley et al. 2012), a hint of the species' resilience. Today's lodgepole environment features fairly dry summers, a short growing season of 60 to 100 days, and frosts in any month; lodgepole grows on soils derived from granite, shale, or sandstone; and it can be found at elevations from 1,500 to 11,500 feet (457–3505 m) above sea level (Fowells 1965). Within these extremes its upper and lower limits conform to the standard latitudinal pattern. For example, in the northern Central Rockies (northwestern Wyoming), forests dominated by lodgepole pine are most common at 5,900 to 10,600 feet (1800–3230 m), whereas they are common at 7,000 to 11,600 feet (2130–3540 m) in the southern Central Rockies (southwestern Wyoming).

All of these dynamic population features—living in diverse habitats, occupying a huge geographic range, having semi-isolated peripheral populations undergoing incipient differentiation, and shifting in distribution—proclaim that lodgepole pine is a swiftly evolving species.

In poor soil, mycorrhizal fungi enable a lodgepole pine to extend the range of its roots and thereby increase the rates at which it absorbs water and nutrients. A symbiotic relationship between a fungus and the roots of a vascular plant, mycorrhizae provide biology teachers with a classic example of mutualism, an intimate relationship that benefits two kinds of organisms. Some species of fungus develop mycorrhizae with the roots of only one species of host tree; others are less partner specific—some lodgepole stands in the Canadian Rockies (southwestern Alberta) host 20 kinds of mycorrhizae (Bradbury et al. 1998).

Lodgepole pine seedlings do poorly in the shade. In many places the shade-tolerant seedlings of Douglas-fir, Engelmann spruce, and subalpine fir eventually replace lodgepole. Another reason that succession forges ahead is that lodgepole incompletely closes the canopy. Even in close-growing stands the lodgepole's tops are whipped by winds, which can displace the upper limbs as much as 16.5 feet (5 m), causing some limbs to abrade and break. Canopies of individual trees do not touch those of their neighbors, crown shyness is reinforced, and resulting light flecks support the establishment of the trees that eventually succeed lodgepole (Jensen 2000; Meng et al. 2006). Where the seeds of such replacement species are available, lodgepole is a temporary species in a transitional stand. In contrast, some lodgepole groves are subclimax, persisting over the long term because they are isolated from the seed supplies of their potential replacements (Fowells 1965). Such a pure stand of lodgepole pine may persist for so long that it assumes the characteristics of a climax forest.

Lodgepole pine is a pioneer species of burned areas. Its episodic establishment can create forest patches with just two or three age classes. Such a stand can have the composition of a tree plantation. Lodgepole is most conspicuous when it grows in such dense, even-sized stands, the so-called doghair thickets. For 50 years or more after a fire, lodgepole seedlings may become established. As the lodgepole canopy grows and admits less light, its own seedlings establish at a slower pace. The mean recurrence interval of such hot, stand-replacing fires in lodgepole pine forests is fairly long, between 100 and 300 years.

Many kinds of animals live in lodgepole pine forests, including birds such as the hairy woodpecker, two species of nuthatch, Clark's nut-cracker, and pine siskin; and mammals such as the red squirrel, snowshoe hare, porcupine, red-backed vole, marten, ermine, coyote, lynx, bobcat, both bear species, and wolverine. Along the trail, though, I found thick lodgepole stands to be quiet, with few animals evident. In dense lodge-pole forests little light reaches the ground and the understory is sparse. This is one reason that, compared to other forest types, lodgepole stands may seem to be biologically depauperate.

Trees in the pine family are pollinated by wind. In such a passive pro-cess the release, transport, and capture of pollen are controlled by micro-climate (Whitehead 1983). Among plants in general, several traits, such as flower structure and location, the timing of flowering and pollen release, and the number, size, and sculptural characteristics of the individual pol-len grains, are adaptations for consummating pollination. At its simplest, the movement of pollen is a function of two variables: wind speed and the pollen's settling velocity. Simply, pollen disperses farther as wind quickens and settling slows. Wind pollination is most effective where the following conditions converge: humidity is low so water is quickly lost from the pollen grains; the odds of rainfall are low; reproductively compatible plants are near each other; unambiguous environmental cues are available to coordinate flowering among trees; and large quantities of pollen are released while wind velocity is within the range that ensures transport and yet minimizes downwind dispersal.

I list these features of lodgepole pine and their environmental context because they will help us understand why lodgepole pine is a prolific, but inconsistent, seed producer. The hit-or-miss character of wind pollina-tion means that lodgepole trees produce good seed crops inconsistently, around every three years (Fowells 1965). As you can imagine, such a mast-yearing habit has consequences for pine seed–dependent animals and the pace of fire recovery.

Lodgepole pines issue winged seeds, which are dispersed by the wind. Vertebrates like chipmunks remove most of the seeds from the ground within a few days (Vander Wall 1994, 2003, 2008). At one site the large seeds of Jeffrey pine disappeared faster than ponderosa's medium-sized seeds, which in turn vanished faster than lodgepole's small seeds. Animals harvest most of the pine seeds during a two-month period between seed-fall and winter.

The harvesting of pine seeds by animals has some interesting consequences for the tree. Several species of bird-dispersed pines commonly grow as multitree clusters. In North America this growth form results primarily from the germination of multiseed caches of the Clark's nutcracker (Torick et al. 1996). In wind-dispersed pines, multitrunk tree clumps also occur but they seem less frequent. Are some of these wind-dispersed, multiseed tree clumps actually multigenet tree clusters? That is, are they clumps of genetically different individuals? In the Front Range of the Southern Rockies (Colorado), tree geneticists analyzed the foliage from 10 tree clumps each of ponderosa, bristlecone, and lodgepole pines. Eight (80%) of the ponderosa clumps, two (20%) of the bristlecone clumps, and four (40%) of the lodgepole clumps were multigenet tree clusters (Torick et al. 1996). Thus, multigenet tree clusters are not restricted to big-seeded, bird-dispersed pine species, like the whitebark pine; they also occur in wind-dispersed pines, like lodgepole.

As I reported in this chapter's opening scene, the severity of wildfire affects the subsequent density of lodgepole seedlings. In Yellowstone in August 1989, a year into postfire recovery, forest ecologists inventoried the density of plants in paired plots (Anderson and Romme 1991). In each pair one site had been burned severely, the other only moderately. The densities of lodgepole seedlings were higher in the moderately burned places. The key variable explaining the difference was the degree to which the seeds were killed by fire. A later study, conducted 10 years after the fires, also concluded that burn severity is an important variable in explaining sapling density (Kashian et al. 2004).

Another factor that influences the availability of lodgepole seeds after a fire is the kinds of cones that are present before the burn. And this takes us to the topic of the different kinds of lodgepole pine cones: some cones open and release seeds in their second year, like the cones of most pine species, while other cones remain sealed by secretions of pitch until they are heated by a fire. Viable seeds have been extracted even from closed cones that were 75 to 80 years old. An asymmetrical cone that sits at an acute angle to its branch indicates such a delayed-release, or serotinous, cone (Tinker et al. 1994).

The word "serotinous" is derived from the Latin *serotinus*, which means "coming late." In our context the word refers to the delayed dissemination of seeds. Other conifer species, like jack pine, which occurs in the Rockies' eastern foothills, also show the serotiny adaptation. Serotiny seems to have been selected in conifer populations where fire has been the dominant ecological disturbance.

Lodgepole pine is categorized as a fire-type conifer. Its serotinous cones must be exposed to temperatures between 113 and 140°F (45–60°C) to melt the resin between the cone scales (Tinker et al. 1994). The heat causes the cone's scales to flex, spread apart, and release its seeds. This is why, after a fire—often within a few weeks—the ground can be sprinkled with tiny lodgepole seedlings.

In response to seed predation by squirrels, natural selection has favored the evolution of tough protective tissues in serotinous cones. Trees with serotinous cones divert a large proportion of their energy into cone tissue, leaving less for actual seed production. It thus makes sense that serotinous cones carry a lighter seed mass than nonserotinous cones.

Some lodgepole pine stands include a mix of trees, some with serotinous cones and others with cones that open at maturity (Tinker et al. 1994). Among Yellowstone's many lodgepole stands the proportion of serotinous trees ranges from 0 to 72 percent, with the greatest frequencies found at the lower and middle elevations of 6,270 to 7,590 feet (1900–2300 m) above sea level. The ratio of serotinous to open-coned trees reflects the nature of the most recent fires. For example, stands recovering from severe burns include trees with a high percentage of closed serotinous cones, whereas stands that originate after a disturbance other than fire, like an epidemic of an insect pest, typically produce a high percentage of open-coned trees.

The association between fire and the percentage of serotiny allows a useful prediction: the density of trees with serotinous cones before a fire is a good predictor of lodgepole seedling density after the fire. Seedling density in burned stands ranged from 7.5 to 10 seedlings per acre (3–4/ha) near Yellowstone Lake, where the percentage of serotiny had been near 0, to more than 18 per square foot (200/m²) in stands with 50 to 75 percent serotinous trees at Cougar Creek in the Madison Valley (the west-central part of the park) (Tinker et al. 1994). Through this process an intense fire in a lodgepole stand with predominantly serotinous cones can generate a doghair stand.

And there's yet another factor at play in determining the frequency of serotiny. It turns out that, at least in Yellowstone, site is also a powerful predictor of the level of serotiny (Turner et al. 1997). Low-elevation sites with substrates of rhyolite, which is a fine-grained volcanic soil, and south-, east-, and west-facing mountainsides are most likely to support a high proportion of serotinous trees (Tinker et al. 1994). Taken together, these findings point to a chain of causes and effects: a specific mix of environmental factors, like soil type and aspect, facilitates a certain disturbance regime, like fire-return interval, that in turn selects for serotiny.

But wait, there are yet two more layers to the serotiny story. While many lodgepole pine trees never produce serotinous cones, other trees grow nonserotinous cones until they reach 20 to 30 years of age and then shift into serotiny (Schoennagel et al. 2003). And still other individual trees seem to grow three types of cones: nonserotinous cones that open at warm temperatures of 77 to 122°F (25–50°C), closed cones that need 113 to 140°F (45–60°C) to open, and intermediate cones that open at 95 to 122°F (35–50°C). This phenotypic variation among trees seems to be at least partially genetically determined.

By working backward from the proportion of serotinous trees, we can reconstruct, at least in general terms, a place's disturbance history. As I've said, the ratio of serotinous to nonserotinous cones depends on the nature of the last disturbance. Nonserotinous trees are favored if the last disturbance was an insect epidemic or a windstorm because most of the serotinous seeds will have remained quiescent in their cones. In contrast, fires yield more serotinous trees because heat opens cones and abundant seeds are dispersed when conditions for establishment are ideal. We therefore have another tool for inferring the past of a Western landscape.

The lodgepole pine is the most common tree of the Rockies. Several of its adaptations, like germination in bare mineral soil and serotiny, are adaptations to the environment available after a wildfire. Its seeds are eaten by birds and mammals, and its cone types indicate a landscape's fire regime. Lodgepole pine by itself will continue to teach us much about how life has adapted to the Rocky Mountains.

CHAPTER 6

Aspen Clones

And the wind, full of wantonness, woos like a lover
The young aspen-trees till they tremble all over.

Thomas Moore, *Lalla Rookh: An Oriental Romance*

ON A HOT, clear July day Nancy and I were doggedly climbing the dusty
trail along the West Branch of the Laramie River, which drains the eastern
flank of the Medicine Bow Mountains (Rawah Trail, Rawah Wilderness,
Roosevelt National Forest, north-central Colorado). Fetching blossoms
of goldenglow and fireweed brightened our passage to Big Rainbow Lake
via Grassy Pass.

Straining, I begged, "Let's stop in the next shade."

The speckled shade of the aspen grove wrapped me in cool air. Lean-
ing against my pack, which in turn was propped against the base of an
aspen trunk, I swigged water as I squinted up through the tree's canopy—
air stirred, leaves trembled, light shafts blinked. Gnats danced through
turbulent dust. Native Americans called aspen "the tree that whispers
to itself." As I rested my heels and squinted up at the leaves, my mind
queried the scene. How and why do "quakies" waggle? Why is aspen so
patchy? And what consequences does this tree's patchiness have for the
animals of its ecosystem?

Also called trembling aspen, a quaking aspen tree in its prime is a beauty
of contrast—a trunk base of rough black and a smooth, white, thin, almost cream-colored bark that overlays a sheer photosynthetic green layer;
thin leaves that are glossy light green on top and silvery below; and an
open, round crown that may reach 100 feet (18 m) high (Grant 1993;

Rosing 1998). Aspen's light-colored bark is thought to reduce the risk of winter sunscald injury, possibly by protecting the cambium, which is the layer of living cells under the bark, from solar heat gain in subfreezing temperatures (Karels and Boonstra 2003).

Let's go ahead and knock off that first question. An aspen leaf trembles because the distal end of its petiole, that is, the leaf stem, is slender, flat, and attached at a perpendicular angle to the plane of the leaf blade (Shaw and On 1979). Plus, each petiole base is loosely connected to the twig (Durrell 1988). These flimsy links yield to the slightest puff, so the whole tree shimmers. Some botanists have suggested an adaptive value of leaf waggling: its function may be to shift the topmost leaves back and forth so sunlight can penetrate to the lower reaches of the tree, allowing the lower tissues to photosynthesize. This idea seems plausible given the tree's greenish bark. When top-canopy leaves flutter, the understory light environment shows more but shorter sunflecks (Roden and Pearcy 1993c). In fact, aspen leaves are efficient at using rapidly fluctuating light (Roden and Pearcy 1993d). Two other hypotheses, specifically that leaf flutter enhances the leaves' carbon dioxide flux and that it cools the leaves, have been tested and rejected (Roden and Pearcy 1993a, 1993b).

Quaking aspen is the most widely distributed tree species in North America (Fowells 1965; Grant 1993; Mitton and Grant 1996; Howard 1996). In the West this native deciduous member of the willow family ranges from Alaska southward through the Rockies (British Columbia and Alberta southward through north-central New Mexico), extending southward as isolated populations into the Sierra Madre Oriental (just north of Santiago de Querétaro, Querétaro state, central Mexico). Its broad distribution is facilitated by its symbioses with diverse ectomycorrhizal fungi (Godbout and Fortin 1985).

The range of aspen in the interior West, where much of the climate is semiarid, appears to be limited not by extreme temperatures but by the availability of water, which it needs to satisfy its high transpirational demands (Jones and DeByle 1985). It is consistent that in the transition zone between boreal forest and prairie (western Canada), quaking aspen seems to be limited by drought. In an area where drought was exceptionally severe during 2001–2002, dead trees were 20 percent of the total aboveground biomass (Michaelian et al. 2011).

At treeline, up against the tundra in Alaska, seed germination increases with experimental warming, suggesting that aspen's treeline may result in part from unsuccessful recruitment under cold conditions

(Hobbie and Chapin 1998). At its northern limit, aspen is found up to only 3,000 feet (910 m) above sea level; at its southernmost latitudes its maximum elevation is 10,000 feet (3048 m) (Fowells 1965; Howard 1996). It grows from the foothills to the subalpine zone on all aspects and slopes (Fletcher 1985). In high, exposed, cold places, aspen assumes a stunted, even prostrate, form less than three feet (1 m) high (Mitton and Grant 1996).

With its broad distribution and wide ecological niche, quaking aspen serves as a major cover type in North America (Howard 1996). In the Rockies, where aspen groves are scattered throughout Engelmann spruce–subalpine fir forests, associated shrub species include mountain snowberry, western serviceberry, chokecherry, common juniper, Oregon grape, Wood's rose, myrtle pachistima, redberry elder, and several *Ribes* species, which include currants and gooseberries. And, as you'll see in a bit, this understory supports a variety of animals.

Although its huge geographic range and success in diverse habitats qualify the quaking aspen as a successful evolutionary entity, it obviously hasn't penetrated everywhere. For instance, some plants outcompete aspen. It seems that lengthening fire-return intervals, one of the consequences of modern fire suppression, has intensified competition between aspen and conifers. In an experiment, a team of tree physiologists found that aspen regeneration was more sensitive to light and soil limits than that of subalpine fir. Aspen is not shade tolerant (Howard 1996). Lessening light and/or shifts in soil chemicals, the kinds of changes that occur as conifers increase in dominance, limit aspen's growth, biomass, photosynthesis, and levels of two families of defensive compounds, phenolic glycosides and tannins (Calder et al. 2011). Thus, increasing dominance of conifers in subalpine forests changes light and soil conditions, which constrains aspen's physiology and growth more than subalpine fir's, which in turn causes more recruitment of conifers and losses of aspen.

Further, some animals limit aspen's distribution. Pocket gophers are medium-sized rodents, roughly eight inches (20 cm) long and weighing 11 ounces (308 g). They spend most of their life underground, although they do surface under the snowpack. During the summer we often saw their leftover earthen tunnels, called eskers, along subalpine trails. Where they co-occur, the Botta's pocket gopher inhibits the aspen's invasion of meadows (Cantor and Whitham 1989). In 32 aspen-meadow associations, the distributions of aspens and gophers were nonoverlapping in 93 percent of the sites. When biologists compared aspen performance in plots where gophers had been removed with that in control areas, the aspen's release from pocket gopher herbivory was swift: aspen tree growth accelerated threefold, vegetative reproduction rose by 2.5 times, and survival increased by a factor of 3.5. These results demonstrate that pocket gophers affect the local distribution of aspen.

Aspen has been expanding its range, seemingly facilitated by changes in climate and land use. In the Upper Foothills Subregion of the Canadian Rockies (west-central Alberta), aspen seedlings have been found up to 660 feet (200 m) higher in elevation than the mature aspen of the original undisturbed forests (Landhausser et al. 2010). Further, aspen is also expanding upslope in places where forestry methods have exposed mineral soils and the climate has been warming.

As an appreciator of Rocky Mountain landscapes, you've no doubt noticed that quaking aspens grow in bunches. An aspen stand may consist of one or more clones (Howard 1996). Aspen groves often occur in depressions, ravines, valley bottoms, or on the lee sides of ridges where snow accumulates through the winter. The presence of aspen is an indication of water near the surface (Eversman and Carr 1992). Its restriction to moist areas is, in addition to its transpirational needs, probably due to the fact that its seedlings cannot tolerate drought. As a deciduous tree, aspen does not efficiently conserve nutrients with its autumnal leaf shedding. But on the other hand, as an aspen stand matures, the organic content, moisture-retaining capacity, and alkalinity of the soil increase (Parker and Parker 1983). Such a pocket of moisture and nutrients explains, at least in part, why aspen does well in depressions.

Aspen groves support some of the most diverse animal communities in the mountains. Large soil invertebrates, like snails, spiders, and ants, are more abundant in aspen groves than in adjacent coniferous forests. The American redstart and chestnut-sided warbler rely exclusively on pure aspen stands (Hobson 2000). Ruffed grouse are associated with aspen—males drum from fallen logs, adults feed on its buds and catkins, and chicks feed on insects in the understory (Gullion and Alm 1983; Stauffer and Peterson 1985a, 1985b). Further, aspen provides habitat for various mammals, including the montane shrew, long-tailed and montane voles, and the long-tailed weasel. In the winter, snowshoe hares eat aspen buds, twigs, and bark; porcupines slice off the smooth outer bark (Howard 1996). Extensive bark stripping in some aspen forests, like the stand in which we rested in the Medicine Bows, can indicate heavy use by elk. Elk browse aspen twigs by scraping their bark, primarily in the winter when understory forage is covered by snow. Bark stripping allows pathogens, like those that cause fungal infections, to penetrate the tree. Black and grizzly bears feed on forbs and berry-producing shrubs within aspen stands (Howard 1996). In some areas the trees also provide bears with denning sites.

Partly because it is shade intolerant and cannot reproduce under its own canopy, quaking aspen functions as an early-successional plant (Howard 1996; Mitton and Grant 1996). While Engelmann spruce and subalpine fir may gradually replace some aspen stands, especially on north-facing slopes, this succession can take centuries (Crawford et al. 1998). In contrast, in some places aspen persists for a long time. For example, between Mount Gunnison and Castle Peak (near Crested Butte, west-central Colorado), aspen stands can be long lived.

Even if we accept the notion that some aspen clones are extremely old, we know they don't live forever. Evolutionary theory predicts that during asexual growth, as in a spreading plant clone, somatic mutations should accumulate and contribute to the senescence of individuals. By combining estimates of clone age from the trees' molecular clock with measures of male fertility, which served as a proxy for senescence, a research team found that the number of viable pollen grains per catkin per ramet decreased with increasing clonal age (Ally et al. 2010). In the Canadian Rockies they collected leaves from natural stands of quaking aspen clones that ranged from 70 to 10,000 years old at Riske Creek and Red Rock. (The latter site, incidentally, was where Nancy and I launched our Waterton-through-Glacier hike.) The pollen analysis revealed a slow but steady loss of fertility with age. Mutations reduced male fertility by 5.8×10^{-5} to 1.6×10^{-3} per year, which translates to an 8 percent annual loss in the number of viable pollen grains in the oldest clones. Fertility was cut by more than three-quarters in the oldest clone and, by extrapolation, would have disappeared entirely after 20,000 years (Meadows 2010). The odds of an aspen lineage going extinct rise as its male sexual fitness declines. So, even though an aspen clone may be extremely old, long life does not imply living in perpetuity.

By the fourth week of September, colors in the high country reach their peak. One of the most stunning sights in the Rockies is the riotous patches of chrome yellow, orange, and crimson blazing across the landscape. Aspen's varying colors have been attributed to differences in local weather conditions, soil composition, and genetic makeup (Walker 1973). More on this in a bit.

As I mentioned earlier, aspen bark can be greenish. Capable of photosynthesis, the chlorophyll in its bark assimilates carbon—even in subfreezing temperatures. Although the photosynthesis in bark contributes only 1 or 2 percent of what the leaves contribute, it could be enough to render the plant a functional evergreen.

Quaking aspen reproduces via both sexual and asexual modes. In some regions, like the boreal forest (northern Canada) and eastern North America, aspen commonly establishes from seed (Howard 1996). In the West, though, aspen germinates only occasionally from its windblown seeds. Each tiny seed has a tuft of hair that allows the wind to carry it. A few parachute for vast distances. Optimum conditions for germination and seedling survival include moist mineral soil, adequate drainage, moderate temperatures, and weak competition (Howard 1996).

Aspen also reproduce vegetatively by root suckers (Fowells 1965; Mitton and Grant 1996). Many aspen in the West produce prolific shoots from their roots, especially after fire kills the adult stem (Bartos and Mueggler 1981; Fletcher 1985; Eversman and Carr 1992). The root system is shallow, with wide-spreading lateral roots that can stretch over 100 feet (30 m). Vertical sinker roots descend from the laterals (Howard 1996). When a stem dies, its shoot-suppressing hormone is inactivated and the new hormonal balance triggers a huge increase of new, fast-growing stems (Grant 1993). Thus, sprouting is hormonally controlled. Auxin, a plant hormone that is transported from the stem to the roots, suppresses sprouting and thereby maintains apical dominance, the process by which the stem tip prevents the development of lateral branches. When stems are killed, apical dominance stops, and cytokinins in the roots initiate root sprouting. Root suckering is also stimulated by nitrate (Wan et al. 2010).

Once trees are established in a stand, their number increases from new shoots that sprout from the old roots. The repetition of this process over centuries allows the stems that grew from one original tree to develop into a large genetic clone (Eversman and Carr 1992; Mitton and Grant 1996). This is why the trees in many places are either all male or all female. It's curious that at low elevations along the Front Range female clones are more common than males. Could this be adaptive?

Let's pause here to clarify two terms. A *clone* is a group of genetically identical individuals derived by asexual, vegetative growth from a common ancestor. A *ramet* is an individual member of a clone, to our eye a single tree. Thus, what looks like an aspen patch on a distant mountain-side may well be a single large clone of many identical ramets.

Suckers issue from buds on shallow lateral roots lying as deep as four inches (10.2 cm) below the soil's surface. A root may travel 100 feet (30 m) underground before sprouting upward (Grant 1993). Even in undisturbed stands a few suckers arise almost every year. A shoot is initially sustained by the parent's root system, and then the derived stem quickly forms its own root.

In the winter range of the Jackson Hole elk herd in the Greater Yellowstone Ecosystem (northwestern Wyoming), aspen ramets have regenerated at low frequencies since 1830, with three peaks during 1860–85, 1915–40, and 1955–90 (Hessl and Graumlich 2002). These three periods coincided with low to moderate elk populations. In contrast, aspen regenerated only sporadically when elk populations were high.

Picture the roots of an aspen tree as having hundreds of dormant shoots, each ready to sprout when encouraged by light and warmth. Fire of moderate severity does not damage roots that are insulated by soil (Howard 1996). In a study of three burn sites, the number of suckers varied from 24,700 to 143,925 per acre (9,880–57,570/ha) in the first year after fire and 17,650 to 53,100 per acre (7,060–21,240/ha) four years post-fire (Brown and DeByle 1987), an annual decrease of about 15 percent. In terms of sucker numbers and growth rates, the success of suckering increases when the root is injured (Fraser et al. 2004), but only up to a point, as suckering is lower on severely burned sites (Wang 2003). New saplings created via this process can shoot up three feet (1 m) in a single summer (Mitton and Grant 1996).

As a clone matures, suckering slows in the dense center and becomes more common in its outer edges where soil and light conditions continue to be favorable. Also, mature trees in the center exude hormones that suppress suckering. An individual stem may live a relatively short life, say 80 to 100 years, but the parent organism—the aspen clone—may persist for centuries, possibly even for several millennia.

As I've said, aspen trees do produce seeds, but they do not seem to germinate well in today's Rocky Mountain environment (Kay 1993; Mitton and Grant 1996). Still, a rare episode of sexual reproduction occurred in Yellowstone after the fires of 1988 (Romme et al. 1997; Stevens et al. 1999). Aspen seedlings were widely distributed over the area that had burned in the park's Northern Range, but the greatest concentrations occurred in riparian zones that had burned down to mineral soil (Kay 1993). In 1989 huge numbers of aspen seedlings sprouted in many burned zones, apparently because of an unusual combination of copious seed production, suitable substrate, and favorable weather. Short-term climate records suggest that rare sexual reproduction has occurred in cool, moist years (Elliott and Baker 2004). In these situations the densities of aspen seedlings averaged 57,751 per acre (142,645/ha)—even reaching 4,700,000 per acre (11,500,000/ha) in one spot (Kay 1993). Further, aspen became established in many areas where it had been absent before the fires. Some investigators went so far as to assert that this flush of aspen seedlings was an extraordinary natural event, namely, the swift range expansion of an ecologically important species in response to a large-scale disturbance (Romme et al. 1997). The cohort of aspen seedlings that germinated after the 1988 fires now seems to be in the early stages of a long-term population shift from genetically distinct individuals with few ramets to few clones with many ramets (Romme et al. 2005).

Because it establishes rapidly in sunny sites from which other trees have been removed by fire, avalanche, or other disturbance, within its ecosystem aspen functions as a pioneer species, one that excels at colonizing newly available sites (Mitton and Grant 1996). Invasion is complete in 5 to 10 years, with its density peaking in 25 to 50 years. Because of its swift establishment and growth, aspen is a principal agent in the reforestation of burned areas. Once established, aspens may nurse the young specimens of other, slower-growing tree species. Evergreens and some hardy species of oak take root under the aspen's protective canopy and thrive in the grove's rich humus. In 50 years the young protectees may crowd and overshadow their aspen nurses. So, in many sites the aspen eventually die off and are replaced by other tree species.

Do Elk Overbrowse Aspen?

Some parts of the Rockies have suffered from poor aspen regeneration. For example, most of the aspen stands in northern Yellowstone were established between 1870 and 1890, but little regeneration has occurred since 1900 (Romme et al. 1995). Environmental managers have been debating the roles of elk versus fire suppression in causing this lack of regeneration. Several studies have started to resolve the issue.

The fires of 1988 burned 22 percent of Yellowstone's Northern Range (Romme et al. 1995). The density of aspen sprouts was greater in burned than in unburned stands in the spring of 1990, two years after the fires, but was approaching the density of unburned stands by the fall of 1991. There were no differences in the browsing intensity between burned and unburned stands. Unbrowsed sprouts were lower than the depth of the snowpack, suggesting that elk browsed nearly all sprouts that were accessible in the winter. The age distribution of 15 aspen stands indicated that the regeneration of large stems had been episodic even before the establishment of the park in 1872 (Romme et al. 1995). The period from 1870 to 1890 was unique: large mammalian predators were present, the numbers of elk and other browsers were low, the climate was relatively wet, and extensive fires had occurred recently. This mix of conditions has not recurred since 1900. Collectively, these observations suggest that the current paucity of aspen regeneration in the northern park cannot be explained by a single factor—either excess elk or fire suppression—rather it seems to involve a complex interaction among several causes.

More recently, though, another research team came to a somewhat different conclusion (Ripple and Larsen 2000). Using data from a previous study and their own aspen increment cores from riparian and random sites, they inferred that 10 percent of today's overstory of aspen in Yellowstone's Northern Range originated before 1871, 85 percent entered the overstory during 1871–1920, and 5 percent did so after 1921. Successful recruitment to the aspen overstory occurred in the Northern Range from the mid to late 1700s until the 1920s, when it ceased. The provocative conclusion was that recruitment to the aspen overstory stopped after the gray wolf, a key elk predator, was extirpated from the region.

Other research teams, using spatial, exclosure, and repeat photography approaches in the Canadian (Yoho and Kootenay National Parks) and Southern Rockies (Rocky Mountain National Park, north-central Colorado), arrived at supporting views (Suzuki et al. 1999; Baker et al. 1997; Kay 1997a). These findings suggest that intense elk browsing, not fire suppression, beaver herbivory, or climate change, limits aspen regeneration in the park's elk winter range.

I think it's clear that overbrowsing, often by elk, has been constraining aspen regeneration in the Rockies.

Vegetative reproduction via asexual suckering makes the clone, not each single stem, the genetic entity of the quaking aspen species. All of the trees in many groves likely issue from one original plant, so, except for a rare somatic mutation, all stems in a bunch are genetically identical. This is why all of the stems of a clone have the same angle between trunk and branches, bark color and texture, leaf size and shape, gender, density of extrafloral nectaries (organs on their leaves that contain nectar), resistance to certain diseases and herbivores, responses to drought, and timing of their leaf-out, color change, and leaf-drop (Griffin et al. 1991; Wagner et al. 2007; Wooley et al. 2007). You can see different clones best in the autumn: each color patch is likely a separate clone. So let's think of natural selection as operating among aspen clones, not among individual stems.

 A Big Old Aspen Clone

Some aspen clones are extremely old, some say even one million years old (Mitton and Grant 1996). More typically, an old one might be 10,000 years old. One such ancient grove goes by a couple of nicknames, the Trembling Giant and Pando, the latter of which is Latin for "I spread." Pando is a male clone that covers 110 acres (44 ha) near Fish Lake, an alpine lake at 8,848 feet (2697 m) above sea level. It is located at the western edge of the Colorado Plateau, just south of the Wasatch Mountains (Fishlake National Forest, south-central Utah). Pando includes 47,000 interconnected ramets and has been estimated to weigh more than 6,500 tons (5850 t) and to be 80,000 years old (Grant 1993).

A team of molecular geneticists has confirmed that the morphological Pando is indeed a single clone (DeWoody et al. 2008). Some biologists have nominated Pando as Earth's largest living thing, at least in terms of mass (Grant 1993). A few researchers even conjecture that all of the aspens living in the Rockies today may be cloned descendants of trees that germinated during the waning years of the Pleistocene epoch, about 10,000 to 12,000 years ago. An aspen clone's longevity is maintained in part because its forest structure supports light surface fires that stimulate suckering and retard invasion by conifers; plus, as I've said, the grove generates the organic matter that holds moisture and nutrients (Parker and Parker 1983).

The clonal nature of aspen has two levels of evolutionary consequences for its herbivorous enemies. First, clones vary in their chemical makeup and therefore in the amounts of nutrients they offer herbivores (Jelinski and Fisher 1991). For cervids, most aspen clones provide adequate levels of calcium, magnesium, manganese, and zinc; some clones offer only limiting levels of protein; and most, but not all, clones are limiting in phosphorus.

And second, aspen clones vary in their antiherbivore defenses. The main secondary compounds in aspen that impact herbivores are phenolic glycosides and condensed tannins in roots, bark, and leaves, and coniferyl benzoate in flower buds. Aspen clones can show up to a 10-fold variation in the level of phenolic glycosides and condensed tannins across a landscape (Lindroth and St. Clair in press). Variation in the level of defensive chemicals among aspen clones contributes to differences in the extent they are defoliated by these herbivorous insects. And genetic differences, in turn, are a likely cause of the aspen's interclonal variation in secondary compounds (Hwang and Lindroth 1997, 1998). These results demonstrate that genetic differences among clones account for different levels of secondary chemicals among the clones, and that this chemical variation, in turn, affects the severity of herbivory.

The kinds and levels of secondary compounds in an aspen clone can represent the products of induced resistance (Clausen et al. 1989; Lindroth and Kinney 1998; Roth et al. 1998; Osier and Lindroth 2004). A sequence of chemical changes provides aspen with an induced short-term resistance against attack by moth caterpillars.

In addition to impacting insect pests, aspen's secondary compounds affect mammalian herbivores. For instance, porcupines eat trees with high levels of phenolic glycosides less frequently than they browse normal plants (Diner et al. 2009). Phenolic glycosides, but not tannins, also influence which aspen are eaten by elk (McArthur et al. 1993; Wooley et al. 2008). As you would expect, the causes and effects run both ways. For instance, browsing by elk can also raise the levels of phenolic glycosides in aspen (Bailey et al. 2007).

What changes take place within an aspen tree as an animal chews on it? In general terms, when a mammal browses on an aspen's bark it induces changes in protein synthesis within the cells of the tree's bark (Thamarus and Furnier 1998). At a finer scale, when a forest tent caterpillar chews on an aspen leaf the wounding induces two segments of DNA within the aspen's genome, called PPO genes, to synthesize an enzyme called poly-phenol oxidase, abbreviated PPO (Haruta et al. 2001). The induction of PPO is systemic, that is, it is induced throughout the plant, including within the cells of the plant's unwounded leaves. The PPO enzyme plays a role in synthesizing the phenolic glycosides tremulacin and salicortin.

Another interesting aspen-herbivore interaction plays out with ruffed grouse, a permanent resident of the Canadian, Northern, and Central Rockies. The buds of quaking aspen's staminate (male) flowers are an important winter food for ruffed grouse, but the bird uses this resource to varying degrees from year to year (Jakubas and Gullion 1990, 1991; Hewitt and Messmer 2000). One hypothesis posits that interannual changes in the chemical content of the buds affect their use by grouse, and this in turn affects grouse population levels. The winter browse pref-erences of ruffed grouse are influenced by both the palatability of plants and their level of digestible nutrients.

It is possible that the grouse's dietary discrimination may be a response to just one kind of molecule in the food. Earlier studies indicated that the main difference between the aspen trees eaten by ruffed grouse and those that went untouched was the level of coniferyl benzoate in their flower buds (Jakubas and Gullion 1990). Coniferyl benzoate, a phenyl-propanoid ester related to cinnamic acid, smells like vanilla. Targeted bioassays have demonstrated that coniferyl benzoate alone does in fact deter feeding by grouse. Coniferyl benzoate and its oxidation products may cause several adverse physiological effects in grouse, including the inhibition of protein digestion, toxic impacts, and antiestrogenic effects.

The findings reported above suggest that aspen's secondary com-pounds deter vertebrate herbivores by being toxic or by reducing the assimilation of nutrients. An alternative yet complementary hypothesis is that secondary compounds influence an herbivore's forage selection by imposing high detoxication costs after absorption. In fact, ruffed grouse do incur such detoxication costs, which they minimize by foraging selec-tively (Guglielmo et al. 1996).

Taken together, these results point to a more complete interpretation of the aspen-grouse relationship: ruffed grouse choose to eat aspen buds with high protein levels and low concentrations of coniferyl benzoate be-cause of this food's high utilization efficiency and low detoxication costs.

⊰⊱

Patches of aspen are one of the iconic symbols of North America's western mountains. The yellow autumn foliage rattles in the slightest breeze. The dancing light on our trails reminds me that quaking aspen is a nimble player in nuanced ecological chemistry and that it plays a role in creating a diverse landscape. Yes, it's a symbol, but this montane icon also helps maintain the Rockies' biodiversity.

CHAPTER 7

Sex-Reversed Katydids

Hunger for protein and salt is what gets millions
of Mormon crickets marching across western North
America—that, and a fear of cannibals.

Jeff Hecht, "March of the Mormon Cricket Cannibals"

ON THE FOURTEENTH of July, 1820, while collecting plant specimens on the summit of Pikes Peak in the Front Range (10 miles [16 km] west of Colorado Springs, central Colorado), Edwin James, the botanist attached to the exploratory Stephen H. Long Expedition, wrote that the air became filled with—of all things—grasshoppers (Evans 1997). From his perch at 14,115 feet (4302 m) above sea level he watched the horde stretch upward to the limit of his vision. Many also fell on the snow and perished. Carcasses of these grasshoppers can still be found embedded in some of the Rockies' existing glaciers, tagged with names like Hopper Glacier in the Beartooth Mountains (Absaroka-Beartooth Wilderness, south-central Montana) and Grasshopper Glacier in the Wind River Range (west-central Wyoming). We now believe that James witnessed a dispersing swarm of the now-extinct Rocky Mountain locust. Arriving in vast clouds on farms of the Great Plains, these insects ate almost everything in their path, even tree bark and clothing hung out to dry. Having consumed all edible items, they would then fly off in search of greener pastures. The multitude that flew over Edwin James in 1820 was presumably one of these irrupting mobs (Lockwood 2004). The last living specimen was seen in 1902.

The Rocky Mountain locust may be extinct, but another mass-dispersing orthopteran is still with us. The Mormon cricket, also a devastating pest of field crops in the Great Plains, crawls en masse through the West in huge cohesive bands (Sword 2012). This animal earned its moniker in 1848 after attacking the Mormon pioneers' first crops in Utah (Beekman et al. 2008). A horde of California gulls arrived, devoured the crickets, and saved the settlers' harvest. The Seagull Monument in Salt Lake City honors those cricket-thwarting gulls.

This insect goes through irruptive phases during which its population density increases and individuals disperse outward, resulting in the species' range expansion. As it transitions in density, its mating behavior also shifts—radically so. The evolution of the Mormon cricket's courtship is teaching us fundamental lessons about what it means to function as a male and as a female.

⊰│⊱

But first, as you've come to expect by now, we need to do a little homework. Dark brown to blue-black and sometimes with pale markings, the Mormon cricket is one to two inches (2.5–5.1 cm) long, sprouts antennae as long as its body, and grows a large shield that extends backward over its abdomen and wings (Borror and White 1970). It is flightless and grows small vestigial wings, which the male uses to create courtship sounds (Beekman et al. 2008). Consequently, it travels on the ground. The female's ovipositor, upcurved and swordlike, is as long as her body (Milne and Milne 1980). Classified in the long-horned grasshopper family, the Mormon cricket is thus misnamed—it is actually a shield-backed katydid (Borror et al. 1981).

The Mormon cricket has a huge geographic range, from the northern Great Plains and southern Canadian Rockies (Alberta) southward into the Southwest (northern Arizona), and from the Missouri River westward into the Mojave Desert (southeastern California). On August 27, 2006, amid erratic boulders, Lewis's monkeyflower, and cotton grass, all nestled in a classic U-shaped, glacier-carved valley, Nancy and I met our first Mormon cricket. A lone female was resting in the trail that skirts the eastern side of Upper Titcomb Lake in the Wind River Range (Titcomb Basin Trail, Bridger Wilderness, Bridger-Teton National Forest, west-central Wyoming). Later, on September 3, 2011, while hiking among the colorful lichens, lance-leaved stonecrop, and moss campion in the alpine at Scenic Point (Mount Henry Trail, southeastern Glacier National Park, northwestern Montana), which sits out on the lip of the Lewis Overthrust, we stepped gingerly through hundreds of them.

Active from June to October, the Mormon cricket is found mainly in open fields. The insect's feeding behavior, marching bands, and cannibalism were studied in three sagebrush sites: (1) among the western meadowlarks, sharp-tailed grouse, and horned larks in the Northern Rockies (Curlew National Grassland, spread around Holbrook, southeastern Idaho) (Simpson et al. 2006); (2) among the Great Basin gopher snakes, gray flycatchers, and black-tailed jackrabbits in the high plains of the Southern Rockies (Browns Park, seven miles [12 km] southeast of Greystone [northwestern Colorado]) (Gwynne 1981); and (3) among the cottonwoods, pronghorn, and prairie dogs of Antelope Flats (4.2 miles [7 km] northwest of Dutch John, Daggett County, northeastern Utah) (Gwynne 1984). For most of the time and throughout most of its range in the West, the Mormon cricket persists in populations of low density. However, during some years and at some places, large and dense, cohesive and coordinated bands of millions of these flightless, voracious katydids march in unison across the landscape at up to 1.2 miles (2 km) per day as they search for food (Sword 2012). A band can be huge, spanning over six miles (10 km) long and a couple of miles (e.g., 3–4 km) wide, with dozens of individuals per square yard (e.g., 30/m^2) (Beekman et al. 2008).

A team of ecological entomologists collected adult Mormon crickets from two places, one with a history of large dispersing bands and the other where individuals do not form bands. In a pioneering study, the investigators attached tiny radio transmitters with a drop of hot glue to the dorsal surface of the Mormon crickets' pronotum and then tracked them as they crawled. An insect's pronotum is a platelike structure that covers all or part of the dorsal side of the thorax. Band-forming crickets were tracked across a high desert plateau in the Blue Mountains (south of Dinosaur National Monument, northeastern Utah and northwestern Colorado), an area with a history of Mormon cricket bands; the non–band formers were monitored in the Poudre River Canyon (north-central Colorado). The individuals in dispersing bands moved faster than insects from non-band-forming populations (Lorch et al. 2005). On average, band formers moved 1,092 feet (331 m) per day versus the non–band formers' 2.3 feet (0.7 m). Further, individuals within bands were directional, that is, they moved along the same bearing. Non–band formers were not directional.

Mormon crickets occur in two phases: solitary individuals are sedentary and cryptic; gregarious individuals form bands, disperse, and display aposematic, or warning, coloration. A team of insect geneticists sequenced two mitochondrial genes, labeled COII and COIII, in crickets from band formers west of the Continental Divide and from solitary, non-band-forming individuals east of the Divide. They found no evidence of gene flow between the two forms, suggesting the existence of two genetically distinct units that broadly corresponded with the solitary eastern and gregarious western populations (Bailey et al. 2005). Molecular clock estimates suggest that the two forms diverged about two million years ago. These findings suggest that the eastern solitary and western gregarious populations are evolving into separate species.

This may remind you of the cross-Divide divergence we saw in the lodgepole pine. How many other seemingly intact species of plants and animals are in the process of diverging genetically on opposite sides of the Rockies? How active, taxonomically inclusive, and geographically widespread is the phenomenon? Should we start thinking of the Rockies as one of Earth's master vicariant forces?

The individuals of a Mormon cricket mob keep a fixed distance from their neighbors, align themselves with their nearest neighbor, and stay in the group. It is within these irrupting, outbreaking bands that the Mormon cricket's cannibalism expresses itself.

The individuals of a marching band turn in unison as a group. Regardless of their position in the band, all individuals show the same changes of direction (Beekman et al. 2008). What determines the direction of a dispersing mob? One hint is that bands in different places travel in different directions. When investigators compared local weather conditions and individual daily movement patterns, they saw no evidence that the directions of band movements were correlated with local wind direction (Sword et al. 2008). This finding is consistent with the idea that whatever cues mediate directionality are more likely to be group specific than they are landscape-level environmental cues. Although it may not satisfy my need for a plausible hypothesis, it is also possible that nothing is responsible. That is, a band may turn randomly. It's just an ongoing mystery.

Contrary to some reports, Mormon crickets do not strip the environment bare of all vegetation; rather, they forage selectively. They eat high-protein foods like flowers, seed pods, the leaves of legumes, carrion, and mammal feces (Simpson et al. 2006). They also eat each other, a habit that can create slick surfaces as they stop to eat crushed conspecifics on roads and then get run over themselves. Members of both genders aggressively compete for the bodies of their own dead, a hint that they crave protein.

In a series of experiments with a wild marching band, insect ecologists found that Mormon crickets preferred foods with protein and salt, suggesting that they were protein- and salt-deprived (Simpson et al. 2006). When they received supplemental protein and salt they became less cannibalistic. Protein also affected how much they marched. Crickets without access to protein spent 50 percent more time walking than did those with protein.

Perhaps the most interesting finding deals with how movement affects cannibalism. Experimenters placed crickets with varying capabilities of moving in the path of an advancing band. Crickets were glued to a flat stone; half of them were alive and able to move their legs and the rest were freshly killed. Consumption of freshly dead crickets began within 21 seconds after the band reached them, whereas this time lag for immobile but motile prey was 165 seconds (Simpson et al. 2006). What caused the difference? Potential victims repelled attackers by kicking them with their hind legs.

Next, the team tethered crickets and varied their motility by compromising their ability to kick. Tethered insects were (1) dead with all legs intact, (2) alive with all legs intact, (3) alive and missing one rear leg, or (4) alive and missing both rear legs. Within two hours band members ate all of the dead and intact insects (Simpson et al. 2006). In contrast, 13 of 14 live, fully intact crickets survived. Insects that were missing both of their back legs fell victim more often than either completely intact or one-legged prey. Thus, motility that was restricted because of missing rear legs had a major impact on the severity of cannibalism.

And why not? After all, to a hungry Mormon cricket a conspecific's body is a handy package of protein and sodium (Simpson et al. 2006). As I said before, the individuals in a marching band are protein- and salt-deprived. Unless crickets are in the band's leading edge, cannibalism may offer the main way to acquire enough nutrients. Consequently, to avoid being eaten, mob members must continually stay ahead of their bandmates. Broadly stated, interactions among individuals play a greater role in inducing the movement, that is, walking-related actions, of band-forming crickets than do internal neurohormonal changes mediated by high rearing density (Sword et al. 2005). The safest individual is one that is mobile and able to repel others with its two rear legs. In this way the threat of cannibalism drives the continuous movement of a Mormon cricket mob.

And there are other factors that determine who's a cannibal and who's a victim. Behavioral ecologists conducted experiments with two Mormon cricket bands at 7,590 and 7,260 feet (2300 and 2200 m) in elevation (21 and 25 miles [34 and 40 km] northeast, respectively, of Vernal, north-eastern Utah) (Bazazi et al. 2010). The crickets' bellies were glued to wooden blocks and then they were placed in various orientations relative to the band's flow. Each individual moved in response to attacks from approaching conspecifics and bit those ahead. An adult Mormon cricket was more likely to approach and attack a stationary individual that was perpendicular to the flow than one that was either head- or tail-on. This suggests that an individual can lower its risk of being attacked by aligning with its mobmates. Further, encounters lasted longer, were more likely to result in an attack, and were more likely to end in a successful attack if other individuals were present around a stationary individual. That is, the presence of individuals attracts others.

With all this food deprivation and cannibalism, if you were one of these flightless katydids, why would you join and stay in a dispersing band? Wouldn't it be better to go off by yourself? It turns out that there is a severe cost to living alone—death via predation. Compared to crickets within bands, which suffered no deaths, crickets removed from their band suffered 50 to 60 percent mortality from predators within two days (Sword et al. 2005). The predators, likely birds and rodents, left telltale spoor: partially chewed body parts in trees and burrows. The likelihood of being killed while living solo far outweighs the odds of being canni-balized as a band member. Thus, one reason individuals join others is to reduce their vulnerability to predators.

So think of a dispersing Mormon cricket band as a forced march of hungry individuals, with all but the few bringing up the rear being threat-ened by cannibals from behind. Here we have a case study of how nutri-tional ecology can explain a landscape-scale mass movement.

A male Mormon cricket that is ready to mate repeats a hoarse chirp from a shrub. In a high-density phase, females respond by moving quickly over the ground toward the male's perch, where they compete for the selective male (Gwynne 1981, 1984). If a female does not approach him soon, he moves to another perch. Sperm are delivered to the female in packets called spermatophores, each holding millions of sperm cells. Male Mormon crickets produce exceptionally large spermatophores, which the females eat after accepting their sperm. Producing these big spermato-phores is costly—a male can lose up to 30 percent of his body weight (Gwynne 1981, 1983). The female deposits her dark brown eggs below the soil surface in midsummer; the eggs then turn gray, overwinter, and hatch in the spring. Up to 100 nymphs, which are immature insects that look like miniature adults, emerge from a single female's clutch.

In developing the theory of sexual selection, zoologists incorporated several basic assumptions (Trivers 1985):

1. Females invest more in their offspring than do the male parents.
2. Males compete with each other for access to females more than females compete with each other for access to males.
3. Females are more discriminating in their choice of sex partners, while males are less selective.
4. Males incur higher mortality than do females.

It is consistent with these assumptions that, in general, male animals produce seemingly unlimited amounts of sperm and mate with every available female (Trivers 1972; Wilson 1975; Dewsbury 1982; Gwynne 1983; Simmons 1995). However, because of the high cost of each of his spermatophores, a male Mormon cricket is limited in the number he can produce. So prudence is expected in how he allocates his ejaculates to females. Among Mormon crickets, aggressive females compete for choosy males, whereas males discriminate among females as potential partners. Thus, compared to animals with conventional gender roles, Mormon crickets are said to be sex-role reversed.

Among animals in general, sex-role reversal is expected when males invest more resources in reproduction than females do (Trivers 1985). An often-cited example is the giant waterbug (R. Smith 1980; Thornhill and Alcock 1983). A female belostomatid will repeatedly approach a coy male. He permits her to glue eggs onto his back, and then he broods the eggs until the nymphs hatch two weeks later. His paternal care includes several specific actions, including exposing the eggs to air, stroking the brood with his legs, and performing push-ups to circulate water over the attached eggs. But the glued-on eggs are heavy and cumbersome, so he is less able to catch prey and escape predators. He cannot spread his wings to fly should the environment deteriorate. Further, being disabled in these ways reduces his ability to inseminate more females. In total, the males of this true bug seem to invest more in reproduction than females do.

Mormon crickets irrupt during phases of high population density. Because food is scarce and the proteins conveyed in a spermatophore are important for the female's reproduction, females compete for access to singing males (Gwynne 1981, 1983). Discriminating males reject most females, preferring large females because they are likely to be more fecund. The Mormon cricket's sex-role reversal contrasts with the standard mating behavior of other katydid species in which males produce small spermatophores, behave promiscuously, and court choosy females.

When several competing female Mormon crickets converge on a singing male, they push past and grapple with each other. In some cases the winning female is able to move behind the male and mount him, and then the pair copulates. In many interactions, though, he pulls away from her after one or two minutes without transferring a spermatophore (Gwynne 1981). Males reject more than two-thirds of courting females (Gwynne 1983).

Why do males reject most females? Females that get mated weigh 0.13 ounce (3.8 g), which is 19 percent more than the 0.11 ounce (3.2 g) of rejected females (Gwynne 1981). This suggests that males are able to assess the female's relative mass. He appears to judge her weight when she clambers onto his back and bounces up and down. There is, in fact, a positive correlation between a female's weight and the number of mature eggs in her abdomen. A heavy female is a good mate choice for another reason—she has demonstrated her ability to accumulate bodily resources during periods of intense competition (Gwynne 1983).

In contrast, during phases of low population densities, Mormon crickets conform to a more conventional mating system, without sex role reversal. Males issue acoustical signals to maintain space around themselves, fight when they encounter each other, and eagerly descend from their calling perch to meet a receptive female. In this situation males reject no females and all females secure a mate.

Roles are reversed at high densities because only then do males become a limiting resource for the females' reproductive success. At high densities band members fight for food plants, seeds, and dead insects, all of which are eaten quickly. In contrast, at low densities females have abundant food and males quickly accrue the nutrients for producing spermatophores. The Mormon cricket's density-dependent mating behavior reflects the ability of individual males and females to change their sexual roles. When the members of a high-density, sex-role-reversed, nomadic band encounter a rich food source, they switch to conventional gender roles: males become less choosy and females revert to being selective.

⁂

The male Mormon cricket provides nutrients to the female via the spermatophore. Among animals in general the feeding of a mate is a specialized form of reproductive investment. Among insects, species in which the males provide nourishment to the females before, during, or after copulation can be sorted into two broad categories (Thornhill 1976). In the first group are females that receive nourishment from a gland in the male's body. This nourishment can include secretions from specialized glands, like those of some orthopterans; spermatophores, like those of our Mormon cricket; and the mating plugs produced by the males of some butterfly species. In the second group are females that receive nutrients from food captured or collected by the male, including nuptial gifts of prey, like a fly in hangingflies; and food other than prey, like nectar in some hymenopterans. Nutrients donated by a male to a female during mating represent an investment by the male in reproduction. Because male-provided food supplements the food the female has gathered, the male-derived nutrients improve the female's fitness. She converts the male-provided food into larger eggs with more nutritional reserves, which can support the development of larger larvae, which in turn develop into bigger adults or increase the likelihood of larval survival over the winter.

As I've said, in most species of animals, eggs are a limiting resource and males invest little in each mating effort. The circumstances may be reversed in unusual cases, like the Mormon cricket's, where males invest more resources in the offspring. Besides the giant waterbug and Mormon cricket, sex-role reversal has been documented in pipefishes and seahorses, poison-arrow frogs, and several species of birds like jacanas, phalaropes, and the Tasmanian native-hen (Wilson 1975; Trivers 1985).

Findings from these and other animal groups support the generalization that whichever sex provides the greater reproductive effort becomes a limiting resource for members of the other gender. In this context, courtship behavior is interpreted as a means for the limiting sex to determine the value of potential partners. That is, one of the main functions of courtship is mate evaluation.

Like male Mormon crickets, the males of other katydid species offer spermatophores that consist of two parts: a large, protein-rich spermatophylax and a sperm-containing ampulla (Gwynne 1983). The spermatophylax is a product of the male's accessory gland. During copulation, while the sperm are moving to her sperm storage organ, the spermatheca, the female detaches the spermatophylax from the spermatophore and eats it. After consuming the spermatophylax, she also removes and ingests the ampulla. Selection should favor males that provide enough material in the spermatophore to ensure the transfer of sperm. In fact, laboratory measurements have shown that the average time spent in spermatophylax consumption is just sufficient to complete sperm transfer.

An increase either in the amount of protein within spermatophylaxes or in the number consumed should increase the female's reproductive output. When the nutritional effects of multiple matings were simulated by increasing the number of spermatophylaxes eaten by females maintained on a low-protein diet, the females produced more and larger eggs. This outcome also supports the idea that males supplement the females' nutrition. The more spermatophylaxes a female eats, the bigger eggs she lays and the longer it takes her male offspring to reach adulthood. In this way courtship feeding yields bigger offspring, which grow into larger adults, which in turn yield offspring with greater fitness.

The mass of spermatophores may vary among individual male Mormon crickets. In the Sonoran Desert (Tucson, southern Arizona), insect behaviorists weighed both parts of the spermatophore, specifically the sperm-containing ampulla and the nutritious spermatophylax, of the decorated cricket, a species in the true cricket family. Each spermatophore weighed a few ten-thousandths of an ounce. Among 55 males, spermatophore mass varied by a factor of 3.7, from 0.00013 to 0.00048 ounce (3.7–13.5 mg). For comparison, a grain of sand weighs 0.00002 to 0.0008 ounce (0.7–23 mg), so we can roughly picture a spermatophore weighing about what a small sand grain does. The ampulla accounted for 17 percent of the spermatophore's mass, while the spermatophylax was 83 percent. Although there was no heritability to the ampulla's mass, there was a genetic component to the variation in the mass of the spermatophylax (Sakaluk and Smith 1988). Thus, there is genetic variation in the level of paternal investment in this true cricket. Extrapolating to the Mormon cricket, males may have been experiencing directional selection for increased spermatophylax size via sexual selection. Presumably, spermatophylax size is stable, so counteracting stabilizing selection, possibly in the form of nutrient costs of investing in a large spermatophylax, has also been at work.

These findings have led some insect behaviorists to hypothesize that the spermatophylax, which is the more nutritious part of the spermatophore, is mainly an adaptation to increase paternal investment. Research conducted in Australia, however, only partly supports this interpretation. Behavioral ecologists studied the vertical bushcricket, an urban katydid endemic to Australia (gardens in Perth, Western Australia). As with the Mormon cricket, offspring are sired by male bushcrickets that have donated nutrients to females. As argued above, food gifts that males present to females are either (1) sexually selected and function to acquire fertilizations, or (2) maintained by natural selection because they increase the fitness of the male's offspring (Gwynne 1986). These hypotheses are not mutually exclusive; rather, it is possible that the vertical bushcricket's nuptial offering arose originally via sexual selection, as a male adaptation that increased the number of fertilizations, and then evolved further by natural selection because it improved the fitness of the male's offspring (Gwynne 1988b).

In explaining the adaptive significance of the mating traits of today's bushcricket, the researchers give more evolutionary weight to natural over sexual selection. The male's spermatophylax is more than twice the size needed to transfer a full complement of sperm and to suppress any further sexual activity in the female. Spermatophylax nutrients extract a cost from a male bushcricket by reducing his mating frequency but provide a benefit by increasing the fitness of his progeny. Two pieces of evidence support the hypothesis that courtship feeding evolved to benefit the male's offspring (Gwynne 1988b). First, increased nuptial food results in an increase in the size of the eggs the females produce. Second, the amount of courtship feeding determines the adult size of the male offspring by influencing their development time, and larger male vertical bushcrickets appear to enjoy increased success in sexual competition.

And like the Mormon cricket, the vertical bushcricket has variable behavior—some bushcricket populations show courtship role reversal. Does the availability of food determine the frequency of spermatophore production and thus the number of males available for mating? Males on a low-quality diet mated less frequently than males on a high-quality diet (Gwynne 1990). Females showed the opposite trend: on a poor diet they increased their mating frequency, apparently to obtain the nutrients of the spermatophores. These results suggest that male parental investment via spermatophores increases in relative importance when the diet is sparse. When rich foods are available there are fewer fertilizable females than sexually active males, male-male competition intensifies, and a polygynous mating system manifests. In these ways, the ratio of fertilizable females to sexually active males, referred to as the operational sex ratio, influences the mating system of the bushcricket, Mormon cricket, and other animals in general.

As I've said, nuptial feeding can be important for the female's reproduction. In the native bush on Mount Eliza, overlooking the Swan River (King's Park, Perth, Western Australia), under conditions of limiting nutrients the females of the nartee bushcricket compete for males and their nuptial gifts, but when foods increase, males aggregate and compete acoustically for females (Simmons 1995). When nutrients are low the number of males capable of donating spermatophores is low, but female demand for spermatophores is high. The reverse is true when nutrient availability is high. Here's yet another case in which the operational sex ratio and sexual roles flip back and forth in unison.

When their population density is high and food is scarce, Mormon crickets irrupt. Hungry females develop more and larger eggs if they supplement their intake with nutrients from the male's spermatophore, so females seek out and compete for males. Offering nutritious spermatophores, choosy males mate with only a few heavily fecund females. With a bit of imagination this story seems relevant to our own behavior. In war-ravaged and other male-deficient societies, women are known to compete for men, just as they do in response to the operational sex ratio on Ladies' Night at your local saloon.

CHAPTER 8

Optimizing Bumblebees

Few aspects of bumblebee life, or human life,
can escape the pervasive influence of economics.

Bernd Heinrich, *Bumblebee Economics*

IT'S AUGUST 15, 2005. Nancy and I are perched—soaking up the panorama—in Burstall Pass, at 7,808 feet (2380 m) above sea level in the saddle between Mounts Sir Douglas and Birdwood, up on the divide that separates the Spray River and Smuts Creek watersheds (Burstall Pass Trail, Peter Lougheed Provincial Park, southwestern Alberta). From this alpine vantage point we drink in a landscape of high-altitude swirled rock strata, valley wetlands, and boreal forest in between. And here, among the pussytoes, Indian paintbrush, and a few other late-blooming flowers, zoom the busy bumblebees. Over the years—and against my initial bias— I've come to associate these industrious insects with the harsh alpine. In this open terrain you can follow the flight of an individual bumblebee as it zips through the boundary layer, stopping along a series of flowers one at a time, seeming so efficient.

In these high places I was often struck with the question, How do these small insects persist in the windy, cold conditions of the Rockies? A general answer is that they succeed in the alpine because of how they integrate their thermal and social adaptations. Bumblebees are endotherms; they generate internal body heat. Their endothermy, in turn, both facilitates and is supported by their social behavior. Bumblebees are eusocial, that is, they are true social insects, characterized by the overlap of two or more generations, a division of labor, cooperative care of their young, and reproductive altruism.

Of Earth's 750,000 insect species, about 2 percent, or 15,000 species, meet the criteria to be called eusocial. Eusocial insects include the wasps, honeybees, and termites. Bees evolved from wasplike ancestors about 100 million years ago. Bumblebees live mainly in temperate and Arctic regions across Europe and Asia, in Africa north of the Sahara Desert, and in the New World from the Arctic Circle to Tierra del Fuego. Of Earth's 400 bumblebee species, about 250 are *Bombus* bumblebees, a eusocial genus, and of these, 50 species live in North America.

Each bumblebee colony is initiated in the spring by a queen that was inseminated the previous fall and survived the winter hibernating in a nearly lifeless state (Heinrich 1976a, 1979a). All of her drones and workers died in the fall. That big bumblebee you spy gathering pollen and nectar in the early spring is probably one of these overwintered queens. After emerging she searches for a suitable site to start a colony. A dark cavity, like a moist tunnel under a rotting stump or an abandoned rodent burrow, will do.

While she is growing her colony a queen bumblebee functions as an endotherm, an animal whose body temperature is maintained by heat produced internally, like a mammal. For example, while she is building her nest an Edwards bumblebee queen maintains a thoracic temperature of 99 to 102°F (37–39°C) throughout the day and night (Heinrich 1972). In contrast, the body temperature of a nonbrooding queen fluctuates with the ambient air. In May, reproducing queens are busy feeding the first broods of their new colonies. Through the summer the queen's only job is to lay eggs. At its peak a colony may grow to several hundred individuals. Eusocial bees require a large and continual influx of food throughout the growing season. At dawn, with frost on the ground and the air at 36°F (2.5°C), foraging workers maintain their thoraxes at around 99°F (37°C) (Heinrich 1972).

Toward autumn, queens develop from specially fed larvae, and these new queens will continue the cycle as the old queen dies. All bumblebees die before winter except for the fertilized queen, who holes up in a hollow tree or under the ground.

In the mountains, bumblebees fly, forage, and care for their brood in harsh conditions, all enabled by their superb thermoregulation. Air temperatures may stay below 50°F (10°C). Bumblebees can fly even at 26°F (−3.6°C), through snowstorms, and in wind and rain (Heinrich 1979a).

As I said, the bumblebee's thermoregulation and social behavior are integrated. Within a bumblebee colony, division of labor is related to the spatial organization of the workers within the nest. In the common eastern bumblebee, in addition to the queen and males, worker bees fell into three groups (Jandt and Dornhaus 2009):

1. About 12 percent of them maintained small zones of spatial fidelity inside the nest, and workers remained at a specific distance from the colony center.
2. Smaller workers maintained tighter zones closer to the center.
3. Individuals that fed the larvae remained in the center of the nest. In contrast, when they were not out gathering food, foragers were found more often along the outer edge of the nest. Individual preferences did not change over time.

To grow, bumblebee grubs need to be maintained at 90°F (32°C) (Heinrich 1990). The honey stomach, a highly distensible sack in the abdomen, serves as both a reservoir for the individual's food and as a bag for carrying nectar to the nest (Heinrich 1979a). Heat produced in the adult's thorax warms its hemolymph, the bloodlike fluid of insects, which is pumped throughout the body. The bee applies its hot abdomen to the brood, much as a parenting bird presses its incubation patch onto its clutch of eggs. A bumblebee queen heats her brood to at least 86°F (30°C)—even in air that is below freezing.

Like other social insects, bumblebees are able to control the climate within their nests. These adaptations provide some independence from their environment and promote growth and survival of the colony. Most bumblebee species nest underground, sometimes in cavities originally dug by small mammals. In a warm spell the brood can get too hot. Within a bumblebee colony an increase in temperature elicits fanning. It's even thermostatically controlled: as the air warms up, the number of fanning bees increases. Further, in this confined space insufficient gas exchange may lead to low oxygen and high carbon dioxide. Increases in carbon dioxide concentration and temperature elicited a fanning response in the buff-tailed bumblebee, while more humidity did not (Weidenmuller et al. 2002). In these ways, bumblebees control both the carbon dioxide level and air temperature within their colonies.

It's not unusual to see bumblebees on the wing above treeline, visiting alpine clover and sky pilot, in frigid weather. In general, bumblebees are adapted to tundra conditions (Heinrich 1979a). To be active, a bumblebee must keep its thoracic temperature between 86 and 111°F (30–44°C). A thick layer of insulating pile on the thorax retains heat, enabling bumblebees to achieve temperatures 65 to 75 percent higher than that of like-sized insects with similar metabolic rates (Heinrich 1979a). In one study, bumblebee queens maintained their thoracic temperatures between 97 and 113°F (36–45°C) while flying through air as cool as 36°F (2°C) (Heinrich 1975a). Some bumblebees can forage at temperatures as low as 32°F (0°C). Within a bumblebee colony the queen is active at lower temperatures than the males and workers are (Lundberg 1980). The ability of the smaller-bodied workers to thermoregulate is more limited, so they do not fly in air cooler than about 50°F (10°C). For comparison, the metabolic rate of flying bumblebees, per unit of weight, is about double that of hummingbirds, which are among the most active vertebrates.

As harsh weather forces other insects into torpor, bumblebees engage in several adaptive behaviors that allow them to heat their bodies and continue their activity. Shivering flight muscles can heat the thorax up to 60°F (33°C) above the air temperature (Heinrich 1990). For a bumblebee to fly, the temperature of its flight muscles needs to be at least 86°F (30°C); swift flight requires 95°F (35°C) (Heinrich 1979a). The capability to shiver and warm up means being able to go out and bring back the nectar and pollen that fuel the colony's growth during cool periods.

Flying on a cold day in the spring, an early queen would have to retain as much heat as possible in her thorax and prevent it from leaking into her abdomen. Circulating hemolymph carries fuel, specifically sugar, from her honey stomach to her muscles. A countercurrent heat exchanger in her petiole recycles the heat back to the thorax without losing it to the abdomen (Heinrich 1990). Resettled on her grubs, she once again allows heat to flow into her abdomen. A couple of definitions are in order. A petiole is the thin waist connecting a bee's thorax and abdomen. A countercurrent heat exchanger is a web of juxtaposed arteries and veins that return heat to the thorax, thereby reducing heat loss from extremities while allowing the hemolymph to continue its transport of oxygen and nutrients to the abdomen.

The power applied to the wings is generated by muscles that pack nearly the entire volume of the thorax (Heinrich 1979a). A bumblebee's flight muscles, contained in a roughly spherical thorax 0.2 inch (5 mm) in diameter, are heated by a metabolism as intense as a flying bird's. When a bumblebee becomes inactive its body temperature returns to ambient. A cost of all this thermal efficiency is the risk of overheating on a hot day, so bumblebees have evolved mechanisms that allow them to dump heat from the thorax to the abdomen, from where it is shed to the air.

 Bumblebees Parasitize Other Bumblebees

A bumblebee colony, with its food and warmth, represents an exploitable resource for some organisms. Its brood, adults, and food attract parasites and predators. A social parasite is a female that enters a nest of a social insect and replaces the queen. The host workers then rear the parasite's offspring. Females of the *Psithyrus* cuckoo bumblebee enter established *Bombus* colonies, kill the queen, and lay their own eggs, and then the *Bombus* workers raise the *Psithyrus* eggs to adulthood.

But first the parasite must overcome the host's defense system. Although a few species of cuckoo bumblebees live in the Rockies, how the *Psithyrus* cuckoo penetrates the *Bombus* host's colony has been better studied in western Europe. There, the cuckoo bumblebee is an obligate social parasite of the tree bumblebee. By using chemical analyses and observing the responses of the host workers' antennae, a team of insect physiologists identified a compound in the insect's cuticle, specifically dodecyl acetate, that female cuckoo bumblebees use to repel tree bumblebee workers during nest usurpation and subsequent colony development (Zimma et al. 2003). We use this colorless liquid, also called lauryl acetate, with its waxy, citrus-rose odor, as a flavoring agent in food.

The source of the energy that fuels the bumblebee's remarkable thermal and social adaptations is nectar. So how do bumblebees harvest nectar? Bumblebee researchers have uncovered a complex, nuanced series of behaviors that enable their foraging.

Let's start with the question, What is it about flowers that attracts bumblebees? A team of bee behaviorists exposed buff-tailed bumblebees to dummy flowers that differed in several characteristics. The bumblebees preferred flowers with two colors over one, large centers over small ones, and a center color similar to that of pollen (Heuschen et al. 2005). These findings suggest that bumblebees have innate preferences for certain colors and sizes of floral color patterns that correspond to visually displayed pollen. Thus, parts of the patterns and colors of flowers mimic the signals issuing from pollen.

As a foraging bumblebee nears, lands, and crawls toward a flower's food reward, the insect is guided by multicolored marks on the flower. These so-called nectar guides, many of which are visible to us only under ultraviolet radiation, reduce the pollinators' handling time, increase visitation rates, and promote pollen transfer. Researchers compared the responses of common eastern bumblebee foragers to artificial flowers that either possessed or lacked starlike patterns. On patterned flowers, bees discovered the reward more quickly and were more likely to find the reward (Leonard and Papaj 2011). Bees persisted in responding to patterned flowers even after rewards ceased, hinting that nectar guides may promote the plant's pollen transfer at the expense of the bumblebee's foraging success.

 ### The Bumblebee's Chemical Footprint

One of the cues that helps a bumblebee decide how much time to spend on a newly contacted flower is its scent. Bumblebees, as well as honeybees, use odor cues deposited on flower corollas by previous visitors (Stout and Goulson 2001). Short-lived repellent scents, thought to be long-chain hydrocarbons secreted by the tarsal glands, indicate flowers that have recently been depleted of nectar, and longer-term attractant scents indicate rewarding flowers. The tarsus consists of the terminal five segments of a bee's leg.

Foraging in a patch of yellow sweet clover (near Winchester, Hampshire, United Kingdom), red-tailed bumblebees avoided flowers recently visited by honeybees for 40 to 60 minutes (Stout and Goulson 2001). By 24 hours after a visit the effect had worn off. Flowers previously visited by conspecifics repelled bumblebees for 40 minutes. During this time nectar was replenished by the flowers. Bumblebees of several species detect each other's repellent scents and avoid flowers depleted by themselves, by conspecifics, or by congeners. This is a neat solution that reduces the time wasted in probing depleted flowers and also allows bees to revisit them after an appropriate time interval, both of which improve foraging efficiency.

Restated as a negative, foraging bumblebees reject flowers where they detect the olfactory footprints of previous visitors. When floral-naive bees were offered a choice between scent-marked and unmarked flowers, individuals neither avoided nor preferred the marked flowers (Leadbeater and

Chittka 2011). This observation suggests that bumblebee workers' response to scent marks is not hardwired; rather, they learn to associate social information with local floral conditions.

Compared to simple flowers, complex flowers require long handling times and the expenditure of more energy. This leads to the question of whether bumblebees respond to scent marks more strongly if they are found on complex flowers, thereby minimizing nonproductive revisits. Bumblebees were more than twice as likely to reject scent-marked long flowers as short ones (Saleh et al. 2006). Further, the effect of the scent marks lingered 60 percent longer in long flowers. The bees often rejected long flowers while still in flight, without direct access to any tactile cues that could indicate floral handling time. These observations suggest that bumblebees decide whether to visit a complex flower by first using their current visual input to recall a memory of floral handling time and then combining this information with a current olfactory cue, the scent mark.

The scent marks left by foraging bumblebees can also be exploited by biologists. A research team has been able to reconstruct a pollinator community from scent marks left by visiting bumblebees. They recorded bumblebees visiting comfrey and later used gas chromatography and mass spectrometry to quantify the unsaturated hydrocarbons left on the flowers. They found that the molecules from the corollas were most like those of the most common bumblebee species, the common carder bumblebee (Witjes et al. 2011). Further, the species composition of the bumblebee communities inferred from unsaturated hydrocarbons on flowers was similar to those actually observed. In this way, the bumblebee species that visit particular plant species can be reconstructed from the organic scent marks they leave behind.

As we saw in the story of scarlet gilia, many plant-pollinator relationships can be interpreted as symbiotic mutualisms (Maloof and Inouye 2000). One lesser-known aspect of mutualisms in general is that one of the partners can be vulnerable to cheating by the other partner. A cheating animal can obtain a reward without providing a service. Within the context of plant-pollinator mutualisms, nectar robbers are birds, insects, and other flower visitors that remove nectar through holes cut in the nectary of the corolla, thereby bypassing the flower's sexual parts. In a study in the Elk

Mountains, western bumblebees robbed nectar from 33 percent of the scarlet gilia flowers (Maloof and Inouye 2000).

In general, flowers with long corolla tubes and nectar spurs, from which nectar is more challenging to extract, are the most likely to be robbed (Maloof and Inouye 2000). The question arises, Do nectar robbers harm their host plants? Of 18 studies on this subject, an equal number indicated negative, neutral, or positive effects of nectar robbing on the host plants. On the positive side, robbers frequently pollinate the plants they visit. This could raise a plant's fitness by increasing its pollen flow and thereby its level of outcrossing (Richardson 2004). Nectar robbers cause visiting insects to fly longer distances between inflorescences, to inspect fewer flowers per inflorescence, and to visit more flowers per unit time, all of which may increase pollen flow and outcrossing. Some individual bees may only rob nectar, others may only pollinate, while some both rob and pollinate. So, whether a nectar robber hurts, helps, or has a neutral effect on a plant's fitness is idiosyncratic, a function of the specific species of plant and insect. Sorry, but a general theory of nectar robbing does not seem to be forthcoming.

Bumblebees can extract nectar from a nectar spur legitimately by entering the front of the flower, or illegitimately by biting or reusing holes in the spur. Do bees switch their foraging method from legitimate visitation to secondary robbing when hole-biting robbers are present? In the Southern Rockies (Colorado), ecologists studied bumblebees with different glossal lengths as they visited flowers. A bee's glossa is its tongue. Although yellow toadflax plants are adapted for pollination by long-tongued bees, short-tongued bees visited them often for small amounts of nectar but switched to secondary robbing in the presence of primary robbers (Newman and Thomson 2005). In this way, primary robbers expand the resources available for normally legitimate secondary robbers.

Flowers Incentivize Their Offering

Another adaptation that plants use to attract bumblebees is floral temperature. Pollinators may perceive floral heat as a reward. Recall that bumblebees foraging in the alpine maintain body temperatures above 86°F (30°C). Given choices between flowers of two temperatures that offer equal amounts of nectar, buff-tailed bumblebees prefer to visit warm flowers, especially if they are 7°F (4°C) warmer (Dyer et al. 2006). They even learn to use the flower's color to predict its temperature before landing. Thus, floral temperature can function as an added incentive to attract pollinating bumblebees.

Another plant feature that encourages insects to transition from flying to probing is found on the petal's surface. For many years botanists wondered about the function of the conical epidermal cells on petals. A team of bee behaviorists observed that foraging bumblebees were able to discriminate between different surfaces via tactile cues. The investigators also found that bumblebees used color cues to discriminate against flowers, like a snapdragon mutant, that lacked conical cells, but only when the flower surfaces were positioned at steep angles, making them hard to manipulate (Whitney et al. 2009). Thus, the function of conical epidermal cells on flower petals is to facilitate the insect's physical handling of the flower.

A colony of social bees produces overlapping generations of adults that visit a succession of plant species. The bees exploit new resources as they become available and make choices among flowers offering more versus fewer rewards. Each individual bumblebee relies on its own experience during foraging, sampling a variety of different flowers in different areas, and then becoming at least temporarily site- and flower-specific. Thus, although the colony can collectively exploit a wide variety of foods, each individual bee sticks to a limited foraging repertoire at any one time.

According to one hypothesis, specialist bumblebee species handle preferred food more efficiently than related generalist species do. In learning the flower-handling skills needed to exploit their specialty plant, monkshood, the naive workers of the consobrinus bumblebee were more efficient than workers of generalist species (Laverty and Plowright 1988). With no previous foraging experience, consobrinus workers began probing near the nectary and quickly located nectar, whereas the foragers of generalist species probed in the wrong places and gave up before finding nectar.

A widely accepted explanation for such flower-constant behavior in pollinators is the learning and memory constraints hypothesis. According to this proposal, pollinators forage more efficiently if they continue visiting the plant species they have recently learned to work effectively (Gegear and Laverty 1995). This idea implies that learning a second flower-handling method interferes with the bumblebee's ability to recall the method it learned previously (Laverty 1994). Because of such an interference effect, bumblebees would have to relearn specific flower-handling actions each time they switch to a different plant species. Switching should temporarily lengthen the flower-handling time, which would decrease the number of flowers visited. In fact, learning a second flower-handling technique did increase the time bumblebees needed to insert their tongue into each nectary by up to two seconds. In another study, bumblebees incurred a 28 percent longer handling time, defined as the time from initial contact until the bee leaves the flower. Thus, flower constancy is interpreted as an adaptation for avoiding the costs of relearning flower-handling actions, thereby increasing foraging efficiency.

Bumblebees can also be loyal to a site. Of the bumblebees arriving at a patch with monkshood and subalpine larkspur, those that returned did so repeatedly for several days. Many bumblebees showed not only area fidelity but also repeatedly flew between the same flower bunches. Bees learn the spatial positions of plant clumps and the flight path between them (Heinrich 1976a, 1976b; Waddington 1983), a foraging strategy called traplining because of its analogy with a fur trapper who routinely checks traps in a set sequence.

Research has provided some details about how a bumblebee develops its trapline (Saleh and Chittka 2007). Bee ecologists compared the performance of two groups of the common eastern bumblebee, one group that foraged in a stable array of flowers, the other within an array that was changed between foraging bouts. Bees in the first group established long-term memories of the array. They started by sampling various routes and then tended to visit flowers in a repeating order, that is, they foraged along a trapline. The routes were formed by linking pairs of nearby flowers, not by attempting to minimize overall travel distance.

Bumblebees traplined in two different ways. Some used a major sequence most often, followed by a minor, lesser-used route, while others used two different routes with equal frequency. In the second group, in which bees were forced to forage in a shifting flower array, the random manipulation disrupted foraging efficiency, mainly because it caused more revisits to previously emptied flowers and longer search times.

Once a bumblebee begins foraging along a specific trapline, is it locked in? Or can it adjust its route? A research team followed buff-tailed bumblebees as they moved through an array of four artificial flowers. Then they sequentially added some new patches of flowers. If bees visited them in the order in which they encountered them they would end up following a long, inefficient route. With experience the bees lowered their tendency to visit patches in their discovery order, instead rearranging flight distances by reordering visitation sequences (Lihoreau et al. 2010). This led each forager to a primary route, its new trapline, and to two or three lesser-used secondary routes. This plastic behavior, the maintenance of route flexibility, allows bumblebees to exploit resources with shifting locations.

Like all adaptations of organisms generally, the behavior of traplining incorporates trade-offs. When buff-tailed bumblebees were trained to forage on five artificial flowers of equal reward, they selected the shortest possible trapline route (Lihoreau et al. 2011). After the investigators introduced a highly rewarding flower to the array the bees readjusted their routes by visiting the most rewarding flower first, as long as the departure distance from the shortest possible route remained short, around 18 percent. When routes optimizing the initial rate of reward were much longer, around 42 percent, bees prioritized shorter travel distances. In the wild, where the locations of rewarding flowers vary through time, it seems to pay bees to prioritize highly profitable sites, both to minimize the total number of flowers visited and to beat competitors. In this way, traplining bumblebees incur a trade-off between minimizing travel distance and prioritizing the most rewarding feeding locations.

Here's another way bumblebees optimize their nectar intake. In an area with numerous simultaneously blooming plant species, some individual bumblebees restrict themselves primarily to one plant species, their so-called major (Heinrich 1975a; 1976b). Other bees at the same site may have different majors. Most individual bumblebees also have second and third specialties, minors, which they sample occasionally. Since the blooming times of plants are shorter than a queen's life span, queens adopt several successive majors during their lifetime (Heinrich 1976b).

The timing of a bumblebee's shift from one flower type to another may reflect an unmet expectation. During an experiment in a test arena, a team of bee behaviorists trained common eastern bumblebees to feed on a single red artificial flower with a specific amount and concentration of sugar solution. When they lessened the reward offered by the flowers of one color, the bumblebees abruptly disrupted their consumption on that flower type and increased their visits to the flowers of another color (Wiegmann et al. 2003). This switch suggests that a foraging bumblebee forms an expectation of a reward and that an unrealized expectation can cause it to sample alternative flowers. In this way an unmet expectation can trigger a bumblebee to switch from its major to one of its minors.

In the preceding paragraphs I have shown that bumblebees forage where they make the most profit, so why do some individuals major on flowers of low nectar production? An area contains many bees that deplete the nectar-rich flowers first, so all flowers eventually come to provide similar amounts of food, especially for young unspecialized bees sampling diverse flowers for the first time (Heinrich 1975a). Thus, when high-yield flower species are already exploited by a dense population of bees, it matters little on which flower the new foragers specialize.

Having foraging expertise with more than one type of flower, that is, visiting one major and several minors, helps an individual bumblebee exploit floral resources that change through time (Oster and Heinrich 1976). Bumblebees that were transplanted to a new area sampled the various species in bloom and then established new majors (Heinrich 1976b). In this way a minor can bridge a bumblebee to a new major.

Within a bumblebee nest, foraging workers vary greatly in size. For workers of the buff-tailed bumblebee (Chilworth, Hampshire, United Kingdom), thorax width corresponded closely with glossal length (Peat et al. 2005). Large-bodied, long-tongued bees seem equipped to feed from deeper flowers, and that is in fact what they do. Although large bees were slower than small bees when handling shallow flowers, they were quicker than small bees when handling deep flowers. These observations suggest that size variation within a bumblebee colony enables the colony as a whole to efficiently exploit a wide range of different flowers.

Here is an insect that prospers in high, cold places. By optimizing its energy management, both in terms of its nectar intake and thermal output, it can maintain a fairly stable body temperature. Uniform body heat, in turn, allows it to maximize the number of new queens and males it produces to go out and found new colonies. And it does all this in harsh montane places with short, cool growing seasons. It fuels that remarkable metabolism by foraging optimally, which is shorthand for a suite of adaptations that includes matching its tongue length to flower depth, majoring and minoring, learning efficient flower handling, and other behaviors that maximize the colony's benefit-cost ratio. Its energy economics, in turn, fuels a complex social life. And this is how their bustling foraging bouts came to entertain me during our high-altitude rest stops.

CHAPTER 9

Flickering Butterflies

Well, I must endure the presence of two or three caterpillars
if I wish to become acquainted with the butterflies.

Antoine de Saint-Exupéry, *The Little Prince*

ACROSS THIS EXPOSED, gusty environment, the vast alpine landscape of Trail Ridge, at 12,045 feet (3650 m) in elevation, which rises between the Big Thompson and Fall Rivers of the Front Range (Rocky Mountain National Park, north-central Colorado), a few butterflies hugged the ground, flitting erratically—to my eye randomly—from one cushion plant to another. Nancy and I often encountered butterflies in the Rocky Mountain alpine. Yet, as with the bumblebees, their presence there seemed so implausible. How do these small, delicate animals persist in such cold, windy places?

Let's set the stage by fluttering through some basic background. Many butterflies have an adult life of less than a week. Within a butterfly population the female's reproductive success is limited in part by the time available for her to search for plants that are suitable for laying eggs (Rutowski 1997).

To exploit the mountains' brief summer season, butterflies raise their body heat in order to fly. To get airborne, many butterflies raise their internal body temperature to between 86 and 104°F (30–40°C) (Kingsolver 1985). Butterflies use two strategies to achieve their takeoff temperatures: active muscular shivering and passive solar basking (Heinrich 1986). You've read about shivering in bumblebees, so here let's focus on basking. As we explore the benefits of basking over the next few pages, try to keep in mind a downside—it exposes the basker to predators.

During cool times sulphur butterflies attain the muscle heat needed for flight by basking in the sun with their wings held together and pointed upward. Solar radiation is absorbed by the undersides of the wings, where it is converted to heat, which is then carried by hemolymph to the torso. Within this general strategy three species of sulphurs native to different altitudes show an interesting trend: (1) Mead's sulphur butterfly is found at elevations between 10,900 and 11,900 feet (3300–3600 m) above sea level; (2) Queen Alexandra's sulphur at 8,910 to 9,570 feet (2700–2900 m); and (3) clouded sulphur at 4,950–5,940 feet (1500–1800 m). The proximal part of the wing makes the greatest contribution to warming the insect, so one would predict that this portion of the wing of these three sulphur species should darken with altitude (Kingsolver 1985). And that is in fact the case not only among these three species, but also among altitudinally separated populations within each species.

Wing darkness can also vary with the seasons. Individuals of some white butterfly species that develop in cool environments have heavily melanized wings. Melanism is the presence of black color in an organism. Dark wings absorb solar radiation and enable flight in cool places. In males of the cabbage white, melanization on both wing surfaces shows seasonal changes (Stoehr and Goux 2008). In response to cool air and/or short days, the ventral hindwing surface becomes heavily melanized compared to that of the warm, long-day phenotype. In this species wing darkness varies seasonally with shifting day lengths, which have been evolutionarily associated with different temperatures.

Although we've suspected genetic influences all along, we're just now gaining glimpses into the inherited controls of butterfly thermal biology. Lepidopterists started by asking, Is there a genetic component that allows female butterflies to search for nectar and oviposit in cold air? The Glanville fritillary lives in open meadows of Europe and temperate Asia. Individual Glanvilles carry different alleles of the Pgi gene, which encodes phosphoglucose isomerase, an enzyme involved in metabolic rate and fecundity. One study showed that compared to homozygotes, females that were heterozygous for the Pgi gene were able to fly at cooler temperatures and oviposit earlier in the afternoon, when the environmental conditions were most favorable and average clutch size was largest (Saastamoinen and Hanski 2008). Although the inquiry into the genes involved in thermoregulation is just getting started, I sense that many discoveries are in store regarding the genetic influences underlying the thermal adaptations of montane butterflies.

Here's a nuanced layer of the basking story. In seven sites in the Southern Rockies (Gunnison and Delta Counties, west-central Colorado), which ranged from 6,072 to 9,636 feet (1840—2920 m) above sea level, the dorsal wings of the clouded sulphur showed more melanism with increasing altitude (Ellers and Boggs 2004). No surprise, but not so fast. Although this wing-darkness idea makes an appealing evolutionary story, we shouldn't always assume that various levels of dark patches are genetically controlled and therefore adaptive. In the woodlands of Europe the speckled wood butterfly also varies in the degree of melanin at the base of its dorsal wings (Talloen et al. 2004). Differences in environmental quality, specifically the degree of drought stress in its host plants, were found to induce differences in wing melanization. Specifically, individuals on drought-stressed plants developed paler wings. In this case coldness had nothing to do with wing darkness. Remember, we should not automatically assume genetic influence and adaptive value, either in our consideration of the dark patches on butterfly wings or in our thinking about other traits of Rocky Mountain organisms.

Another adaptation of the sulphur's thermoregulatory strategy is fur on the ventral side of its thorax (Kingsolver 1985). The thorax, where temperature is more closely regulated than it is in other body parts, is covered by a hairy layer of modified scales that functions as insulation. At higher altitudes and more northern latitudes this pile may be thicker.

As its thermal needs change through the day, the Arctic blue fine-tunes its posture and the time it spends basking (Heinrich 1986). This tiny butterfly carries its 0.0008 ounce (0.023 g) on a wingspan of 0.8 inch (20 mm). For comparison, a swallowtail can weigh 0.01 ounce (0.3 g), 13 times heavier. At 10,230 feet (3100 m) high in the Sierra Nevada (east-central California), Arctic blues spend 94 percent of their time in the morning basking and 6 percent flying; near noon they bask a quarter of the time. Near midday most bask dorsally, with wings held horizontally, but 30 percent in the morning and 60 percent in the evening bask laterally, with wings held vertically. Thus, butterflies' thermoregulation includes behavioral adjustments.

Viewed at a simple level, the way the wings of a basking butterfly convey heat to the body can be sorted into two general strategies: (1) absorbing solar radiation and conducting that heat through the wing tissues to the body, or (2) reflecting solar radiation from the wings onto the torso, where some of it is converted to heat (Rawlins 1980; Kingsolver 1985). You'll recognize the sulphurs mentioned above as examples of the former. Within the context of this dichotomy between absorbing and reflecting, butterfly species can be even more finely sorted into four basking attitudes:

1. At rest, dorsal basking species extend their wings horizontally, like a fixed-wing airplane. Only radiation striking the base of a dorsal basker's wings helps raise its body temperature. Thin wings are poor conductors of heat, so most of the heat created by radiation hitting a wing more than an eighth of an inch (0.3 cm) distal to the thorax is lost.
2. Lateral baskers hold their wings together vertically over their body.
3. Reflectance baskers are intermediate between dorsal and lateral baskers; they bounce solar radiation off their upper wing surfaces onto their body. Reflectance baskers rest with their wings in a *V*.
4. More recently, another basking method has been discovered (Kemp and Krockenberger 2002). In the South Pacific, males of the great eggfly butterfly perch with their wings fully spread and angled downward with the edges pressed against the substrate. They adopt this posture when their thoracic temperature drops below 93°F (34°C), and it allows them to warm faster than standard dorsal basking would. This so-called appression basking is interpreted as a modified form of dorsal basking. The warmth gained via appression seems to come from the lessened flow of cooling air under the wings and around the body. I wonder, will this behavior eventually be detected in any Rocky Mountain butterflies?

Sulphur butterflies are reflectance baskers whose wing-color patterns are adapted to local climatic conditions (Kingsolver 1985). In reflectance basking, light wing areas send more radiation to the body than do dark areas. Two sulphur species live at an elevation of 9,570 feet (2900 m) on the western flank of the Sawatch Range (near Crested Butte, west-central Colorado). The western sulphur is a broad V-basker, the color of its wing margin does not affect its body temperature, and it has extensive dark areas there. In contrast, the green-veined white butterfly is a narrow V-basker. Its outer wing margin, which does affect body temperature, has light coloring.

In the spirit of the epigraph, let's not ignore the thermal needs of caterpillars. In the Sierra de Guadarrama (central Spain), larvae of the Apollo butterfly were studied along a 2,310-foot (700 m) elevational gradient (Ashton et al. 2009). With increasing altitude, the caterpillars chose more open microhabitats, specifically those with more bare ground and dead vegetation, suggesting that they used hotter sites in cooler environments. When the air was cooler than 81°F (27°C), larvae occupied open sites that were warmer than ambient air; in warmer air they chose shaded, cool microhabitats. This is an example of how butterfly caterpillars actively regulate their body temperature.

Although it may seem surprising initially, an excess of heat has also shaped the adaptations of some montane butterflies. Because of intense insolation and stagnant air, a butterfly in the boundary layer can overheat. For all species of sulphurs studied so far, at body temperatures above 104 to 108°F (40–42°C), individuals stop flying and show heat-avoidance behaviors, like seeking shade and orienting parallel to the sun (Kingsolver and Watt 1983).

I mentioned at the start of this chapter that female butterflies spend much of their short adult lives searching for plants that are suitable for laying their eggs. They deposit only part of their total egg production in a single bout, thereby hedging their bets. Newly hatched larvae move short distances, if any, in search of food plants, so an ovipositing female's choice of host plant is critical to her reproductive success. As you'd expect, because of variation in nutrients and secondary compounds, plant species and individual plants within the same species differ in how well they support caterpillar growth (Thompson 1988). This is why female butterflies are choosy about where they oviposit.

Although a butterfly species capable of vast dispersal can persist as a single population, even in fragmented habitat across a vast montane landscape species that exhibit intermediate levels of dispersal may persist as metapopulations. A metapopulation is a set of more or less distinct, yet slightly interconnected, local populations (Wilson 1975; Harrison et al. 1988). Take the Gillette's checkerspot, for instance. This lovely butterfly, with a wingspan of 1.75 inches (4.4 cm), sports a wide orange-red submarginal band on the upper side of both wings. It lives in moist mountain meadows connected by riparian corridors, all set within the lodgepole pine forests from the Canadian Rockies (southeastern British Columbia and southern Alberta) southward into the Central Rockies (western Wyoming) (E. Williams 1995).

The semi-isolated populations of the Gillette's checkerspot participate in metapopulations in which local extinctions and recolonizations recur infrequently. After the Yellowstone fires of 1988 butterfly ecologists chose eight unoccupied patches of presumably suitable habitat, four of which had burned, and introduced a single Gillette's egg mass into each. Larvae survived to diapause in four of the sites, but only one of these introductions became established and formed a new colony (E. Williams 1995). The single new population grew swiftly for two years, but then it too decreased and disappeared. These observations led to three conclusions: most single isolated egg masses do not yield adults the following year; a single isolated egg mass is enough to colonize an open habitat; and recently burned sites provide acceptable habitat for this butterfly.

The fragmented habitats of Europe have also offered case studies of butterfly metapopulations. On the Åland Islands, an archipelago of southwestern Finland situated between the Baltic Sea and the Gulf of Bothnia, the Glanville fritillary persisted as 400 small populations on dry meadows that were home to its larval host plants, narrowleaf plantain and spiked speedwell (Kuussaari et al. 2000). Genetic influences on oviposition preferences were detected in five of its metapopulations.

Dispersal within a metapopulation includes both immigration and emigration, that is, the coming and going, respectively, of individuals among local populations. In general, the reasons animals disperse are manifold, including avoiding competition with kin and escaping harsh environmental conditions. In current metapopulation theory, habitat geometry, which combines habitat patch areas and interpatch distances, has been used as an indicator of dispersal. However, habitat quality is also important for predicting metapopulation dynamics.

In an attempt to further understand the metapopulation concept, a team of butterfly biogeographers conducted an experiment on the bog fritillary in the Lienne River Valley (Liège Province, southeastern Belgium) (Baguette et al. 2011). Assigned to the brush-footed butterfly family, this handsome species features wings with dark zigzags and dots on an orange background. Its wingspan is 1.5 inches (3.8 cm). This fritillary is found throughout the north-temperate regions of the world; in the Rockies it occurs from the Northern Rockies (western Montana) southward into the Southern Rockies (central Colorado). In the Lienne study area the bog fritillary was a specialist on meadow bistort, the host plant of its caterpillars and the only nectar source for adults. Butterflies lived in discrete patches of wet hay meadow. Seven habitat patches were interspersed with seminatural vegetation and artificial grasslands. This metapopulation was almost isolated from other metapopulations in the landscape. Investigators lowered the quality of certain habitat patches and left other patches untreated. Compared to the initial habitat, treated patches saw more butterfly emigration and untreated patches saw less. This butterfly's response seems to allow for a fine-tuning of dispersal rates to changes in habitat quality.

The Gillette's checkerspot and Glanville fritillary are examples of butterfly species that persist as metapopulations. Again, think of a metapopulation as a population of populations. Whether any particular small local population can be considered as a member of a more widespread metapopulation depends on whether the patch interacts with other patches via at least occasional movements of individuals. At any given moment each habitat patch may or may not contain a population: old populations occasionally become extinct; empty patches are infrequently colonized by immigrants that form new populations (Wilson 1975). Species persist as metapopulations as long as new populations are founded at a rate that balances the extinctions of established ones (Harrison et al. 1988).

Nine metapopulations of the silver-studded blue butterfly occurred in three environmental regions, or biotopes, of Britain (northern Wales): five metapopulations lived in heathland, one in mossland, and three in limestone grassland. The silver-studded blue's regional distribution was limited by its inability to colonize suitable habitat farther than a few miles (e.g., 5–8 km) from an existing metapopulation (Thomas and Harrison 1992). Extinctions and colonizations of its populations were frequent. Further, turnover was greater in heathland than in grassland, mainly because habitat patches were smaller in the former.

As you've seen, some butterflies, like the Gillette's checkerspot and Glanville fritillary, are so mobile that they cross ordinary physical barriers between habitat patches and participate in a vaster metapopulation. Other butterfly species, though, are more sedentary. The Edith's checkerspot lives in colonies throughout the grasslands and chaparral-covered hills of Jasper Ridge (Stanford, central coastal California), between the Coast Range and the Pacific Ocean. It has also been found in the high mountains of the West. At Jasper Ridge the vast majority of checkerspots stayed in the area where they were initially marked (Emmel 1976). This site loyalty was unexpected because there were no insurmountable physical barriers separating the grassy patches of their colony. When they were chased these butterflies easily flew over the intervening shrubby chaparral. Although population densities varied annually, the locations of the main concentrations of checkerspots remained static through seasons and over years. These findings suggest that the barriers to the Edith's dispersal were intrinsic, meaning constrained by the genetic predispositions of the organism, not imposed by extrinsic environmental barriers.

This kind of limited dispersal ought to apply to some of the Rockies' butterflies. In the face of high winds, alpine butterflies generally confine themselves to circumscribed areas. Lepidopterists have never seen the alpine butterfly called the anicia checkerspot blown off a mountaintop; rather, individuals fly up into the wind, descend back into the boundary layer, and return to their original position (Ehrlich and White 1980). In this species, long-distance passive dispersal by wind seems unlikely.

So if it's not physical barriers, what limits the Edith's dispersal? It may be factors that impact their reproductive success. Shortly after emerging, females are mated and plugged by the first successful male (Emmel 1976). The copulation plug is presumably a male adaptation that inhibits further mating by the female (Rutowski 1997). Males that change areas seem less likely to find a virgin female than those that stay home. A female is stimulated to oviposit by only one species of food plant, yet to survive to the diapause stage most larvae require a site where two species of food plants intermingle (Emmel 1976). Since the food plants dry up toward the end of the flight period, larvae from eggs laid by late-mated or transferred females would not have enough time to reach the body size needed for a successful summer diapause. Female Edith's that disperse leave fewer offspring because the two larval food plants co-occur more frequently in presently inhabited areas than they do elsewhere. Thus, there seems to have been long-term selection for staying put and not dispersing.

Amazingly, each butterfly species, even each population, seems to conform to a unique dispersal regime (Watt et al. 1977). Only some Queen Alexandra's sulphurs disperse, but those that do move an average of 0.8 mile (1.3 km). The extent of dispersal by Scudder's sulphurs is influenced by the geometry of their bog and riparian habitats. While some populations of the Mead's sulphur show plenty of dispersal, others approach isolated island status. Their dispersal radius ranges from 0.2 to 0.4 mile (0.3–0.7 km) in different populations, but the proportion of individuals dispersing varies greatly. These and other reports buttress the generalization that each butterfly population conforms to its own idiosyncratic dispersal regime.

Returning to the Glanville fritillary on the Åland Islands, a network of 1,502 habitat patches contains the species' entire distribution in Finland (Hanski et al. 1995). A local population lives in each of 536 dry meadow patches. As is typical of a metapopulation, this species persists in a balance between local extinctions and recolonizations. In one area of six square miles (15 km²), the species occupies 50 discrete habitat patches (Hanski et al. 1994). Empty patches are smaller than occupied ones; small populations are especially prone to extinction (Nieminen et al. 2001). At 16 percent extinction per year, population turnover is high. Fritillary density increases with decreasing isolation and with decreasing patch area, trends that are consistent with migration playing an important role in local dynamics. In this case there is no large mainland population to export a consistent supply of colonists, so this metapopulation survives in an extinction-colonization equilibrium. The Glanville fritillary shows that, in spite of frequent migration, it is possible to have suitable yet empty patches in a metapopulation because of the difficulties brought on by isolation, like locating mates, attracting conspecifics, and migrating in nonrandom patterns.

Along a 15-mile (25 km) stretch of chalk hills in Britain (North Downs, Surrey), 69 habitat patches seemed suitable for the silver-spotted skipper (Hill et al. 1996). In 1982, 48 were occupied. Then, over nine years 12 patches were colonized, 7 went extinct, and 9 stayed vacant. Patches that were colonized were large and close to large populations; in contrast, populations living in small, isolated habitat patches were more likely to go extinct. Sixty-seven percent of the movements between patches were less than 165 feet (50 m), with the longest being 3,530 feet (1070 m). In sum, these skippers are most likely to move between habitat patches that are large and nearby.

Inbreeding depression, the reduced fitness that results from the mating of close relatives, is caused by the pairing of deleterious recessive alleles. Recall from your introductory biology class that some genes have alternate forms, called alleles. In the Åland Islands the extinction risk incurred by small Glanville populations increased with the degree of inbreeding (Nieminen et al. 2001). A downward spiral ending in extinction starts with a small habitat, which supports a small population, which leads to excessive inbreeding, which causes low rates of egg hatching and larval survival, which in turn yields few larvae. In the Glanville's case the species' entire metapopulation might suffer from increased local extinctions aggravated by inbreeding effects.

For a long time the Edith's checkerspot was not known to occur in the Rockies. Then a population was discovered between 8,910 and 10,890 feet (2700–3300 m) in elevation on a south-facing slope of the Sawatch Range (Ehrlich and White 1980). Here it occupied a lush meadow dominated by big sagebrush. Abundant nectar was offered by paintbrush, which was also its larval host. From year to year the population's size fluctuated by an order of magnitude, between 200 and 2,000 individuals.

The average flight distance of male Sawatch Edith's was 558 feet (169 m) (Ehrlich and White 1980). This movement is partly explained by their flights between areas of abundance on the face of a slope and a seep in the valley floor where they probed the moist earth, possibly to obtain sodium (Arms et al. 1974). Other long movements of males were among the isolated rock outcrops where they basked.

The Sawatch Edith's checkerspot seems to persist in widely scattered populations (Ehrlich and White 1980). The butterfly's minimal requirements include the appropriate larval food plant, access to nectar sources, and some undetermined soil chemicals. Edith's were concentrated on ridge patches isolated by areas where individuals were never seen. As at Jasper Ridge, there is little reason to believe that there is much movement among the Sawatch's populations. Further, populations at different elevations were out of synchrony. For example, the Almont (8,910 feet [2700 m]) and Almont Summit (9,570 feet [2900 m]) populations were separated by only 0.9 mile (1.5 km), yet the former was at the end of its flight season while the latter was peaking (Ehrlich and White 1980). This degree of asynchrony has precluded successful interbreeding and may be facilitating the evolutionary divergence of the Sawatch Edith's checkerspot into two separate species.

In many cases, areas that were apparently suitable for Sawatch Edith's were going unoccupied. A population in the Gunnison River basin (Jack's Cabin, halfway between Gunnison and Crested Butte, Colorado) was composed of hundreds of individuals in 1976 but was extinct in 1977, possibly due to a severe drought (Ehrlich and White 1980). There was no influx of individuals from regional populations 1.2 to 6 miles (2–10 km) away, which held plenty of butterflies.

Picture a montane landscape sprinkled with patches of butterfly habitat. The founding, persistence, and extinction of hundreds of small butterfly populations conjure in my mind an image of a Christmas tree. Each color-ful light turns on and off at its own intensity, rhythm, and duration…the flickering butterflies of the Rockies.

CHAPTER 10

Axolotls

Many animals are potentially cannibalistic.
Such individuals occasionally may have to choose
between eating a relative or a nonrelative.

David Pfennig, Paul Sherman, and James Collins,
"Kin Recognition and Cannibalism in Polyphenic Salamanders"

HERE'S A PASSAGE from my field journal:

> 3 Sep 03—Climbing switchbacks most of the day, we hiked 12–13 miles from Palisade Meadows to Cherokee Lake [headwaters of Middle Trout Creek, San Juan Mountains (Continental Divide Trail, Weminuche Wilderness, southwestern Colorado)].... White-throated swifts jetted by while flycatching. Cherokee Lake was full (1 indiv/2 sq m) of medium-sized (4–5 in) passive (periodically swam slowly along bottom for 1–2 ft) tiger salamander (?) larvae with large gills (neotenic?). In this krummholz live gray jays, white-crowned sparrows, red-shafted flickers, and the ubiquitous American robin. Many chipmunks throughout. We agreed this was one of our best days yet!

That evening from the hillside overlooking Cherokee Lake, through binoculars I was able to follow the salamanders as they wiggled slowly through the clear water. Although they struck me as drab and passive, these amphibians have taught us a lot about how flexible life histories enable persistence in the extreme environments of the Rockies.

Let's first slither into some salamander biology. Although the mountains' cold climate, droughty soil, and short growing season are anathema to typical amphibians, a few species—the long-toed and tiger salamanders, spotted and leopard frogs, and the boreal toad—do thrive in some parts of the Rockies (Whitney 1998; Koch and Peterson 1995).

Up to one foot (0.3 m) long, with a broad head, two small protruding eyes, and a large mouth, the tiger salamander is one of the largest terrestrial salamanders in North America (Petranka 1998). Its highly variable colors range from large light spots, bars, or blotches on a dark background to a network of spots on a light background (Behler and King 1979).

Distributed from the East to the West Coasts of North America, from the boreal forest (southern Canada) southward to the southern end of the Sierra Madre Occidental (Puebla, Mexico), and from near sea level up to above 12,000 feet (3658 m) in elevation, the tiger is the most widely distributed salamander in North America (Koch and Peterson 1995). As you might expect, such a ubiquitous creature lives in a wide variety of habitats, including montane forests, grasslands and sagebrush plains, damp meadows, lakes and ponds, and the quiet waters of rivers and streams. Individuals dwell beneath debris near water, in crayfish burrows, and in fishless waters, and they are often seen at night after heavy rains (Behler and King 1979). On the basis of the adults' highly variable color patterns some herpetologists have suggested that the species includes seven subspecies (Collins et al. 1980), some of which I expect will eventually be promoted to the species level.

The tiger salamander is a sit-and-wait predator, lurking quietly and then seizing earthworms, large insects, and other amphibians—even small mice (Stebbins and Cohen 1995; Koch and Peterson 1995). In fishless waters the tiger salamander fills the ecological niche of top predator (Holomuzki and Collins 1987; Holomuzki et al. 1994). At 12,080 feet (3682 m) high in a cirque atop Galena Mountain in the Elk Mountains (Mexican Cut Nature Preserve, 5 miles [8 km] northwest of Gothic, west-central Colorado), adult tiger salamanders continue living in ephemeral ponds after the breeding season presumably because of the twin benefits of plentiful and nutritious fairy shrimp and only slight competition from other salamanders.

The amphibian life history has traditionally been divided into four stages: egg, aquatic larva, terrestrial nonreproductive subadult, and reproductive adult (Sexton and Bizer 1978). Two to four weeks after they are laid, tiger salamander eggs hatch into larvae half an inch (1.3 cm) long, which then metamorphose in the summer at about four inches (10.2 cm). The larvae gather in schools; if scattered by a disturbance they reaggregate (Koch and Peterson 1995).

Even though tiger salamanders produce unpalatable skin secretions (Stebbins and Cohen 1995), they are eaten by a variety of predators, including leeches, trout, garter snakes, great blue herons, and coyotes—and by other salamanders (Koch and Peterson 1995). Their aposematic behaviors, meaning those actions that warn of distastefulness, include spreading their hind legs and waving their tail.

The tiger salamander is unique in its order, Urodela, in that the tadpoles of two of its subspecies feature a trophic polymorphism. That is, individuals develop different feeding anatomies (Collins et al. 1980; Collins 1981). Both kinds eat invertebrates, but whereas typical larvae rarely eat other salamanders, cannibal morphs mainly do so (Collins and Holomuzki 1984). Compared to the typical morph, cannibalistic larvae have a large body, a broad flat head with a large skull, and an extra row of large conspicuous teeth on its vomers, which are the paired bones that support the anterior roof of the mouth (Petranka 1998). These features enable cannibals to eat large prey items, including salamander tadpoles. At 2.8 inches (7.1 cm) in snout-to-vent length, which is the distance from the tip of the nose to the anus, cannibal morphs are half again longer than the typical salamander's 1.9 inches (4.8 cm).

The tiger's cannibal morph has been reported in the Midwest and West, including Arizona, Colorado, and Texas. So why aren't cannibals found throughout the species' entire range? One hypothesis posits that disease has limited the spread of cannibalism (Pfennig et al. 1991; Collins et al. 2003). Members of the same species often share lethal pathogens (Jancovich et al. 1997), so cannibals, which experience an ultimate intimacy with conspecifics, are more likely to acquire pathogens and die from disease than typical morphs. In this way, disease may be constraining the spread of genes that predispose individuals to cannibalism.

The availability of conspecifics as prey and their level of relatedness to the presumptive cannibal are proximal cues, that is, immediate stimuli, that influence which morph develops (Loeb et al. 1994). Tiger salamander larvae reared in mixed-brood groups are more likely to develop into cannibal morphs, and at an earlier age, than those reared in groups of pure siblings (Pfennig and Collins 1993). It is therefore not surprising that in the lab, cannibal larvae preferentially eat less-related larvae (Pfennig et al. 1999). These and other findings implicate kin selection as the evolutionary reason that cannibalistic tiger salamanders discriminate their kin.

Experimentally occluding a tiger salamander's nares eliminates its kin discrimination, so olfaction is the key sense by which cannibals identify their own kin (Pfennig et al. 1994). Further, individuals in lineages with cannibals are best at discriminating kin, providing another hint that the cannibal morph's ability to recognize relatives evolved by kin selection.

And don't dismiss cannibalism as a minor effect—it can be intense. Cannibalism by the largest size classes occurs mainly on young-of-the-year (Wissinger et al. 2010). Those small larvae that survive have more injuries, lower activity levels, and lower growth rates in the presence of cannibals. These impacts on individuals can be so severe that they annihilate a whole new generation and thereby depress the population.

The tiger salamander's typical and cannibal larvae are examples of an environmentally induced developmental polymorphism (Collins and Cheek 1983). As they develop, large larvae interfere with the feeding behavior of small individuals (Rose 1960; Wilbur and Collins 1973; Ziemba and Collins 1999). More specifically, big larvae depress the feeding rate of small ones and this causes a widening in the range of larval body sizes (Ziemba et al. 2000). In addition to the number of prey larvae and degree of kinship, an individual larva's relative position in its local size distribution and the amount of size variation among all of the larvae also influence whether a larva develops into a typical or cannibal morph (Maret and Collins 1994).

From March to June in the north and at altitude, adult tigers migrate to their breeding waters after snowmelt and mate in temporary pools, fishless ponds, and stream backwaters. Breeding is cued by rain (Hill 1995). In swarming rituals males deposit spermatophores, or packets of sperm, on the substrate (Stebbins and Cohen 1995). A male produces 8 to 37 spermatophores per courtship episode with a single female. He releases pheromones from his exposed cloacal papillae and wafts them toward her with his tail undulations. She is attracted. In a tail-nudging walk with her nose near his vent, he leads her over the spermatophore. After she plucks up the capsule with her vent the sperm swim into her spermatheca, a storage chamber in the roof of the cloaca.

As eggs pass down the oviducts they are fertilized by sperm from the spermatheca. She can lay more than 7,000 eggs, usually on aquatic plants. The eggs of some salamander species, including the tiger, may house green algae, which apparently penetrate the eggs after they are laid (Stebbins and Cohen 1995). This presumed symbiotic mutualism, in which the embryos gain oxygen released by the algae and the algae gain carbon dioxide respired by the embryos, may speed the embryos' development and reduce larval mortality.

Tiger salamanders occasionally set off on a mass march, probably as they are dispersing from a site of high density (Varley and Schullery 1998). Group movements usually take place at night after a rainstorm in the spring or late summer. Some individuals slither for miles (e.g., 5–7 km). In several areas of Yellowstone (Yellowstone National Park, northwestern Wyoming), like the Little America Flats and the banks of the Yellowstone River in the Hayden Valley, roads can become slick from all the squashed salamander bodies (Koch and Peterson 1995).

A typical amphibian life history includes a metamorphosis. That is, regardless of environmental conditions individuals invariably transform from a gilled, swimming, fishlike larva to a lung-breathing, terrestrial, miniature adult. And in fact, over most of its geographic range the tiger salamander conforms to this norm: larvae lose their gills, grow larger legs and feet, develop lungs, become land-based adult salamanders, and then breed.

But in some places tiger salamander larvae do not follow the typical life history pattern. They do not transform into the adult stage—yet they still mature sexually and breed. This phenomenon is called neoteny, an intriguing, somewhat unusual life-history pattern. One way to think about neoteny is that gonadal maturation outpaces somatic development. The egg hatches and the larva looks like a tadpole, with long, feathery, external gills, large head, and a long, eel-like body; yet the internal reproductive organs mature inside the outer larval features (Varley and Schullery 1998). A tiger salamander larva that does not transform and breeds in neotenic form is called an axolotl (Koch and Peterson 1995), the Aztec word for "water monster." Axolotls reach a total length of 7 to 15 inches

(18–38 cm). Also called a water dog or mud puppy, and seeming more like a fish than an amphibian, the axolotl has been promoted by biology teachers as a classic example of neoteny.

And it gets even more complex. Tiger salamander larvae actually come in three types. Those that regularly transform are called type 1; those in which metamorphosis is facultative, type 2; and obligate neotenes that do not transform are type 3 (Stebbins and Cohen 1995). The ratio of the three morphotypes varies among populations. All three types are found in some populations of the barred tiger salamander, a subspecies of the Great Plains; many populations have larvae of types 1 and 2; and some populations of the gray tiger salamander, a northern subspecies, are predominantly of type 3 (Stebbins and Cohen 1995).

What is causing all this variation in life histories? The current answer is that it's a mix of local environmental conditions and genetic predispositions. In temporary waters there is usually not enough time for the developmental delay that causes neoteny, so neotenic larvae are found most often in semipermanent or permanent waters (Stebbins and Cohen 1995).

But perhaps the most important environmental factor associated with this reproductive polymorphism is water temperature. Physiologically, cold water retards growth, which either slows the thyroid gland's release of thyroxin, a hormone essential to metamorphosis, or inhibits the ability of body tissues to respond to thyroxin (Stebbins and Cohen 1995). Neotenic tiger salamanders are often found in the cold waters of high elevations or northern latitudes. For example, at Yellowstone's lower elevations (e.g., 5,700 feet [1737 m]), metamorphosis occurs during the summer, but at 7,500 feet (2286 m), where the growing season is not long enough to produce adults, only axolotls are found (Varley and Schullery 1998).

Here's a more detailed case study. Throughout the Southern Rockies (Colorado), the water temperature of ponds is correlated with the life-history patterns of their resident tiger salamanders. In order of decreasing water temperature, ponds that averaged 62°F (17°C) hosted populations with the standard life history, ponds at 60.5°F (16°C) featured metamorphosis in the second warm season, at 56°F (13°C) the salamanders transformed in their third year, and ponds at 55°F (13°C) supported neotenes (Sexton and Bizer 1978).

What ultimate evolutionary conditions could have selected the genes for neoteny? In addition to the permanence of the aquatic habitat and the length of the growing season, a wide variety of other local environmental factors may influence the frequency of neoteny. Food shortages, scant levels of iodine, severe temperature fluctuations, aridity, lack of cover on land, and competition have also been implicated (Collins et al. 1993; Stebbins and Cohen 1995).

And one other possibility has been offered, namely, the harshness of the terrestrial conditions for the adults compared to the larvae's relatively benign aquatic habitat (Semlitsch and Gibbons 1985). Theoretically, if mortality is greater in adults than in larvae and both stages experience equal fecundity, delayed metamorphosis could be favored by natural selection.

Although, as I've said, several ultimate environmental factors have been proposed to favor the evolution of neoteny, a proximal developmental cause could be an individual's genes. The Mexican axolotl, a related species, is an obligatory neotene (Rosenkilde and Ussing 1996). In this species geneticists identified a major gene that triggers the development of neoteny (Voss and Shaffer 1997).

The opposite ends of a gradually changing series of life-history pathways can be scored as distinct morphs, each exploiting its own kind of environment (Sexton and Bizer 1978). Populations conforming to the standard amphibian life history function as colonizing morphs because they are capable of exploiting both terrestrial and ephemeral aquatic habitats at different stages in their life history. In contrast, tiger salamanders with the neotenic life history maintain stable populations in permanent ponds. Both the standard and neotenic morphs retain the capacity of producing the alternate form, so the progeny of the colonizing morph in cooler, more permanent situations can become neotenic. This helps explain why the neotenic consolidating form exploits only permanent waters, while the metamorphic form exploits both temporary and permanent situations.

As with the alternate forms of a trait in all kinds of organisms, the tiger salamander's two morphs surely come with advantages and disadvantages. What are the evolutionary costs and benefits that accrue to each morph? Metamorphic adults grow more than neotenic adults. Compared to neotenes, metamorphs have higher biomass and more calories in their stomachs. In some places the diets of metamorphs consist primarily of fairy shrimp, whereas the neotenic diet includes a variety of benthic and terrestrial invertebrates. There's a simple reason for this dietary difference: fairy shrimp occur only in temporary ponds and thus are unavailable to axolotls in permanent ponds. Because they forage on fairy shrimp and incur only weak intraspecific competition in their temporary ponds, metamorphs gain a growth advantage over neotenes. Neotenes experience higher levels of intraspecific competition with large larvae in permanent ponds than metamorphs do in temporary ponds. Axolotls should have less fitness relative to metamorphs, primarily because metamorphs can move into the best habitats for growth. Thus, facultative neoteny may be maintained by the differences in fitness accrued by each morph in its respective environment.

Following this logic, in some places neoteny seems to be a flexible adaptation that evolved in varying environmental conditions (Sexton and Bizer 1978). It permits persistence where the conditions on land are inhospitable. For those populations in which neotenic breeding is not genetically obligatory, individuals can give rise to larvae that transform, providing the option of dispersing to new breeding sites and avoiding the predation and competition of permanent waters. Alternatively, the progeny of colonists may resort to the neotenic mode should the conditions at a new site favor it. Some breeding or nonbreeding larvae can grow large before metamorphosis, shortening the hazardous growing period on land. The tiger salamanders of the Gunnison River basin (west-central Colorado), which live at 9,000 to 11,000 feet (2743–3353 m) above sea level, show this kind of life-history flexibility (Stebbins and Cohen 1995).

Three hypotheses—the neotene advantage, best of a bad lot, and dimorphic neotenes—have been offered to explain the evolution of such facultative neoteny. As I write, data on larval growth patterns suggest that both the neotene advantage and best-of-a-bad-lot proposals seem most plausible. Thus, it is possible that the tiger salamander's environmentally induced developmental polymorphism could reflect the action of more than one selective mechanism.

As you've seen, facultative neoteny is an environmentally cued polymorphism in which a salamander's adult morphology depends on the interaction between its genotype and the larva's environment. Within the population some individuals transform into terrestrial metamorphic adults, while others retain larval characteristics like gills, remain fully aquatic, and mature as neotenic adults. Both genders exhibit the polymorphism, so some interbreeding can occur between the two morphs. At Galena Mountain the short growing season imposes a minimal time window for foraging and reproducing. The breeding season is only 10 to 14 days per year, and larval development takes 14 months to 5 years. Neotenic males have a shorter minimum time interval between breeding events than metamorphic males, whereas neotenic females have a longer minimum time interval than metamorphic females. Thus, neotenic males breed more frequently than metamorphic males, and metamorphic females breed more frequently than neotenic females. Neotenic males may breed more frequently than metamorphic males because they are always in the breeding habitat, compared to metamorphic adults that migrate annually between breeding ponds and terrestrial burrows. These observations suggest that sex-specific fitness payoffs and sex-ratio biases can influence the maintenance of the tiger salamander's neoteny-or-metamorphosis polymorphism.

When we look across the vast spectrum of Earth's living things, we can detect the workings of neoteny in many of them. Some plants provide interesting examples. The red larkspur was studied in the Coleman Valley and Crane Canyon (Sonoma County, northwestern California), while the coastal larkspur was studied at Bodega Head and Cheney Gulch (also Sonoma County) (Niklas 1994). The red larkspur, which is pollinated by hummingbirds, features flowers with strongly tubular corollas that are strikingly similar to the buds of the bumblebee-pollinated coastal larkspur. Also, the growth rates of red larkspur's sepals and petals are slower than the coastal larkspur's. The flower of the hummingbird-pollinated red larkspur is thus interpreted as a neotenous derivative of the bumblebee-pollinated coastal larkspur's flower.

In animals, some evolutionary biologists have argued that many major groups arose evolutionarily through the process of neoteny. For example, because juvenile millipedes and all adult insects have six legs, insects are thought to have arisen via neoteny from the larva of a millipede-like ancestor (Futuyma 1979). Similarly, chordates had their origin in the tadpole larvae of tunicates. Neoteny can also result during the artificial selection of domestic species. A long-term experiment with the domestication of the silver fox revealed that certain developmental steps had become retarded, resulting in adult animals that retained juvenile morphology and behavior (Trut et al. 2004).

These and other examples share a common evolutionary pattern. When the rates of development of specific tissues change, the adult phase of the parent species becomes the phase through which the embryo of a new species passes, eventually delivering a new adult form. A new species can arise by the relative speeding and slowing of the development of various body parts. In modern evolutionary theory the slowing and speeding of development, reflecting the mutations of genes that regulate growth rate, are thought to be an important mechanism of evolutionary change.

And neoteny is even implicated in our own origins. Humans and chimpanzees diverged from a common ancestor five million years ago (Lewin 1982). When human and chimpanzee proteins are compared, little difference is found—only 1 part in 100 is different. Outwardly observable differences are produced by the timing of the assembly of the building blocks, not by different kinds of ingredients. That is, many of the differences between chimp and human anatomies and behaviors can be traced to the mutations of our two species' regulatory genes.

How might modern humans have emerged from an ape ancestor by the alteration of development rates? Several of our features do, in fact, seem to be neotenic (Futuyma 1979; Lewin 1982). Adult humans have a bulbous cranium like baby apes and monkeys. The mature human's vertical face, small brow ridges, and small jaws and teeth are typical of those of fetal apes. Our heads are balanced atop our backbones, with the opening for the spinal cord at the base of the skull, as in embryonic apes; in adult apes, the spinal opening is toward the rear of the skull. Our big toe is straight, strong, and nonopposable, as in embryonic apes. And finally, the growth in the number of our brain cells is switched off later in development than it is in apes, so we mature with bigger adult brains.

Those sluggish salamanders in cold ponds high in the Rockies are offering our minds some new ideas with which to contemplate the origins of our brains.

CHAPTER 11

Tadpole Kin

The clever men at Oxford
Know all there is to be knowed.
But they none of them know one half as much
As intelligent Mr. Toad.

Kenneth Grahame, *The Wind in the Willows*

I BEGIN THIS STORY with three reports from my field notes, arranged from north to south. On August 16, 2005, along the stretch of the Spray River where it passes between Leman Lake and Bryant Creek (Palliser Pass Trail, Banff National Park, southwestern Alberta), Nancy and I stepped gingerly through a mob of slowly crawling (no, not hopping) boreal toads.

From August 4, 2002: "Hiked from Park Creek (upper) to Lake Isabel, with Vigil Peak looming above at the southern end of the Lewis Range [Lake Isabel Trail, Glacier National Park, northwestern Montana]." "Rainy, cold! Wet vegetation-overgrown trail led to soaking wet, cold feet. The lake is *full* of boreal toad? tadpoles; large, meandering, sinuous schools of tadpoles."

And on July 1, 2000, I wrote "Hiked 5–6 mis [Lamar River Trail, Yellowstone National Park, northwestern Wyoming] to 3U3, a pleasing campsite on an island in Lamar River" [in the shadow of Little Saddle Mountain]. "We took an afternoon walk upriver, found 2 toads with yellow mid-sagittal stripe, toad egg strings in River's backwater."

We encountered this animal on many of our Rocky Mountain hikes— sometimes in teeming abundance—so I've gotten to know the boreal toad fairly well.

The boreal toad is two to five inches (5.1–12.7 cm) long and features a stocky body; short, blunt head; warty skin; prominent parotoid glands behind each eye; a light brown background; and a distinct thin, cream-colored stripe down the middle of its back (Koch and Peterson 1995). The parotoid is an external skin gland that secretes a predator-deterring neurotoxin, the milky alkaloid called bufotoxin. A dorsal bump overlies each parotoid poison gland.

As an interesting aside, we now see that alkaloids function as predator deterrents in both plants, like lupine, and animals, like this toad. Could this be an example of convergent evolution in different kingdoms? Or does it reflect alkaloid synthesis by a plant, and its subsequent bioaccumulation through herbivorous insects and predatory toads? Regardless of the origin of the similarity, it's impressive.

This widespread amphibian can be found from sea level to above 11,800 feet (3597 m) and ranges from southern Alaska southward to northern Baja California, and from the Rockies westward to the Pacific Coast.

The boreal toad breeds in beaver ponds, temporary pools, slow-moving streams, and, as I reported above, in lakes and backwater channels of rivers (Koch and Peterson 1995). During the breeding season mature males develop dark thickened swellings on the upper surfaces of their thumbs. These so-called nuptial pads help them during amplexus, when they hold on to a female during mating. Females lay an average of 12,000 eggs, which they deploy in two long, gelatinous strings.

The boreal toad is an explosive breeder, its mating season lasting just one or two weeks (Olson et al. 1986). More than 250 breeding adults may converge on a single site. At three places in the Cascade Range (western Oregon), the sex ratios of breeding adults favored males, with the male-to-female ratio varying from 1.5 to 2.6. Males actively search for females on the water's surface and clasp other toads regardless of their gender, but they neither defend territories nor give mating calls. Sometimes ravens feast on throngs of these preoccupied toads. At one communal site more than 20 percent of the breeding population was eviscerated (Olson 1989).

The larvae of many toad species are distasteful to predators and aggregate in densely packed schools (Waldman and Adler 1979). Tadpoles of the boreal toad show this social behavior—they can form huge aggregations. One band of tadpoles was reported to be 1 yard (0.9 m) wide by 330 yards

(300 m) long (Koch and Peterson 1995). That long, sinuous school of tadpoles I saw at Lake Isabel was probably one of these superorganisms.

Among animals in general, living in a group can confer several benefits to individual members. For a toad tadpole, life in an aggregation could bring one or more of the following advantages (Waldman and Adler 1979; Blaustein and Waldman 1992):

- Efficient feeding—Groups of tadpoles stir the substrate and suspend food particles, allowing each larva to filter food out of the water.
- Enhanced thermoregulation—The tadpoles' collective black bodies may function as a thermal sink, elevating body temperatures and quickening the growth of individual tadpoles.
- Less competition—Large schools may swamp small groups of tadpoles.
- Predator avoidance—Group living could enhance early detection and avoidance of predators. Within a group the reactions of peripheral tadpoles could alert the inner ones.
- Alarm signals—When preyed upon, a tadpole that releases alarm chemicals could warn siblings, thereby increasing the inclusive fitness of both the sender and receiver via kin selection.
- Nepotism—Kin selection may account for the aposematic coloration of distasteful individuals. When a predator samples and rejects one tadpole, that individual's relatives may incur fewer attacks.

Because this is the first mention of an alarm substance, here's a bit of supplementary information on the fifth item above. In response to chemicals released from an injured conspecific, boreal toad tadpoles show an immediate behavioral reaction. They also develop antipredator shifts in their life history. Ecologists raised groups of tadpoles with either non-predatory water boatmen, chemical alarm cues from injured conspecifics, or predatory backswimmers that had been fed toad tadpoles. Tadpoles raised with the latter two types of stimuli metamorphosed more quickly than those raised in the presence of water boatmen (Chivers et al. 1999a). The accelerated metamorphosis shows that boreal toads can facultatively alter their life history. Quickening the time to metamorphosis seems adaptive, as it could lessen exposure to aquatic predators.

After they metamorphose, toadlets disperse across the landscape. In the early 1990s such a gang dispersed across the floodplain of Nyack Flats along the Middle Fork of the Flathead River (near the West Entrance to Glacier National Park). A similar mass dispersal occurred on

July 25, 2002, when thousands of juvenile one-inch-long (2.5 cm) boreal toadlets emerged from the ponds near Sullivan and caused the closure of the North Fork Road (northwestern Glacier National Park). By July 27 it had subsided. With this latter report I've now documented that the mass dispersal of two amphibian species, the tiger salamander and boreal toad, can dangerously lubricate Rocky Mountain roads.

What's going on with these mass movements? One idea is that synchronized metamorphosis and mass dispersal overwhelm predators and thereby reduce each individual's risk of being eaten. Herpetologists tested this so-called predator-swamping hypothesis by measuring the level of synchrony of metamorphosing boreal toads in either the presence or the absence of toad-eating garter snakes. They measured the time to emergence from the water, the number of metamorphs emerging together, and the spatial tightness of the aggregations before and during emergence. When they considered all three factors, the researchers did indeed detect a synchronizing effect (Devito et al. 1998). They interpreted the synchrony as an adaptation in which the toads emerged sooner in the presence of the predator, regardless of whether each individual toad had reached the point at which it was better suited to terrestrial versus aquatic life.

While killing and feeding on a boreal toad tadpole, predators like the giant water bug inflict damage that releases an alarm substance from the larva. In laboratory experiments tadpoles avoided the side of an aquarium where a predator was feeding on a conspecific tadpole (Hews 1988). Further, naiads of the shadow darner, that is, the aquatic larvae of a dragonfly, were less efficient at capturing tadpoles that had been exposed to their species' alarm substance.

In the Cascade Range, boreal toad tadpoles live in the same waters with backswimmers, giant water bugs, common garter snakes, rough-skinned newts, and rainbow trout. The first three species kill and eat toad tadpoles, whereas the latter two find them unpalatable. When they are exposed to live members of the three predatory species, groups of tadpoles respond with antipredator behaviors; they don't when they are near the nonpredators (Kiesecker et al. 1996). When presented only with the predators' chemical cues, the tadpoles still responded in the same defensive way. These observations demonstrate that boreal toad tadpoles use chemical cues to distinguish between predatory and benign animals.

Juvenile boreal toads, that is, the small land-traversing and still-growing toadlets, avoid chemical cues from snakes that have eaten juvenile toads, but they do not respond to stimuli from live earthworms, conspecific juveniles, or snakes that have eaten conspecific tadpoles (Chivers et al. 1999b; Belden et al. 2000). So here's the surprising conclusion: boreal toadlets can distinguish between the chemical cues issuing from predators that have consumed tadpoles and the chemicals from predators of juvenile conspecifics.

Among animals in general, cannibalism can be widespread, especially, as we saw with the Mormon cricket and axolotl, under conditions of high density and food scarcity (Fox 1975; Crump 1983; Pfennig 1997). The possible benefits of eating one's own kind include the energy and nutrients gained and the elimination of competitors and other cannibals, but potential costs include risking injury, acquiring parasites or pathogens, and eating one's genetic relatives (Meffe and Crump 1987; FitzGerald 1991; Heinen and Abdella 2005).

According to one hypothesis cannibalism should be favored at a point in the life cycle where food needs are high and mortality is severe (Crump 1983). Tadpoles developing in temporary waters would seem to be candidates. In toad species that breed explosively the larvae of one age class may be well developed by the second breeding. If food is limited the flush of new eggs or tadpoles may provide excellent nourishment for the older, bigger larvae. Amphibian eggs are high in calcium and phosphorus, both of which are needed for skeletal development in a growing toad. It is possible that the defenses of tadpoles that deter invertebrate and fish predators may actually have originated as anticannibalism adaptations.

But wouldn't cannibals be eating their own kin? Where explosive breeding congregations are composed of hundreds of adults, the odds are remote that a cannibal would be closely related to a potential victim (Crump 1983). In fact, field experiments strongly suggest that the opportunity for boreal toad tadpoles to interact with siblings is low and that tadpoles frequently mix with many nonkin (Blaustein et al. 1990). In nature, tadpoles probably encounter groups consisting of individuals from numerous sibships, often hundreds of them. In such a situation the odds of eating kin are tiny because of the overwhelming dilution by unrelated tadpoles.

Kin recognition, the ability to distinguish between genetic relatives and nonkin, can be inferred when an animal behaves differently toward genetic relatives (Gamboa et al. 1991). Anuran species show wide variation in their ability to discriminate between kin and nonkin. In North America, for instance, kin recognition has been demonstrated in tadpoles of the southern spadefoot toad; American and boreal toads; and in the red-legged, wood, and Cascades frogs (Waldman 1982, 1984; O'Hara and Blaustein 1985; Blaustein et al. 1990; Blaustein and Waldman 1992). In contrast, other anurans—the Pacific tree frog, spring peeper, and spotted and leopard frogs—lack kin recognition capability.

Kin recognition in the absence of an opportunity to learn one's kin is interesting because it can facilitate the evolution of altruism, one of the hallmarks of true social behavior (Blaustein 1983; Waldman 1987, 1988; Pfennig 1997). The essence of inclusive fitness is that, regardless of how they sense their degree of relatedness, individuals behave more favorably toward one another the tighter their genetic relationship is.

Near Lost Lake, set in the subalpine forest of the Pacific Northwest (20 miles [32 km] southwest of the town of Hood River, northwestern Oregon), boreal toad tadpoles associated more with full siblings than with paternal half sibs, and with maternal half sibs over nonsibs (Blaustein et al. 1990). Tadpoles did not associate more with full sibs than with maternal half sibs. Sibling preferences formed early in development, perhaps even before hatching, by behavioral recognition rather than by differential habitat selection. Tadpoles preferentially formed schools with familiar sibs over both familiar and unfamiliar nonsibs, showing that sibling discrimination is not based merely on familiarity. Boreal toad tadpoles reared exclusively with sibs preferred to associate with sibs over nonsibs throughout development, but tadpoles reared with sibs and nonsibs showed no preference (O'Hara and Blaustein 1982). Thus, a boreal toad tadpole is able to discriminate its own siblings from the hundreds of others it encounters.

While it's still within the female anuran's body, the jelly surrounding the eggs incorporates a specific suite of chemicals (Blaustein et al. 1990). It is also possible that environmental chemicals may be incorporated into the jelly after the eggs are laid. Either process would label all of the eggs in a clutch with the same chemical compounds. In this way the eggs of a female's clutch would come to share a molecular identity—a unique chemical signature on which the tadpoles could imprint and then use to identify relatives. In fact, some preliminary data do suggest that tadpoles distinguish sibs from nonsibs by using waterborne chemical cues sensed by smell or taste.

As I've said, for animals in general, kin recognition is considered a key step in the evolution of various social behaviors like nepotism and altruism (Waldman 1987). Four possible causes have been proposed to explain the evolution of kin recognition (Blaustein 1983; Lacy and Sherman 1983; Blaustein and O'Hara 1986; Waldman 1986; Waldman et al. 1988). The first mechanism is spatial distribution. If relatives occur in predictable places, like a home site or a specific type of habitat, altruistic acts could be selected if they are directed toward individuals in that place. Second, familiarity and prior association can create kin recognition. Individuals of the same litter or those that share the same nest may learn to recognize each other. Third, in a process called phenotypic matching, an individual learns and later recalls some of the unique outward features of relatives or of itself and then assesses the level of similarity between a conspecific's body and its own. And fourth, genes called recognition alleles may create a phenotypic marker, like a particular lineage's chemical or odor. So far, the empirical evidence seems to favor the latter two ideas, namely phenotypic matching and recognition alleles, which we can think of as the effect and cause, respectively, of a single adaptation.

Because toad tadpoles are unpalatable to some predators and are conspicuous when aggregating, their social behavior could result from kin selection (Blaustein et al. 1990). A predator that tries to eat a noxious tadpole subsequently avoids other similar-looking nearby individuals. If individuals sort into groups of relatives, then kin could benefit if the predator samples a distasteful member and then avoids the rest of the bunch.

Yet another benefit of kin recognition may be the avoidance of inbreeding (Blouin and Blouin 1988). Defined as the mating of related individuals, inbreeding generally describes mating between first cousins or closer relatives. Among birds and mammals the offspring of inbred matings are often less fit than outbred progeny. This is presumably why many species have evolved behaviors that lower the odds of inbreeding, including kin avoidance, widespread dispersal, and kin recognition. In some amphibians, kin recognition abilities can persist even after metamorphosis (Blaustein and Waldman 1992). In natural populations, because adult toads rarely mate with siblings even though close kin are readily accessible as mates, it is possible that kin recognition may reduce inbreeding.

And now, coming full circle, we can link the behaviors of cannibalism and kin recognition. Tadpoles that are able to recognize their relatives might direct their cannibalistic predation toward nonkin (Blaustein and Waldman 1992). If cannibals recognize kin they should generally avoid eating them if nonrelatives are available.

So how do we explain the fact that the small larvae of the American toad are cannibalized by their larger siblings? Although eating one's brothers and sisters would seem maladaptive, under some life-history scenarios larvae could be selected to eat their own siblings if it speeds the cannibals' development (Waldman 1988). Small individuals with poor odds of metamorphosing in a drying pond may sacrifice themselves, thereby accelerating the growth of their larger sibs and permitting them to metamorphose sooner or at a larger size (Degani et al. 1980). In other words, provided eating one's kin yields a net fitness benefit to the overall lineage, selection may have favored runts that preferentially allow themselves to be cannibalized by larger sibs rather than by nonsibs (Pfennig 1997).

Growing evidence points to the presence of kin recognition in a wide variety of animals (Lacy and Sherman 1983; Lewin 1984b; McCracken 1984; FitzGerald and van Havre 1987; Waldman 1988; Waldman et al. 1988; Blaustein et al. 1991; FitzGerald and Morrissette 1992; Toth et al. 2011). To list a few vertebrate examples, kin recognition has been detected in fish such as the guppy, coho salmon, and three-spined stickleback; amphibians like the smooth newt, Cascades, red-legged, and wood frogs, and American and boreal toads; birds such as the bank swallow and Canada goose; and mammals such as the Mexican free-tailed bat, Belding's ground squirrel, house and deer mice, Norway rat, muskrat, and, of course, primates.

In my own family and probably in yours, there is a yearning to understand the source of kids' eye and hair colors, and an interest in extending the links of the family tree and in discovering the provenance of heirlooms. Nationally, genealogy is a growth industry. The boreal toad is teaching us a bit about why we show such a passion for knowing the sources of our own body features (e.g., my Roman nose), our family names (I'm actually George III), and the history of Great-Grandmother's rocking chair (in which I wrote this book).

CHAPTER 12

Scent of a Mouse

*The popular scenario whereby
the first rattlers warned away trampling herds
of American bison...is probably incorrect.*

Harry Greene, *Snakes: The Evolution of Mystery in Nature*

IN OUR MORE THAN 1,300 Rocky Mountain trail miles (2080 km), despite the hype that greeted us everywhere, Nancy and I came across only one rattlesnake. While a lone male lazuli bunting was singing his heart out from the tops of big sagebrush, we set up camp under a canopy of paper birch. This cozy spot was nestled in the riparium along lower Camas Creek in the Salmon River Mountains (Middle Fork Salmon River Trail, Frank Church–River of No Return Wilderness, Salmon National Forest, east-central Idaho). After we settled in, a juvenile rattlesnake slithered leisurely by between our tent and cooking area.

We appreciated the viper's patterned camouflage and fine-tuned movements, but this was one campsite where we didn't venture about barefoot after sunset. And that's because rattlesnakes are out hunting small rodents at night. Not merely a simple sequence of strike-poison-swallow, the predatory life presents these hunters with three problems: detecting a mouse at night, injecting venom and quickly releasing the mouse to avoid its sharp teeth, and then finding it again in the dark. The rattlesnake has evolved elegant adaptations to successfully meet these needs. It turns out that how a rattlesnake kills and eats a mouse is a complex, nuanced, and fascinating story.

But first, let's set the stage by reviewing a little rattlesnake biology. In North America's fossil record the family Viperidae, the vipers, and a

group of its member species, the rattlesnakes, date from the Middle
Miocene and Lower Pliocene, about 15 million and 5 million years ago,
respectively (Cook et al. 1994). Rattlesnakes of the genus *Crotalus*, from
the Greek work *krotalon*, meaning "rattle," are found only in the Americas, from the southern Canadian Rockies (southwestern Alberta and
southeastern British Columbia) southward into southern South America
(southern Argentina). North America hosts 19 species of rattlesnakes.

The western rattlesnake, our main subject here, is a relatively large
snake, with adults growing up to 65 inches (1.7 m) long, although most
are in the range of 35 to 45 inches (0.9–1.1 m). The western rattlesnake features a broad, triangular head; vertical, elliptical pupils; a stout midbody;
keeled scales that lend a roughened look; and a rattle at the end of its tail
(Koch and Peterson 1995). Along its dorsal surface, dark brown blotches
are narrowly bordered with white. All of this is set against a background
color that can vary from green to gray (Conant 1958).

The western rattlesnake is the only poisonous reptile in most of our
Western forests. Within the species' vast range, from the Great Plains
(Iowa) westward to the Rockies and from the Canadian Rockies (British
Columbia and Alberta) southward into the Chihuahuan Desert (north-
ern Chihuahua state), this serpent lives in a wide variety of habitats, in-
cluding mountain forests, talus slopes, and at treeline.

Western rattlesnakes may den—sometimes in large numbers—in
mammal burrows, south-facing talus slopes, and caves (Koch and Peterson 1995). In the northern part of the species' range they overwinter
communally. The mass of entangled snakes, which may be as large as a
watermelon, helps hibernating rattlers conserve heat and moisture. While
dormant, their body temperature fluctuates between 36 and 45°F (2–
7°C) (Macartney et al. 1989).

In the spring the hibernaculum, or communal den, gradually warms.
The vipers emerge in April and May and then spend most of their summer
foraging (Koch and Peterson 1995). Both sexes emerge simultaneously
(Graves and Duvall 1990). In a study in the Snake River Canyon (Snake
River Birds of Prey National Conservation Area, 20 miles [32 km] south
of Boise, southwestern Idaho), the rattlesnake's activity peaked from late
May through early June (Diller and Wallace 1996). They mate in mid to
late summer (Macartney and Gregory 1988). Several kinds of predators,
including hawks, badgers, and coyotes, prey on western rattlesnakes.
Other mortality factors include winter-kill, especially of young-of-the-
year, and, of course, persecution by humans (Gannon and Secoy 1984).

After emerging from their dens they disperse along fairly straight paths to individual hunting areas (Koch and Peterson 1995). Some rattlesnakes migrate up to 10 miles (16 km) between their hibernaculum and summer hunting grounds. Pregnant females often remain within 0.6 mile (1 km) of the den and aggregate in a rookery. The species is viviparous, which for our purposes I define as giving birth to live young rather than laying eggs. In the first half of their active season, snakes search for small mammal prey on traditional hunting grounds (King and Duvall 1990). Males search for mates in the second half of the active season.

By late October most rattlers have returned to their den (Koch and Peterson 1995). Individuals return to the same den site year after year. According to one hypothesis the adults migrate to their home dens first via celestial cues and then use conspecific chemical signals as they get closer (King et al. 1983). Young snakes seem to follow their mother's scent trail to the hibernaculum.

Among western rattlesnakes, gravid females allow large animals to approach closer than males do, suggesting that pregnant females rely on visual crypsis to avoid predators, possibly because pregnancy limits their mobility (Kissner et al. 1997). Camouflage is achieved because the snake's markings resemble a random sample of its substrate's color pattern (Endler 1988). Compared to large snakes, small individuals may be slower and allow closer approaches, which may be why they wait to rattle until the threat is close. Among gravid females, cooler individuals allow closer approaches than warm ones do. In sum, reproductive status, body size, and body temperature influence whether a rattlesnake protects itself with passive camouflage or active defense.

If a threat persists the rattlesnake will escalate its defense. It may start by trying to move away; then it will intensify its reaction by coiling, cocking, and head hiding; and finally it might climax by striking (Duvall et al. 1985; Koch and Peterson 1995). Whether a snake is near or far from protective cover and whether it is in a group or alone both affect the intensity of its defensive behavior. All these actions suggest that rattlesnakes assess the odds and possible severity of a potential attack. If the snake cannot escape it defends itself by striking and injecting venom, but it is usually reluctant to do so.

The rattle, an epidermally derived organ made of highly modified scales, is moved by specialized shaker muscles (Fenton and Licht 1990). In the evolution of rattlesnakes the rattle arose only once (Cook et al. 1994), so all modern species are descendants of that early prototype.

The rattle's buzzing, hissing noise is produced when its loose but interlocking segments strike each other as the tail is shaken vigorously by the specialized muscles (Cook et al. 1994). When a rattlesnake shakes its rattle the small muscles on either side of its tail contract at up to 90 times per second, a rate similar to that of a hovering hummingbird's wings (Friederici 2008). This makes the rattlesnake's shaker muscles some of the fastest repeatedly shortening muscles among all land-based vertebrates. The rattle's sound features a rapid onset, medium-intensity broadband tones from 2 to 20 kHz, and an unchanging frequency pattern (Fenton and Licht 1990). To my ear it sounds somewhat like maracas. A rattle's loudness and dominant frequencies are determined mainly by the diameter of its most proximal free segment (Young and Brown 1995).

A disturbed rattlesnake usually does not rattle but remains camouflaged and goes unnoticed. One hypothesis posits that the rattle evolved as a signal to warn large animals, like bison, about the viper's venomousness so the snake would not be stepped on (Cook et al. 1994; Koch and Peterson 1995). (Yeah, I know, that runs counter to this chapter's epigraph.) An alternative idea is that it originally evolved as a caudal lure. Rattling seems to be designed to frighten the signal receiver, perhaps by startling it (Fenton and Licht 1990). In fact, snakes of many species vibrate their tail when threatened, regardless of whether they have a rattle. So the rudimentary rattle may have been selected because it exaggerated the sound of this preexisting movement.

In the eastern part of the Columbia Plateau Province of the Northern Rockies (northern Idaho), mature male western rattlesnakes carry sperm in their distal vas deferens, or sperm duct, from late March to October (Diller and Wallace 1984). Ovulation occurs from mid-May to mid-June. The follicles of mated females undergo vitellogenesis, or yolk production, before hibernation (Macartney and Gregory 1988). Upon emerging in the spring, reproductive females have large yolked ova, each up to 1.4 inches (35 mm) long.

During the breeding season, male rattlesnakes occasionally engage in a combat dance (Koch and Peterson 1995). Two males will approach each other, rise up, entangle their necks, sway from side to side, and attempt to throw each other down (Hersek et al. 1992). This type of ritualized fighting occurs when a receptive female is nearby. The larger male or the one with a prior history of dominance usually prevails and mates with the female.

Males begin searching for mates in mid to late summer (Koch and Peterson 1995). Males that probe along straight-line paths locate and mate with more females than those following curvier routes (Duvall and Schuett 1997). Females usually breed every other year or less often. They store sperm in their reproductive tract until the following spring. Among pregnant snakes, follicle number is positively correlated with body size (Graves and Duvall 1993). Females deliver 4 to 21 young, with a mean of 5.5 (Diller and Wallace 1984).

Pregnant females maintain a high and relatively constant body temperature of about 86°F (30°C) by frequenting warm microenvironments, especially rock piles near their den (Koch and Peterson 1995). They spend most of the summer in gestation, during which they may not eat. Pregnant female timber rattlesnakes coil together in groups of 5 to 30 snakes (Eliot 2004). Snakes in rookeries are relatively sedentary and maintain higher body temperatures than nonpregnant conspecifics (Graves and Duvall 1993). Membership in the group seems to convey thermal benefits (Graves and Duvall 1993).

Females give birth to miniature, functionally competent rattlesnakes, each 6 to 11 inches (15–28 cm) long, in September and early October (Diller and Wallace 1984). Mothers may remain with their young until after the snakelets shed their skin for the first time, which usually happens by 10 days of age (Koch and Peterson 1995). After parturition the emaciated female sets out to renew her fat stores. The longer it takes her to recoup body mass, the longer the time between breeding episodes (Charland and Gregory 1989).

During their first year the rattlesnakelets grow an average of 13 inches (33 cm), and then their growth slows. Males that are longer than 20 inches (51 cm) in snout-to-vent length and that are equipped with four or more rattle segments are probably sexually mature; most females that exceed 22 inches (56 cm) in length and carry five rattles are adult (Diller and Wallace 1984). Rattlesnakes reach sexual maturity at five to seven years of age and produce their first litter when they're six to eight years old.

Western rattlesnakes hunt from mid-April to early October (Wallace and Diller 1990). A rattlesnake's predatory behavior is well suited to life in exposed places—the snake curls in a shady place, burning little energy and avoiding a thermoregulatory battle, while not exposing itself to hawks.

This sit-and-wait predator spends most of its time in a resting coil under a sagebrush or rock, or in a burrow, waiting in ambush along trails frequented by small mammals (Koch and Peterson 1995).

How does a rattlesnake decide where to assume a resting coil? A sit-and-wait predator like a rattlesnake invests a lot of time in waiting for prey, so it would pay an opportunity cost if there were better sites for ambushing prey. Thus, it is important that ambush predators choose a site where profitable prey, like large or nutrient-rich animals, are likely to be encountered. One way to accomplish that would be to use cues from past feeding events.

And, in fact, this is what they do. Timber rattlesnakes, born in the laboratory to wild females that had been caught in the Central Appalachians (northeastern Pennsylvania), were more likely to select ambush sites next to the chemical trails left by prey with which they had had a previous feeding experience (Clark 2004). This finding suggests that these ambush predators learn to recognize the chemical scent of profitable food items and then later use that memory when choosing an ambush site. The western rattlesnake ought to be doing the same thing.

The western rattlesnake eats a large variety of animal prey, including lizards, birds, and small mammals (Wallace and Diller 1990; Koch and Peterson 1995). In some places snakes less than a year old feed exclusively on vagrant shrews. Small individuals of the Great Basin rattlesnake feed mainly on lizards, whereas adults eat mammals (Glaudas et al. 2008). Where they co-occur, adult rattlesnakes prefer Townsend's ground squirrels.

A rattlesnake locates a rodent with its eyes and tongue, and with heat-sensitive pores called loreal pits, which are situated on the sides of its head. A snake tongue is a delivery mechanism for the paired chemosensors inside the snout called Jacobson's organs. These organs connect to the mouth via two tiny openings, the vomeronasal fenestrae, which are located in the palate. The tongue samples environmental chemicals by flicking. It darts out, sometimes oscillating, and then is retracted into the mouth, often after the tips have contacted the ground or some object (Schwenk 1994). Odor molecules adhering to the tongue are delivered to the vomeronasal fenestrae and then make their way to sensory epithelia in the Jacobson's organs.

For a snake to detect a prey animal by chemosensory tropotaxis, which is the simultaneous comparison of the intensity of a chemical on both sides of the body, it must be able to sense the molecules at two points (Schwenk 1994). This function is served by the paired tips of the forked tongue. The distance between these paired sampling points, the tongue's tips, is a function of the tongue's width and fork depth and the degree to which its tines are spread. The chemical source must leave a gradient steep enough that a difference can be sensed between the separated tips of the forked tongue. The aerial trails of molecules left by prey or by other passing rattlesnakes, both known targets of tongue flicking, are narrow and not highly volatile and thus can provide a chemical gradient of the appropriate width. In essence, the function of a reptile's forked tongue is to detect the edge of a chemical trail.

That makes for a neat story, but it has been challenged. When a team of comparative psychologists unilaterally severed the vomeronasal nerves, which should disrupt trailing ability, they found no change in several measures of trailing (Parker et al. 2008). This finding was inconsistent with the edge detection hypothesis. Alternatively, the deeply forked tongue may be a chemosensory adaptation to increase odor-sampling area, and snakes may detect only the concentration of a chemical trail.

Now that I've offered both sides, I'm free to state my preference. I lean toward the edge detection hypothesis for several reasons. Taxa with deeply forked tongues, like snakes and teiid lizards, are proficient trail followers (Schwenk 1994). Tongue tips are widely spread during trail-following behavior, and tines are spread rapidly and widely just before they contact the substrate. When the edge of a trail is exceeded by one tongue tip during a tongue flick, the snake swings its head back into the molecular swatch before the next tongue flick. These observations are consistent with the edge detection hypothesis. Still, it'll be fun to watch this debate play out.

Small mammals lick themselves during grooming, so it makes sense that a hunting rattlesnake would be sensitive to rodent saliva. And, in fact, western rattlesnakes were found to respond to rodent saliva with high rates of tongue flicking (Chiszar et al. 1997). They also struck applicators bearing saliva more frequently than they struck controls. Prairie rattlesnakes did not use urinary cues; rather, they followed trails left by materials from a mouse's integument, like its skin and fur (Chiszar et al. 1990).

Another adaptation rattlesnakes use to hunt is the loreal pits, which are seated between the snake's snout and eyes (Koch and Peterson 1995).

Loreal pits are sensitive to infrared radiation, the wavelengths emitted by warm objects. This sense allows the viper to accurately strike a warm body in complete darkness (Schmidt et al. 1993).

To understand how a loreal pit works, let's talk a bit about how a lens works. The simplest way to manipulate light to form a coherent image is to place a small hole in front of a retina. If the hole is small enough, light from the source falls on only a limited part of the retina, while light from other sources falls elsewhere. An image thus becomes focused. The smaller the hole, the more precise the definition of the direction from which light arrives, and the clearer the image.

The snake's infrared-sensing cells are contained within its loreal pits. The side walls of a pit form a pinhole, limiting the angle at which infrared radiation enters the pit. The two pits' fields of view cross in front of the head. By adjusting the direction of its head until both pits receive the same intensity of infrared radiation, a snake comes to point its head directly at a warm prey animal, even in total darkness.

Over the millions of years of their predator-prey arms race, ground squirrels and rattlesnakes have coevolved adaptations and counteradaptations that enable and thwart, respectively, their actions toward each other. A hunting rattlesnake poses little threat to an adult ground squirrel, but the snake is a major predator of the rodent's pups (Rowe and Owings 1990). In defense of its young an adult ground squirrel may approach and harass—and even attack—a rattlesnake. The snake responds by rattling and striking. Because warm snakes show less hesitation, swifter movement, and finer accuracy, and because large snakes can strike farther and keep their fangs embedded longer, a ground squirrel would benefit by having information about the snake's body warmth and size. Warmer snakes rattle with shorter latencies, faster click rates, and higher amplitudes (Rowe and Owings 1996). Body temperature also affects the rattling sound: at higher body temperatures the rattle is not as loud and its pitch is higher (Cook et al. 1994). Larger snakes produce rattling of higher amplitude and lower frequencies. Thus, rattling provides cues to the rodent about the viper's warmth and size, and therefore the level of risk the snake poses (Swaisgood et al. 1999b).

Ground squirrels elicit such information from a rattler by probing—perhaps by shoving stones at the snake and inducing it to rattle. As encounters escalate the rattlesnake becomes the target of more harassment.

Where they co-occur west of the Rockies (Oregon and California), adult California ground squirrels actively confront and harass Pacific rattlesnakes, a subspecies of the western rattlesnake (Swaisgood et al. 1999a).

California ground squirrels wave their tails to appear larger to, and thereby to intimidate, hungry snakes. It's been recently discovered that the rodents shunt body heat to their waving tails, from which they emit infrared radiation (Rundus et al. 2007). Using a thermal-imaging device, a team of behavioral ecologists discovered that the rodents add an infrared component to their tail flagging when confronting Pacific rattlesnakes but flag their tails without infrared emission when confronting infrared-insensitive gopher snakes. Simply, squirrels warm their tail when encountering rattlesnakes (McNaughton 2008). The hot tail may increase the apparent size of the rodent.

Although a rattlesnake uses visual and infrared cues to aim its strike, the strike lunge itself is released by the prey's odors as sensed by the viper's vomeronasal system (Graves and Duvall 1985). During a strike, venom flows through the sharp, hollow fangs into the puncture wounds (Koch and Peterson 1995). Rattlesnake venom has two biological functions: immobilization and digestion (Mackessy 1988).

Rattlesnakes inject more venom into large rodents than into small ones (Hayes et al. 1995). Venom metering seems to be adaptive for several reasons. First, injecting too much venom into a small animal would be wasteful. This could temporarily deplete venom reserves and leave the snake unprepared for additional prey. Second, larger animals are less affected by a given amount of venom than smaller ones. If insufficient venom is injected, large prey may flee too far to be recovered. And third, because of the lower surface-to-volume ratio of larger prey animals, snakes may obtain digestive benefits by injecting greater quantities of proteolytic venom into larger prey.

So far so good, but here's a counterintuitive twist: a highly toxic venom does not work best for an adult snake. This is because the prey's quick death would preclude the venom from being distributed throughout the entire body, and this in turn would reduce the digestive effectiveness of the venom's proteases, enzymes that break up cellular proteins (Mackessy 1988). In contrast, less toxic venom immobilizes prey via venom-induced shock, while still allowing the digestive enzymes to be distributed by the prey's still-beating heart.

Rattlesnake venom is a complex oral secretion, both in its chemical composition and its pharmacological effects (Mackessy 1988). Venoms contain various kinds of enzymes (Minton 1987). Proteases, which are common in rattlesnake venoms, are important because they degrade structural proteins, which then, once the prey is swallowed, expose the prey's viscera to the snake's stomach enzymes. Some of these proteases break down proteins in the cell membranes of capillaries, which then fall apart and allow hemorrhage to ensue ("Dissecting Rattlesnake Damage" 1978).

Juvenile rattlesnakes, like the little guy we encountered along Camas Creek, eat a lot of lizards (Mackessy 1988). The venom of a juvenile rattlesnake is more toxic to sagebrush lizards than the adult's venom is. In contrast, snakes longer than 19 inches (50 cm) take mainly mammals. As a snake grows it feeds on increasingly larger mammals and secretes a functionally different venom with a rising level of protease and a decreasing toxicity.

The Ongoing Evolution of Venom

There are hints that rattlesnake venom is evolving swiftly (Grenard 2000). The bites of rattlesnakes in the West are becoming more toxic, requiring medical intervention with larger doses of antivenin (Tennesen 2009a, 2009b).

The various kinds of toxic molecules in snake venom can be sorted into three main categories: cytotoxic components that kill cells, a hemotoxic fraction that affects blood, and neurotoxic ingredients that attack nerves. It's the proportion of neurotoxins that has been increasing recently.

What could be causing such a swift evolution? It is possible that an evolutionary arms race between ground squirrels and rattlesnakes is driving it. A team of toxicologists assayed the ability of rock squirrels from two sites (both in south-central New Mexico), where prairie and western diamondback rattlesnakes co-occurred, to inhibit the digestive and hemostatic activities of the rattlesnakes' venoms. The rock squirrel's blood serum reduced the metalloprotease and hemolytic activity of the venoms from these two rattlesnake species more than it reduced these elements in the venom from the allopatric northern Pacific rattlesnake (Biardi and Coss 2011). "Allopatric" refers to nonoverlapping geographic ranges. This finding suggests that rock squirrels defend themselves against metalloproteases and other proteases after envenomation from at least two rattlesnake species they are likely to encounter naturally. Therefore, prey resistance influences the evolution of snake venom, a conclusion that supports the predator-prey arms race hypothesis.

Whatever the underlying causes, the ongoing evolution of venom seems to be widespread. It is occurring in several species distributed across the continent (Tennesen 2009b). We may not know what's causing it, but it's certainly an example of evolution that is occurring now, nearby, and in a system that affects our well-being.

Rattlesnake venom seems to be highly variable—between species and populations, within species, and by age within populations. Here's an example. Across its vast range, taxonomists have split the western rattlesnake into eight subspecies. A toxicologist extracted venom from specimens of all of the subspecies. Analytical tests showed that myotoxins, disintegrins, and PLA_2 were common in most venoms (Mackessy 2010). Here are those definitions: myotoxins cause muscle necrosis; disintegrins inhibit platelet aggregation; and PLA_2 causes inflammation and pain. In contrast, two categories of metalloproteases, PIII and PI, were common in only five subspecies. Metalloprotease activity varied by 100-fold among the subspecies. There was a 15-fold difference between the most and least toxic venoms. The most likely adaptive explanation of all this variation is that it relates to the characteristics of different prey animals in the subspecies' ranges.

Mice are always struck and released regardless of their size or the size of the snake (Mackessy 1988; Hayes 1991). After striking a sharp-fanged rodent and injecting venom, a rattlesnake withdraws. Rather than trying to finish the prey off on the spot and risk an injury to its eyes or face, the snake pulls back and waits for the poison to take effect. The strike-and-release of an adult rattlesnake represents a compromise between avoiding the retaliation of the sharp-toothed rodent and losing the food animal altogether (Mackessy 1988).

During the brief 0.3-second-long strike, the snake acquires a memory of the unique chemical cues of that individual prey animal, which it then retains for at least 60 minutes (Melcer and Chiszar 1989; Lavin-Murcio et al. 1993). As I mentioned before, this chemical search image guides the snake in following the unique molecular spoor left by the envenomated animal. The rattlesnake is able to discriminate the poststrike trail of an envenomated mouse from the odor trails of other, unstruck mice (T. Smith et al. 2000).

After a strike an adult prairie rattlesnake changes the orientation of its head, bringing it closer to the departure bearing of the prey (Lee et al. 1988). As you now know, during poststrike trailing an adult snake is thought to use its forked tongue as a chemosensory edge sampler and its vomeronasal organs as the major sensors (O'Connell 1983). Envenomated prey may dash away over complex terrain (T. Smith et al. 2000). In one experiment adult mice that had been envenomated by western prairie rattlesnakes traveled an average of 73 inches (1.9 m) during 78 seconds before becoming immobile (Estep et al. 1981). This distance hints at the extent of trailing that confronts a rattlesnake in the dark. Envenomated mice die in three to eight minutes, which is about as long as snakes wait before starting their search, supporting the hypothesis that the predator's behavior is designed to avoid contacting a still-living rodent (Melcer and Chiszar 1989).

If a snake does not strike a mouse immediately before being exposed to the trails, trailing behavior will not occur. In contrast, if the snake first strikes the mouse it follows its olfactory trail with precision (Golan et al. 1982; T. Smith et al. 2000; R. Clark 2006). This suggests that the vomeronasal use of chemical information is blocked before the strike, possibly because tongue flicking would be conspicuous to an alert prey animal (Chiszar et al. 1983).

Striking eliminates the block. When a trail is present, frequent tongue flicking facilitates locating the trail and following it to the carcass. Once the trail is located the snake confines its head to within 0.8 inch (2 cm) of the odoriferous cues and 75 percent of its tongue flicks are directed to the trail. Although trailing frequency declines over time, some rattlesnakes can maintain the selective poststrike trailing behavior for up to 24 hours after striking the prey animal.

In one experiment, western rattlesnakes struck mouse carcasses that had been misted with either water or diluted perfume, and then the envenomated carcasses were removed. Later, snakes were presented with a pair of nonenvenomated carcasses, each doused with one of these liquids. Snakes preferred the carcass with the same odor as the prey they had struck, even an hour after the strike (Melcer and Chiszar 1989). Snakes even preferred the carcasses of mice that had been eating the same diet as the mouse that had been struck. These results further demonstrate that a rattlesnake acquires chemical information from its rodent prey during its brief predatory strike and then uses that memory to search for the prey (Lavin-Murcio et al. 1993). Rattlesnakes of closely related species recognize each other's envenomated prey, but distantly related species do not (Chiszar et al. 2008). The vomeronasal system plays the critical role of mediating this poststrike prey discrimination (Stark et al. 2011).

In summary, visual and thermal cues trigger and orient a rattlesnake's strike, whereas chemical cues direct the poststrike actions (Haverly and Kardong 1996).

The western rattlesnake has taught us a lot about detecting a mammal at night with infrared radiation, metering specific amounts of venom, and following a chemical trail through the air, all adaptations we could copy and put to practical uses. So I'll close this chapter with a naked plea. Isn't it odd that we worry more about being bitten by a rattlesnake than about being killed in a car? The former mishap is not only vastly rarer, but the serpent gives us a warning. These fascinating creatures also eat rodents, which tend to increase in numbers after we conduct a rattlesnake roundup. Can we please cut them a break?

CHAPTER 13

The Ultra-Overwinterer

*I was hiking one day over a stretch of boulders
splotched with gray lichens when suddenly at my feet
a rock the size of a coconut started to walk.*

Frank Craighead Jr., *Wilderness U.S.A.*

I RETAIN A FEW faint memories of a magical bird.... In the summer of
1968, probably July, while a student along Yellow Bay off the western
flank of the Mission Range (University of Montana Biological Station,
14 miles [22 km] northeast of Polson, northwestern Montana), on one of
my weekend hikes in the Lewis Range (Glacier National Park, northwestern Montana), I came across a ptarmigan in the alpine. My aging 35-mm
Kodachrome slides show the bird in summer camouflage. In one picture
the bird's bill is parted—it was panting on that bright sunny day—even
though it was standing on a snowfield. I also recall being impressed by its
fearlessness.

And here's a fresher image. On July 28, 2002, as Nancy and I were
closing in on Piegan Pass along the trail from Many Glacier to Reynolds
Creek (Cataract Creek Trail, Glacier National Park), a lone white-tailed
ptarmigan stood quietly along a steep section of the trail. It looked like
one of the place's rocks, like a round mass hugging the ground. Across its
sleek, smooth surface, individual feathers were hard to discern as it slowly,
seemingly fearlessly, walked around. I felt like I was in the presence of
alpine imperiousness—no ice storm or freezing gust would disrupt its day.
So I've been fascinated by this slow, lethargic bird for several decades—
by how it survives life on the edge, and how it reproduces in these cold,
windswept, treeless places.

At the last glacial maximum so much of the Earth's water was locked up in ice that the ocean's surface subsided 280 to 430 feet (85–131 m) (Stanley 1986). The drop in sea level exposed a wide tract of land between Siberia and Alaska, a land bridge that linked Eurasia and North America for 70,000 years. The connector and its abutments go by the name of Beringia. In part because it was free of large glaciers, Beringia functioned as an intercontinental biological filter—it allowed only certain cold-adapted species to pass. Some plant species, like sagebrush, needle-and-thread grass, and bluegrass, dispersed eastward from the Old World across Beringia to the New. Elk, grizzly bear, and humans, also Eurasian emigrants, crossed into North America about 13,000 years ago.

The grouse line, in contrast, originated in North America and exported forms westward to Eurasia (Johnsgard 1973; Lucchini et al. 2001). Most of the North American and Eurasian grouse species originated in the late Pleistocene epoch, 300,000 to 20,000 years ago, before Beringia's final drowning. Grouse and quail may have arisen from cracid-like ancestors during the mid-Tertiary period, roughly 34 million years ago. Cracidae is a family of tropical birds that includes chachalacas and curassows.

The Rockies are rich in grouse species; there are six of them. Blue grouse are unusual among American birds in that they migrate to lower elevations in the spring and move upward in the autumn. In the summer they court, mate, and nest on lower slopes; in the fall they return to higher ground where, through the winter, they feed on fir needles and buds and shelter under snow-laden evergreen branches. We trekked among these fearless, approachable birds along the Middle Fork of the Salmon River and one of its tributaries, Big Creek (Frank Church–River of No Return Wilderness, east-central Idaho). Sage grouse assemble late in the growing season and retire to valleys where they feed on sage leaves. In the mating season sharp-tailed grouse gather at a meeting place, where the calling males boom through dawn and dusk. All males join the dance, circling, bowing, and squatting in an accelerating whirl. The spruce grouse, also called "fool hen," is, like the blue grouse, unwary. Encountering both of these species on the trail, I wondered how such tame animals survived Native American hunters. The willow ptarmigan, a bird mainly of the Arctic tundra, ranges southward into the Northern Rockies.

The sixth species of grouse and the subject of this chapter, the white-tailed ptarmigan, lives in the Rocky Mountain alpine where it shares the heights with rosy-finches and American pipits (Pearson 1917) as well as hoary marmots and mountain goats. Measuring 12 inches (30 cm) long and weighing 14 ounces (392 g), this is the smallest member of the grouse family. The white-tailed is a fairly common resident of the alpine zone from the Canadian Rockies (northern British Columbia and central Alberta) southward into the Northern Rockies (northwestern Montana), and in the Southern Rockies (Colorado and northern New Mexico) (Peterson 1990; Wassink 1991). It attains some of its higher densities in the Front Range of the Southern Rockies (Rocky Mountain National Park, north-central Colorado). At the southern end of its range, it is found only at the highest altitudes, usually above 10,000 feet (3048 m), while at its northern extreme it lives at lower altitudes but still usually in mountainous terrain. Its geographic distribution is superimposed on the pika's.

Alpine habitats are extreme environments that feature strong winds and cold temperatures, short breeding seasons and limited food availability, and potentially severe predation. A specialist of those extreme windswept summits, most white-tailed ptarmigans remain above treeline throughout the year (Brooks 1967). Although some birds occasionally descend into subalpine habitat when deep snow covers their alpine food plants, this small grouse is the only bird that generally spends its entire life in the alpine (Wassink 1991).

In the Sierra Nevada (east-central California), the white-tailed's breeding habitat includes willow shrubs taller than 12 inches (30 cm), and a cover of boulders, mosses, and subshrubs. It uses primarily the Arctic willow community on rocky, north-facing slopes. Brooding hens prefer moist meadows while flocks occupy sites with abundant boulders. After the nesting season, the hens use depressions within their breeding territories.

When a predator flies over, feeding ptarmigan issue a cluck, stop and sit, and then roll their heads sideways to watch the sky (Ulrich 1984). Once the intruder leaves they resume feeding. Although others have written that they rarely fly to avoid predators and that they just sit still, we have flushed several coveys along the trail. For instance, in the Maligne Pass, perched between Replica Peak and Endless Chain Ridge (Maligne Pass Trail, Jasper National Park, west-central Alberta), we flushed a flock of five, which then swiftly slipped into a krummholz thicket.

Over an annual cycle the plumage of the white-tailed ptarmigan alternates between summer brown and winter white. Summer birds are camouflaged with mottled browns and grays (Pearson 1917). Brown patches are often the size, shape, and color of old willow leaves. Adult birds seem to know when they are molting in the spring and autumn, as they remain on the periphery of snowbanks, half-and-half environments that match their transitional plumage. In the winter, except for their black bills, claws, and eyes, they are pure white (Ulrich 1984). In a neat piece of seasonal engineering, air spaces replace pigment granules in the white feathers of winter, so these provide more insulation than the summer's dark feathers. Each form of seasonal plumage functions as a different kind of camouflage. Pattern camouflage, like the white-tailed's winter whites, looks like the background; the summer plumage is an example of disruptive camouflage, a jumbled pattern that breaks up the animal's outline.

In the spring, males return to their former territories in the alpine and within a few days are joined by females. Each breeding male defends a territory of one-half to two acres (0.2–0.8 ha). The largest territories are occupied by the oldest and most aggressive individuals. Mating begins in early May and females usually nest in July. A female will not start to nest until she has completely changed to summer plumage. Even though the white-tailed ptarmigan is monogamous with a lifelong pair bond, most females raise their young alone. In defense of her camouflaged chicks the ptarmigan mother may feign a broken wing. Falcons, nutcrackers, and weasels may find the eggs when the hen is off her nest, but it is bouts of extreme weather that kill the most eggs.

The white-tailed ptarmigan is classified as a socially monogamous species, an exception within the highly polygynous grouse subfamily (Benson 2002). But it's not unwaveringly so. In the Lewis Range of the Northern Rockies (Glacier National Park), white-taileds were nearly completely genetically monogamous. Of 58 chicks with their putative fathers identified, 3 (5 percent) were the result of extra-pair copulations. Three of 18 clutches (17 percent) contained extra-pair offspring. It seems that males are able to guard their female mates from most extra-pair copulations because of the high visibility across their habitat and their habit of foraging alongside their mate.

A team of wildlife biologists studied the reproduction of white-tailed ptarmigan in the Southern Rockies, specifically in the Front, Collegiate, and San Juan Ranges (Colorado) (Giesen et al. 1980). Several adaptations functioned to squeeze their reproductive cycle into brief windows of favorable weather. Adult males began defending their breeding territories in early to mid-April. Females, which return to their mate and territory of the previous year, arrived in late April to early May. Within the territory the females selected natural depressions in snow-free sites on moderate, south-facing slopes. The average size of nest bowls was 6.0 × 5.2 × 1.4 inches (151 × 130 × 36 mm). Picture a teacup saucer with an inch-and-a-half rim.

At a median elevation of 11,870 feet (3597 m), nests were built of dead leaves and stems of willow, spruce, grass, lichens, and a few small white feathers. Most nests were located in krummholz or within 825 feet (250 m) of treeline. In order of decreasing frequency, nests were built in rock or boulder fields, turf, evergreen krummholz, and willow krummholz. Krummholz, both willow and spruce, protected the incubating hens from the wind and also concealed them. Most nests in krummholz were at the edge of a shrub clump or near an opening, the latter likely allowing a quick departure.

Copulation occurred three to seven days before the eggs were laid. The pair remained bonded until late in incubation. The interval between the deposition of successive eggs was 26 to 30 hours. The oval eggs, which averaged 1.7 × 1.2 inches (43.7 × 29.7 mm), were lightly to heavily blotched or spotted with reddish brown on a creamy brown background. Clutch size averaged 5.9 eggs, with a range of 2 to 8. As clutches neared completion the females spent more time on the nest, and incubation started when the last egg was laid. The clutches of older adults were larger than those of yearlings, 6.2 versus 5.5, respectively.

If we define the incubation period as the time from the deposition of the last egg to the hatching of the clutch, the white-tailed's incubation period was 23 to 26 days (Martin and Wiebe 2004). Hatching started in the first or second week of July, with a median hatch date of July 15. In this statewide study area almost two-thirds of the hatch occurred within a two-week period. The main nest predators were coyotes and weasels. Females raised one brood per season. Older females that failed in early to midincubation produced replacement clutches.

In two populations of white-tailed ptarmigan in the Park Range (north-central Colorado), males had a strong tendency to return to the place where they had been raised, a behavior called philopatry. Their median dispersal distance between hatching and breeding was three-fourths of a mile (1.3 km) (Giesen 1993). Females, in contrast, dispersed three times farther, across a median distance of 2.4 miles (4.0 km). This sexual difference in dispersal is one reason why 51 percent of yearling males but only 13 percent of yearling females recruited into their parents' population. The short dispersal of males contributes to the colonization of vacant habitat patches within the expanse of their metapopulation.

Birds everywhere must meet the physiological needs for breeding, but white-tailed ptarmigans do so in the alpine's extreme conditions. Even though they show quite a lot of resilience in some reproductive functions, when the snowmelt is extremely delayed their breeding success is depressed. In one particularly slow-warming spring, mean snow depth in May was 34.4 inches (87.3 cm) and snow persisted through most of June (Martin and Wiebe 2004). This squeezed the birds into a severely shortened breeding season. In this year the first egg was laid 18 days later than the site average of June 7. Females started laying eggs with less body reserves compared with females at the same stage in normal years. Since alpine birds are ground nesters they need some snow-free ground to start laying and thus need to be flexible in reproductive timing. The ability to adjust its breeding schedules to local conditions is critical to the white-tailed's persistence. These findings suggest that white-tailed ptarmigans assess a variety of risks before committing to reproduction (Martin and Wiebe 2004).

Before white-tailed hens start incubating, males accompany their mates 90 percent of the time. During this phase the males spend 26 percent of their time looking out for predators (Artiss and Martin 1995). That's a lot of wariness. Two hypotheses have been offered to explain the male's preincubation vigilance (Artiss et al. 1999). First, the protection-of-paternity hypothesis posits that male vigilance minimizes the odds of being cuckolded. Accordingly, male vigilance should be most intense when hens are fertile and there are plenty of potentially competing males. And second, according to the predator-detection hypothesis, the function of the male's vigilance is to decrease the predation risk to his mate, which in turn would allow the female to increase her foraging efficiency. I suspect both hypotheses apply to white-taileds.

Whereas some males stay near the nest where they may confront and distract intruders, incubating hens remain still, hidden by their camouflage. So far, that description strikes me as pretty normal, but here's an amazing adaptation: when the hen does leave the nest it's with excruciating slowness. She achieves invisibility by moving so slowly that the predator's eye does not detect her motion.

All of the eggs in a white-tailed ptarmigan's nest hatch simultaneously and the chicks start foraging almost immediately, traits characteristic of precocious birds. If the mother spies danger she issues warning clucks and her chicks freeze in place. At eight weeks of age they reach the full adult mass of about a pound (0.5 kg).

Of all possible conditions in the alpine the most stressful period for a white-tailed hen is when she is incubating in cold weather. In the Sierra Nevada the snow depth in the spring can vary from 20 to 170 inches (51–424 cm) (Clarke and Johnson 1992). Chick survival and brood success were found to be negatively correlated with snow depth, supporting the idea that the white-tailed's nesting success is depressed by deep snow, probably due to its impact on the availability of food, cover, and nest sites.

Do Ptarmigan Hens Build Eggshells from Their Bone Calcium?

Alpine environments are generally poor in calcium, so one might expect alpine birds to incur a shortage of this nutrient in their diet. In such a calcium-poor environment, how does a female white-tailed ptarmigan build her eggshells? Based on the bird's physiological constraints, ptarmigan hens have three possible options for meeting the breeding season's acute demand for calcium: (1) seeking calcium-rich foods just before egg laying; (2) storing calcium in their skeletons over a longer time and then mobilizing those reserves when they are needed for forming eggshells; or (3) both.

A team of bird ecologists collected white-tailed ptarmigans in the alpine of the upper Animas River basin in the San Juan Mountains (near Silverton, southwestern Colorado) and studied their leg bones (Larison et al. 2001). The microanatomy and chemical composition of leg bones cycled annually in hens, but not in males. Specifically, hens stored a lot of calcium in their leg bones during the months before breeding, depleted it during egg laying, and then subsequently recovered the lost bone structure and composition. These findings are consistent with the second hypothesis, that females store calcium in their leg bones before the start of egg laying and then draw on these reserves to build eggshells.

Although this story is intuitively appealing, it has been challenged (Reynolds 2003; Larison 2003). So here's yet another provocative question about a Rocky Mountain organism that awaits a definitive study.

Sticking with their mother, newly hatched white-tailed chicks begin scouring through an array of new foods. How does a naive hatchling learn which items are nutritious? In a nutshell, hens teach their chicks. White-tailed mothers issue a food signal, a multimodal display that includes vocalizing and tidbitting (Allen and Clarke 2005; J. Clarke 2010). Tidbitting is a display in which a bird, like a courting male or parenting female, picks up a bit of food and offers the morsel to another, like a female or chick, respectively. Our barnyard roosters do it all day long.

To understand the function of the white-tailed's tidbitting display, animal behaviorists studied hens and their chicks in the Southern Rockies (Rocky Mountain National Park) and the Sierra Nevada. Hens foraged in patches where certain plant species were abundant and called their chicks to these sites. The plant species that triggered a hen's food calls had more protein than did random mixtures of plants. Through tidbitting, these food types came to dominate the chicks' diet. Chick feeding mirrored the calling rates of their mothers, so the chicks were led into eating high-protein foods. The relative proportion of each plant species in the chicks' diet increased with the food calls associated with that plant species, but not with that plant's relative availability. The chicks of hens that often uttered food calls ate diets higher in protein than chicks of hens that rarely called. As they grew and foraged farther from their mothers, the chicks maintained their food preferences. These observations demonstrate that the white-tailed hen's food call is a form of cultural transmission in which information about available foods is taught to the chicks.

On Vancouver Island (off the western coast of British Columbia) and in the Ruby Range (10 miles [16 km] northwest of Kluane Lake, southwestern Yukon Territory), a few white-tailed ptarmigan hens adopted chicks that were not their biological offspring (Wong et al. 2009). In these two places adoption rates were 13 and 4 percent, respectively. By now, this far into the book, the evolutionary questions that should be shouting at you are, Who is adopting whom? And what is their genetic relationship? Invoking the theory of kin selection, an obvious prediction would be that hens adopt their sister's chicks. Or wouldn't it make a great story if hens were adopting their grand-chicks? Another mystery awaiting further research.

As we saw in the butterfly story, alpine habitat is spatially fragmented and forms an archipelago of high-altitude habitat islands. What are the roles of dispersal and recruitment in maintaining populations of

white-tailed ptarmigan in their fragmented universe? At four sites in the
Southern Rockies (Colorado), almost all recruitment of both sexes, especially females, was of birds produced next to the local population (Martin
et al. 2000). So the sustainability of white-tailed populations depended
more on recruiting females than it did on gaining males. In general,
patterns of recruitment were not correlated with the local survival of
adults or production of young the previous year. More than 95 percent
of the recruits were yearlings. The dispersal of adults, even though infrequent, was also important to achieving interpopulation connectivity.
A bird is recruited where it overwinters. The white-tailed ptarmigan's
well-developed external recruitment, as well as the consequent genetic
exchange, would seem to allow this bird to persist in small populations in
the face of the Rockies' challenging fluctuations.

But, based on some other findings, we shouldn't automatically invoke
the metapopulation model to explain the distribution of ptarmigan
throughout the Rockies. On Vancouver Island the white-tailed ptarmigan
lives year-round in alpine patches separated by unsuitable low-elevation
habitat, yet the system does not appear to function as a metapopulation.
On one hand, in seven study sites the average movements as measured by
radiotelemetry were 0.4 to 1.9 miles (0.6–3.2 km), which was much less
than the 10.8 miles (18 km) between sampling sites (Fedy et al. 2008).
If fact, movement between sites was never detected; molecular data also
showed isolation by distance. And yet, on the other hand, genetic results
showed connectivity among most of the seven sites. Thus, even though
the distribution of white-taileds was geographically subdivided, they did
not fit a typical metapopulation model. The inconsistency between the
inferences derived from radiotelemetry and those from genetics might be
due to rare and acute, so-called episodic, dispersal events.

Ornithologists assessed the influence of the white-tailed's fine-scale
habitat selection on population performance in two subdivided populations on Vancouver Island (Fedy and Martin 2011). The island's center has
more continuous and larger habitat patches than the southern region. The
hens' breeding success was consistently higher in the central region than
in the southern region. The central region also had a higher proportion
of successful hens than did the south, 87 versus 55 percent, respectively.
These findings suggest that the white-tailed ptarmigan's population performance is influenced by a combination of coarse-scale habitat configu-
ration—the metapopulation idea—and several fine-scale habitat features,

like food availability, distance to surface water, and cover from predators. Here's yet another reminder that we should not automatically apply the metapopulation model to the white-tailed ptarmigan.

White-taileds spend the winter in separate flocks—males remain in the alpine, while females winter in willow thickets below the treeline. Using the fringed feathers on their toes as snowshoes, they walk across snowy summits seeking places where the wind has exposed the nutritious buds of low-growing willows, birches, and aspens.

Guanella Pass (southwestern Clear Creek County, north-central Colorado), in the Front Range of the Southern Rockies, lies between Mount Evans and Square Top Mountain. Ornithologists studied a wintering population of white-tailed ptarmigan in this high mountain pass (Hoffman and Braun 1977). Winter use sites were at or above treeline, at elevations of 11,468 to 12,062 feet (3475–3655 m) above sea level, usually at the head of a basin. Willow bushes were rarely completely covered by snow. Most birds started arriving during October 20–26 and remained until April 19–30. Genders segregated by habitat: males wintered closer to breeding areas, in krummholz dominated by clumps of willow and Engelmann spruce; females wintered at lower elevations near or at treeline in dense, tall stands of willow.

On the wintering area 80 percent were females and 65 percent were adults (Hoffman and Braun 1977). Climate influenced the timing of arrival and departure to and from these winter use sites. Birds of all ages and both sexes exhibited a high fidelity, specifically a 60 percent return, to the wintering area. Thus, like their attachment to breeding sites, individual ptarmigan are also loyal to their wintering areas.

Wherever ptarmigan occur on Earth, willows provide much of their winter diet. In winter the Icelandic ptarmigan strongly prefers snowbed willow (Gardarsson and Moss 1970). In October in interior Alaska the main food of rock ptarmigan is tealeaf willow (Moss 1974). In the Southern Rockies (Colorado), white-taileds eat mainly willow species during the winter (Weeden 1967).

But these food plants impose a cost. Willow shrubs contain secondary compounds, toxic chemicals that may start a series of effects in ptarmigan: depressing the quality of the bird's diet, inhibiting its fattening, increasing its risk of starving, and thereby raising the odds of falling prey (V. Thomas 1987). Further, detoxication of these poisons may impose an extra metabolic price on the birds, which may cost them energy that

otherwise could be allocated for predator defense and holding off starvation.

Ptarmigan exploit the insulative value of snow by diving into the
snowpack and tunneling a short distance to rest in a sheltered place (Marchand 1987). In a harsh storm they may scratch out a small depression
in the lee of a rock or in krummholz and let the snow drift about them
until they're completely covered. In such a spot they may spend anywhere
from a few hours to three days, benefiting from the snow's insulation. By
roosting in the snow, they can evade severe cold, and the ambient temperature usually remains above their lower critical temperature (Stokkan
1992), which is the lowest temperature an organism can tolerate without
losing functions. They even forage on the ground while they're under the
crust. If the temperature in a ptarmigan's snow burrow remains 9°F (5°C)
warmer than the surrounding snow and 55°F (25°C) warmer than the air
above the snowpack, a roosting bird can reduce its heat loss by 45 percent. Carbon dioxide does not seem to accumulate in a ptarmigan's snow
burrow, in part because the bird enters hypothermia. It is able to drop
its body temperature by almost 8°F (5°C), and its depressed metabolism
generates less carbon dioxide.

Ptarmigan do not store fat; rather, they feed regularly in short bouts,
acquire just enough energy reserves to persist through the long winter
night, and practice energy conservation (Stokkan 1992). The white-
tailed ptarmigan may well be the most thermally efficient of all Rocky
Mountain birds. Low temperatures have little effect on its energy budget.
Ptarmigan have a highly insulative white winter plumage that minimizes
heat loss. Its entire feet are heavily feathered and function as snowshoes;
countercurrent heat exchangers minimize heat loss from its legs; and it
expels little heat or moisture in its breath. However, a disadvantage of all
these efficient heat-retaining adaptations is that the bird cannot survive
air temperatures as high as its own body temperature, 101°F (39°C), for
more than an hour. Here's another example of an alpine organism with
poor heat dissipation.

The ptarmigan's wintertime energy uses are similar to those of other
Arctic and alpine endotherms. Three species of North American grouse
and the snowshoe and European hares accumulate little fat and few protein reserves, have little resistance to fasting and must feed regularly for
short bouts, and emphasize energy conservation to maintain their energy

balance (V. Thomas 1987). This is a nice example of the evolutionary convergence of metabolic adaptations.

Completing the homework for this story dumped me into a state of unabashed awe. In various sports there are a few practitioners who outdo the rest. Ultramarathoners run 60 miles (100 km) or more, not the standard 26.2 (42). Ultralight backpackers carry 15 pounds (6.8 kg) wearing light hiking shoes, not the 45 (20.2) with stiff boots like I did. So I nominate the white-tailed ptarmigan—a year-round alpine resident that saves energy in snow tunnels, annually cycles between pattern and disruptive camouflage, features vigilant males and female micromovements, grows snowshoes, and endures brutal storms by going hypothermic in its snow cave—as the Rockies' ultra-overwinterer.

CHAPTER 14

Hummingbirds
Micromanage Their Energy

Darting, hovering helicopter
Fueling at a flower,
Tell me how your engine-heart
Generates such power!

Joel Peters, "The Frustrated Engineer"

HERE'S ANOTHER FLASHBACK to the summer of 1968. I'm watching birds above Yellow Bay along the eastern shore of Flathead Lake, which lies at the northern end of the Mission Range (near the University of Montana Biological Station, 12 miles [19 km] south of Bigfork, north-western Montana). Several weeks ago the ornithology professor approved my research topic, a field study of the territorial behavior of the calliope hummingbird. In a clear-cut with slash piles, shrubs, and scrub trees, which is bordered by coniferous and mixed deciduous-coniferous forests and cherry orchards, two male calliope hummingbirds engage in midair combat. By mapping and then connecting their points of conflict I've been able to draw the boundaries of their territories. All this buzzing, swooping, chasing! And ever since, I've been fascinated by how these improbable tiny jeweled darts manage to fuel their high-energy lifestyle—even through the Rockies' frigid nights!

In the paleontological record the first hummingbirds, defined by mor-phological specializations for hovering flight and nectar eating, arose in the early Oligocene epoch, 37 to 24 million years ago (Mayr 2004). As you might expect, protohummingbirds appear in the fossil record after the emergence of flowering plants. Classified in their own New World family, Trochilidae, which is one of the largest bird families, the 341 species of hummingbirds are found from the Chugach Mountains overlooking the Gulf of Alaska (Anchorage, southern Alaska) southward to Isla Grande de Tierra del Fuego (southern Chile and Argentina) (Gill 1990; Osborne 1998). The 13 North American species make up a single recent lineage within this tropical-centered family (Bleiweiss 1998).

The smallest of birds, hummers weigh 0.07 to 0.11 ounce (2–3 g). Most species are brilliantly iridescent, with the males of most showing a brightly colored throat patch called a gorget. The species also have a variety of colors and bill shapes.

A dominant theme in hummingbird evolution, counterintuitive though it may be, is their vigorous expansion from lowlands up into the mountains (Altshuler and Dudley 2002). In a trend relevant to the Rockies, hummingbird evolution has featured a progressive invasion of higher and higher habitats. This presented ancestral hummers with a challenge: life at altitude is constrained by air of low density, scant oxygen, and cold temperatures, yet hovering flight is one of the most energetically expensive forms of animal locomotion (Altshuler et al. 2004a). Thus, flight at altitude presents twin, confounding constraints: higher lift is needed, yet low oxygen availability limits metabolic power output (Altshuler and Dudley 2002).

Part of the solution is biochemical. Hummingbirds' need for less oxygen to burn the sugar in nectar partially compensates for the aerodynamic costs of life at altitude. Hovering at altitude by rufous and Anna's hummingbirds is facilitated by the biochemical fact that the oxidation of carbohydrate requires less oxygen than when fat is used (Welch et al. 2007).

Other parts of the solution lie with anatomy and physiology. In the Cordillera Vilcabamba, a small range along the eastern slope of the Andes, in south-central Peru (which, by the way, includes the Inca site of Machu Picchu), a team of hummingbird researchers mist-netted 43 species of hummingbirds and then measured and filmed several aspects of their morphology and flight. The hummers' body mass increased slightly with increasing elevation, possibly an adaptation to conserve body heat in colder air (Altshuler et al. 2004a). Yet, a bigger body at altitude adds more aerodynamic cost because more lift must be generated to keep a heavier body aloft in thinner air. Among hummingbirds over an elevational range of 12,870 feet (3923 m), from 1,320 to 14,190 feet (400–4300 m) above sea level, high-elevation hummingbirds show two adaptations that enhance aerodynamic performance: an increase in relative wing size and greater wing stroke amplitude (Altshuler and Dudley 2006). That is, their wings are larger relative to their body and they reach farther with each wing stroke during hovering.

To summarize, compared to lowland species, high-altitude humming-birds have a suite of adaptations that enable them to succeed up high, including a larger body, more wing area, and greater stroke amplitude during flapping. They also do more perch feeding and less hovering. It'll be interesting to see how closely this Andean story applies to our Rocky Mountain hummers.

Hummingbirds are the only vertebrates that can hover in still air for an extended time (Altshuler et al. 2004b). The evolution of hovering was allowed by unique anatomical structures. Hummingbirds flex their wings at the wrist during the upstroke, but only slightly. Picture wings that are more rigid than those of other birds (Tobalske et al. 2007). They have fused radial wing bones and flight muscles with a high density of capillaries. The birds also sport several novel physiological functions, like high rates of wingbeat, heartbeat, and oxygen consumption (Altshuler and Dudley 2002; Suarez and Gass 2002).

The members of both genders are about equal in body size (Lack 1968). Hummingbirds are promiscuous, their pairing is brief, and males take no part in nesting. Females build nests of plant down bound with cobwebs and adorned with lichens or small leaves and then lay two eggs 36 to 48 hours apart. Relative to those of other birds, their eggs are small. At hatching the chicks are blind and helpless, typical of altricial birds. Females do all of the rearing of young.

All hummingbirds have long, extensible tongues for reaching nectar (Gill 1990). You'd expect Rocky Mountain hummingbirds to sip nectar from penstemons, paintbrushes, and columbines, but they actually pursue a more diverse diet. Hummers eat lots of insects, especially when they are feeding protein-needy chicks. They are versatile insect predators, picking them off bushes, tree trunks, and the undersides of branches (Constantz 1968a). Hummingbirds even hawk tiny insects in midair, sometimes picking individual dance flies—at 0.4 inch (10 mm) each—out of a swarm.

In some places hummers feed on tree sap. Along Bear Creek, at the foot of the Front Range (Bear Creek Nature Center, Colorado Springs, central Colorado), broad-tailed and rufous hummingbirds fed on drip-pings from bacteria-induced lesions on the undersides of Gambel oak twigs (Kevan et al. 1983). These exudates were not only high in amino acids, they also contained a high ratio of sucrose to the sum of glucose and fructose, which—get this!—is typical of the nectars of hummingbird-pollinated flowers.

Still, most of a hummer's feeding happens in flowers. Like bumble-bees, the individuals of some hummer species are nectar robbers (Ornelas 1994). They draw nectar through a hole in the base of a flower's corolla tube, functionally circumventing the flower's sexual parts. The hummer's serrated bill has been interpreted as an adaptation for grasping and cut-ting a flower's tough tissues (Ornelas 1994). Two benefits may accrue to the nectar robber: rich resources that would otherwise be unavailable, and the need to burn less energy than it would spend in a standard flower visit.

Among birds in general, the males of species like hummingbirds, in which copulation is not preceded by a long-term bond, feature colorful plumage and elaborate courtship. A courting male calliope humming-bird, with its iridescent body and purple-red gorget, swoops back and forth like a pendulum (Ulrich 1984). The dive displays were thought to serve two functions: courting females and defending a territory (E. Arm-strong 1942). Along Flathead Lake I found that a male calliope's typical display flight included three to five "cycles," each tracing a *J* (Constantz 1968b). The top of the *J* was 40 to 50 feet (12–15 m) above the ground; the *J*'s bottom, the low swoop, was 5 to 10 feet (1.5–3.0 m) high. The male hovered for three to five seconds at both ends. As the bird hit high G-forces at the bottom of each *J* it emitted a loud, sharp "bzzt!"

The calliope's courtship display included several steps. With a female perched low in a deciduous bush the male zipped through several *J* cycles directly above her, each pass bottoming out close to her (Constantz 1968b). Plus, I occasionally witnessed an astonishing behavior: he de-scended to the now hovering female, they put their bills tip to tip, and then they spun like a horizontal pinwheel for about two seconds. There-after, she returned to her perch and he resumed *J*-displaying above her. Males of the rufous hummingbird also direct their *J*-displays at females (Hurly et al. 2001).

Female hummingbirds collect the sticky silk off spider webs and use it to fashion cup-shaped nests, flying around and around their half-built nest, playing out the thread from their beaks and wrapping it around the outside of the nest (Attenborough 1998).

My paper on the growth of nestling rufous hummingbirds contained the first published data for the growth of a temperate-zone hummingbird (Constantz 1980). Near Flathead Lake, a rufous hummingbird nest, made of lichen stuck together with spiderweb, was built adjacent to a clearing on a 20-foot-high (6 m) down-sweeping bough of a Douglas-fir tree (Constantz 1968a). Each of the pair of eggs weighed 0.025 ounce (0.7 g). From 3 to 12 days of age, chicks grew swiftly and gained 0.01 ounce (0.3 g) per day. Eyes were completely open at 13 days and the chicks began to practice flying at 15 days. It's interesting that chick mass leveled off on day 13 and practice flying started at day 15, hinting at a trade-off between allocating energy to bodily growth and developing flight muscles. The nestlings' peak weight, attained 59 percent of the way through the nestling phase, was similar to the weight of adult female rufous hummers, at a mean of 0.13 ounce (3.7 g). Thus, chicks added no mass during the latter 41 percent of their life in the nest. Young hummingbirds practiced flying while clinging onto the nest's rim with their feet to avoid being swept upward by their whirring wings.

That summer, in 1968, I studied two other rufous nests, both in the Lewis Range (Glacier National Park, northwestern Montana). They had been built on drooping red cedar limbs four feet (1.2 m) above the ground. In all three cases, as the chicks grew the nests changed from cup- to saucer-shaped. Nests with chicks six days old were cup-shaped and measured 1.4 inches (3.6 cm) in outside diameter, whereas those from which the chicks had recently fledged were nearly flat and had an outside diameter of 1.9 inches (4.8 cm) (Constantz 1968a). By calculation, nest area changed from about 1.5 to 2.8 square inches (10.1–18.1 cm^2), an increase of 82 percent. Thus, unlike the rigid nest of a songbird, a rufous nest is pliable and can be flattened by the movement of its users. The chicks' legs develop muscular competence as the nest flattens, and the chicks can then use the platform for practice whirring (Attenborough 1998). I bet similar changes happen to the nests and bodies of other species of Rockies hummers.

In a stand of lodgepole pine in Jackson Hole, which lies just east of the Teton Range (Jackson Hole Biological Research Station, near Moran, northwestern Wyoming), with the air temperature at 13°F (−21°C) and its branch at 39°F (4°C), a female calliope hummingbird tenaciously incubates her eggs. In this freezing spot she maintains her body surface at 54°F (12°C) and eggs at 91°F (33°C) (Morse 1980). Because of her high surface-to-volume ratio, the heat lost from the back of this incubating hummer could be substantial, especially at night. This is one reason females build their nests beneath overhanging branches, like the ones I studied. Such a semisheltered nest cuts the incubating bird's heat loss by half (Gill 1990). Hummers lower their heat loss even more by building substantial nests. A mother's energy needs drop by an extra 13 percent with a minor 0.002-inch (0.05 mm) increase in nest thickness. By carefully selecting a nest site and constructing a well-insulated nest, an incubating hummingbird can reduce her heat loss in the mountains.

The hummingbird's style of flying—buzzing wings, hovering in place, moving vertically and horizontally—consumes more energy than the movements of nearly any other animal, except perhaps the activities of bumblebees and shrews. The wings of a ruby-throated hummingbird beat up to 80 times per second. Its heart beats 200 to 600 times per minute, escalating to 1,200—an amazing 20 beats per second!—when the bird is feeding or agitated. Even at rest a hummer burns a lot of fuel, in part to keep its flight muscles warm and ready for takeoff. A hummingbird eats five to eight times per hour, may visit 1,500 flowers during an average day, and consumes more than half of its total weight in food per day. Its high-octane fuel is nectar.

Hovering is a hummer's costliest activity. The resting metabolism of a hummingbird, as measured by the rate of oxygen consumed per unit of body mass per unit of time, is 12 times that of a pigeon, 25 times a chicken's, and 100 times an elephant's (Welty 1982). The resting metabolism of Anna's and Allen's hummingbirds, which weigh 0.13 to 0.15 ounce (3.8 to 4.3 g) each, ranges from 19 to 28 cubic inches of oxygen per ounce of body weight (11–16 cc O_2/g) per hour, whereas hovering consumes 119 to 147 cubic inches (68–85 cc O_2/g). Thus, a hovering hummingbird burns five to six times more energy than one at rest.

At three inches (7.6 cm) long and weighing one-tenth of an ounce (2.8 g), the calliope hummingbird is North America's smallest bird (Brooks 1967; Wassink 1991). This small, hot animal, with its high surface-to-volume ratio, loses a lot of heat as it flies through cold mountain air (Chai et al. 1998). Even though the muscular work of flight produces heat, wings flapping through cold air exacerbate the body's cooling. This is one reason some Rocky Mountain hummers are unable to maintain their metabolism during unseasonably late blizzards—and freeze to death.

Because their flying method differs from that of most other birds as radically as helicopters differ from airplanes (Altshuler et al. 2004b), a hummingbird's thin wings are not contoured like the airfoil of a standard bird wing. Compared to those of other birds, the long bones of a hummer's wing are shorter, the joints at the wrist and elbow are less mobile, and the paddle-shaped wings swivel more at the shoulder (Welty 1962). Hummers beat them so the tip of each wing draws a figure eight lying on its side. The wing moves forward and downward into the front loop of the eight, creating lift, and then twists 180 degrees and generates more downward thrust as it comes up and back. The wing's varying pitch is made possible by the extraordinary rotation of the humerus, the bone between the shoulder and elbow. This alternating, helical movement is inefficient, but the bird is partly compensated by the fact that each wingbeat creates a trailing current of air against which its succeeding reverse stroke moves. This gives it the advantage of cutting through air of higher velocity and hence of producing greater lift. Restated in terms of aerodynamics, with each stroke the bird retrieves from the air some of the kinetic energy it created during the preceding antagonistic stroke.

Researchers have recently discovered another subtle efficiency that partly compensates for the hummingbird's flapping inefficiency. Aerodynamic theory predicts that airflow over a hummingbird wing should be dominated by a stable, attached leading-edge vortex. A vortex is a mass of fluid swirling in a circle with a vacuum in the center. One would expect that when the translational movement of the wing ends, as at the end of the downstroke, the vortex would be shed and the lift would stop until the energy of the vortex was recaptured in the following half-cycle translation. Not so with hummers. In the hummingbird wing, partly because the leading-edge vortex is generated within 0.12 inch (3 mm) of the wing's dorsal surface, bound circulation is not shed as a vortex at the end of translation (Warrick 2009). Rather, the vortex remains attached and persists after translation has ended. This is augmented by the rotation of the wing that occurs between the wing-translation half-cycles. The result is a nearly continuous lift through wing turnaround. This form of aerodynamic gain is unknown in other vertebrates. The hummingbird's uninterrupted lift contributes to its weight support, stability, and control, all of which lower the energy demands of hovering.

The keel, a thin, platelike, bony extension of the sternum, is the chief anchor of a bird's pectoralis, or flight muscle (Welty 1962). Compared to other birds of similar size, hummingbirds have enormous keels, partly because the inefficiency of their small wings means that they must be fanned more vigorously, and partly because they use both up and down strokes to power flight. The pectoralis of other birds accounts for 15 to 25 percent of their body weight (Hartman 1961), but the hummer's pectoralis may account for up to 30 percent of its body weight. Its enormous keel and pectoralis are further hints that the hummingbirds' twisting, vibrating wings are grossly inefficient biomechanically compared to the wings of other flying birds.

Even though hovering flight is metabolically expensive, the advantage of being able to hang in one spot is that it allows quick flower visits. A ruby-throated hummingbird can visit 37 jewelweed blossoms per minute versus a bumblebee's 10.

How Do You Measure a Hummingbird's Metabolism?

You might be wondering how hummingbird researchers measure the metabolic rate of such a tiny bird. Simply, a bird physiologist puts a mask on the bird. A mask that encloses the whole head can serve as a useful tool to measure a bird's gas exchange rates because it frees the rest of the body, permitting flight movements (Welch 2011). Mask respirometry works to study the hovering energetics of hummingbirds because these birds are small, hover in place, and eat nectar. In essence, hummingbird feeders with sugar solution are modified to function as respiratory masks that the birds voluntarily breathe into while hovering. One of the take-home conclusions from feeder-mask respirometry has been that hovering hummers function at some of the highest metabolic rates among vertebrates.

Hummingbirds fuel their hovering flight mainly with newly consumed sugar. A team of zoologists mist-netted broad-tailed hummingbirds in the Central Rockies (Albany County, southeastern Wyoming), took them to the lab, and manipulated their diet and fasting schedule in ways that allowed them to estimate the relative contributions of carbohydrates and fat to the fueling of hovering. Immediately after fasting, the hummers burned internal fat, after which they used more carbohydrates (Welch et al. 2006). By 20 minutes after their first meal, dietary sugar was supporting 74 percent of the bird's hovering metabolism. Similarly, when broad-taileds were feeding, assimilated sugar fueled 90 percent of their metabolism (Carleton et al. 2006). In rufous and Anna's hummingbirds, the burning of newly ingested sugars increased over 30 to 45 minutes and then accounted for all of the fuel oxidized (Welch and Suarez 2007). Thus, hummingbirds fuel their hovering flight mainly with recently ingested sugar, a capability that is unique among vertebrates.

Powering the flight of a small hovering body through thin, cold, montane air requires a high metabolic rate. Specifically, hummingbirds that stay in energy balance by foraging at near-freezing temperatures, like our Rockies hummers, burn an average of 62.5 W/kg ($62.5 \ m^2/s^3$) per hour. At this writing, this is the highest known metabolic rate of all energetically balanced vertebrates (Gass et al. 1999).

Let me explain these units of measurement. The unit W/kg (m^2/s^3) stands for watts per kilogram (meter squared per second cubed), which is a measure of specific power, that is, the power produced per unit mass of fuel. Here's a human example to put it in context. While training, competitive cyclists apply this idea when they compare their power-to-weight ratios. For example, to reach the top of Cheyenne Canyon, which is located in the Southern Rockies along the southern flank of Kineo Mountain (three miles [4.8 km] southwest of Colorado Springs, central Colorado), in 20 minutes, a biker must generate four watts of power for every kilogram ($4 \ m^2/s^3$) of her body weight (Carmichael, n.d.). A foraging hummingbird generates 15.6 times more power than a mountain-climbing cyclist!

In late summer, on the southward leg of their migration, rufous hummingbirds stop to refuel on floral nectar in subalpine meadows. Whereas their short on-site foraging bouts are fueled by the oxidation of carbohydrates, like sugar, hummers rely on fat to fuel the long-distance legs of their migratory flights (Suarez and Gass 2002). Because refueling runs on sugar, migrants that stop over at montane meadows are able to accumulate fat. This is how, on cold mornings in subalpine meadows, refueling hummers achieve net energy gain despite the high energetic costs of flight and thermoregulation.

In these montane habitats the birds are challenged to achieve a daily net energy gain, especially with near-freezing morning temperatures. When hummers were offered a solution of 15 to 20 percent sucrose, they were not able to stay in energy balance and lost mass (Gass et al. 1999). They did, however, achieve a net energy gain on 30 percent sucrose, which is close to the amount found in the nectar of hummingbird-visited flowers. This finding hints that the hummingbird's thermal and flight needs and the sugar content of flower nectar have coevolved.

By June male calliope hummingbirds are well separated from each other, with an average of more than 100 yards (90 m) between their territorial centers (Tamm et al. 1989). The functions of a male calliope's territory include mating and feeding; the function of a female's territory is nesting only.

This returns us to my findings about hummingbird territories. After plotting the locations of the male calliopes' display and defensive behaviors, I connected the outermost points to reveal their enclosed territories. Each male's territory held several assets, including display, mating, and feeding grounds; a prominent perch; and peripheral trees that provided cover from the elements and protection from predators (Constantz 1968b).

I then estimated the areas of the two territories. One was 74×99 yards, or 7,326 square yards ($67 \text{ m} \times 90 \text{ m} = 6030 \text{ m}^2$), and the other was 85×61 yards, or 5,185 square yards ($77 \text{ m} \times 55 \text{ m} = 4235 \text{ m}^2$), which together average 6,159 square yards (4927 m^2) (Constantz 1968b). To picture this space imagine a square measuring 78 yards (70 m) per side. The distance between their prominent perches was 100 yards (91 m), which agrees with the report above.

The theory of economic defendability offers a framework for interpreting the hummingbird's territoriality. According to this idea an animal should defend an area only if its energy gains minus its defense costs are more than they would be if the animal were not territorial. When the value of a resource is small, birds should not protect it since excluding others would not increase its worth enough to offset the defense costs. At the other extreme, when a resource is plentiful a bird is not expected to defend it because the bird's energy needs are adequately met even with others sharing it. Thus, birds are predicted to maintain territories that hold intermediate levels of resources.

But it's not quite that simple. While the territorial behavior of post-breeding hummingbirds can be explained in such energetic terms, the behavior in breeding males seems to be different. That's because the male's territory also functions in courtship. In a meadow at 2,640 feet (800 m) in elevation nestled in the North Cascades (15 miles [25 km] southwest of Penticton, Ashnola Provincial Forest, south-central British Columbia), male calliope hummingbirds could have obtained energy faster by foraging in nearby undefended areas than by foraging in their own territories (Armstrong 1987). In June there were no productive flowers in their territories, so males did nearly all of their foraging outside their territories. The main function of territoriality in the male Anna's hummingbird was reproduction rather than food defense (Powers 1987). These observations suggest that during the breeding season, male hummingbirds select territories with prominent perches near females' nesting areas, a resource that presumably outweighs the benefits of defending high-quality nectar.

Despite the high energy value of nectar, sipping a lot of it creates a physiological problem. When energy demands are high, hummingbirds consume more than three times their body mass in fluid per day (Beuchat et al. 1990). This requires them to process a large volume of dilute liquid (del Rio et al. 2001). The metabolic rate of a 0.16-ounce (4.5 g) Anna's hummingbird in a moderate climate is 7.65 calories (32 kJ) per day. To satisfy this energy need requires 0.22 fluid ounce (7.4 ml) per day of nectar with 25 percent sucrose by weight. This amount of liquid is equal to 1.6 times the bird's own body mass, which is almost five times the amount (0.05 fluid ounce [1.6 ml]) needed per day by a generic bird this size. An Anna's that consumes 0.22 fluid ounce (7.4 ml) of nectar per day must excrete 0.15 fluid ounce (5 ml) of urine per day, equal to 111 percent of its body mass. At its highest rate of intake, 0.45 fluid ounce (15 ml) per day, an Anna's must excrete each day a volume of urine equal to three times its body mass, a level far exceeding some of the highest rates of urine production by amphibians. And among terrestrial vertebrates, amphibians excrete the most dilute urine. These values mean that hummingbirds have one of the highest rates of water flux of any endothermic vertebrate.

During diuresis, which is the increased excretion of urine, hummingbirds lose a lot of electrolytes and minerals, particularly calcium. Yet nectar does not provide a hummer, especially an egg-laying female, with enough of these trace nutrients. They've evolved an interesting solution:

in the Coast Range (western Oregon), female rufous hummingbirds eat soil (Adam and Des Lauriers 1998). And I've read other reports of hummers eating nutrient-rich materials, like mineral dust and wood ash. These observations suggest that hummingbirds compensate for their high losses of micronutrients by eating foods other than nectar, like certain soils and insects.

There are few animals in which the interactions among nutrient intake, energy expenditure, and osmotic balance are so tightly coupled—and with so little margin for error.

If you hang a hummingbird feeder, you know that hummers show aggressive, in-your-face audacity. They fight for food not just because they need immediate energy but also because they're driven to accumulate enough body reserves to be able to fly between North and Central America. The principal wintering grounds of several of our Western hummers, including the broad-tailed, calliope, and rufous, are in northern Central America (Mexico southward into Guatemala).

Southbound rufouses arrive in California weighing 0.11 to 0.12 ounce (3–3.5 g), gain about 50 percent more body mass during one or two weeks on a refueling territory, and then resume their trip (Calder 1987). While stopping over in the Southern Rockies (Colorado), a rufous can increase its weight by up to two-thirds (Calder 1998). All of its increase in body mass above 0.12 ounce (3.5 g) is fat, which, as you now know, is used to fuel migratory flight. A fully fattened rufous can fly 610 miles (976 km), from the Maligne Range (Jasper, west-central Alberta) to the Greater Yellowstone Ecosystem (Yellowstone National Park, northwestern Wyoming) or from Yellowstone to the Sangre de Cristo Mountains (Santa Fe, north-central New Mexico). This means that a migrating rufous can fly the geographic span covered by this book with just one refueling stop!

To deal with energy challenges, hummingbirds evolved an adaptation that lowers their energy needs. Partly because of nighttime torpor, a rufous hummingbird can gain mass four to eight times faster than it would if it didn't go into torpor. Think of torpor as a form of physiological dormancy, a period when an animal's body temperature drops below its normal level (Barclay et al. 2001). Torpor occurs in only a few bird

families other than hummingbirds, like the swifts, nighthawks, and doves
(McKechnie and Lovegrove 2002).

Since many flowers bloom for short times, small pollinators could
face severe energy problems. Acute fluctuations of weather and food have
presumably selected for torpor in hummingbirds (Calder 1994). The
Anna's hummer expends 10.3 Kcal (43,096 J) during 24 hours, as opposed
to 7.6 Kcal (31,799 J) when torpid, an energy saving of 26 percent, equal
to the nectar of 370 fuchsia blossoms. It makes sense that incubating females do not enter torpor.

Some ecologists have noticed an association between specific foods
and the ability to enter torpor. All of the birds capable of torpor eat fruits,
nectar, or insects (Schleucher 2004), foods that are only temporarily
available. This association makes food specialization a prime candidate as
an ultimate factor that favored the evolution of torpor in birds.

Torpor is especially crucial during cold montane nights. A hovering
0.11-ounce (3.2 g) Costa's hummingbird consumes 73 cubic inches of
oxygen per ounce (42 cc O_2/g) of body mass per hour (Gordon 1972).
When a Costa's is in torpid hypothermia, with its body temperature at
68°F (20°C), its oxygen consumption rate is about one one-hundredth
as great (0.68 in^3/oz [0.39 cc/g]), about the same as the standard metabolism of a 0.1-ounce (3 g) lizard at the same temperature. Further, body
temperature drops from 107 to 65°F (42 to 18°C), heart rate slows to 50
beats per minute, and breathing lowers from four breaths per second to
actually stopping for brief periods (R. Peters 1983). On nights cooler than
60°F (16°C), a torpid hummer can save up to 98 percent of the energy it
would have spent to fuel a normal body temperature (Wassink 1991). At
air temperatures likely to be encountered at night, rufous hummers can
save energy by entering torpor (Hiebert 1990). For these reasons, torpor
is interpreted as an adaptation for surviving cold nights.

Out on the trail, I usually heard a hummingbird before I saw it. If I was
lucky I saw the iridescent dot beelining it above the horizon. A tiny, hot
bird was optimizing the balance between its energy intake and output
according to a strategy that would eventually get it to Central America—and ultimately back to North America to fledge chicks next year. No
Rockies animal micromanages its energy budget on a more precarious
tightrope.

CHAPTER 15

Hay-Stacker

*The warrior charged, the dandy held his ground,
and the two tumbled in a squeaking, furry mass,
down into the boulders.*

John Winnie Jr., *High Life: Animals of the Alpine World*

UNDER A HEAVY PACK on a steep, narrow trail up unstable talus, and beat up by gale-force winds—I was scared. In several spots the gusts actually lifted me up the trail. I focused on the ground to hold off vertigo. Fighting off a bout of fright, I found myself yearning for the comforting cry of a pika. And in this mood Nancy and I slowly worked the trail from Swiftcurrent Lake along the eastern flank of the Lewis Range on our climb to Piegan Pass (Cataract Creek Trail, Glacier National Park, northwestern Montana). Ahh, relief when I saw one scurrying over boulders—following a straight-line course, focused, without deviation—carrying a plant sprig. His normal industry reassured me.

Also called conies, little chief hares, hay-stackers, and rock rabbits (Brooks 1967; Durrell 1988; Streubel 1989), pikas wear the mottled camouflage of gray-brown rock. About seven and a half inches (19.1 cm) long and weighing 5.7 ounces (160 g)—the size and shape of a guinea pig—the tailless, roly-poly pikas grow rock-gripping fur on the soles of their feet (Milne and Milne 1962; F. Craighead 1973; Hunt 1976). Pikas also distinguish themselves behaviorally with their piping squeak, an innocent childlike expression, and their diligent gathering of plants.

Not a rodent, the pika is actually North America's smallest lagomorph, the mammalian order better known for rabbits and hares (Brooks

1967). North America's ancestral pika seems to have come from Asia during the late Pliocene epoch, about two million years ago (Hunt 1976; Mead 1987). A study of pika mitochondrial genes supports a single invasion of North America. Several modern species of pika live in the alpine of Asia and North America (Streubel 1989).

Pikas initially spread southward along montane corridors during a pre-Wisconsin glacial stage (Hafner and Sullivan 1995). The Wisconsin glacial age, which lasted from 110,000 to 10,000 years ago, was the last major advance of North America's Laurentide Ice Sheet during the Pleistocene epoch. During a subsequent interglacial, pika populations were fragmented into isolated montane refugia. With that comment I hope your brain switched on the metapopulation concept, which I'll talk about in a bit.

During the late Pleistocene, perhaps 20,000 years ago, the pika was more widespread in the West than it is today (Beever 2002). Since then, climatic warming has led to the extirpation of most low-lying populations, leaving behind scattered relictual high-elevation populations.

Local extirpations are continuing. Over the last few decades, 7 of 25 pika populations in the Great Basin have gone extinct. From the Late Wisconsinan and Early Holocene to today, the pika's total altitudinal increase has been 2,584 feet (783 m), about half a mile (Grayson 2005). As climate and vegetation changed, low-lying populations went extinct and the species' distribution came to resemble its modern fragmented range at high elevations.

What specific environmental factor has caused these local extirpations? It turns out that places where pikas have disappeared experience higher summer temperatures and higher frequencies of extremely warm days than sites where they persist (Wilkening et al. 2011). Relative forb cover is also positively related to pika persistence. These results strongly suggest that mean summer temperature has been the main cause of the extirpations. And this conclusion, in turn, supports the hypothesis that extirpation is caused by chronic heat stress during the summer, when the pikas are running around gathering food for winter.

Pikas live in rock piles, mainly at and above treeline, at elevations of up to 12,000 feet (3658 m). Prime pika habitat consists of talus islands adjacent to vegetation suitable for grazing (Streubel 1989; Johnson and Crabtree

1999). A talus slope is made of boulders up to 3.3 feet (1 m) in diameter. Of all the places we've backpacked in the Rockies, the Teton Range (Grand Teton National Park, northwestern Wyoming) seems to support the most conies. Pikas perch on boulders with a good view. If they stray too far from their rock pile, they become vulnerable to hawks, weasels, and coyotes (Streubel 1989; Eversman and Carr 1992).

In contrast to the pikas at altitude, some persist in a few places in unusual, low-lying habitats. In the eastern Snake River Plain (Craters of the Moon National Monument, southern Idaho) at 5,200 to 6,500 feet (1590–1990 m) above sea level, and on the northeastern flank of Medicine Lake Volcano in the Cascade Range (Lava Beds National Monument, north-central California) at 4,000 to 5,400 feet (1230–1650 m), pikas live at exceptionally low altitudes (Beever 2002; Rodhouse et al. 2010). In these two places, with climates 18 to 24 percent drier and 5 to 11 percent warmer than those formerly experienced by the now-extirpated lowland pika populations of the Great Basin, lava tubes and caves have provided rock rabbits with cool refugia—presumably ever since the Pleistocene.

Pikas are vocal animals. Adults emit at least nine distinct acoustic signals. In size and form their repertoire more closely resembles that of many rodent species than it does the calls of other lagomorphs (Conner 1985a). For example, the similarity of the pika's and marmot's alarm signals hints at an evolutionary convergence (Niko'skii and Formozov 1983). The pika's elaborate vocal repertoire may have been shaped evolutionarily by its visually disruptive environment and unusual social organization.

The pika's best-known call is its single, short, querulous, shrill whistle (Streubel 1989)—"Eep!" to my ear. It reminds me of the squeal I hear when I step on my dog's squeaky toy. What is the role of this high-pitched ventriloquistic call? "Eep!" advertises territory and warns of predators. When a predator like a marten approaches, the members of a pika colony emit nonstop warning calls. If the threat is a weasel, though, they are silent—weasels are small enough to enter the pikas' retreats ("Climate Change and the Pika" 2009). At Niwot Ridge, perched along the Front Range in the Southern Rockies (Roosevelt Forest, 22 miles [35 km] west of Boulder, Colorado, pikas recognized each other's "Eep!" (Conner 1985b). When a resident disappeared, neighbors intruded more often and persisted longer within the newly vacant territory (Conner 1984).

A playback of a recording of the missing resident's short call inhibited further trespassing.

Do pikas that live in different places issue distinct calls? Even though they may exhibit little genetic differentiation, the calls of pikas from different places do indeed vary (Conner 1982b). A mammalogist recorded the short calls of pikas in seven Southwestern sites (all in New Mexico, Utah, and California) and then analyzed the recordings for their fundamental frequency, note duration, internote interval, and number of notes per call. He found significant differences between widely separated groups (Conner 1982b). It seems that the geographic variation between widely separated populations was caused by their different evolutionary histories, which in turn had been maintained by geographic barriers to interbreeding. The pika's different calls do not seem to be true dialects (Conner 1982a). Overall, these findings are consistent with a metapopulation model.

More recently, a team of biogeographers recorded pikas in four places in the Canadian Rockies (all sites in Jasper National Park, southwestern Alberta) and then measured 21 features of the calls. These populations, separated by up to 55 miles (92 km), did show differences in their call structure. After testing and rejecting the acoustic adaptation hypothesis, that is, that population-specific sound characteristics were selected in different environments, they concluded that the calls' geographic variation reflected genetic divergence (Trefry and Hik 2010). The data also led to another interesting conclusion: the high-frequency harmonics, which show greater variation between individuals than within them, provide the information that pikas use for recognizing individuals. Both the Southwestern and Canadian Rockies studies support the idea that different forms of pika calls in various places do not represent adaptations to environmental constraints; rather, they have diverged by drift across space.

With pika calls encoding valuable information, an individual might benefit from eavesdropping on its neighbors. Ethologists studied the responses of collared pikas to both conspecific and heterospecific vocalizations in an alpine valley of the Ruby Range (southwestern Yukon) (Trefry and Hik 2009). The collared pika, a congener of our American pika, lives from southeastern Alaska southeastward into the Mackenzie Mountains (District of Mackenzie, northwestern Canada). After the researchers played back the alarm calls of heterospecific mammals, specifically the hoary marmot and Arctic ground squirrel, collared pikas increased their vigilance. They also discriminated between individual pika callers. Information from neighborhood sources, issuing from individuals of both its own species and other species, may affect when and where a pika forages, how it avoids predators, and whether it practices nepotism.

In alpine ecosystems the pika functions as a keystone species. They dig burrows that become the homes of various other small animals, disturb soils that sustain diverse plant species, and serve as prey for several kinds of alpine predators (Smith and Foggin 1999). The latter two functions account for much of the nutrient cycling and energy flow above treeline.

Pikas may even have played a crucial role in restoring North America after the Pleistocene glaciers retreated. In the forefront of Lyman Glacier in the North Cascades (Yakima County, south-central Washington), the fecal pellets of small mammals like pikas contain spores of mycorrhizal fungi (Cazares and Trappe 1994). The periglacial terrain in front of the ice has been colonized by pine and willow species that depend on these mutualists. Thus, fungus-eating animals like the pika inoculate newly deglaciated soils with the mycorrhizae that foster early plant succession.

The pika also exerts keystone effects through its grazing. By feeding around talus, pikas impose a gradient of grazing pressure that extends outward from the talus edge (Roach et al. 2001). In an alpine area at 9,900 feet (3000 m) above sea level on the Beartooth Plateau (northeast of Yellowstone National Park, northwestern Wyoming), a team of ecologists studied the effect of the pika's grazing on the site's plant community. At three talus-meadow interfaces, pikas traveled different distances for forage, depending on the structure of the talus slope. They fed preferentially on plants within the talus, fed in the surrounding meadow when intratalus vegetation was rare, and ranged even farther when haying.

When habitat structure forced them to move out from the talus, within 3.3 feet (1 m) of the talus edge they depressed plant biomass by up to 80 percent and increased the relative abundance of cushion plants and sedges (Roach et al. 2001). It turns out that intense grazing gives a competitive advantage to cushion plants and sedges. In contrast, without herbivory forbs tend to dominate. In this way, pikas determine the plant community in their immediate environment.

Pikas do not hibernate in the winter but continue leading an active life in their rocky labyrinths beneath the snow (Brooks 1967). A pika features several morphological adaptations to the harsh winter environment: a compact body with a low surface-to-volume ratio that slows the loss of heat; small limbs, ears, and tail, also with low surface-to-volume ratios; nostrils that close in cold weather; and fur-clad soles (Streubel 1989). Further, to retain body moisture in the dry alpine it concentrates its urine into nearly crystalline form (Hunt 1976). A patch of brilliant red-orange, nitrogen-loving jewel lichen can flag a rock that is being doused by pika urine (Eversman and Carr 1992).

Warm temperatures of around 78 to 85°F (26–29°C), even in the shade, can kill a pika (Beever 2002; "Climate Change and the Pika" 2009). Its thick fur inhibits evaporative cooling; its small feet and ears, short legs, tiny tail, and small nose dissipate little heat. Evolution has almost erased the pika's ability to cool itself.

As this chapter's epigraph reports, pikas are aggressive. In their loose colonies each individual calls from atop tall boulders within its own territory. Typical territories are 50 to 100 feet (15–30 m) across and cover 500 to 900 square yards (400–720 m²). In rough terms, picture a square measuring 75 feet (23 m) per side. A pika seldom ventures more than 30 feet (9 m) from its rockslide lair. The biggest, most aggressive individuals own the largest territories bordering the best vegetation. A pika's territory, which it scent-marks by rubbing its cheek glands and urinating on rocks, includes a cache of edible plants called a haypile or haystack.

Pikas trespass into their neighbors' territories. Sometimes their intent is to steal hay. Kleptoparasitism, defined as the stealing of resources from another animal, may benefit the thief by reducing the costs associated with normal foraging, specifically by lowering search and handling times and by reducing the risk of predation (McKechnie et al. 1994). Members of both genders rob equally. Some individuals thieve repeatedly, year after year, while others never steal (A. Smith 1997). Pikas also appropriate the plant material from the haypiles of deceased neighbors.

In addition to stealing, other forms of intrusion include attempts to become familiar with neighbors of the opposite sex and probes by foreign conspecifics deciding where to settle. All these various forms of trespassing make for busy, aggressive lives: in mid-July territorial disputes and chases break out at least once an hour.

Pikas live singly until the mating season, which spans from March through May. Females breed for the first time as yearlings (Streubel 1989). A female in estrus leaves her territory in search of a male. In spite of their high levels of philopatry and social tolerance, inbreeding among pikas is not extreme. In a pika metapopulation fragmented throughout the 100 refuse talus islands of a gold-mining ghost town (Bodie State Historic Park, 15 miles east of Bridgeport, Mono County, east-central California) at 8,415 feet (2550 m) above sea level on the eastern side of the Sierra Nevada, DNA fingerprints revealed that mated pika pairs were similar to each other at the level of second-order relatives (Peacock and Smith 1997b). That is, they were as closely related as half siblings, first cousins, or grandparent-grandchild pairs. Pikas had colonized the talus islands around 1900; each talus pile supported 2 to 50 animals (Peacock and Smith 1997a). At these levels of relatedness, individuals share on average one-fourth of their genes, which could offer enough genetic similarity for kin selection to have delivered some altruism. These pikas mated with individuals with intermediate levels of genetic similarity, which begs several questions. Do they choose to mate with cousins or are they making the most of a marginal situation? If the former, how do they assess their level of relatedness? By smell? By their "Eep" call? Alternatively, what triggers mate rejection?

After a 30-day gestation female rock rabbits give birth in the spring to litters of two to six babies (Streubel 1989). Young are weaned in four weeks, and then a second litter arrives in early July. First-litter offspring enjoy better odds of surviving than those in second litters. Severe springtime weather can cause pregnant females to absorb their embryos. After the mated pair have cooperatively raised their young through the summer, the parents resume single life in the fall.

Ecological constraints, such as the limited availability of meadow near talus and the short summer season that places a premium on early litters, have apparently led to the evolution of the pika's facultative monogamy (Smith and Ivins 1984). Males can't monopolize enough limiting resources to attract several females, nor can they defend groups of females, because females repulse each other.

In midsummer juvenile pikas disperse because they are driven out by dominant individuals, or they leave because of their own social intolerance, or both (Gaines and McClenaghan 1980). By autumn a young pika has established a territory around its own homestead and has assembled a haystack (Milne and Milne 1962).

Along Cooper Creek, which runs along the flank of White Rock Mountain (Elk Mountain Wilderness, near Crested Butte, central Colorado), the home ranges of adult male and female pikas were found to be about equal in size (Smith and Ivins 1983). Adjacent home ranges were normally occupied by members of the opposite sex. Throughout the summer, juveniles remained on their natal home range, where they were involved in both agonistic and affiliative behaviors with their mothers and putative fathers. Most animals that established residency were juveniles, and of these almost all settled within 165 feet (50 m) of the center of their natal home range.

Females are the main dispersers (Brandt 1985). Why would this be the case? One hypothesis posits that sexual differences in natal dispersal are a consequence of the pika's mating system. If males defend resources to attract mates, then females rather than males should be selected to disperse. Males are hampered in acquiring a breeding space away from their birthplaces by the territorial activities of resident adult males, but because females do not defend territories they are free to disperse to areas with better resources and fewer male relatives. Of the three major hypotheses proposed to explain the evolution of dispersal in birds and mammals—competition for mates, inbreeding avoidance, and competition for resources—results for the pika support the last, where the key resources are the territory's assets, like a rock pile and adjacent vegetation (Peacock 1997).

The movements of marked juveniles demonstrate that pikas do not disperse far from their natal populations (Peacock 1997). Even though DNA fingerprints are consistent with a philopatric settlement pattern, pikas do not cluster with relatives. There is little genetic differentiation between populations 1.2 miles (2 km) apart. The average similarity of DNA fingerprints among adults is similar to the values reported for other outbred mammal species.

A pika metapopulation is supported by a dynamic equilibrium between the extinctions and colonizations of its small member populations (Gaines and McClenaghan 1980). In fact, some population biologists consider the pika metapopulation to be the best mammalian example of a classic metapopulation with significant population turnover (Moilanen et al. 1998). According to one hypothesis the stability of pika populations is a result of their food-based territoriality, parent-offspring conflicts, and sibling rivalry, all of which function to limit, and thereby steady, their local density.

The pika's low genetic variability is consistent with the geography of its populations in the Southern Rockies because it persists as stranded isolates on mountaintops. Some of these small populations incur so much inbreeding that individuals are even more closely related than a parent is to its offspring.

The pika is a generalist herbivore that simultaneously selects two diets: summer foods that are eaten immediately and winter foods that are stored for later consumption (Dearing 1996). That is, pikas engage in two distinct types of foraging behavior: grazing, which is eating food on the spot; and haying, which is collecting food for long-term caching (A. Smith 1997).

Pikas divide their foraging trips equally between grazing and haying (A. Smith 1997). Grazing pikas stay within six feet (1.8 m) of their talus and thereby create a zone on the edge of the meadow that is trimmed like a lawn. In contrast, a haying pika is more adventuresome, collecting plants up to 60 feet (18.3 m) from the talus. Grazing pikas are cautious as they eat grass, but haying ones are foolhardy while they collect stalks, leaves, and flowers. In Paintbrush Canyon in the Teton Range (Paintbrush Canyon Trail, Grand Teton National Park), during September 9–10, 2006, haying pikas were so preoccupied with carrying and stacking plant sprigs that I was able to approach to within four feet (1.2 m) of several of them.

Because they need food through the winter, pikas spend much of their time during the summer caching vegetation (Milne and Milne 1962; Durrell 1988; A. Smith 1997). In mid-July a pika begins cutting large quantities of mosses, grasses, wildflowers, and other plants. Near the center of its territory it assembles the plant material into a large pile tucked under a rock overhang (Brooks 1967). I measured the dimensions of a haypile, one that seemed typical in size, along our Paintbrush Canyon walk. With hay spilling out from under its cover of rock, this stack was 53 inches (135 cm) long, 30 inches (76 cm) wide, and 30 inches (76 cm) high. This translates to a volume of 27.6 cubic feet (0.8 m³), slightly more than a cubic yard. A few pikas assemble more than one haypile. Stored under rocks to shield it from snowmelt, the hay serves as wintertime food (Morrison et al. 2009).

A pika's haystack may contain a bushel (35 L) or more of dried plants, up to 50 pounds (23 kg) of hay, most of which the animal gathers within 100 feet (30 m) of its home boulders (Brooks 1967). As I've said, these haystacks, which are built in the same location year after year, are defended vigorously against intruding neighbors.

At Niwot Ridge pikas store an average of 350 days worth of food in their haypiles, yet during an average winter they consume only about 180 days of food (Dearing 1997b). Such seemingly oversized haypiles have also been reported in other pika populations. Why a pika doesn't store just enough food to get it through the winter, or maybe just a little more as a buffer against an unusually severe winter, strikes me as curious. Plus, you may recall that Clark's nutcrackers overstore pine nuts. Is there a pattern of caching animals in the Rockies accumulating excess wintertime foods? If so, why? Here's a mystery begging for a definitive study.

The excess, and therefore uneaten, items of a haypile decay to form patches of fertile soil embedded within the rock talus (Aho et al. 1998). Do these nutritious leftovers improve the soil and aid plant growth? Three findings from an alpine cirque called Cody Bowl, on the eastern flank of Rendezvous Mountain in the Teton Range (Teton National Forest, seven miles (11 km) northwest of Jackson, northwestern Wyoming), seem relevant. First, soils derived from haypiles had higher carbon and nitrogen levels than other nearby soils did. Second, two plant species, sky pilot and mountain sorrel, contained higher nitrogen levels in their tissues when growing on haypile-derived soils. And third, plant biomass increased with soil nitrogen, suggesting that vegetation was nitrogen-limited. By affecting the levels of nutrients in the soil and hence what is available to plants, the pika qualifies as an ecosystem engineer, a term applied to other landscape-altering Rocky Mountain animals, like the beaver, bison, and grizzly bear.

The pika's hay gathering is an example of a type of optimal behavior called central-place foraging (Roach et al. 2001). Many animals forage at distant sources and carry pieces of food back to a central place (Wetterer 1989). The central-place foraging hypothesis predicts that at short distances from the central place, the optimal load mass should maximize the net return per unit of collecting time. In contrast, over long expanses the optimal load mass should maximize the animal's net return per unit of travel time. With increasing distance from the talus, the intensity of the pikas' foraging decreases and selectivity increases, consistent with the proposal's predictions (Huntly et al. 1986). While a pika is haying, it is cost effective for it to carry as large a load as possible (A. Smith 1997). The Rockies host other central-place foragers—bumblebees, water shrews, and red squirrels.

Both the abundance and species richness of plants increase with distance from a pika's talus (Huntly et al. 1986). Whether a pika ingests or caches reflects differences in the costs and benefits of these activities. Higher proportions of forbs and tall grasses are hayed than are grazed. More plants suitable for harvest grow farther out in the meadow (A. Smith 1997), so haying pikas travel farther into the meadow from the talus than grazers (Roach et al. 2001). A downside of venturing farther from the talus is greater exposure to predators.

We come now to this lagomorph's most interesting adaptation: pikas manipulate the toxic chemicals in their haystacks (Dearing 1996). Pikas add specific plants to their haypiles in a definite sequence (A. Smith 1997). Sometimes they bypass certain plants because of their secondary compounds. For example, during the flowering season, columbine leaves hold a lot of toxic chemicals, but in late summer the plant shunts these compounds to its roots (A. Smith 1997). In late summer pikas harvest a wide variety of plants, including lichens and mosses, yellow paintbrush and alpine avens, and pine needles and conifer twigs. Some of these food items are high in secondary compounds like phenolics. It seems possible that pikas hay these items but don't eat them because of their effectiveness at preserving the cache. Pikas choose some plants that inhibit bacterial growth and thereby function as a haypile preservative.

Food stored for an extended time may change in value by ripening and spoiling (Gendron and Reichman 1995). When selecting food for its winter haypile, pikas should consider the value that each food item will have when it is eaten, not its merit at the time it is collected. It follows that a pika should adjust the composition of its cache to reflect food perishability.

Although they produce salivary proteins that bind tannins, captive pikas that consumed a high-tannin diet of the leaves of alpine avens digested less dry matter, protein, and fiber (Dearing 1997a). They also excreted higher concentrations of detoxication by-products. Thus, alpine avens tannins are poisons that may reduce the pika's ability to digest food.

As we've seen in previous stories, like those of lupine, aspen, and butterflies, herbivorous animals avoid plants with high levels of secondary compounds because the animal is harmed by ingesting these chemicals. The observations I've reported here, considered in the context of this widespread phenomenon, suggest two hypotheses about the pika's haymaking. First, the presence of secondary compounds in the pika's cached plants helps preserve these plants, as well as other plants within the same haystack that lack secondary compounds. And second, pikas overcome the digestion issues imposed by plant defensive compounds by storing these foods until their toxins have degraded.

The pika is a generalist herbivore that ingests low-phenolic plant matter in the summer while simultaneously haying high-phenolic vegetation for winter use (Dearing 1997c). A common food in the winter diet, alpine avens, contains high levels of phenolics, which deter bacterial growth. Halfway through the winter storage period, the phenolic concentrations of cached plants have decreased to levels equal to those of plants readily consumed by pikas in the summer. In fact, a pika increases its intake of alpine avens from its haypile only after the plant's phenolic levels have decreased, which happens well into the winter. Further, when the phenolic concentrations of alpine avens were artificially reduced, pikas preferred them over plants with natural levels. These results demonstrate that pikas manipulate the chemistry of their haystacks by storing plants rich in toxic secondary compounds and then delaying their consumption of these plants until the toxins have decayed (A. Smith 1997).

Among montane animals food caching is a common strategy, so the manipulation of the toxic chemicals in cached foods may be more prevalent than we currently realize. What other Rocky Mountain animals manage the secondary compounds in their food caches? Perhaps Lewis's woodpecker, Clark's nutcracker, common raven, water shrew, red squirrel, pre-Columbian Native Americans? Here are more exciting research opportunities.

I enjoy pikas, so when I hiked through what seemed to be an ideal pika talus slope and didn't hear one I felt shortchanged. I asked, "What's wrong with this site?" or asserted, "There's gotta be one in there!" In silence I prayed it wasn't a case of extirpation by climate warming. Silence signifies a depauperization of the audio environment, a depression of life (Beever 2009). As both an ecologist and a backpacker, I need the acoustic iconic "Eep!" to continue as part of my Rocky Mountain experience.

CHAPTER 16

Two Fat Marmots, One Fat Rock

Gaping right at me, he let out a sonic blast
that I actually felt strike my face.
My ears were ringing…I was all but deaf.

John Winnie Jr., *High Life: Animals of the Alpine World*

ROUNDING THE BEND of a trail along the lower end of Rainbow Lake—in the headwaters of Norris Creek, a tributary of Raspberry Creek that, in turn, drains the eastern slope of the Park Range (Rainbow Lake Trail, Mount Zirkel Wilderness, Routt National Forest, north-central Colorado)—Nancy and I surprised two big ol' fat marmots basking on a big round boulder. The pair snapped to attention, shouted piercing calls, and then slinked under the rock. The marmot's sharp warning scream has taught us a great deal about the evolutionary paradox of altruism.

After a short wait, one slowly emerged and resumed its belly-press on that sun-warmed rock. What a life.

Mammalogists recognize several species of Western marmots. Olympic marmots live in their namesake mountains of the Pacific Northwest (northwestern Washington). Hoary and yellow-bellied marmots range widely along the Western Cordillera, the latter at lower elevations.

A hoary marmot–like precursor originated in the Himalayas early in the Pleistocene epoch, possibly 1.7 million years ago, dispersed to the northeast, crossed Beringia, and then colonized much of northern North America. Today's exclusively alpine hoary marmot has a grizzled muzzle and weighs 20 pounds (9 kg), making it the largest member of the squirrel family. It lives from Alaska southward into the Northern Rockies (Montana and Idaho).

Marmots live in groups. The standard description of a hoary marmot colony is a family with one dominant male, one to six breeding-aged females, and the young from the current and two previous years. More than one female will move in if the male's rocks are surrounded by ample vegetation. Each colony includes several burrows. Females breed every other year. The hoary marmot's long, shrill call inspired its nickname, "whistler." The alarm calls, which propagate from colony to colony, almost always mean that a predator has been spotted, often a golden eagle. As you might gather from the epigraph, a marmot's loud, high-pitched cry could force a predator to abandon its attack.

More recently, though, a team of biologists found that the hoary marmot's mating system is more flexible than previously thought. Theory predicts that regions with limited resources should promote monogamy. The team studied hoaries at altitudes of 5,445 to 6,270 feet (1650–1900 m) in a valley of the Ruby Range (near Kluane National Park, southwestern Yukon Territory), at the northern limit of the species' distribution. Following tradition, the researchers assumed the hoary's northern populations to be monogamous. However, they discovered that the marmots' mating system was actually facultative (Kyle et al. 2007), meaning that they used different systems under different conditions. They varied between monogamy and polygyny within and among social groups. This flexible mating system may reflect, at least in part, local variation in resources.

In some extreme montane sites hoary marmots may spend more than 80 percent of their lives in hibernation. In mid- to late September, members of the colony hole up in a burrow. In their communal bundle of fur each individual drops its body temperature to less than 40°F (4.4°C) and maintains its heart and respiration rates at just a fraction of their active rates. Hibernating whistlers live solely off their fat reserves, losing 40 percent of their body weight by the time they arouse in mid to late June.

The geographic distributions of the hoary marmot and its close relative, the yellow-bellied marmot, overlap in the Northern Rockies. Yellow-bellieds live from the Canadian Rockies (central British Columbia) southward through the Southern Rockies (northern New Mexico). We met quite a few of these guys along trails in the Wind River Range (west-central Wyoming). I think they're pretty: reddish-brown back, golden belly, and small fur-covered ears. Native Americans used their skins for clothing (Haines 1955). In contrast to hoaries, yellow-bellieds weigh at most only 10 pounds (4.5 kg), and they have thinner coats and smaller fat reserves, making them poorer heat conservers but better heat dissipaters.

Also called whistle pig and rockchuck (Streubel 1989), the yellow-bellied marmot, at 24 inches (61 cm) long, is a social, diurnal ground squirrel. Yellow-bellieds typically use two aboveground microhabitats: meadows, where they forage, and rocks near the burrow, where they sit (Melcher et al. 1990). Throughout the Greater Yellowstone Ecosystem (northwestern Montana) yellow-bellieds are found from low-lying valleys to the alpine, where they usually inhabit open, grassy areas, almost always near rocks (Johnson and Crabtree 1999). This kind of habitat is patchy, so some of their populations are somewhat isolated from each other. On the one hand, the habitat patches and their temporal stability favor some genetic drift; on the other hand, a high rate of gene flow between marmot colonies, including the dispersal of most young, and avoidance of inbreeding suggest that the social system retards genetic impoverishment (Schwartz and Armitage 1980). The presence of genetic heterogeneity among colonies suggests that drift is ongoing. This local diversity enhances the genetic variance of the overall population. Taken together, these results suggest a species that is undergoing gradual evolution.

Within a colony of numerous adults each individual restricts itself to its own home range. Compared to hoaries, yellow-bellieds have greater spacing among themselves, less frequent social interactions, and more aggression. While half of male hoaries are monogamous, all yellow-bellied males are polygynous. The adult male-to-female sex ratio in whistle pig colonies can reach 1:18. This is one reason why yellow-bellied societies are less socially stable than the hoary's. Competition among females in a yellow-bellied colony can be so intense that they cannibalize each other's offspring.

Some yellow-bellied colonies come and go over the years. Based on 42 years of data collected in the Elk Mountains (near Rocky Mountain Biological Laboratory, Gothic, west-central Colorado), a team of ecologists was able to sort 49 sites into three categories: those with persistent marmot colonies; those with intermittent colonies, which periodically went extinct; and those that never hosted marmots. They discovered that environmental variables associated with visibility and safety, but not with

food, allowed the correct classification of sites into these three categories (Blumstein et al. 2006). Safety-related features were associated with
visibility, like the continuity of the view at marmot height; and cover, like
the number and sizes of rocks. These findings suggest that safety from
predation is the most important factor in the long-term persistence of a
yellow-bellied marmot colony.

Yellow-bellieds eat grasses, forbs, seeds, and insects (Streubel 1989). In
the Sierra Nevada (east-central California), yellow-bellieds also prey on
pikas (Petterson 1992). They avoid eating certain poisonous plants, like
larkspur and lupine. Further, in the spring and early summer, rockchucks
choose forbs over grasses because of the former's high concentrations of
phosphorus, sodium, and possibly protein, and low levels of fiber and
cellulose (Carey 1985).

Marmots are imperfect endotherms, that is, their body temperatures
fluctuate even when they're active. Lizard-like sunbathing, as my two fat
marmots were doing, helps them boost their body temperature before
they venture out to forage (Travis and Armitage 1972). From late morning
to midafternoon on sunny days in the Elk Mountains, the temperature of
the foraging areas often exceeded the upper limit of the yellow-bellied
marmots' thermoneutral zone (TNZ) (Melcher et al. 1990). The TNZ
is the range of ambient temperatures over which an endotherm does not
have to expend a lot of energy to control its body temperature. Think
of an animal's TNZ as its temperature tolerance range, or loosely, as the
thermal range in which it is comfortable. During these stressfully hot
periods marmots spend more time underground, shorten their foraging
bouts, and tolerate the acute warming of their bodies.

Perhaps it's this kind of thermal flexibility that has allowed a low-
elevation population to adapt to a warmer habitat. In contrast to the
species' normal montane-mesic populations, a lowland-xeric population
of yellow-bellieds in the Columbia River basin (near Grand Coulee Dam,
eastern Washington), at 1,297 feet (393 m) above sea level, had smaller
bodies. Further, at high ambient temperature they had a lower metabolism and higher evaporative water loss (Armitage et al. 1990).

Yellow-bellied marmots seem to incur their main mortality during
hibernation (Streubel 1989). In the summer, though, almost all of their
deaths are attributed to predation by golden eagle, coyote, badger, marten, and grizzly bear (Andersen and Johns 1977; Armitage 1982; Van
Vuren 2001). Badgers seem to kill mainly young marmots (Armitage
2004). When badgers are nearby, the members of a marmot colony issue

alarm calls more frequently, forage less often, and are more vigilant than when badgers are absent.

 Desynchronized Phenologies

In the springtime a marmot emerging from hibernation needs immediate food. What happens when an animal comes out of hibernation on a new schedule but its food plants reactivate per their regular date? Over the last few decades yellow-bellied marmots have been emerging from hibernation earlier than they have before. In 1999 in the East River valley of the West Elk Mountains (Gunnison County, Colorado), at 9,719 feet (2945 m) above sea level, marmots emerged 38 days earlier than they did in 1976 (Inouye et al. 2000). That's an average forward creep of 1.7 days per year! They're emerging earlier in an apparent response to warmer spring air temperatures.

But that's only half of the story. Phenology refers to the seasonal timing of an organism's activity, like a tree shedding its leaves in the fall or a migratory bird reappearing in the spring. These days, when marmots emerge there is plenty of leftover snow. When marmots emerge into a snow-covered landscape with no plants to eat, they have to spend more time functioning at full metabolic pace and drawing on their remaining fat reserves. This may increase their stress. For example, prolonged snow cover decreases both litter size and the frequency of reproduction. The combination of warm air and lasting snowpack will desynchronize the phenologies of mutually dependent plants and marmots, and possibly those of other hibernating animals. Where will this leave our montane fauna?

Yellow-bellied marmots mate within two weeks after they emerge from hibernation (Streubel 1989). After a gestation period of 30 days females give birth once a year to four or five young. In the upper East River valley, at 9,570 feet (2900 m) above sea level, 24 percent of the yellow-bellied litters were communal. These communal litters were produced by closely related members of a matriline (Armitage and Gurri-Glass 1994), so kin selection was presumably operating. Pups are weaned at 25 to 30 days of age. Females can produce litters while they are 2 to 10 years of age (Schwartz et al. 1998).

❊

Because yellow-bellied marmots live in semi-isolated populations sprinkled through a metapopulation, dispersal can be a key behavior that contributes to outbreeding and minimizes inbreeding depression, both of which play a role in the long-term sustainability of the semi-isolated populations. Yet a dispersing marmot moving across strange terrain incurs predators, malnutrition, the uncertainty of locating suitable habitat, and other, aggressive marmots. If dispersing is so dangerous, why do they do it?

To resolve this question let's refresh the definition of dispersal—the one-way movement of an animal away from its home area. In the Elk Mountains the survival of dispersing yellow-bellieds was 73 percent, 16 percent less than the 87 percent survival of philopatric marmots (Van Vuren and Armitage 1994). Thus, dispersers suffered higher mortality than did philopatric marmots of comparable age, reinforcing the idea that there is a survival cost to dispersing. So, again, why do marmots disperse? For selection to maintain both leaving and staying, the average reproductive success of dispersing and philopatric individuals needs to be equal. Stay-at-home females may incur inbreeding and inbreeding depression, which suppresses reproductive success; for males the cost of philopatry may be more severe, including breeding suppression by the dominant male and the risk of fatal aggression. Thus, from a cost-benefit point of view the reproductive benefits, like higher levels of fecundity or offspring survival, must be offsetting the survival costs of dispersal.

Among marmot species, the timing of juveniles' dispersal is a key selective factor in the evolution of their social behavior. According to one hypothesis, in environments where the growing season is short, as it is at altitude, it is adaptive for juvenile marmots to remain at home and postpone their dispersal (Gaines and McClenaghan 1980). Let's compare the timing of dispersal in three marmot species, each living in a different environment (Barash 1974). Groundhogs live at low elevations in the East, where there is a long growing season. Their offspring disperse at weaning near the end of their first growing season, adults are solitary and aggressive, and males and females interact only to mate. In contrast, the highly social Olympic marmots live at high altitudes in colonies that include several adults, two-year-olds, yearlings, and young-of-the-year. They disperse as two-year-olds and mature sexually at three years of age. The members of an Olympic colony show neither dominance nor aggressiveness. Between the extremes of the groundhog and Olympic marmot lies the yellow-bellied marmot. Yellow-bellieds live at intermediate elevations and feature an in-between social organization. Less solitary than ground-hogs, individual yellow-bellieds do maintain distinct home ranges. Their infrequent social interactions lead to considerable aggression. They disperse as yearlings and mature sexually at two years of age.

In this three-species series, the postponement of sexual maturity and dispersal seems to be an adaptive response to shorter growing seasons. As elevation increases and growing season shortens, the lengthening interval from birth to dispersal reflects an increase in the time required to accumulate enough body weight to meet the demands of dispersal and independence, and eventually of successful reproduction.

What causes a marmot to leave its colony? That is, what are the prox-imate stimuli of dispersal? In yellow-bellieds, although the timing of dispersal by yearling males is independent of the intensity of aggression, there is a positive association between the level of friendliness and delay of dispersal (Downhower and Armitage 1971). Simply, when friendliness is common yearling males stay longer in their natal colony. Yearling males also delay dispersal when they are underweight. These findings suggest that the genial actions of others and a young male's body condition inter-act to influence the timing of his dispersal. In contrast, the severity of belligerence alone explains female dispersal: when attack levels are high young females disperse sooner; when colony mates are peaceful they stay longer.

Using radiotelemetry and mark-recapture data from a long-term study, a team of ecologists found that the dispersal of females was less likely when three conditions were met: the mother was present; amicable behavior with the mother and play behavior were more frequent; and spatial overlap was greater with the mother, with matriline females, and with other yearling females (Armitage et al. 2011). These social conditions show that cooperation among kin, expressed via cohesive behaviors and focused on the mother, discourages dispersal and thereby promotes philopatry. Cooperation among kin is a crucial factor that influences staying put in marmots.

Throughout the Rockies true hibernators include some species of bats and chipmunks, the western jumping mouse, and marmots. At altitude, yellow-bellied marmots may hibernate for up to eight months, from early September to May (Streubel 1989). Body temperature falls to 40°F (4°C), and the pulse holds at just a few percentage points of its active rate. To avoid freezing, hibernating animals occasionally warm their bodies to normal temperatures and arouse. But reactivation burns a lot of body fat.

In the yellow-bellied marmot, population dynamics are functionally linked to social behavior. The group's density, age structure, and sex ratio influence the behavioral characteristics of residents and potential recruits, the way in which space is shared, and the number of years residents live together (Armitage 1977). In these and other ways, the yellow-bellied marmot's polygynous mating system is both the cause and effect of its demography (Schwartz et al. 1998).

Most yellow-bellieds live in colonies consisting of a dominant territorial male, his harem of several females, and their young-of-the-year and yearling offspring (Schwartz and Armitage 1980). A large patch of suitable habitat may sustain several marmot colonies. In contrast, small peripheral sites with marginal habitat may hold one or a few marmots and incur a high turnover, poor reproductive success, and a more rudimentary social structure.

When closely related yellow-bellieds meet, they often nuzzle and expose their cheek glands, or they may raise their tails and expose anal glands. Agonistic behaviors include alerting, fleeing, and chasing. In the East River valley, when a yellow-bellied marmot colony included adults that had been resident the previous year, pugnacious acts were infrequent and there was a lot of amicable behavior (Armitage 1977). In contrast, new immigrants trigger more hostile acts and fewer friendly ones. A shift from aggression-targeted immigrants to amicable residents signals a more integrated society.

Social behavior also shifts with population changes. As a population increases in size, aggression intensifies and amicable behaviors decrease; in contrast, emigration reduces conflict (Armitage 1977). This plays out seasonally as June's intense agonistic behavior between adults and yearlings drops to nil after the yearlings have dispersed.

The intensity of social behaviors is related to the use of space. High rates of aggression continue as long as the home range of a dominant female overlaps the home ranges of other females, but after females have partitioned the habitat few social interactions occur (Armitage 1977). A few especially friendly females may even maintain overlapping home ranges.

One particular type of aggression centers on the burrow. In the Central and Southern Rockies (Yellowstone National Park, northwestern

Wyoming; and near Rocky Mountain Biological Laboratory, Gothic, Colorado; respectively), dominant yellow-bellied marmots buried subordinate colony members in the subordinates' own burrows (Armitage and Downhower 1970). Dominant females moved toward a subordinate female, chased her into the latter's burrow, scratched soil around the burrow entrance, carried rocks to the entrance, and dropped them into the burrow. Both the chaser and chased were rearing pups. Some burrows were completely blocked with rocks and soil. Dominant, excited females, often flagging their tails, kicked stones or sticks into the burrow entrance. Burying another female sounds like a straightforward example of reproductive competition.

Infanticide may be another adaptation that improves individual reproductive success. Several field biologists have seen adult yellow-bellied marmots killing newly emerged young who are still within their natal home range (Brody and Melcher 1985). Again, this strikes me as a direct way to reduce competition and improve one's fitness.

In the yellow-bellied marmot, friendly behaviors include greeting; allogrooming, or the grooming of one individual by another; and mutual reciprocal grooming. The longer a colony has been together the more friendly behaviors increase and agonism decreases. Aggression is more intense between unrelated individuals. To signal his dominance the resident male waves his tail.

Marmots cheek-mark objects with perioral secretions, which are fluids released from tissues around the mouth. Cheek marking is a form of signaling in which an individual rubs its muzzle with a secreted chemical against an object. Most cheek marking occurs within 10 feet (3 m) of the main burrow system (Brady and Armitage 1999). Adults cheek-mark more than yearlings do. In yellow-bellieds, cheek marking slackens as the season progresses. Marmots investigate strange secretions longer than familiar ones, and familiar scents longer than unmarked objects. Cheek marking communicates burrow occupancy, reinforces territorial defense, and provides cues to young-of-the-year on the safe areas within a home range.

A major social behavior of female yellow-bellieds is the formation of matrilines, groups consisting of long sequences of mothers and their daughters (Armitage 1984, 1998). The social behaviors of philopatry and daughter recruitment help to generate matrilines (Armitage and Schwartz 2000). By facilitating the acquisition of resources, matrilines provide their female members with a fitness advantage. Although the total number of residents may not change, the space occupied increases when matrilines divide. With the fission of large matrilines, newly independent females experience higher reproductive success than they would have if they had remained in their birth family.

Within a yellow-bellied matriline adult females suppress the reproduction of younger females (Armitage 1998). Although dominant females seem to benefit from retaining subordinate females, the adaptive significance of accepting a subordinate role is not as obvious. In some situations submissive behavior may be a form of behavioral altruism, selfless behavior favored through kin selection. In the yellow-bellied marmot, matrilineal bifurcation is associated with the splitting of a single space into two or more spaces, each of which is shared by individuals related by 0.5 (Armitage 1984)—that is, on average they share 50 percent of their genes. In addition to benefiting the dominant female, reproductive altruism would benefit the subordinate individual by increasing her inclusive fitness.

The matriline strikes me as a social system in which natural, kin, and group selection have all played roles in shaping individual behavior (sensu Wilson 2012). Individual female marmots show the effects of this dynamic equilibrium among the three levels of selection. A female's behavior seems pluralistic, as she pursues her own reproductive success while also behaving altruistically to contribute to the group's inclusive fitness.

Turning to the male's behavior, I said before that the yellow-bellied marmot is primarily polygynous. The male adaptations that enable polygyny include dispersal, the inclusion of several females within each male's territory, and hibernation in an area where females are present. Because dominant females limit the number of subordinate females that reproduce and males strive to increase the number of breeding females in their territories, intersexual conflict is inevitable (Downhower and Armitage 1971).

The members of a marmot colony communicate often with each other. An alarm call, defined as a vocalization that communicates danger to other members of one's group, may be stimulated by an approaching predator, territorial invader, or backpacking human. Most alarm signals are general in scope, while a few are narrowly specific (Wilson 1975). In general, animal signals can be grouped into two types, discrete or graded, which you may think of as digital or analog data, respectively. A discrete signal is projected in a simple on-or-off manner; a graded signal is more intense and prolonged the greater the motivation behind it. An example of a graded signal is a squirrel intensifying its warning signal from slow waves of its tail to violent total-body twitching.

In evolutionary biology, alarm calls have traditionally presented us with a challenge because they seem to be examples of altruistic behavior (R. J. F. Smith 1986). Among fishes, chemical alarm signaling has been documented in freshwater minnows and darters and marine gobies (R. J. F. Smith 1973, 1979, 1989). They release a chemical alarm after their skin has been damaged by a predator. Chemical alarm cues also exude from the skin of some salamanders (Lutterschmidt et al. 1994). In many bird species a member of the flock may give an alarm call when it sees an aerial predator (Gyger et al. 1986). The whole flock immediately takes off and heads for cover, or the birds freeze if they already are in cover (Charnov and Krebs 1975). White-tailed deer flag their tails (Hirth and McCullough 1977; Bildstein 1983; LaGory 1987).

With a predator still 990 feet (300 m) away several species of ground squirrels set up waves of alarm calls, which increase in intensity and duration as the intruder gets closer (Wilson 1975). Findings indicate that nepotism, the helping of relatives, is the most likely function of the Belding's ground squirrel's alarm call, implicating the action of kin selection (Dugatkin 1997). At a meadow at Tioga Pass, in the Sierra Nevada (eastern edge of Yosemite National Park, east-central California), the average genetic relatedness among female Belding's ground squirrels is high. Daughters mature and breed near their birthplaces, whereas males usually emigrate before their first winter. In the round-tailed ground squirrel, which lives in human-modified areas of the desert Southwest (e.g., Arizona), the kin-based prediction is also supported, as individuals whistle more often when they are near genetic relatives (Dunford 1977).

Marmots issue alarm calls that vary according to the situation. Three marmot species, the Olympic, hoary, and Vancouver Island, produce four roughly similar but specifically distinct loud alarm vocalizations (Blumstein 1999). The microstructure of the calls, specifically their shape and duration, and whether the calls are repeated to create multinote calls, vary as a function of the caller's distance from the alarm stimulus and the type of alarm stimulus. Thus, these three species issue alarm calls associated with the caller's risk. I suspect that a repertoire of at least similar sophistication will be found in yellow-bellieds.

Yellow-bellied marmots issue individually distinctive alarm calls (Blumstein and Daniel 2004). Each call encodes information about the sender's identity, age, and sex (Blumstein and Munos 2005). The key variables that enable discrimination are repeatable, whereas those that do not are less repeatable. Statistically, each call contains 3.37 bits of information about identity. Defined as the smallest piece of information that can exist in alternative states, a "bit" in this context could be the frequency or temporal length of a note. Compared to other species for which signals have been similarly analyzed, marmots do not seem to have undergone strong selection for individually distinctive calls. However, the fact that receivers do discriminate among individual callers indicates that receivers benefit from making the distinction and, thus, that listening for differences does confer fitness advantages.

So now you know that a yellow-bellied marmot can distinguish among the calls issuing from different adult females. It can also discriminate between the calls of individuals in different age and sex categories. Calls from juveniles elicit a greater response, in the form of more vigilance and less foraging, than do calls from adult females. This discrimination conveys survival benefits because the receivers are able to identify when young, presumably vulnerable, marmots are calling and then respond with enhanced vigilance.

Marmots respond even to the calls of other species; they have been observed responding to the alarm calls of pikas. Yellow-bellied marmots and golden-mantled ground squirrels also respond to each other's antipredator calls (Shriner 1998). If two species have a predator in common they could gain important information about the risk level from another species' alarm call.

In an interesting twist to this alarm-call story, it turns out that animal alarm systems can be exploited by cheaters. On Jutland (Denmark), great tits give alarm calls in the winter even though predators are not present, causing competitors to flee and leaving the food for the cheater (Moller 1988). A dominant individual issues alarms deceptively if another dominant bird is present on a concentrated food source; if a subordinate individual is present the boss simply displaces the meek bird with threat displays. Subordinate individuals give false alarm calls if either dominant or subordinate tits are present. Thus, regardless of its position in the local social hierarchy, each individual is both manipulator and manipulated. False alarms seem to be cried most often when food is scarce or when the birds need to feed quickly, for instance before an oncoming snowstorm. Deceptive calling can be effective—as long as it's not attempted too often. I wonder how often false alarms echo through the canyons of the Rockies. Do cliff swallows, common ravens, chickadees, warblers, bats, pikas, marmots, or other group-living animals of the Rockies utter false alarm calls? Here are more research questions calling out to the next generation of behavioral ecologists.

Among squirrels in which the males give little or no parental care, and in which matrilineal kin groups are the basic population unit, there are similarities in the form and in the female sex- and age-specificity of alarm calls (Sherman 1977). Colonial marmots communicate through whistling, screaming, and teeth chattering, the latter being used to signal aggression. The shrill cry communicates warning. The alarm calls of many mammals are mostly nonspecific, but yellow-bellied marmots produce different alarm calls in response to different kinds of predators (Blumstein and Armitage 1997). Marmots vary primarily the rate, and potentially a few frequency characteristics, as a function of risk level.

Invoking kin selection theory, behavioral ecologists have interpreted the alarm calls of ground squirrels as benefiting the caller's inclusive fitness (West Eberhard 1975; Blumstein et al. 1997). That is, kin selection is thought to have played an important role in the evolutionary origin and consequent maintenance of marmot alarm calls (Maynard Smith 1965). However, a more parsimonious hypothesis is that a parental animal cries out an alarm simply to warn its own offspring. After the young emerged from their burrow, female yellow-bellied marmots with pups called more than females of other ages and breeding classes (Blumstein et al. 1997). Specifically, 42 percent of the variation in call rate was a function of whether the caller was a female with her own pups aboveground. This result suggests that alarm calling is a form of direct parental care and that kin selection may not be necessary to maintain alarm calling in the yellow-bellied marmot (Blumstein and Armitage 1998). In this debate I'm attracted to the middle ground: my biological intuition tells me that both natural and kin selection have contributed to the evolution of the yellow-bellied marmot's alarm call. The harder question is, What are the relative contributions of each?

※

Let's close this story by returning to those rotund yellow-bellied marmots we found sunning themselves along the trail. As we worked our way along a mountain path, it wasn't unusual to be announced by warning calls—the acoustic wave preceded us. I almost always heard marmots before I saw them. Now we know that the callers were most likely females warning their nearby offspring and possibly their sisters and their young of an approaching dangerous animal. Over the last few decades the study of alarm calls in many kinds of animals—and the consequent rejection of genetic altruism hypotheses—have lent crucial support to the theories of evolution by natural and kin selection.

CHAPTER 17

Intimidating Bitches

I've even seen a wolf,
with an air of not wanting to miss out,
howl while defecating.

Barry Lopez, *Of Wolves and Men*

IT WAS DAY TWO of our first Yellowstone trek. Camped along Eagle Creek, which drains the eastern flank of the Absaroka Range (Eagle Creek Trail, Washakie Wilderness, Shoshone National Forest, northwestern Wyoming), we were jolted alert at two in the morning by a wolf cutting loose with a full-blown howl. Just 30 yards (27 m) from our tent, it was classic—plaintive, semimusical, drawn out, tapering to an end. It was hard to fall back to sleep, not because of fear of the wolf but because of the sheer honor of it all…and that smugness you feel with being in the right place at the right time. I'll use howling as an iconic entrée for exploring the wolf's complex social life.

On the trail the next morning, fresh wolf tracks were going our way.

The gray wolf is the largest natural member of the dog family (Mech 1970). From tip of nose to end of tail, males range from 5 to 6.5 feet (1.5–2.0 m) long and females 4.5 to 6 feet (1.4–1.8 m). They stand 26 to 32 inches (66–81 cm) tall. Adult males average 95 to 100 pounds (43–45 kg) and females are 80 to 85 pounds (36–38 kg), so females weigh about 85 percent as much as males. Compared to the coyote, the gray wolf is larger and stouter, projects a more robust muzzle tipped with a larger nose pad, and has shorter, less pointed ears. Most wolves are mottled gray with tawny legs and flanks (Mech 1991). Slender all over, the wolf's sinuous and graceful body is carried high on long legs.

The wolf precursor arose in the Arctic. About half a million years ago it moved southward into Eurasia, where it became almost indistinguishable from today's gray wolf. It then crossed Beringia, dispersed southward, and about 13,000 years ago became a common member of the North American fauna. Once one of the most widely distributed mammals, the gray wolf until recently lived throughout Earth's Northern Hemisphere. In the Rockies the gray wolf is now restricted to the mountains from Alaska southward through the Canadian Rockies into the Northern Rockies (Idaho, Montana) and the Greater Yellowstone Ecosystem (southwestern Montana and northwestern Wyoming). It lives in a huge variety of habitats: tundra, forest, savanna, plains, desert (Mech 1970).

There are few other mammals that roam as far as a gray wolf—up to 40 miles (64 km) per day. In the boreal forest of the Upper Midwest (northeastern Minnesota), a wolf pack used a range 43 miles in extent (Mech et al. 1971). Major travel routes, which have been used by many wolf generations, usually form closed circuits. The trails frequented by adjacent packs can interconnect as a network over a vast landscape.

Occasionally, wolves prey on earthworms, lizards, and mice; they also pluck berries, scavenge carrion, and cannibalize injured packmates. In the autumn along the Kunsoot River on Denny Island, off the coast of the Pacific Northwest (west-central British Columbia), they eat a lot of salmon (Darimont et al. 2003; "As the Wolf's World Turns" 2009). But normally wolves kill large mammals. Animals the size of beavers or larger compose 59 to 96 percent of their food items. Prey species include white-tailed and mule deer, moose, caribou, elk, bison, mountain goat, and bighorn sheep (Mech 1970; Mech et al. 1971; Kunkel et al. 1999; D. Smith et al. 2000; Kunkel and Pletscher 2001).

Within a prey population, wolves kill selectively. During the winter in the Salmon River Mountains (central Idaho), elk were the primary prey, followed by mule deer. Wolves preyed more on elk calves and old individuals (Husseman et al. 2003). Among mule deer they selected fawns. In Yellowstone, wolves selected elk based on their vulnerability as a result of age, sex, and season and thus killed mainly calves, old cows, and bulls that had been weakened by winter (Stahler et al. 2006). Further, the nutritional status of prey animals, as indicated by the percentage of fat in their femur marrow, was poorer in wolf-killed prey. Some wolf biologists have suggested that the wolf's long chases and low capture rates require them to favor vulnerable prey.

The wolf body is an awesome killing machine. Its head is adapted for catching, killing, and eating. The large skull tapers forward. Of its 40 teeth, the largest are the canines, which can measure up to 2.3 inches (5.8 cm) long (Mech 1970). Massive jaws are powered by strong masseter muscles; their powerful bite exerts three-fourths of a ton (0.68 t) of crushing pressure. Although a wolf can run up to 35 miles (56 km) per hour and maintain a chase for 20 minutes, its conformation—narrow chest, forelegs and hind legs on the same side that swing in the same line, and long legs that allow speed and enable travel through deep snow—is really designed for trotting.

Wolves are boom-and-bust, feast-or-famine feeders: they engage in intense activity, rest for several days, and then hunt again (Fontaine 1999; Stahler et al. 2006). In one study, the kill rate averaged one deer every 11 days. In Yellowstone, packs killed an elk every two to three days. In the wintertime in the boreal forest (northeastern Minnesota), the kill rate varied from one white-tailed deer every 6.3 to 37.5 days per wolf, with a rough average of about one deer every 10 to 13 days (Mech et al. 1971). The average kill rate during more usual winters was one deer every 18 days. The rate was lower for a wolf in a pack of five than it was for a lone wolf. This predation rate yielded a rough long-term average of 5.6 pounds (2.5 kg) of venison per wolf per day.

After a kill, packmates eviscerate and eat the most nutritious organs first, then the major muscles, and finally the bones and hide (Stahler et al. 2006). From one end to the other a wolf's digestive tract is adapted to process meat. The stomach has a huge capacity: each individual can gorge on 10 to 20 pounds (4.5–9.0 kg) of meat. Wolves eat all of the prey—even snow soaked in blood. And then, each member, engorged and bulging, finds a comfortable spot, plops down, and goes to sleep.

Wolves locate prey in three main ways (Mech 1970). The first method, and the one they use most often, is direct scenting. When wolves are downwind of an animal and catch its scent, the lead animals suddenly stop, and all pack members stand alert with their eyes, ears, and nose pointed upwind. They assemble nose to nose, wag their tails for 10 to 15 seconds, and then veer straight upwind toward the prey animal. Wolves also come upon prey in chance encounters, which are more likely where prey live at high densities. Finally, wolves will follow fresh tracks by hold-ing their noses to the ground.

Stalking, a quick burst, and then a short chase are the main steps for overcoming a prey animal. During a stalk the wolves close the gap, be-come excited yet maintain restraint, quicken their pace, wag their tails, and peer ahead intently (Mech 1970). With a stealth approach wolves can sometimes get close, like within 75 feet (23 m), if the quarry is not facing them.

When predator and prey encounter each other the prey animal may respond in one of three ways: it may approach the wolves, stand its ground, or flee. Some prey animals, like moose and elk, face the approach-ing predator. As soon as the wolves see that the prey has sensed them and is not running, they usually end their stalk. The wolves quickly abandon this testing process if the prey responds like a healthy animal. After the wolves give up, the prey animal may stop, turn, and watch its back trail, conserving energy for another quick dash. If the prey's response is abnor-mal, feeble, or suggestive of a young or old animal, the chase is on.

Capture comes with a sudden rush (Mech 1970). Preying on a big animal is risky—wolves suffer broken legs and cracked skulls. Contrary to popular stories wolves seldom, if ever, hamstring their prey. As soon as the quarry is stopped the wolves try to grab its head, usually by the snout. While the victim is focused on the wolf hanging onto its nose, other pack members grab the rump, flanks, and throat. The prey animal is killed within a few minutes.

I've read some suggestions that wolves use higher mental processes while hunting. Here's an example. Muskoxen are challenging for wolves to overcome because they live in herds and possess formidable horns and hooves. Wolves try to kill their calves, which seek protection within encir-cling adults. On the Fosheim Peninsula on the western side of Ellesmere Island (Nunavut Territory), Arctic wolves, a subspecies of the gray wolf, used a two-pronged approach (Mech 2007). The wolves split up and ap-proached the prey from two directions. Two members would sneak up while the rest of the pack waited and watched. The wolves appeared to be using elementary cooperation and strategy, as well as showing insight and purposiveness. To avoid a misunderstanding, let's define those last two terms: insight—perceiving a solution; purposiveness—deliberate behav-ior with an objective. Further, waiting in ambush implies that the wolves expected the muskoxen to become available eventually. These observations hint that wolves may use foresight, understanding, and planning during their hunting behavior.

Wolves endure low rates of hunting success. In one study the members of a pack detected 131 moose, tested 77 of them, attacked 7, and killed 6 — a predation efficiency of 4.5 percent. This equals a kill rate of 1 for every 22 moose encountered. During five winters in the Canadian Rockies (Banff National Park, Alberta), the average kill rate of wolf packs was 0.33 kills per day per pack, 70 percent of which were elk (Hebblewhite et al. 2003). On Yellowstone's Northern Range, wolf kill rates during winter were 1.9 kills per wolf per month, of which 90 percent were elk (Smith et al. 2004).

One reason for these low success rates is that wolves usually cannot capture a prime, healthy prey animal. This is why they kill young, old, and inferior prey animals, which they accomplish mainly through a process that seems mechanical. One study reported higher incidences of abnormalities and pathologies of the mandibles and lower limbs among white-tailed deer killed by wolves than in human-killed deer (Mech and Frenzel 1971). This finding is consistent with the dogma that wolves selectively remove debilitated prey.

Male wolves 4.5 to 5.5 years old had the best scores. The positive effect of male age on hunting success seems to reflect both increasing experience and greater size. At older ages, though, the predatory skills of Yellowstone wolves dropped (MacNulty et al. 2009). And this, in turn, can impact the pack: a high proportion of senescent individuals depresses the pack's kill rate.

❄

Wolves use various forms of vocal communication, including the howl, whimper, growl, bark, and social squeak (Mech 1991). Once one begins howling, other pack members often approach and join the chorus. Tail wagging, excitement, and friendliness accompany the howling. As hinted by this chapter's epigraph, once howling starts it's impossible not to join in. Under a temperature inversion and with slow winds a wolf can hear another's howl from six miles (10 km) away (Larom et al. 1997; Harrington and Asa 2003). By calculation, a pivoting wolf can be heard throughout a circle of 113 square miles (294 km^2)!

After decades of research we have gained some understanding of the functions of the gray wolf's long, low, mournful howl (Mech 1970, 1991).

First, the howl identifies the howler. It may also indicate the howler's activity, for instance whether it is resting, walking slowly, or pacing. Second, howls reassemble pack members that have become separated. Third, wolves howl as a group when they hear the wail of a strange pack. Packs reply more often when they have something to defend, like pups or a fresh kill. Think of chorus howling as a threat to potential intruders. And fourth, howling seems to synchronize the packmates' behavior. When they awaken and stretch, they may urinate, nose each other, and break into a group howl.

Most of the communication between wolves, though, is transacted not through howling but by scent marking, which is the urination, defecation, and rubbing of certain body parts on objects and the investigation of those odors by other wolves (Mech 1991). Objects repeatedly scent marked, called scent stations, include rocks, logs, and other conspicuous objects. When a pack discovers the urine of a stranger, members become excited. Scent marking seems to serve as territorial advertisement and individual identification (Lewis and Murray 1993). There are twice as many scent stations around the edges of a territory as in its center. Scent marking also functions in courtship—alpha females scent-mark more as the breeding season approaches. Wolves use urine and feces as vehicles for pheromones. A wolf removes food from its store and then urinates there to tell another wolf not to bother with the empty food cache. Wolves have complex scent glands inside their anus. When they defecate, these secretions, which carry a mixture of chemicals unique to each individual, coat the scat.

On the Central Massif in Ourense on the Iberian Peninsula (Montes de Invernadeiro Natural Park, Galicia, northwestern Spain), gray wolves deposited 60 percent of their feces at crossroads and 72 percent on conspicuous substrates (Barja et al. 2004). These and other kinds of prominent locations seem to increase the effectiveness of the scat as visual and olfactory marks.

In the Rockies, gray wolves mate in February. Breeding is strictly seasonal (Asa and Valdespino 1998). The pack's dominant male and female are called the alpha wolves. Wolves are monogamous with strong and long-lasting bonds, placing them in the category of obligate monogamy.

The evolution of such mating exclusivity has been favored by two environmental constraints: (1) solitary females cannot rear their litters without the aid of conspecifics, and (2) the habitat's carrying capacity is not sufficient to allow more than one female to breed at the same time in the same place. In general, mammals with obligate monogamy tend to show several common traits (Kleiman 1977): there is little sexual dimorphism; adults have infrequent sociosexual interactions except during the early stages of pair bond formation; young exhibit delayed sexual maturity in the presence of their parents, so only the adults breed; older juveniles help rear their younger siblings; and the adult male aids in rearing the young by feeding, carrying, defending, and socializing the offspring.

Among animals in general, monogamy is related to parental investment. A male is more likely to invest in young if he is certain he is their father. Canid species are unusual among mammals in that they are primarily monogamous (Kleiman 2011). In the gray wolf the continuing association of the monogamous pair increases the odds of parental investment (Asa and Valdespino 1998).

In the autumn, testosterone levels increase in all adult males, while the dominant male increases his territorial scent marking (Asa and Valdespino 1998). During proestrus, which is the period immediately before the female's estrus, the alpha pair spends a lot of time together and repeatedly double urine-marks, which seems to be important in forming and maintaining the pair bond.

Usually only the alpha individuals breed; mating attempts by others are spurned (Mech 1970). The alphas become the parents, while the pack's other adults, if any, serve as aunts and uncles. In the presence of their parents the sexual maturation of young wolves is delayed. Instead of breeding, older juveniles help rear their younger siblings. This suite of social behaviors suggests that the evolution of helping within packs has resulted from kin selection among packs.

The bitch has only one estrus, one chance to conceive, per season. Even though the gray wolf's strictly seasonal reproduction is normal for temperate-zone species, its single ovulatory cycle, called monestrum, is rare (Asa and Valdespino 1998). In compensation, a relatively long period of estrus allows multiple copulations. The adaptive significance of monestrum may be related to the wolf's social system in that it eliminates the chance for more estrus periods in subordinates, which could otherwise intensify social conflict. If estrus recurred in subordinates, the alpha fe-male would need to be more aggressive, and this would strain the pack's cohesion.

Wolves engage in a long courtship that features sniffing, head rub-bing, snout pushing and grabbing, and the male's snuffling and licking of the female's genitals. He initiates three times as many courtship acts as she does. To thwart a mating attempt she tucks her tail between her legs and sits on it; if receptive she stands firmly, turns her tail to one side, and exposes her vulva. He mounts her from behind (Mech 1991). After he has inserted his penis, its base swells and her vaginal sphincter con-tracts. They remain physically locked together back to back for up to half an hour.

To help us interpret the function of the copulatory lock, let's refer to the theory of sperm competition. From the alpha male's point of view the copulatory tie may prevent other male pack members from gaining sexual access to the female (Asa and Valdespino 1998). During copulation most members of the pack rush over to the pair excitedly and mill around. Because other pack members sometimes try to get in on the mating or otherwise harass the coupled pair, just before copulation the mated pair may move away from the main pack for a few days (Mech 1991). Thus, the copulatory lock seems to be a male adaptation to ensure paternity.

Before giving birth the bitch searches for shelter (Mech 1991). The den may be in a hole in the ground, in an old beaver lodge, or even on top of the ground. She may also usurp a den from a smaller animal like a fox. Dens are often reused for several years. After 63 days of gestation females give birth to two to six pups of about a pound (0.5 kg) each.

Father helps by feeding, defending, and socializing the pups. The off-spring are raised cooperatively by all pack members, which also contribute babysitting, nursing, and solid food. Aunts and uncles actually compete to care for the pups. All adult pack members, even males, guard and play with the pups and feed both the bitch and her pups (Mech 1991; Asa and Valdespino 1998). Nonparental males, like an older brother or uncle, care for the pups by providing food, defending the den, babysitting, playing with and guarding the pups, and caring for the mother.

Female wolves are capable of pseudopregnancy, a hormonal state in which they exhibit the same outward behaviors they would if they were pregnant, even though they are not (Mech 1991). Because of the endo-crine similarity to pregnancy, all females that ovulate are hormonally primed to show maternal behavior. Some may even lactate. Through the process of pseudopregnancy, a pupless female may turn into a wet-nurse.

When pack members return from a hunt, pups nip their faces to stimulate the regurgitation of meat chunks. Both the alpha male and younger members feed the alpha female. When food arrives she either grabs it or begs it away. Later, unmated females that were previously harassed by the pack may serve as dry nurses for the litter and keep males out of the den. After serving in such a nursemaid role a former outcast may rise in rank within the pack's hierarchy. The contributions by pack members during this sensitive period are crucial to the alpha female because they enable more pups to survive.

In the spring, prolactin, a hormone that causes nurturing behavior, surges in all adult wolves (Asa and Valdespino 1998). In nonparental males the hormone stimulates them to care for pups. There is a parallel hormonal mechanism in human males, in which fatherhood, and even lactation, are supported by low testosterone and high prolactin levels.

Twenty to 40 percent of the packs with two or more adult females produce two litters (Mech 1991). In some packs the subordinate pair's pups do not survive, but in others the litters merge and are raised together. Here's yet another hint that kin selection has been at work.

At 9 to 12 weeks of age gray wolf pups are weaned and moved to a rendezvous site (Mech 1991). Each rendezvous site includes about 30 square feet (2.7 m^2) of vegetation-leveled activity area, a field of vision of up to 300 feet (91 m), a shady spot, beds and open water, and a system of trails, all within an area of up to one acre (0.4 ha). Think of it as a den above the ground, a place that provides the adults with a safe place to socialize with the growing pups. Pups use rendezvous sites for about 17 days, until mid-September, and then begin traveling with the pack. Pups grow quickly, so by late in their first autumn they look like adults.

The unit of wolf society is the pack, a group of bonded individuals that travel, hunt, and rest together (Mech 1970). In general, large-bodied canids evolved social groups with sophisticated cooperation because it allowed them to kill large-bodied prey (LeBoeuf 1978). The basic wolf pack consists of a mated pair and their young (Asa and Valdespino 1998)—a nuclear family that stays together while the offspring learn how to live on their own. Many packs consist of an alpha pair, their last litter of pups, and the offspring of a few previous litters, for a total of 5 to 20 members. Plus, as I mentioned earlier, some packs may include one or more adults besides the breeding pair.

How much ground a wolf pack covers can vary widely. In the Northern Rockies, territories range from 140 to 2,400 square miles (350–6000 km²). In the Canadian and Northern Rockies (southeastern British Columbia and northwestern Montana), the Magic Pack covered 718 square miles (1795 km²), and in south-central Alaska, territory size averaged 658 square miles (1645 km²) (Ballard et al. 1987). For a rough idea, picture a square measuring 26 miles (41 km) per side.

Normally, a lone wolf that intrudes into a pack's territory is detected, attacked, and killed—but sometimes a pack accepts an alien. Genetic data confirm that new wolves are occasionally incorporated into existing packs (Asa and Valdespino 1998). For example, when the alpha bitch dies a female from outside the pack may move in, assume the behavior of an alpha female, and produce pups the next year in her predecessor's den.

Within a pack, individual wolves interact through a peck order. Initially discovered in chicken flocks, the peck order, also called a dominance order or social hierarchy, can be visualized as a social ladder in which each member occupies a position (Mech 1970). The highest-ranking individual threatens all other members of the group without retaliation, the second highest accepts aggression from the highest member and bullies all lower-ranking individuals, and so on. The bottom animal harasses no one and is pecked by all.

Within each wolf pack there are two separate dominance hierarchies, a male order and a female order (Mech 1970). The highest-ranking male is referred to as the alpha male; the top female is the alpha female. As I've said, within a pack the alpha male and alpha female are usually the only individuals that reproduce. Dominant wolves get the choicest food and best resting places and also show leadership during a hunt. In addition to the alpha pair, remember that the rest of the packmates can be assigned to one of three other classes: (1) mature subordinate animals, (2) juveniles, which do not become part of the pack nucleus until their second year, and (3) lone wolves, which rank so low they avoid the main pack.

Social status is established early in life (Mech 1991). Pups begin play fighting with their littermates at three weeks of age (Mech 1970). The heaviest pups hold an advantage. These early competitions eventually lead to an order of dominance among littermates. Although rank may be established early, say by 30 days of age, a disturbance in living conditions or the loss or addition of a member can trigger a realignment.

Many of the interactions between pack members function to keep or raise a wolf's position in the hierarchy. Each individual maintains a watchful interest in its packmates. Status quarrels are not private affairs; rather the whole pack takes part (Mech 1970). A dominant wolf approaches a subordinate; raises its tail, ears, and mane; may bare its teeth and growl; and enlarges itself—the subordinate diminishes itself; lowers its tail, body, and ears; and whines. The inferior animal may also lie down, roll over, or paw solicitously at the dominant individual. As you read that description you pictured your dog, right?

Each pack has a leader, defined as the individual that most influences the behavior of the others (Mech 1970). The pack leader is the most aggressive wolf during a hunt, breaks trail through deep snow, arouses others from sleep, guards the pack by repelling intruders, and is able to reverse the pack's direction. Although it may appear that the leader acts independently of its packmates, the leader is actually influenced somewhat by the behavior of the other pack members.

Which wolves serve as pack leaders? A wolf's rank is partly related to its age. The oldest of both genders are usually alphas, the oldest offspring next, and yearlings and pups are lowest. An alpha animal may hold its position for up to eight years.

A team of ecologists analyzed the behavior of gray wolves in three packs during the winter in Yellowstone. Breeding wolves, mainly dominant individuals, performed the scent marking (Peterson et al. 2002). Dominant breeding pairs provided most of the leadership, which is consistent with what happens in other social mammals. Dominant breeders led traveling packs 71 percent of the time. During travel, breeding males and females led packs equally. A change in behavior was prompted almost three times more often by dominant breeders than by nonbreeding individuals. Dominant breeding females triggered pack activities almost four times more often than subordinate breeding females. Breeding wolves sometimes led from nonfrontal positions. Among subordinates, leadership was shown by subordinate breeding females and other individuals just before they dispersed from their natal packs. Subordinate wolves more often led packs that were large and held many subordinate adults.

To maintain its social rank a wolf must constantly assert itself (Mech 1970). Dominance displays range from peaceful self-assertion to physical

battle. An air of self-assurance alone is usually enough to enforce the status quo. Actual fights are rare and usually occur between contenders for
the alpha position. Bared teeth, forward mouth corners, a wrinkled and
swollen forehead, and erect and forward ears assert a full threat by a dominant wolf. There are two extremes in tail position: threatening, when the
tail is raised above the back; and submissive, when the tail is held low and
tucked between the legs or curved alongside. Submission is critical for the
group's harmony (Mech 1970).

Alpha wolves pay a price for their high rank—they incur a lot of stress.
Among mammals in general, stressed individuals have high levels of glucocorticoid hormone. The hormone functions in metabolic pathways
that produce ATP and diverts energy from physiological processes not
needed for immediate survival, like digestion, growth, and reproduction.
This response may benefit the animal in the short-term but is harmful if it
becomes a chronic condition.

Over two years a team of animal behaviorists followed three wolf
packs, the Druid, Leopold, and Rose packs, through Yellowstone. When
the wolves defecated the biologists collected their scat and analyzed it for
glucocorticoid hormone. In all packs during both years, the alpha individuals of both sexes had higher levels of fecal glucocorticoid than their
subordinates did (Sands and Creel 2004; Creel 2005). One hypothesis
explaining the high glucocorticoid levels in dominant wolves is that the
hormones are associated with the physical activity needed to maintain
dominance. Yet the rates of aggressive behavior were not related to glucocorticoid levels. This suggests that dominant wolves incur subtle, continuous costs of maintaining their high rank. This reminds me of the price
humans pay in bodily health for living under chronic stress and conflict.
In wolves, a possible consequence could be high levels of stress hormones
that suppress the immune system. The top dog may pay for its high rank
with a shorter life. Thus, this social system may actually include a counterintuitive outcome—a positive advantage, namely less stress and longer
life, for subordinates.

With the advent of noninvasive genetic sampling, the study of the
wolf's society has entered a new phase. An opportunity to sample an
entire pack presents itself in the summer when the members localize at
a rendezvous site. A team of wildlife biologists collected 155 to 296 scat
and hair samples from each of five rendezvous sites in two places in the
Salmon River Mountains (central Idaho) (Stenglein et al. 2011). They de-

tected 5 to 20 wolves per pack, for a total of 65 individuals. According to the genetic material in the scat samples, the members of each pack were closely related to each other. All packs included at least two years of off-spring from the current breeding pair.

I was surprised by a couple of these findings. First, three of the packs, or 60 percent, included additional breeding adults. That seems like a lot, although it is a small sample size. And second, the scat analysis method detected multiple cases of inbreeding, like parent-offspring and full-sibling pairings. This is surprising, exciting stuff. I can't wait for the next generation of insights into wolf society.

As Nancy and I were making our way across the Thorofare on our approach to the southeast arm of Yellowstone Lake, we saw a single wolf trot effortlessly across a meadow. It was leaving a fresh carcass that was already hosting several scavenging ravens and a bald eagle. Just enough time to break out the binocs, shuttle them back and forth, and break into a big smile. A brief 15-second view that left another inspiring Rocky Mountain memory...

CHAPTER 18

The Counterintuitive Grizzly

*In my first interview with a Sierra [grizzly] bear
we were frightened and embarrassed, both of us,
but the bear's behavior was better than mine.*

John Muir, *The Grizzly Bear: Portraits from Life*

WE REVELED in meadows of chest-high, full-blooming beargrass, dallied to inspect sulphur flower, and stepped carefully across stone stripes all along the climb to Cut Bank Pass (North Fork Cut Bank Creek Trail, Glacier National Park, northwestern Montana). Here, on the Continental Divide at the crest of the Lewis Range, we took a break amid cushion plants of pussy paws, ice-encrusted krummholz, and one fearless hoary marmot. We had been passing the binoculars back and forth, taking turns scanning the unnamed valley between Mount Morgan and Tinkham Mountain, when Nancy declared, "There's just gotta be a grizzly down there somewhere!" So it was only fair she spotted them first.

Just off a tongue of rock talus a sow foraged among shrubs, eating plant tops and pausing occasionally to sniff the air. On a flat rock nearby her twin cubs sat up on their haunches, lazily scanned back and forth, and then lay on their backs and rolled around. That ursine family entertained us for an hour.

The grizzly bear is known as a fast and powerful animal, a vicious cannibal. So back in the library I was surprised to learn that it grazes on grass, picks individual seeds from pine cones, and licks moths off rocks. I was most startled when I read—I had to read it twice!—that sows adopt cubs. I wondered, Would I be able to use evolutionary theory to reconcile the massive power and altruistic behavior in this beast?

Bears differentiated from dogs in the mid-Miocene or early Pliocene epoch, 14 to 5 million years ago (Storer and Tevis 1955). All fossil and modern species of the genus *Ursus*, which includes North America's polar, black, and grizzly bears, descended from the Auvergne bear, a small forest-dwelling bear that lived in Europe during the Pliocene, 5 to 2 million years ago (Schwartz et al. 2003). Auvergne bear begat Etruscan bear, which begat the Rockies' two modern bear species, grizzly and black, about a million years ago (Schullery 1992). The earliest fossils of the grizzly bear are 500,000 years old and were collected from the Zhoukoudian Cave in Asia (27 miles [45 km] southwest of Beijing, China). It colonized Alaska during the Wisconsin glacial period, 26,000 to 13,000 years ago, and then, as the continental ice sheet receded in the Early Holocene 11,000 years ago, the grizzly bear expanded into North America.

The range of the modern grizzly bear is classified as Holarctic, that is, it has been found across Earth's northern lands (Storer and Tevis 1955). Once upon a time in North America, grizzly bears lived from the Arctic Circle (Alaska) southward to northern Central America (southern Durango state, central Mexico) and from the Mississippi River westward to the Pacific Ocean. Assuming the descriptions in Lewis and Clark's journals represent the pre-Columbian condition, its present range of 20,000 square miles (52,000 km^2) is a mere 6 percent of what it was at that time (Botkin 2004).

Which Bear Is It?

If the number of times I was asked along the trail is any indication, people earnestly want to know which bear species they saw, black or grizzly? So here I offer some general distinguishing features (Gunther 1998).

Griz are bigger than blacks. The grizzly bear is about 3.5 feet (1.1 m) tall at the shoulder. In the Rockies, grizzly boars weigh 387 to 539 pounds (176–245 kg), and sows are 251 to 334 pounds (114–152 kg) (Schwartz et al. 2003). Black bears average 3 feet (0.9 m) at the shoulder; males weigh 210 to 315 pounds (95–134 kg), females 135 to 160 pounds (61–73 kg). Thus, within the same sex and region, griz are roughly 17 percent taller and almost twice as heavy as blacks.

Their fur colors are similar, so this feature is not as helpful. Grizzlies vary from black to blond, usually with white-tipped fur. Their silver-tipped, or grizzled, appearance is created by pale-tipped guard hairs (Schullery 1992; "Threatened Species" 1995). They may have a light brown girth band. Blacks can also vary from black to blond; about half are black with a tan muzzle.

Blacks have short, curved claws suited for climbing trees, whereas grizzlies' are longer and less curved. The grizzly's front claws, which are heavy, broad, and long (2.4 to 3.7 inches [6.1–9.4 cm]), function in digging for bulbs and rodents—and in fighting other grizzlies (Storer and Tevis 1955). The shoulder hump of the griz, possibly its most distinctive feature, betrays the large muscles that power its digging.

I'm guessing these diagnostics leave you less than completely satisfied. If they sound imprecise, I understand. We face the same problem trying to distinguish coyotes from wolves: both species of these respective pairs are closely related and variable. This leaves us with relative indicators, not certainty. Sorry.

Bears are stocky, sport tiny tails, and move about on stout legs and fully plantigrade feet (Storer and Tevis 1955). That last item means that they walk on the entire foot so the track shows the palm and toes. The grizzly bear's most common gait is an ambling walk with a side-to-side rolling of its body (Storer and Tevis 1955). We followed one such swaggering grizzly ass as it sauntered down the middle of a road—as if it owned it!—on the eastern slope of the Canadian Rockies (Kananaskis Country, southwestern Alberta). For fast travel a grizzly breaks into a gallop, like a loping horse. Explosively quick, a grizzly bear can accelerate from 0 to 30 miles (48 km) per hour faster than most high-performance sports cars.

Depending on the season, grizzly bears may favor riparian zones, wet seeps, alpine slabrock, or wet meadows. Plus, any time they're aboveground they seem to be attracted to avalanche chutes (Waller and Mace 1997). For grazing, Yellowstone grizzlies prefer open or young stands of lodgepole pine on wet and fertile sites (Mattson 1997b). The Clark Range (Waterton Lakes National Park, southwestern Alberta) is one of the few areas that offer all of North America's major bear foods, especially huckleberry and soopolallie, or buffaloberry (McLellan and Hovey 1995).

Grizzly bears are opportunistic omnivores with unspecialized digestive systems (F. Craighead 1979; Gunther 1994; "Threatened Species" 1995). Even though they lack a caecum, which functions to digest cellulose in other mammals, plant matter still makes up 80 percent of the grizzly's annual diet (Gunther 1994). They compensate for this alimentary shortcoming by foraging on vegetation at its most digestible state—while it's young and tender. Grizzlies eat many kinds of plants: mushrooms, grasses, cow parsnip, biscuitroot, clover, elk thistle, blueberries, buffaloberries, aspen buds, and pine nuts (Servheen 1983; Hamer et al. 1991; Gunther 1994; Mattson 1997a).

Through their foraging behavior, grizzly bears function as ecosystem engineers (Tardiff and Stanford 1998). Grizzlies dig for a variety of starchy plant roots, small mammals, and insects. A study of bears in the subalpine meadows of the Lewis Range, for instance, found that bears till the soil as they forage for glacier lily bulbs. Some digs covered more than 18 square yards (15 m²), of which 12 percent was actually disturbed. Some digs overlapped with previously dug areas. Bears turned over chunks of sod at a uniform depth, about four inches (10 cm), and then exposed and nipped off the bulbs. Some chunks of soil were left intact, so many glacier lily bulbs were left to resprout.

Bear digging created patches where the distribution and abundance of ground cover plants differed from those of adjacent undisturbed areas. After digging by bears, glacier lilies were the first plants to reappear and dominated the sites after disturbance, accounting for 41 percent of the total plant cover. Nitrate was higher in two-thirds of the digs compared to the level in intact meadow. Glacier lilies growing in digs had higher concentrations of nitrogen in their tissue and produced twice as many seeds as plants in undisturbed meadow. Higher nitrogen levels rendered the bulbs more nutritious and digestible. Soil that has been previously tilled is easier for bears to dig in. Thus, there are several reasons grizzlies return to dig in the same places. In this way, the bear's digging enhances the fitness of one of its preferred foods. Would it be a stretch to say that grizzly bears farm glacier lilies?

For meat, grizzly bears switch with the seasons (Gunther 1994; Green et al. 1997; Mattson 1997c). For example, in some places they eat winter-killed and weakened ungulates in the spring, newborn elk from May through June, adult elk in the summer, and army cutworm moths from late summer into midautumn. Other animal foods that griz will also eat include wood-boring larvae, yellow jacket nests, trout, snakes, and mice.

As you can tell, a dominant theme of the grizzly bear's diet is variety—among seasons, across the landscape, between adjacent sites. In some cases even different individual bears in the same place with access to the same foods eat different things. On Chichagof and Admiralty Islands in the Alexander Archipelago (southern Alaska), for example, most brown bears fed on salmon during late summer and autumn, yet one subpopulation of bears did not use salmon (Hildebrand et al. 1996). When spawning salmon arrived in late summer and autumn, most bears shifted to fishing, but the minority group maintained its land-based diet. Could this be a case of cultural inheritance? Did they stay with what they learned as cubs? Or was there a genetic component to their different tastes?

Nuts of the whitebark pine offer a high-quality food with energy levels equal to those of fleshy fruits (Mattson and Jonkel 1990). Whitebark nuts are good bear food for four other reasons. First, the seeds mature by August and are available until the bears enter winter-sleep, a state similar to hibernation but with a shallower metabolic depression. This corresponds with the bears' hyperphagic, or heavy-eating, state, a time of intense feeding during which they accumulate enough fat to sustain themselves during winter—and then through their springtime hypophagia. Second, whitebark pine nuts contain a highly digestible lipid that contributes to efficient fat accumulation. Third, the seeds are durable, that is, they have a long shelf life and provide a high-quality food through the upcoming spring and summer. And fourth, whitebark cones and seeds contain estrogenic compounds that may influence the sows' delayed implantation.

The intensity at which grizzly bears consume whitebark pine nuts varies through space and time, from near zero in the Mission Mountains off the southeastern edge of Flathead Lake (Flathead Indian Reservation, northwestern Montana), to a level that contributed to 28 percent of their fecal volume in Yellowstone (northwestern Wyoming) (Mattson and Jonkel 1990). In Yellowstone a bumper crop of whitebark pine nuts occurs in one of every six years; there was good seed production in two of seven years in the Scapegoat Mountains (70 miles [112 km] southeast of Polson, northwestern Montana). When they can get whitebark pine seeds grizzlies consume little else.

Grizzlies also steal pine nuts. Recall from the introduction that red squirrels cache seed-bearing whitebark pine cones in middens. Bears search out the squirrels' middens and excavate their cones (Mattson and

Reinhart 1997). Even moldy cones from deep within the pile are eaten. Bears are known to excavate squirrel middens in the Northern Rockies (northern Idaho and the East Front of Montana) and Central Rockies (Yellowstone National Park) and in the Sierra Nevada (Yosemite National Park, east-central California).

Right about now you may be trying to picture, like I was, how this beast gets seeds out of a pine cone. Griz have several ways. They may scrape away cone scales with their claws and then lap up the nuts with their tongues (Mattson and Jonkel 1990). Or they can hold the cones between their paws, go around the cone with their teeth and strip the shells off the nuts, spit the shells out, and then go around one more time extracting the nuts in one pass. This second method doesn't take long— just a few seconds per cone. And then there's a third way: the bear crushes the cones with its paws or breaks them in its jaws, spreads out the cone debris with its paws or muzzle, delicately licks up the nuts, and expels the cone scales out the side of its mouth. All gingerly movements for such a massive animal!

As I've said, in some places and in some years when the whitebark pine is masting, that is, producing heavy seed crops, pre-winter-sleeping grizzlies feed from August through October almost entirely on pine nuts. Because whitebark pines generally occur in the subalpine, mainly in remote areas, a large nut crop keeps the bears where they are less likely to encounter humans. One study found that during years with small whitebark seed crops, management trapping of grizzlies was 6.2 times higher, mortality of adult females 2.3 times higher, and mortality of subadult males 3.3 times higher than normal (Mattson et al. 1992), presumably because the bears ranged closer to human facilities. Further, in years of nut crop failure, grizzlies are twice as likely to turn up near buildings (Mattson and Jonkel 1990).

The abundance of whitebark pine nuts also impacts the bear's populations. Compared to their mortality rate in mast years, mortality in Yellowstone grizzlies is double in years when the whitebark crop fails (Pease and Mattson 1999). Consequently, some bear populations decline after the crop fails and increase after mast years. In order of importance, over the two decades between 1975 and 1995, grizzly bear mortality rates were correlated with season, whitebark nut crop, sex, whether they had ever been trapped for management purposes, and age. Thus, fluctuations in the size of the whitebark pine's nut crop explain a lot of the variation in the Yellowstone grizzly's population. An underlying reason for this pattern is that the abundance of whitebark nuts is positively correlated with the bear's litter size (Schwartz et al. 2006).

Grizzly bears have historically congregated during July through September on McDonald Peak in the Mission Mountains and in the headwaters of the South Fork of the Flathead River (Scapegoat Wilderness) (both in northwestern Montana) to feed on insects, specifically dense aggregations of ladybird beetles and army cutworm moths (Klaver et al. 1986).

Yellowstone grizzlies also feed on massed insects above treeline in the Absaroka Range. In these alpine areas, they feed on insect aggregations at 6 known talus sites and are suspected to do so at 12 other locations (Mattson et al. 1991). These sites tend to be above 11,055 feet (3350 m) in elevation, offer southern or western aspects, and are on slopes steeper than 30 degrees. At these places the bears eat adult army cutworm moths almost exclusively. Sows with cubs and subadult grizzlies are underrepresented at these places, probably because they're avoiding boars (Mattson and Jonkel 1990). Grizzlies also seek aggregations of ladybird beetles or army cutworm moths in the Lewis Range and East Front (northwestern Montana) (White et al. 1998). Finally, in a few places, grizzlies forage on a surprising insect: they pick Rocky Mountain locusts, a species of extinct grasshopper, out of melting glaciers. Now that's an unexpected consequence of climate change!

During July adult army cutworm moths fly from low-lying farmlands up into the mountains, where they feed on alpine flowers. The fat content of the abdomen of these soft-bodied, highly digestible insects can reach 64 percent (Mattson et al. 1991). The moths are abundant during the bear's hyperphagia. A grizzly bear can consume up to 1,700 moths per hour, which can translate to 40,000 moths a day (White et al. 1999). One month of moth eating can yield 300,000 calories (1,255,230 J). By mid-October the leftover moths return to lower lands to lay their eggs.

Within any given area individual grizzly bears know each other, form a social hierarchy in which each animal recognizes its own position, and behave accordingly (F. Craighead 1979). Individual recognition is based mainly on scent and to a lesser degree on sight. At close range bears communicate their intent through the nature of their walk, the position of their ears, and via head, body, and mouth movements.

An individual's rank changes through time. For example, although the rank of a particular boar may not shift drastically from one season to the next, over a longer stretch the vigorous young males move upward in position as they grow in size and strength. Sows with cubs are more aggressive than barren ones; they will attack boars that approach them and their cubs, and thereby temporarily occupy high positions.

Each grizzly bear roams through a home range (F. Craighead 1979). In the Swan Range (northwestern Montana), which is part of the Kootenay Mountains, the annual home ranges of adult males and females were 307 square miles (768 km^2) and 50 square miles (125 km^2), respectively (Mace and Waller 1997). Movement patterns can be extremely variable among and within populations. The seasonal, annual, and life ranges of bears that use dependable, high-quality foods are generally smaller—for example, 10 to 80 square miles (25–200 km^2)—than those of bears in places without dependable concentrated foods—for example, 80 to 760 square miles (200–1900 km^2) (Schwartz et al. 2003). Home ranges also differ between the sexes: males cover 46 to 3,268 square miles (115–8171 km^2) and females range over 9.6 to 974 square miles (24–2435 km^2).

Stressed Teeth

In the 1880s, about 10 years after the establishment of Yellowstone National Park, grizzly bears began feeding at the park's garbage dumps (Haroldson et al. 2008). After more than 80 years of supplementing the bears' food, the dumps were permanently closed between 1968 and 1979. Were the dump closures traumatic for the bears? An early part of the answer is that after this resource was fenced off, the bears died at a higher rate and increased their annual home range areas more than fivefold (Badyaev 1998).

More recently we have learned another part of the answer. Fluctuating asymmetry, a pattern of bilateral variation in a sample of individuals, can be used to estimate the effects of developmental accidents (Van Valen 1962). The asymmetry of bilateral traits indicates an individual's resistance to stress because it results from the inability to develop in precisely determined paths.

A behavioral ecologist examined how closing the dump affected developmental stability by comparing the dentition of bears born before and after dump closure. Developmental stability of canine teeth, which are under directional sexual selection for increased size in males, was more responsive to environmental stress compared to that of male premolars or female dentition, which are under stabilizing selection (Badyaev 1998). That is, the developmental stability of canines responded more to stress than did the other teeth.

The increase in relative asymmetry in male canines during the post-closure period wasn't the only thing that changed. Canines, premolars, and skull length were also smaller in males born after the dump closed.

Teeth revealed that closing the dumps was traumatic. This specific anthropogenic stress may represent an extreme case of the occasional food shortages that wild bears incur naturally. Mast and berry crop failures, low salmon runs, and scarce food after fire are known to affect the growth, mortality, and fecundity of bears. The record's in the teeth.

Grizzlies mate from May through July. In Yellowstone, sows mate for the first time at 3.5 to 5 years of age, thereafter every 2 or more years (Knight and Eberhardt 1984). In one type of courtship a pair becomes isolated on a high point, and the male then herds the female by remaining below her and displacing her upslope when she tries to descend (Hamer and Herrero 1990; Brady and Hamer 1992). These movements are interpreted as the male's attempt to sexually monopolize an estrous female and as the female's testing of the male's vigor. Over the course of a month a dominant boar may exert himself in several strenuous fights and sexual encounters—after which he can be completely exhausted (F. Craighead 1979).

The grizzly bear's mating system is classified as polygamous (Steyaert et al. 2012), defined as mating with multiple partners. During a given mating season the adults of both sexes mate a variable number of times with a variable number of partners. Females usually mate with three or four males; a few males may mate with up to eight females, but many obtain no matings.

A genetic study of 30 grizzly families in Alaska revealed that each cub in a litter can be sired by a different boar (Craighead et al. 1995). No single male was responsible for more than 11 percent of the offspring, and no more than 49 percent of the mature males bred successfully. Thus, there is large variation in the reproductive success of the males within a grizzly population. This indicates that the male-male competition component of sexual selection is intense, a behavioral constraint with interesting consequences, as we'll see in a bit.

Unlike those of most mammals, the embryos of bears do not immediately implant in the wall of the uterus; rather, they remain unattached in embryonic arrest (Ramsay and Dunbrack 1986; Steyaert et al. 2012). Implantation is delayed for about five months, until the sow enters her den in the autumn (F. Craighead 1979). Gestation is only six to eight weeks long, which seems adaptive for a fasting, winter-sleeping animal. From mid-January to early February, sows give birth to naked, blind, helpless neonates; they are eight inches (20 cm) long and weigh up to 12 ounces (336 g) (Biel 1996).

A bear's litter mass is one-third to one-tenth that of similar-sized mammals (Ramsay and Dunbrack 1986), a comparatively tiny litter weight that, like the short gestation, reflects the sow's inability to meet the needs of fetal metabolism while she's in a state of winter dormancy without food.

Griz's winter den, blanketed by snow except for a small breathing hole, is well insulated (Ramsay and Dunbrack 1986). Cubs nurse while nestled in their mother's fur. By the time the family emerges in the spring the cubs have reached the weight expected of similar-sized mammals. This catch-up in growth suggests an analogy between the maternity den and the mammalian uterus.

The timing of den entry and the duration of winter-sleep are roughly correlated with latitude (Schwartz et al. 2003). In the north, grizzlies enter dens earlier and remain inside longer than they do at more southerly latitudes. For example, average denning periods were 203 days at 62°N, in the southern Selwyn Mountains (southeastern Yukon Territory), and 136 days at 44°N, in the northern Teton Range (northern Grand Teton National Park, northwestern Wyoming).

In their den the cubs do not enter a deep winter-sleep, like the sows; rather, they sleep at normal metabolic levels (Biel 1996). The cubs nurse and grow quickly. By 40 days of age they are 12 inches (30 cm) long and weigh two pounds (0.9 kg), their eyes are open, and their milk teeth are erupting. When they emerge in the spring, cubs weigh five to eight pounds (2.3–3.6 kg), about the size of a rabbit. Cubs nurse until August and then begin taking solid food. In their first autumn, at 20 to 40 pounds (9–18 kg) each, the cubs enter the den with their mothers. In June of the next year the sow stops producing milk, weans the yearlings, and chases them off. The duration of lactation varies widely, but 1.5 to 2 years is common. By the end of their second year cubs weigh 100 to 200 pounds (45–90 kg) and den with each other but apart from their mother. By their third summer the cubs are pursuing separate lives.

Even though sows provide a vigilant, vigorous defense, some grizzly boars do kill cubs (F. Craighead 1979; Mattson et al. 1992; Steyaert et al. 2012). Can infanticide possibly be adaptive? An initial hint comes from the observation that infanticide occurs during specific seasons. First-litter mothers incurred higher odds of losing their cub(s) than did multilitter sows (Zedrosser et al. 2009). The critical times for these first-time sows to lose their cubs were the premating season, which spanned from birth to just after leaving the den, and the mating season. During these two periods cubs were lost due to different reasons. Before the mating season, food conditions seemed to be the biggest cause, whereas during the mating season the main reason was infanticide by boars.

The hypothesis of sexually selected infanticide posits that the killing of cubs is a male adaptation (Bellemain et al. 2006a). However, because this behavior does not benefit females, sows are expected to have evolved counterstrategies that protect their cubs from infanticidal boars (Steyaert et al. 2012). Some female behaviors, like aggressive defense, leaving the group, and showing pseudoestrus and mating, mitigate the boars' killing of their young (Packer and Pusey 1983). However, when the death of her offspring is inevitable a sow may minimize her long-term fitness loss by terminating her pregnancy or abandoning her infant.

A team of ethologists used field observations and genetic tests to describe the mating strategies used by both sexes of brown bears in Scandinavia (Sweden and Norway) (Bellemain et al. 2006a). The results supported the sexually selected infanticide hypothesis: (1) infanticide shortened the time to the mother's next estrus, (2) infanticidal boars were not the fathers of the killed cubs, (3) the perpetrators of infanticide sired the next litter, and (4) all of the cases of infanticide occurred during the mating season. Contrary to expectation, resident adult males commonly committed infanticide, but perhaps they avoided killing the cubs of females they had mated with.

Sows have their own counterstrategy. DNA tests showed that at least 14.5 percent of litters with at least two cubs resulted from multiple paternity; up to 28 percent of litters with at least three cubs were also the product of more than one father (Bellemain et al. 2006a). Female promiscuity, which may confuse a male as to his paternity, can be interpreted as a female adaptation that discourages infanticide. Paternity confusion counters infanticide, either directly by mate recognition or indirectly by multiple paternity.

Implementing this counterstrategy forces a grizzly sow to make a choice. Should she mate with a high-quality boar based on his phenotype or with a potentially infanticidal male as a counterstrategy to infanticide? Among the males that were available to females, the largest, most heterozygous, least inbred, and geographically nearest males were more often the fathers of the female's next litter (Bellemain et al. 2006b). These observations suggest that females select the closest males as a counterstrategy to infanticide. Further, sows seemed to exercise a postcopulatory cryptic choice. That is, even though females allow themselves to be bred by potentially infanticidal boars, they may select for fertilization the sperm of a different, more preferred male, one they choose based on inferred genetic quality. A female's possible compromise, then, may be to allow insemination by an infanticidal boar but fertilization by a high-quality male. This provocative hypothesis needs more testing.

Infanticide is a prerequisite of cannibalism (Mattson and Reinhart 1995). Cannibalism, defined as intraspecific predation, is a normal behavior in a wide variety of animals (Fox 1975). In mammals infanticide occurs regularly in rodents, lions, and several primate species. In these mammals, males kill infants of unfamiliar females when they first encounter them but subsequently are unlikely to kill their own genetic offspring. Several factors, like low food supply, high population density, the availability of vulnerable individuals, high stress, and flight behavior, can trigger a cannibalistic strike. Some of these stimuli may sound familiar from the stories of cannibalism in Mormon crickets and axolotls.

So here's an evolutionary interpretation of infanticide in the grizzly bear. Infanticide contributes to male reproductive success in three ways: it stops the female from investing in the offspring of another male; speeds the female's return to sexual receptivity; and, coupled with cannibalism, yields a protein-rich food.

※

Once upon a time in a land far away, specifically in the spring of 1971 in Alaska, a grizzly sow emerged from her den (Tait 1980). A few days later one dead and one live cub were left at the site. The sow had deserted her cubs, possibly because of human smell and noise. At least two other incidents of cub abandonment have been reported in the Northern Rockies (Montana). Is cub abandonment an unusual behavioral pathology or could it possibly be an adaptation?

When we consider how life histories have evolved, we assume that an organism's reproductive strategy involves a trade-off in allocating resources to current versus future reproduction (Williams 1966; Tait 1980). It is possible that a sow could increase her lifetime fitness by rejecting her current cub and having a larger litter in her next breeding season. If this is true, cub abandonment could contribute to individual reproductive success.

For female grizzlies along the McNeil River (Alaska), the ratio of current cost to future benefit was met, so abandonment there was interpreted as an adaptation (Tait 1980). For bears in the more southerly Lewis Range, though, smaller litter sizes precluded desertion as an adaptive tactic in the absence of adoption. In short, if a sow and her cub are threatened but she has good odds of producing two or three cubs the next year, abandoning today's cubs may yield greater reproductive success in the long run.

A few grizzlies have been seen pursuing a contrasting strategy—adoption. The recruitment and care of dependent young from another parent have been confirmed in only a few mammals (Wilson 1975; Rapaport and Haight 1987). Male African wild dogs care for pups after their mother has died. Their small pack size makes it probable that males are close relatives. Male hamadryas baboons take on juvenile females, a tactic for accumulating a harem; adult chimpanzees foster young orphaned siblings; and, of course, humans adopt unrelated babies.

In the upper reaches of Alum Creek (Yellowstone National Park), either two grizzly sows occasionally switched cubs or the cubs changed mothers (F. Craighead 1979). In some places one or more cubs followed one sow for a while and then a few days later kept to the other sow. In another study, permanent cub adoption occurred in 3 (3 percent) of 104 litters (Barnes and Smith 1993). These four adopted cubs represented less than 2 percent of the 254 cubs originally identified in litters. In another case a female grizzly with a cub less than a year old permanently adopted another new cub whose mother had died, and these two cubs were then weaned as two-year-olds (Barnes and Smith 1993). The Yellowstone bear named Owl Face was the first grizzly sow ever confirmed to have adopted the cubs of another female (F. Craighead 1979). These and other anecdotes of adoption in bears (Alt 1984; Haroldson et al. 2008) provoke some questions: What is the adaptive significance of adoption by female grizzly bears? Does adoption happen between sisters? Is kin selection at play here? I hope someone is working on these questions.

I saw my first grizzly bear in the Lewis Range in 1968. Even though the animal was a quarter mile away and walking in the other direction, I still remember feeling unsettled, like I was trespassing on its trail—and I can still recall that wave of awe that swept over me. Some Native Americans who held the grizzly bear sacred felt the same way (F. Craighead 1979). The youth of the Nez Perce found strength in the spirit of the grizzly bear.

While following fresh grizzly prints through the charred landscapes of Yellowstone, I was surprised by flashbacks—of being on patrol in Vietnam, scanning back and forth like a metronome, wary of what is around this corner, on the other side of that thicket. This sense of being thrown back into combat surfaced unbidden as we hiked on a backcountry trail threading its way through fallen and cut boles, a path that functioned as a long, thin game concentrator. Most humbling was a boar's huge hind pawprint—13½ inches (34.3 cm) long from claw tip to heel butt, compared to normal rear prints of about 10 inches (25 cm) long (Halfpenny 2001)—that we encountered on the trail as we returned from Slough Creek (Buffalo Plateau Trail). Raw power lingered in that fresh track. There is value in being humbled by the Great Bear, of experiencing the insecurity that comes with being a prey item. Of "putting yourself out there." It's definitely a way to learn about yourself.

The grizzly bear is the most powerful terrestrial predator in North America, yet it grazes clover and laps insects. Boars practice infanticide, and sows can both abandon and adopt cubs. Welcome to the counterintuitive grizzly.

CHAPTER 19

The Bearded Climber

Having only a scrap of momentum behind them
they reached out, hooked one hoof on an overhead shelf,
and hauled themselves up by it alone.

Douglas Chadwick, *A Beast the Color of Winter:*
The Mountain Goat Observed

As I mentioned in the ptarmigan story, in 1968 I summered in the Mission Range along the eastern shore of Flathead Lake (University of Montana Biological Station, near Bigfork, northwestern Montana). Ostensibly there to study ornithology, specifically hummingbirds, I also spent several long weekends adventuring in the Lewis Range (Glacier National Park, northwestern Montana). It was there I discovered the form of ecosystem immersion called backpacking. On one of those treks I lingered in Gunsight Pass, hanging between Sperry and Jackson Glaciers along the Continental Divide (St. Mary River Trail). The mountain goats were putting on a show—muscular billies struck majestic poses on angular rocks, shaggy nannies rubbed their fur onto krummholz, kids bounded among boulders. All set against the backdrop of Lake Ellen Wilson, which in turn was nestled in a classic glacier-sculpted valley. I look back on that episode as one of the formative experiences of my life as an ecologist.

Mountain goats live on high, treeless, windy, steep rocks. For them to successfully eat, keep warm, and reproduce in these alpine places, evolution has surely stretched mammalian adaptations to extremes. How do mountain goats cling to life?

The mountain goat is actually not a true goat in the genus *Capra*; rather, it is assigned to the Rupicaprini tribe, which also includes the European chamois (Milne and Milne 1962; Brooks 1967; Chadwick 1983). And rupicaprids, in turn, are assigned to the family Bovidae with bison, African antelopes, and the domestic cow. The mountain goat has been assigned to various placements within the tribe and has stubbornly resisted a consistent phylogenetic position (Winnie 1996; Festa-Bianchet and Cote 2008; Shafer and Hall 2010).

Rupicaprids have been around since the early Miocene epoch, 20 million years ago. After arising in the Himalayas an ancestral rupicaprid crossed Beringia during the Pleistocene, perhaps 40,000 years ago (Festa-Bianchet and Cote 2008). Pressures from predators and other grazing species may have pushed the original American rupicaprid into higher, steeper places. The earliest mountain goat fossil is at least 100,000 years old. During cold phases the species extended its range southward along the Western Cordillera into the northern reaches of the Sierra Madre Occidental (north-central Mexico). Since then the climate has warmed, so natural populations of the modern mountain goat occur from Alaska southward into both the Pacific Northwest (Washington) and Northern Rockies (Idaho and Montana). At the southern end of their range they live near and above treeline but in the north they venture down to sea level.

Mountain goats are 3.5 feet (1.1 m) tall and feature a rectangular torso perched on four short legs. They have a small head, humped shoulders, a shaggy white coat with a full beard, and hooves adapted for jumping on uneven terrain (Brooks 1967; Walker 1973). Superficially they look like a shaggy white goat. Their skull is thin boned and light compared to the massive cranium of bighorn sheep (Chadwick 1983). As hinted by this chapter's epigraph, they show tremendously developed shoulder muscles. Billies average 240 pounds (108 kg), nannies 180 pounds (81 kg) (Winnie 1996).

Both male and female mountain goats feature small, spiky, sharp horns that are 8 to 11 inches (20–28 cm) long (Milne and Milne 1962; Chadwick 1983). A true horn consists of an inner core of bone that is an extension of the skull's frontal bone, the piece underlying the mammalian forehead. The bony core is permanent, not deciduous like antlers, and continues to grow throughout life. Encasing the core is a sheath of keratin, an epidermal fingernail-like covering derived from fused hair.

In mountain goats, horns are important social organs (Chadwick 1983; Cote et al. 1998; Festa-Bianchet and Cote 2008). Billies feature thicker, more gradually sweeping, and longer horns than similar-sized nannies. In both genders the length and circumference of the horns are positively correlated with body mass, chest girth, and hind foot length. As you'll see in a bit, among males body mass is probably more important than horn size for mating success.

Mountain goats feature several adaptations to alpine conditions (Chadwick 1983; Winnie 1996). Dense, fine wool underlies long, thick guard hairs. While they're shedding in the summer the animals look bedraggled. Goats rub against stiff plants and leave tufts of loose fur hanging in the vegetation. In terms of body shape mountain goats are comparatively flat and wide at the base, creating a low center of gravity. Their large forequarters are suited for quick pivoting and hoisting themselves up cliffs. They have strong, compact hindquarters. The lateral flex of the leg joints allows the angle of the hooves to conform to the slope of the terrain, a fit that maximizes surface contact.

In terms of geography and elevation, the mammal whose natural distribution is closest to the mountain goat's is another Pleistocene relict, the hoary marmot (Chadwick 1983). Sometimes marmots and goat kids follow one another, play together, and rest side by side—a pleasing image that captures a long-shared evolutionary history. This picture, however, gives me an opportunity to make a general point: just because two species have experienced similar evolutionary pressures in a common place does not necessarily mean they have coevolved. I suspect that the hoary marmot and mountain goat do not feature any adaptations that have been shaped by mutual coevolution.

Throughout glaciated North America there was a period called the hypsithermal interval, roughly 9,000 to 5,000 years ago, when the climate was warmer, and usually much drier, than it is today. During the hypsithermal, vegetation zones shifted upward, treelines ascended, and alpine patches dwindled. These habitat constrictions seem to have delivered today's patchy distributions of the mountain goat and hoary marmot. The evidence suggests that the goats and marmots spread into their present ranges from the south when the Cordilleran Ice Sheet melted, and then they died out in low-lying places during the hypsithermal.

Today's mountain goat still lives under Pleistocene conditions, intimately bound to cold winters, permanent snowfields, and the droughtiness of alpine habitats. With its vast exposures of rock strata stacked like blocks, the Lewis Range is prime mountain goat country. The goats prefer alpine meadows, forb-dominated outcrops, and mineral licks on slopes greater than 40 degrees mixed with vertical or near-vertical cliffs (Singer and Doherety 1985; Demarchi et al. 2000). Mountain goats do not stay where the average daily summer temperature gets above 60°F (15°C).

Although grasses and grasslike plants are major winter forages, this efficient herbivore will eat any plant that grows in its habitat, including lichens, sedges, flowering plants, and trees (Adams and Bailey 1983; Chadwick 1983; Winnie 1996). As a ruminant it can extract nutrients from twigs and tough alpine plants (Milne and Milne 1962).

Near the southern end of the Lewis Range (2.5 miles [4 km] east of the Walton Ranger Station, which, by the way, was the takeout of our Waterton-Glacier through-hike), the outside cutting edge of the Middle Fork of the Flathead River has exposed a bank of gray clay with minerals like gypsum, kieserite, and sulfates ("Goat Lick Overlook" undated). Goats come from all around to eat the minerals. Calcium, potassium, and magnesium in the lick may help replace minerals lost from their bones during winter (Singer and Doherety 1985). The licks also provide carbonates that buffer the pH of the rumen after their food changes in the spring from fibrous winter forage to lush spring growth (Ayotte et al. 2006). Young goats learn the trails to the licks from their elders. These licks are so important that their geographic distribution influences the movements of populations of mountain goats and other ungulates.

When they are at least two and a half years old, male mountain goats mature and take part in the rut, which runs from late October into early December (Chadwick 1983). During this mating season billies compete by poking each other in the rear. The so-called dermal shield, a patch of tough skin on the rump nearly an inch (2.5 cm) thick, protects the billies from each other's sharp horns.

In polygynous ungulates the rut imposes a trade-off between time spent on maintenance and time devoted to reproduction; one specific cost is less foraging time (Pelletier et al. 2009). Simply put, breeding males are predicted to pay a bodily price during the rut because they eat less. Field observations on the mountain goat are consistent with this so-called foraging constraint hypothesis. During the period of the prerut to the rut, sexually active males spend less time foraging and lying down because they spend more time at mating-related activities. This phase is so stressful that it has earned its own name, rut-induced hypophagia.

The lengths of mountain goat horns exhibit fluctuating asymmetry (Cote and Festa-Bianchet 2001b), a concept I introduced in the grizzly bear story. As a reminder, fluctuating asymmetry is a population condition in which individuals lack identical left and right sides, and the side that is abnormal varies randomly among individuals. In the eastern foothills of the Canadian Rockies, specifically at Caw Ridge in the Front Range (18 miles [30 km] northwest of Grande Cache, west-central Alberta), greater horn symmetry characterized six classes of mountain goats: juvenile (one- and two-year-old) males, adult females in good condition, heavy adult females, dominant females, females that produced an offspring the year they were captured, and females with high long-term reproductive success. Note that adult males are not on the list. These results suggest that the asymmetry of horn length indicates individual quality in females, but not in adult males. This reinforces my previous statement that horns are not a primary determinant of mating success in male mountain goats.

So if horns are not important in mating, what mating tactics do male mountain goats use? During three ruts at Caw Ridge a team of mammalogists studied a marked population to determine how age and social rank affected the formation of consort pairs (Mainguy et al. 2008). Think of a consort pair as a temporary male-female alliance. Some males participated in coursing, an alternative mating behavior that consists of trying to disrupt a consort pair in order to gain temporary access to the female, often by chasing her. Males in consort pairs were at least four years old and most of them, 86 percent, were in the top half of the dominance hierarchy. The age and social rank of males were positively related to the age of females and to the total number of young produced by the tended female. Ninety-one percent of all matings were between males and females engaged in consort pairs. Only rarely did a coursing male successfully mate a female. These results suggest that although coursing males had a little mating success, consort pairs, which consisted of older, dominant males and experienced females, produced most of the offspring.

A few females give birth at three years of age, but most do not reproduce until they are five (Festa-Bianchet et al. 1993). High-quality nannies, based on their longevity, success in the previous breeding opportunity, body mass, and social rank, were more likely to reproduce compared to low-quality females (Hamel et al. 2009a). Low-quality females were also less likely to reproduce two years in a row.

Given this variation among females, what causes some to be superior breeders? For one thing, environmental conditions early in life shape a female's reproductive performance. At Caw Ridge the quality of individual female mountain goats, as measured by their mean annual reproductive success over a lifetime, was reduced by unfavorable weather, low resource availability, and high population density during the year of their birth (Hamel et al. 2009b). Statistically, early-life conditions accounted for 35 to 55 percent of the variation in individual female quality. Thus, variation in female fitness reflects partly the environmental conditions of early life. And here's another factor: milk is expensive. The high energetic costs of lactation can incur trade-offs with other life-history traits, especially in young females that reproduce while they are still growing.

Within the Caw Ridge population births were highly synchronized, with 80 percent of the kids born within two weeks of the first birth (Cote and Festa-Bianchet 2001a). Compared to a mother's firstborn offspring, kids born to nannies with previous breeding experience were heavier during their first summer. Early-born kids were heavier than the later born. This kind of variation is important because at one year of age heavy females survived better than light ones. These results suggest that female mountain goats have a short time window—a brief period with the most productive forage—in which to give birth to a kid that will have decent odds of living through its first winter.

Nannies pay a price for having a kid. One of the assumptions in the theory of life-history evolution is that an investment in one function, like growth, maintenance, or reproduction, causes a lower allocation to one or both of the other functions (Williams 1966). For example, shunting nutrients to a growing fetus may cause a lessening investment in the mother's somatic tissues. To assess whether reproduction affects the survival and future reproduction of female mountain goats, a team of ecologists analyzed 18 years of longitudinal data from the marked goats at Caw Ridge (Hamel et al. 2010). Reproduction did, in fact, reduce the odds of parturition and offspring survival in the following year; however, female survival was independent of previous reproduction. These findings hint that natural selection has favored the long-term survival of females over the life of their current offspring.

A life-history trade-off also manifests between offspring mass and the mother's subsequent reproduction. When resources are limited, current maternal investment should reduce subsequent reproductive success or survival. At Caw Ridge ecologists used longitudinal data collected from marked females between 1990 and 2009 to assess whether offspring mass affected maternal survival and future reproduction (Hamel et al. 2011). Offspring mass at weaning was positively correlated with survival of old nannies, suggesting that mothers produced lighter kids, and hence allocated lower reproductive effort, in their last breeding season. Offspring mass did not affect survival of young and prime-aged mothers, but females that weaned heavy offspring incurred lower odds of subsequent reproduction in years of low population density. Because offspring survival is correlated with weaning mass, the nannies' allocation to reproduction involves a trade-off between current and future fitness. These results suggest that in this iteroparous mammal, allocation to current offspring mass reduces the odds of subsequent reproduction.

After a gestation of six months, nannies give birth to one kid, sometimes two, in late May or early June (Chadwick 1983). Ten minutes after birth the agile kids are standing; they're jumping within 30 minutes; and one-day-old kids climb on rocks, logs, and their nannies. Two-day-old kids spin and butt in ways that suggest the combat between billies. By day four, kids are biting off plant stalks and keeping up with their nannies over broken terrain. Kids are weaned at four weeks and stay with their mothers for 10 or 11 months.

As a species that typically lives in small populations and conforms to a polygynous mating system, the mountain goat could be vulnerable to the deleterious effects of inbreeding. In a long-term study at Caw Ridge a team of ecologists was able to infer relatedness from genetic markers (Mainguy et al. 2009). Breeding pairs producing offspring that survived to one year of age were less genetically related than expected under random mating. Parental relatedness was negatively correlated with offspring heterozygosity. Further, heterozygous yearlings experienced higher survival to two years of age. Kids that survived to yearling age were produced mainly by less genetically related parents. These findings confirm that, like living things in general, mountain goats avoid inbreeding depression by mating with less related individuals because the offspring of such outbred matings have higher fitness.

Young male mountain goats leave their natal groups, but young females stay. Some behaviorists have proposed that the males leave spontaneously or are expelled by the aggressive behavior of adult females (Romeo et al. 1997). At Caw Ridge a team of animal behaviorists found that two- and three-year-old females received 50 percent more threats than males, specifically 2.4 versus 1.6 threats per hour, respectively. Therefore, adult females do not force young males from the group. So the reason males leave is a mystery.

Kids stay with their nannies for varying lengths of time (Chadwick 1983). A 33-year study of wild mountain goats uncovered a relationship between climate and the length of time nannies retain their offspring (Dane 2002). Harsh weather depresses the production of forage plants, and the consequent limited food availability requires mothers to extend parental care for longer periods, which limits them to breeding every other year. This kind of reproductive flexibility contributes to individual reproductive success in the alpine's unpredictable environment.

Most mountain goats live in pairs, but large groups, with up to 50 animals, do sometimes occur (von Elsner-Schack 1986). Local herds consist of several bands plus a few solitary individuals. A typical goat band contains a nanny, a kid, and perhaps one or two yearlings and two-year-olds. Although a band may look superficially like a family unit, the movements of marked goats have surprised us: bands are actually loose associations of shifting individuals (Chadwick 1983).

Mountain goat society is organized as a dominance hierarchy in which each individual defends a mobile personal space. Rank is straight-forward: big goats dominate small ones (Chadwick 1983). Body size, physical strength, and horn size increase with age, so young goats usually yield to older ones. An individual typically takes part in three or four conflicts per hour (Chadwick 1997)—every day, all year long! The odds of winning one of these encounters are strongly and positively related to age (Cote 2000b).

In an unhunted population of mountain goats in the Canadian Rockies (west-central Alberta), females interacted aggressively more often than other ungulate species. Further, the goats' dominance ranks were less stable through time and less age related (Fournier and Festa-Bianchet 1995). Reversals in position are frequent, and individual ranks change between years. An individual's position one year is not a good predictor of its rank the next year. But here's a curious result: the best morphological predictor of rank is horn length in some years and body mass in others. I'm surprised that age is only a weak predictor of dominance status. Collectively, these observations suggest that any particular mountain goat hierarchy is ephemeral, that it responds to frequent contingencies. Shifting band membership and changing ranks mean that mountain goat society is loose and flexible.

As I've said, mountain goats fight each other (Chadwick 1983, 1997). In more than 95 percent of the conflicts the adults decide whose personal space is preeminent without touching one another. But threats would lose their effectiveness if the daggers weren't brought into action every so often. Goats use their horns as both defensive and offensive weapons. Dominance battles are head-to-tail (Winnie 1996). They attempt to gore each other in twirling, horn-to-rump conflicts. Each billy is protected by its dermal shield, which is so tough that some Indians fashioned it into breastplates for deflecting arrows.

Dominance relationships are important in mountain goat society (Cote 2000b). In the Canadian Rockies (west-central Alberta), an animal behaviorist studied the aggressive behavior of 40 marked adult females over four years. The females were organized in a linear hierarchy in which rank was related to age but not to body mass, horn length, or body size. Aggressiveness toward younger adult females increased with both age and social rank. The rank of adult daughters was determined by their age, not by their mothers' rank.

From one year to the next a band keeps to the same seasonal ranges (Chadwick 1983), each of which is labeled with a network of obvious paths. The oldest goat's knowledge of the areas is passed on to younger ones. A nanny is faithful to her traditional home range year after year, but at about three years of age billies move to a separate range. Thereafter, males seldom associate with females outside the rutting season. Differences in food preferences, foraging behavior, habitat selection, or social preferences have been implicated in this sexual segregation.

Square Butte (Chouteau County, north-central Montana), an isolated volcanic formation rising from the prairie, supports a high density of mountain goats (J. Williams 1999). From the butte, goats disperse across 2.4 miles (4 km) of low-lying prairie to two other high-elevation habitats. As we've seen in other places, males are more likely to disperse than females; juveniles, which are one to three years old, are more likely to disperse than adults. Because the focus of competition among males is usually access to females, dispersal of males can be triggered by limited breeding opportunities, whereas for females it takes low forage to stimulate dispersal.

Mountain goats succumb to a variety of forces. Survival to one year of age averages 60 percent (Festa-Bianchet et al. 1993). Because of their high surface-to-volume ratio, kids are particularly vulnerable during severe winters. At least half of the yearlings lost from the population are killed by predators. Most mortality of kids occurs from September into November and appears to be due to predation by wolves, cougars, and grizzly bears. A 10-year-old mountain goat is nearing the end of its natural life. Teeth wear down to the gumline, and some goats are killed by avalanches, others fall to their death, and many starve in winter. Overall, predation is a major source of mortality of young goats, while low nutrients retard growth and limit the reproductive performance of adults.

Wildlife biologists evaluated the roles of sex and age, as well as the winter and summer climates, on the odds of mountain goat survival in coastal Alaska (White et al. 2011). Using 31 years of data collected from 279 radio-marked goats in nine study areas, they found that old animals, defined as nine years and older, incurred lower survival than younger ones. Males had lower survival than females, though differences existed only among prime-aged adults, which were five to eight years old, and old goats. Winter exerted the strongest impact on survival. Old animals were more sensitive to winter's effects than young or prime-aged animals. These findings reveal that the integrated effects of climate, sex, and age affect the survival of mountain goats.

While foraging, a mountain goat exposes itself to predators. So how do the nannies balance foraging and safety? A team of zoologists assessed the kind and amount of vegetation relative to the distance to escape terrain (Hamel and Cote 2007). They found that females of all reproductive categories spent more time foraging near steep rocks than they did away from them. In June, a time when offspring were vulnerable to predators, nannies with kids foraged 66 feet (20 m) closer to escape terrain than barren females. The amount of forb and shrub forage increased with distance to escape terrain, but its quality did not vary. For grasses and sedges, digestible content decreased closer to escape terrain, yet protein increased. These collective results suggest that females incur a trade-off between safety and forage amount, and to a lesser degree between safety and forage quality. Therefore, by foraging in safe areas, nannies with kids pay the price of foraging on less digestible plants.

※

Also called the winter-colored beast, mountaineer, and bearded climber, the mountain goat is the Rockies' premier alpinist. Some individual goats spend their entire lives in rocks above the treeline (Milne and Milne 1962; Walker 1973). In the winter, mountain goats graze withered alpine plants that have been stripped of snow by the wind. On hot summer days they seek shade and dig into snowbanks to cool their bodies. In all seasons they station themselves on exposed outcrops to detect predators.

When a field biologist observed mountain goats for a total of 4,400 hours, equal to 366 12-hour segments, he observed 29 missteps that were serious enough to throw a goat off balance (Chadwick 1983). Five of these were on dangerously steep slopes. He also saw 291 aggressive encounters in dangerously steep spots, of which 39 caused a goat to lose its footing and fall. Of these, 18 were directly pushed over the edge, 18 others were forced to make a frantic leap to escape and lacked adequate footing to land on, and the rest were either innocent bystanders bumped off a ledge by combatants or an aggressor slipping in haste. These observations confirm that, although unusual, aggression between mountain goats does cause falling injuries.

The bearded climber is a beast of precipitous terrain (Chadwick 1983). The steepest pitch at which a pile of loose rocks will remain in place without sliding is called the angle of repose. In terms of physics it is the point where the inertia of particles at rest equals the pull of gravity. Not much talus stays put at angles steeper than 40 degrees. Mountain goats spend 70 percent of their time on slopes greater than 40 degrees, and 10 percent of their time on rock 60 degrees and steeper. And they actually use steep slopes more in the winter! In the Pahsimeroi Mountains of the Lost River Range (central Idaho), for instance, 60 percent of the goats winter on slopes of at least 50 degrees. This seasonal pattern makes sense because steep surfaces shed snow.

The winter-colored beast is a ruminant with four stomachs (Winnie 1996). Each stomach houses an ecosystem with cellulose-digesting bacteria. In the Lewis Range the tough leaves of beargrass provide important winter food for mountain goats. They're able to survive on this nutrient-poor vegetation because their gut bacteria turn cellulose into sugars. As they are carried along with food through the gut, the bacterial populations grow and are digested, thereby adding protein to the diet. If the ruminant host cannot find enough to eat, its bacteria will starve, and then later, even when food becomes plentiful, the goat host could starve on a full stomach. For a mountain goat, winter is a race against thinning forage of diminishing nutritional value, decreasing gut bacteria populations, dwindling body reserves—and its own slowly dissolving skeleton.

In the winter, mountain goats do not hibernate, migrate, or live under snowbanks (Milne and Milne 1962)—they seem oblivious to the cold. Rather, they patrol the rocky ledges, habitats that are higher, rockier, and steeper than the bighorn sheep's. South-facing and sun-catching, with broken terrain on 30-degree slopes, and parallel to dominant winds— these sites are the last to be covered with snow in the fall and the first to green up in the spring (Winnie 1996). These alpine grazers seek out such blustery, windswept slopes, sites featuring wind chill factors of −75 to −180°F (−59 to −117°C). In the winter, kids feed in snow craters dug by their nannies. Spring thaw reveals the broken bodies of accident victims and the emaciated carcasses of goats that succumbed to starvation.

The mountain goat's thick coat has two layers: (1) the outer, hollow, air-filled guard hairs seven or eight inches (18–20 cm) long that keep out wind and snow, and (2) a three-inch-thick (7.6 cm) insulating layer of soft, interwoven, woolly underfur that slows the escape of heat (Milne and Milne 1962). The coat offers another bonus: hunters say that it's hard to drag a goat carcass across snow. The surface of each guard hair has over-lapping scales that form a rough surface and increase the friction of an animal that might be sliding on steep rock.

Because much of its life plays out on cliffs, the mountain goat depends on its climbing skills. Goats literally cling to life. A secret to the mountain goat's climbing success is a suite of anatomical features (Winnie 1996). The distance between its front and rear legs is relatively short. With its short lower-leg bones and muscular shoulders a mountain goat can stand with all four hooves close together on a small spot, which is important in negotiating a tight place. Its massive forequarters relative to its compact rear give it unparalleled pulling power. The mountain goat is relatively short legged. The two main metapodial bones, located in the palms and fleshy part of the foot, are fused and elongated into the cannon bone, which gives leverage for propulsion when running and leaping. Longer than eight inches (20 cm) in deer, the cannon bone of the mountain goat is only four inches (10 cm) long. These proportions create a body with a low center of gravity. What is lost in speed is made up by superb balance and maneuverability.

A mountain goat climbs with three-point suspension (Chadwick 1983). Lifting one limb at a time a goat frequently pauses to assess the situ-ation, tests the footing, and if needed turns back and selects a different route. Slow, sure consistency allows life on rock steeper than the angle of repose. Because they are most likely the ones to find themselves in a tight spot, kids do most of the go-for-broke climbing. Although a kid might take four or five missteps per year, it salvages the situation almost every time.

The length of a goat's hoofprint is short compared to its width. The track's squarish imprint is created by the hoof's spreading tips. The sides of the toes consist of hard keratin, like that of a horse hoof. Each foot's two wraparound toenails are used to catch and hold on to cracks and tiny knobs (Chadwick 1983). The front edge of the hoof tapers to a point, which digs into dirt or packed snow when the goat is going uphill. In contrast to a horse's concave hoof, which causes the animal to walk on the rim of its toenail, a goat's hoof has a flexible central pad that protrudes beyond the nail. The pad's rough texture provides friction on smooth rock or ice yet is pliant enough to impress itself into irregularities on a stone. Four hooves × 2 toes per hoof = 8 gripping soles per animal.

As goats descend a slope the toes spread widely, adjusting tensions to fine-tune the grip (Chadwick 1983). This feature makes them more likely to catch onto something. It also divides the downward force of the weight on the hoof so that some of the animal's total weight is directed sideways. Because there is less net force on each downward line, the foot is less likely to slide. Think of it as the fanning out of downward forces over numerous points of friction.

During our treks we didn't often see mountain goats. But of all the Rocky Mountain mammals we encountered, mountain goats triggered the most unmitigated reverence. Their combined anatomy, physiology, and behavior caused me to stop and drop everything for a lucky view. And to be tolerated by them, as I was at Gunsight Pass long ago, continues to be one of my life's high honors.

CHAPTER 20

Antler Indicators

Elk actually rob minerals from their skeletons
to fuel production of their annual antlers.

Ron Spomer, *The Rut: The Spectacular Fall Ritual of*
North American Horned and Antlered Animals

WE WERE CAMPED along the edge of the vast wetland at the tip of Yellowstone Lake's Southeast Arm (Trail Creek Trail [yes, that's its real name], the Thorofare, Yellowstone National Park, northwestern Wyoming). The dusk of September 11, 1999, resonated with shrill bugling, and cracking racks woke us through the night. During the days, Nancy and I would win occasional glimpses of elk bulls with their harems of cows before they would quickly retreat into the lodgepole pine stands. The first query that popped into my mind was, How in the world do they wiggle those huge antlers through the thicket? Further, the antlers seem bigger than what is needed to repel predators, shove rival bulls, and impress the lady elk. So what is the adaptive significance of the elk's humongous antlers?

Elk are also called wapiti, the Shawnee word for "white rump." The earliest fossils of elk in North America south of the Pleistocene ice front have been dated to 13,000 years ago. The subspecies known as Rocky Mountain elk is distributed along the Western Cordillera from the Canadian Rockies (British Columbia and Alberta) southward into the Southern Rockies (New Mexico) (Carrera and Ballard 2003). Lewis and Clark mentioned "large gangs of Elk" in the mountains (DeVoto 1953). Except for the Roosevelt wapiti on Vancouver Island, there is a high level of shared genes throughout the elk of North America, from Alberta eastward into Ontario and southward to Yellowstone, suggesting that today's patchy herds were once part of a vast, continuous, interbreeding population (Polziehn et al. 2000).

An elk cow can weigh more than 600 pounds (270 kg), the largest bulls as much as half a ton (450 kg) (Rosing 1998). Like those of the mountain goat and other montane ungulates, the elk's nutritional needs through the winter and early spring have shaped the evolution of several of its adaptations. Through the winter an elk incurs progressive nutritional deprivation and increasing catabolism, or destructive metabolism, of its body's protein. Restated loosely, to make it through the winter and into spring it digests parts of its own body. The most severe food deficits and body-protein breakdown occur in situations where the elk population is dense and the snow is deep (Delgiudice et al. 1991).

To answer my question about antler size, we first need to understand the elk's mating behavior. Polygyny is the type of mating system in which a male breeds with more than one female. The elk is one of Earth's most polygynous species. Elk rut in the autumn when they collect in large bands. A thick neck, swollen shoulders, broad chest muscles, and large antlers are advantageous during the bulls' head-crashing disputes (Rosing 1998). Dominant bulls, like our night-long combatants at Yellowstone Lake, spend little time eating or sleeping. The bulls' maximum body weight and prime condition coincide with the start of the rut—thereafter they lose up to 17 percent of their weight. By rut's end a bull may have lost 100 pounds (45 kg) and may be a mere shadow of the king bull that bugled in September; he therefore enters winter in a weakened state.

Antler Mechanics

With their antlers interlocked, two bulls wrestle, trying to force each other to the ground or to pierce each other with their antlers. During combat their antlers undergo severe impact and bending yet do not break. The antlers of mammals are extremely tough and resist fracturing more than their other skeletal bones. Stated in terms of mechanics, antlers undergo high impact loading and large bending moments without fracture.

To grow its antlers a bull diverts fluids and minerals from its body. Antlerogenesis, the growth of antlers, uses a lot of calcium and phosphorus. In the red deer, antlers need 3.5 ounces (100 g) of bone material per day to grow, compared to those of growing fawns, which need 1.2 ounces (34 g). This amount of minerals cannot be obtained from food; rather, much of it comes from the long bones of the animal's own legs and ribs.

Antlers are deciduous, shed and regrown every year, making them the only mammalian bone capable of regenerating. This regrowth every year requires exceptionally fast tissue growth. In fact, antlers show the fastest growth of all natural calcified tissues, with peak rates measured at 0.8 to 1.6 inches (2–4 cm) per day. This amounts to 31 pounds (14 kg) in six months. And fast tissue growth requires fast importation of minerals. This growth process results in antlers with low mineral levels and high collagen content, a ratio that contributes to their low stiffness and yield strength.

A materials engineer would say that an antler's ability to resist fracture is due to its low material stiffness, low yield strength, and high nonlinear response (Vogel 2003). In translation, this means that compared to that of a normal bone, an antler's ability to resist breaking is due to its greater flexibility, the lower level of stress at which it permanently deforms, and its increasingly higher strength with increasing strain.

An antler's ability to withstand large impacts suggests that its strain rate–dependent behavior is greater than it is for skeletal bone. Strain rate is defined as the rate of change in strain with respect to time. A team of materials engineers evaluated this idea by measuring the compression of elk antlers over a range of strain rates (Kulin et al. 2011). The antlers did, in fact, exhibit higher compressive strength at increased strain rates; they sustained compressive strains that were 10 times greater than those sustained by mammalian long bone.

What features give antlers such toughness? When a team of materials and mechanical engineers assessed the mechanical properties of elk antler (Chen et al. 2009), they reported that antler bone is less mineralized but has a higher toughness than skeletal bone (McKittrick et al. 2010). The organic content, especially type-I collagen, is higher in antler compact bone, resulting in stiffness two to three times lower than that of human cortical bone. This confers higher measures of extensibility and work to fracture.

Another team of materials scientists also studied antler fracture toughness (Launey et al. 2010). They found that antler in the transverse orientation is one of the toughest biological materials known. In terms of mechanical engineering, its resistance to fracture, that is, its ability to limit crack growth, is due to a combination of gross crack deflection/twisting and crack bridging via uncracked "ligaments" in the crack wake. Antler material is anisotropic, meaning it is directionally oriented. An example of an anisotropic material is wood, which is easier to split along its grain than against it. Antler's biological composites, anisotropic because they are made of longitudinal tubules and structural protein fibers, exhibit a toughness that is several orders of magnitude higher than that of a single-phase mineral.

Students of biomimicry have noticed the elk antler's impressive fracture resistance (Kulin et al. 2011). Biomimicry is the science of replicating naturally occurring systems for creating objects and processes for human use (McKittrick et al. 2010). The antler material's high resilience to impact loading may inspire the development of energy-absorbing, impact-resistant composite materials, like better car bumpers and football helmets.

This brings us to the spectator sport of watching wolves kill elk. How much predation pressure do wolves actually exert on elk? Wildlife biologists estimated wolf kill rates in the Canadian Rockies (Banff National Park, southwestern Alberta) for the winters of 1986–2000 by using snow tracking and radiotelemetry locations of 429 kills during 195 sampling intervals covering 1,294 days (Hebblewhite et al. 2003). Mean kill rate by wolf packs was 0.44 kills per day per pack, 52 percent of which were elk. This means that a wolf pack killed an elk every 4.4 days, which strikes me as a moderately intense rate.

Elk bulls vent their lust through frenzied displays and bugling. In New Zealand the roaring of male red deer, which is the same species by a different common name, causes cows to enter estrus sooner. In the Rockies the intensity of bugling shows two daily peaks, at dawn and dusk, from late September through early October. The screech holds clear and high before crashing down into a series of grunts (F. Craighead 1973), which to my ear sounds like "A-a-a-aai-e-eeeeeeeee! E-ugh! E-ugh! E-ugh!" Larger bulls have deeper calls, so a cow can probably evaluate a male's size and thereby his social rank from the pitch of his bugle.

During the rut bulls attack trees and shrubs; they urinate copiously, drenching themselves and rolling on urine-soaked grass; they extend their muzzle upward and draw back their lips to expose the lower incisors. Bulls posture, chase, circle, clash antlers, and push and shove, with the weaker ones giving way. Bulls are injured and occasionally killed in these battles. The antler's fourth tine is called the dagger point because it is so deadly.

The purpose of all this hyperactivity is to gather, defend, and sexually monopolize a group of cows. A dominant bull may police a harem of up to 60 cows. One factor that affects harem size is the number of bulls (Bender 1996). The harem boss does not necessarily breed all of his cows. Males that fail to win a cow may skulk around the fringes of a harem. Sexually mature but antlerless males, termed hummels, are known to develop in red deer populations (Darling 1937). From an evolutionary point of view, while stag males rely on superiority in male combat, a hummel invests resources saved from combat in other functions like agility and the stalking of females. I haven't seen a report of such antlerless sneak males in North American elk, but I predict they're out there.

Some of our Rockies bull elk equipped with antlers are known, however, to exhibit sneak mating behavior (Lung and Childress 2007). And it's these sneakers that drive, in part, the bulls' hypervigilance during the rut. Vigilance in socially foraging animals, like elk, may function to detect predators or to monitor the behavior of conspecifics. A team of behavioral ecologists observed elk of both sexes in three age classes during breeding and calving seasons in two areas of Yellowstone that differed in predation risk due to the density of wolves. Male aggression increased from 1 percent of their active time in the spring calving season to more than 7 percent in the fall breeding season, suggesting that the main function of the bulls' vigilance is to monitor conspecifics. Reproductive male vigilance would be a benefit in detecting the approach of a sneak male or the separation of a cow from the harem. When a subordinate male approaches, the dominant male moves quickly to intercept the intruder before he reaches the herd. Bulls, especially breeders with a harem of cows, increase both vigilance and aggression during the fall rut.

Throughout the animal kingdom many species feature alternative male mating behaviors (Waltz and Wolf 1984; Austad 1984; Maekawa and Onozato 1986; Taborsky et al. 1987; Goldsmith 1987; Alcock and Houston 1987; Kuwamura 1987; Forsyth and Montgomerie 1987; Hutchings and Myers 1988; Beani and Turillazzi 1988; Alexander and van Staaden 1989; Shuster and Wade 1991; Magnhagen 1992; Lucas and Howard 1995;

Kanoh 1996; Stockley et al. 1996; Waltz and Wolf 1998). One kind of male is superior in combat and allocates great resources to assert his superiority; the other male type is poor at fighting and wastes little energy in developing weaponry (Gadgil 1972; Crespi 1988). Dimorphic males may represent different genetically based strategies. In the social systems of some populations, sneak males parasitize combat males (Waltz 1982). Theoretically, the ratio of the two types within a population should stabilize when the reproductive success of males that opt out of aggression equals the fitness of those invested in weaponry. A common form of alternative mating behavior includes some males that court females in breeding territories versus other males that act as nonterritorial sneakers (e.g., in the field cricket [Cade 1981], Gila topminnow [Constantz 1975], tree lizard [M'Closkey et al. 1990; Thompson et al. 1993], and the ruff, a sandpiper [Lank et al. 1995]).

Before we explore the next layer of the elk's mating system, let's revisit natural selection and one of its subtypes, sexual selection. Natural selection is the process of differential reproductive success among the individuals of a population that produces change in inherited traits over several generations. There are three requirements for a trait to evolve by natural selection: (1) there is variation in the trait, (2) genetic differences underlie the variation, and (3) the different forms convey differences in individual fitness. That is, the genetically influenced traits of today's organisms result from reproductive competition among their ancestors.

Classically, sexual selection, which you can think of as natural selection in a mating context, is a consequence of two general types of behavior: competition between males for females and female choice among males (Lewin 1984a). Male-male competition is behavior in which males struggle with each other to fertilize eggs; female choice is behavior in which females choose which of several males will fertilize their eggs.

With these theories refreshed let's look at four hypotheses that purport to explain the evolution of elaborate mating structures like the elk's huge antlers. First, the runaway selection model states that females choose males with traits that confer initial survival or reproductive advantages (Lewin 1984a; Enquist and Arak 1993). With continued selection by females the feature becomes exaggerated, sometimes even to the detriment of the male bearer. A balance is achieved, that is, the structure stops evolving to bigger and bigger sizes, when the feature's survival costs equal its reproductive benefits.

Second, in the handicap model, sexual selection favors traits that promote male reproductive success at the expense of survival (Zahavi 1975; Bell 1978; Lewin 1984a; Pomiankowski 1987; Eberhard 1993; Zahavi and Zahavi 1997). The development of such traits is linked to superior genetic qualities in males. The sexually selected traits must be costly to produce. Both the runaway and handicap models predict that over many generations, sexual selection will push males into the precarious position of jeopardizing their own survival, perhaps by going into metabolic deficit or by being more vulnerable to predators.

According to the third hypothesis, the truth-in-advertising model, the display of male traits varies among individuals in such a way that the degree of expression of the traits is linked to the males' overall genetic fitness (Kodric-Brown and Brown 1984; Eberhard 1993). Because the exaggerated expression of these traits requires the allocation of limited resources to reproduction, the feature reflects age, nutritional condition, social status, and resistance to predators and pathogens. Such characteristics honestly advertise desirable attributes that can be passed on to male offspring. By my interpretation, the evidence for the truth-in-advertising hypothesis is growing.

And now on to the last hypothesis, fluctuating asymmetry, which you'll recall we explored in the chapters about the grizzly bear and mountain goat. Among animals in general, duplicate bilateral structures are usually symmetrical. For example, the two sides of your face may appear to be mirror images of each other. In contrast, asymmetry in a bilateral character means the two sides of an organism differ from each other.

Among animals, asymmetries can be sorted into three types. First, in directional asymmetry the trait's measurements assume a skewed distribution. Here's a hypothetical example: among elk, one branch of the antlers, say the right half, is always bigger. Second, in antisymmetry one side is always developed, but the developed side varies from left to right, like handedness in humans. Either the left or right side is fully functional. Both of these kinds of asymmetries seem to be adaptive. The third type of asymmetry, fluctuating asymmetry, is characterized by incomplete development on one side that is randomly determined (Van Valen 1962; Palmer and Strobeck 1986). In contrast to the previous two types, fluctuating asymmetry is not interpreted as an adaptation; rather, it seems to reflect the organism's inability to perfectly control its own development (Ames et al. 1979; Thornhill 1993; Clarke 1995).

Fluctuating asymmetry, a population phenomenon in which a morphological trait deviates randomly from perfect bilateral symmetry,

indicates a propensity for the development of a character to stray from its
genetically programmed outcome (Van Valen 1962; Watson and Thornhill 1994). A structure with fluctuating asymmetry betrays an underlying
violation of homeostasis. It thus makes sense that fluctuating asymmetry
is high among inbred and genetically impoverished populations.

Fluctuating asymmetry has been detected in many kinds of living
things (Wayne et al. 1986; Patterson and Patton 1990; Kieser and Groeneveld 1991; Solberg and Saether 1993; Thornhill 1993; Eggert and Sakaluk
1994; Cordoba-Aguilar 1995). Beetles defoliate boreal willows, which
then develop leaves with fluctuating asymmetry (Zvereva et al. 1997).
Dung flies that catch houseflies have more symmetrical forelegs than
dung flies that miss (Liggett et al. 1993; Swaddle 1997). Male European
earwigs with symmetrical cerci, which are tail pincers, are more successful
in mating females than similar-sized but asymmetrical males (Radesater
and Halldorsdottir 1993). California grunion exposed to high levels of
the insecticide DDT develop asymmetrically (Valentine and Soule 1973).
Rainbow, cutthroat, and brook trouts that are genetically homozygous
have high fluctuating asymmetry (Leary et al. 1983, 1984). In nestling
barn swallows the presence of a certain parasite, specifically the tropical
fowl mite, causes asymmetrical growth of its tail feathers (Moller 1992).
In the Swan Valley (northwestern Montana) of the Northern Rockies,
masked shrews born under the environmental stresses of a logging op-
eration developed asymmetrical mandibles (Badyaev et al. 2000). In the
little brown bat the length of the forearm, a body part that is vital in foraging, shows less fluctuating asymmetry than the length of the tibia, the
main leg bone, which is used for the less critical function of hanging in
roosts (Gummer and Brigham 1995).

Fluctuating asymmetry occurs even in humans. Facial attractiveness is
negatively correlated with fluctuating asymmetry (Gangestd et al. 1994).
The relation for men, but not for women, is statistically significant. Two
findings complement this picture. First, facial attractiveness is negatively
correlated with a composite measure of fluctuating asymmetry based on
seven bilateral nonfacial traits (Watson and Thornhill 1994). And second, when computerized facial images are used, fluctuating asymmetry
of faces is negatively correlated with opposite-sex attractiveness ratings
in both sexes. Together, these two findings suggest that symmetrical faces
are more sexually attractive than asymmetrical faces and that facial symmetry is associated with overall body symmetry.

To repeat, fluctuating asymmetry results from the failure of a bilateral trait to develop identically on both sides of the body. Since both sides of a bilateral trait are produced by the same genome, it follows that the degree of asymmetry reveals an individual's inability to control its development (Swaddle et al. 1994; Merila and Bjorklund 1995). Factors causing deviation from symmetry include a wide variety of genetic and environmental stresses. High levels of inbreeding and homozygosity are examples of genetic stresses that increase a population's level of asymmetry. The more environmental stress a fetus experiences, the more fluctuating asymmetry will eventually be apparent in its adult body (Emlen et al. 1993; Bortolotti and Garielson 1995). Symmetrical growth can be disrupted by a number of environmental disturbances, including diseases, pollutants, extreme temperatures, and food deprivation.

We're now in a position to integrate hypotheses about sexual selection and fluctuating asymmetry. I propose that the degree of fluctuating asymmetry is an honest indicator of a bull elk's quality and thus can be sensed by females as they discriminate among males (Moller 1994; Nilsson 1994).

To evaluate this hypothesis let's start by reviewing how elk antlers develop. To see how antler development is affected by environmental conditions, a mammalogist assessed the effects of several factors on 215 male elk ranging from 1.5 to 14.5 years old that had died during five winters in the Central Rockies (National Elk Refuge, northeastern edge of Jackson, northwestern Wyoming). Bulls infested with scab mites had antlers with more points, greater beam circumference, and heavier mass than unafflicted males. The development of antlers and infestation with scabies were positively correlated with age. Antler size was correlated with the temperatures in March and April during the year they grew, which is considered a nutritional effect, and weather conditions while the males were in utero. Population size, adult sex ratio, and winter feed levels did not influence antler size.

The Pacific Ocean Affects Elk in the Rockies

Elk numbers are affected by many factors—local weather, like the amount of summer rainfall; food quality, such as the level of nitrogen in summer grass; food quantity, like the amount of browse available during winter; winter severity, measured by temperature and snow depth; the elk's own population density; the kind and amount of predation, like the number of calves killed by grizzly bears versus the intensity at which gray wolves attack old cows; and the animals' tendency to form small versus large herds.

And here's an unexpected one. A recent study suggests that elk populations in the Rockies are affected by events out in the ocean. We've known for a while that the North Atlantic Oscillation, a large-scale climatic phenomenon in the northern Atlantic Ocean that controls the strength and direction of storms across the north Atlantic, affects the northern populations of continental animals, including ungulates like red deer in Scandinavia (Norway) and white-tailed deer in the Maritimes (New Brunswick) (Hebblewhite 2005).

An ecologist examined the influence of the North Pacific Oscillation, a similar marine effect, on elk population dynamics in the Canadian Rockies (Banff National Park, southwestern Alberta) (Hebblewhite 2005). He analyzed a 15-year data series of three elk subpopulations exposed to different levels of wolf predation.

The North Pacific Oscillation was strongly related to local climate, including a positive correlation with snow depth and a negative correlation with winter temperatures. Greater activity of the North Pacific Oscillation caused greater winter severity, slowing elk population growth rate regardless of predation pressure from wolves. However, through its interaction with winter severity, elk population growth was depressed more in areas with wolf predation. That is, the effects of the North Pacific Oscillation were weaker in the absence of wolf predation. Minus wolves, the North Pacific Oscillation reduced elk population growth rate, suggesting that overall climate was important. With wolf predation, snow depth was more important than the North Pacific Oscillation, confirming that wolf predation is more intense in deeper snow. These findings demonstrate that the climate of the Pacific Ocean influences the population dynamics of elk in the Rocky Mountains.

As you know, a set of elk antlers grows quickly, up to half an inch (1.3 cm) per day, and can eventually weigh up to 50 pounds (23 kg). Antler tissue is sensitive to food intake. Thus, a rack of antlers serves as an indicator of year-to-year changes in food supply and of the male's ability to find adequate food (Kodric-Brown and Brown 1984; Geist 1986).

Let's apply these theoretical and empirical ideas to the question of why bull elk grow such huge antlers, starting with antler size. It seems to me that absolute size can be explained by the first two proposals, namely the runaway and handicap hypotheses. That is, antler massiveness has been the subject of runaway selection by female choice and handicap selection through male-male competition.

However, the antler's architecture, specifically the geometry of its branches and points, calls for a different explanation. I propose that cows evaluate a bull's success in foraging, his parasite load, and indicators of his developmental stability by the degree of asymmetry of his antlers' tines. A large and complex rack magnifies, and thereby makes more obvious, any asymmetries among the tips of the antlers' tines. With this proposal, I am integrating the truth-in-advertising and fluctuating asymmetry hypotheses: the degree of symmetry of the tine tips truthfully advertises the underlying genetic and bodily functions that play crucial roles in the bull's fitness.

This proposal is testable. A tool for evaluating the level of stress is the fecal glucocorticoid assay, which provides a sensitive, noninvasive means to study the physiological responses of wildlife to stressors (Millspaugh et al. 2001). In the southern Black Hills (Custer State Park, western South Dakota), the amount of human activity, like vehicle use on primary roads, was positively correlated with the elk's fecal glucocorticoid levels. In some elk populations, high glucocorticoid concentrations have been detected during the summer peak of recreational activity.

In another study, conservation biologists tested for associations between snowmobile activity and fecal glucocorticoid levels in wolves and elk in Yellowstone and elk in two other areas (Creel et al. 2002). In wolves, fecal glucocorticoid levels were higher in areas and times of heavy snowmobile use. For elk, daily variation in fecal glucocorticoid levels paralleled variation in the number of snowmobiles. Also, glucocorticoid levels in elk were higher in response to snowmobiles than they were to wheeled vehicles.

Crowding has been shown to induce stress responses, and high glucocorticoid levels reduce immune function and raise disease susceptibility (Forristal et al. 2012). The levels of fecal glucocorticoid metabolite were strongly correlated with local elk density.

These research findings lead me to several testable predictions. First, there should be a positive correlation between glucocorticoid concentrations during the season of antler formation and the degree of fluctuating

asymmetry of the bulls' antlers. Second, there should be a positive correlation between genetic heterozygosity and antler symmetry. Third, cows
should be able to detect the asymmetry of tines on large antlers more
readily than they can on a small rack. And fourth, cows should choose to
mate with bulls sporting more symmetrical antlers over males with more
asymmetrical tines. Here are more research questions offered by a Rocky
Mountain organism.

So a bull elk's antlers may indicate his ability to buffer stresses during
the antler-forming season. The last time I came across a bull elk, I found
myself using binoculars to scan his antlers for evenness. Even though I
noticed a few asymmetries in coat color, skin cuts, and even in eyelid
droopiness, I didn't detect much deviation from bilateral symmetry in
his rack. Perhaps to a cow in estrus he is a walking set of tine points—his
body, and even the bulk of his antlers, are merely out-of-focus tagalongs.

CHAPTER 21

Rock Artists

*All birds, even those of the same species, are not alike,
and it is the same with animals and with human beings.
The reason why WakanTanka [the Breath Giver] does not
make two birds, or animals, or human beings exactly alike
is because each is placed here by WakanTanka to be an
independent individuality and to rely upon itself.*

Shooter, a Teton Sioux, undated; intuiting the notion
of initial variation, a prerequisite of evolution by natural selection

IN ALL OUR Rocky Mountain treks, this had been one of the easiest sections of trail. Sauntering up through Big Creek Canyon in the Salmon River Mountains (Frank Church–River of No Return Wilderness, Payette National Forest, central Idaho), Nancy and I paused every now and then to admire the blazing star flowers, listen for Lewis's woodpeckers, and scan the heights for a mountain lion.

Suddenly, they reached out and grabbed me. I was emotionally jolted—like you feel the instant you realize someone has been watching you. The seven red prehistoric figures had been painted on the small smooth patches of an otherwise roughly fractured cliff face: tick marks, as if counting something; a doglike quadruped; a radiating burst suggesting the sun; two nondescript smudges; a llama-like animal; and a symbol reminiscent of the logo on New Mexico's license plate. The shock faded, and then analytical questions surfaced: Was there a message here? Or were they just pictographs for art's sake? And who were these rock artists, anyway?

Once upon a time, actually not all that long ago, North America's archaeologists basked in the comfort of a consensus paradigm (NGS 1972;

239

Gugliotta 2013). Three independent lines of evidence—teeth, mitochondrial DNA, and language—suggested that the most likely ancestors of the First Americans were the Sinodont, or Chinese, late Stone Age hunter-gatherers (Thomas 1999; Fagan 2000). Further, the theory went, Sinodont mammoth hunters moved eastward across the Siberian tundra 20,000 years ago, then onto Beringia about 14,000 years ago (Hoffecker et al. 1993).

An analysis of mitochondrial DNA suggested that Native Americans originated from a single dispersal to Beringia, probably from eastern Central Asia, about 43,000 to 30,000 years ago (Bonatto and Salzano 1997). This finding supported a model for the peopling of the Americas in which Beringia played a central role. After the colonization of Beringia, people dispersed southward through an ice-free corridor and went on to colonize the rest of the American hemisphere. The ice sheets regrew from 20,000 to 14,000 years ago, closed the ice-free corridor, and isolated the First People south of the continental glaciers.

Six research teams used genetics, specifically the study of the mitochondrial DNA of living and ancient people, to probe the question of where the First Americans came from (Balter 2011). Their findings supported the earlier conclusion that the Paleoindians, the ancestors of today's Native Americans, stemmed from a single Asian source population.

At the end of the last glaciations, about 12,000 years ago, Siberians finished their dispersal across Beringia, edged southward through a newly ice-free corridor (Fagan 2000; Mann 2005), and then fanned out in all directions (Fladmark 1986; Hoffecker et al. 1993). Within a mere 500 years fire-making and flint-knapping First People had spread southward through the entire American hemisphere (Dorfman 2000).

This theory of colonization is supported by the obvious similarities—medium skin color, dark brown eyes, straight black hair, and wide cheekbones—between the Mongoloid people of eastern Asia and Native Americans. For these and other reasons, American Indians are interpreted as a distinct branch of Asian stock.

From the Alaskan end of Beringia the invaders dispersed either around the coast north of the Brooks Range (northern Alaska) or up the Yukon River valley (east-central Alaska), neither of which was covered by glaciers during the last glaciations. Hemmed in on the west by the Cordilleran Ice Sheet and on the east by the Laurentide Ice Sheet, dispersing people slipped southward through an ice-free corridor (Fladmark 1986;

Fagan 2000; Mann 2005). This passageway ran along the eastern flank of the Rocky Mountains from the interior of Alaska southward through the Canadian Rockies (western Alberta) (Krech 1999).

When did people settle temperate North America? For decades archaeologists held that the 13,500-year-old stone spear points found in Blackwater Draw (five miles [8 km] southwest of Clovis, east-central New Mexico), an ephemeral stream on the large mesa called Llano Estacado, were the earliest evidence of human settlement on our continent (Hoffecker et al. 1993; Dorfman 2000; Mann 2005; Gugliotta 2013). This finding anchored the Clovis-first model, but there are now competing ideas.

The Cactus Hill site near the Eastern Shore (Richmond, Virginia) has been conclusively dated at 18,000 years old (Dorfman 2000). There is also the 17,000-year-old rock shelter at Meadowcroft (southwestern Pennsylvania) (Hoffecker et al. 1993; Adovasio and Page 2002). Although the conservative view is still that First People arrived about 13,500 years ago, a growing rebel camp advocates for an arrival of 17,000 to 18,000 years ago. And a few archaeologists even advocate for a first arrival at 40,000 or more years ago. Despite evidence from these potentially paradigm-busting findings, many archaeologists continue to hold that there is no unequivocal evidence of human occupation in the New World before 14,000 years ago (Thomas 1999; Fagan 2000). This ecologist interprets the sister discipline of archaeology to be in paradigm breakdown—First People arrived 11,500, 18,000, or 40,000 years ago (Krech 1999; Mann 2005).

There is also energetic debate about the immigration route(s). Some archaeologists argue that in addition to walking across Beringia, some people made their way to North America from Asia by boat along the edge of the land and ice (Fladmark 1986; Mann 2005). A few archaeologists even support a transatlantic dispersal. Integrating these two notions leads me to a bicoastal hypothesis: most of the peopling of the Americas occurred across and along Beringia, while some boated across the Atlantic Ocean.

Further confounding this intellectual freefall, some data indicate that people invaded North America in several waves (Hoffecker et al. 1993). The three-migration model, that First Americans arrived in three separate immigration events across Beringia in the Late Pleistocene, is supported by studies of dentition, languages, and genetics (Cassells 1997; Fagan 2000; Mann 2005).

In summary, archaeologists are arguing vigorously about when humans colonized North America, their route(s) of immigration, and the number of colonization episodes. I'm jealous: my archaeologist friends are swimming in a chaotic but exciting sea.

The first humans to have occupied the New World are called Paleoindians (Thomas 1999). Responsible for the oldest known cultural tradition in North America, Paleoindians lived here from 11,500 to 8,000 years ago. It was the Paleoindians who, soon after arriving, swept southward through the Americas. Paleoindians are the ancestors of modern Native Americans.

Archaeologists have traditionally recognized three major cultures within the Paleoindian tradition: Clovis from 11,500 to 11,100 years ago, Folsom from 11,000 to 10,200 years ago, and Plano from 10,000 to 8,000 years ago (Thomas 1999; Plew 2000).

I just wish it were that simple. Before we explore the human progression through these prehistoric stages in the Rockies, I need to acknowledge the temporary nature of the story. For example, a research team (Jenkins et al. 2012) has recently unearthed projectile points in the Paisley Caves, in the Summer Lake basin at 4,520 feet (1380 m) above sea level in the arid northern Great Basin (five miles [8 km] north of Paisley, south-central Oregon), that suggest that a newly recognized culture, the Western Stemmed tradition, coexisted with Clovis people. It's beginning to look like America was possibly initially colonized by genetically different groups, that is, parallel cultures with divergent technologies.

So for now, because the story is in flux, let's follow the traditional account. The Clovis projectile point was the first kind of flaked stone weapon in the world that was designed to provide a single hunter with a dependable means of killing a large mammal (Thomas 1999; Gugliotta 2013). In fact, Clovis spear points have turned up fairly consistently within mammoth skeletons (Hoffecker et al. 1993; Thomas 1999; Fagan 2000). The most distinctive part of the Clovis toolkit is the fluted Clovis spear point, a beautiful blade four to five inches (10–13 cm) long and almost perfectly symmetrical (Plew 2000; Mann 2005). It resembles the upper third of a bayonet. Its nearly parallel sides curve to a sharp point; its faces were carefully thinned to improve penetrating power (Thomas 1999). Possibly to provide a firmer grip on a wooden shaft, the broad faces were further thinned by detaching flakes, thereby producing flutes, or troughs, which extended one-third to one-half of the point's length (Cassells 1997; Fagan 2000). The spear's shaft was made from a long, straight tree branch. Clovis points have not been unearthed in Asia, so this tool type seems to have been a New World innovation. In addition to distinctive fluted projectile points, the Clovis toolkit included bifacial knives; steep-edged, unifacial end scrapers; and spurred scrapers.

To avoid close encounters with large dangerous prey, Paleoindians used a spear thrower, called by its Aztec name, atlatl, to hurl the weapon from a safe distance and yet with enough force to penetrate the tough hide of a mammoth (Plew 1986; Janetski 1987; Fagan 2000; Plew 2000). An atlatl consists of a bone or stout stick two to three feet (0.6–0.9 m) long, with one end shaped into a turned-up hook. The spear was laid along the stick so the hook sat in the spear's butt. Grasping the other end of the stick, the hunter used it as an extension of his arm to hurl the spear with whip-snapping action.

As I've said, Clovis technology swept across the continent with astonishing rapidity. The thin layer of fluted points covering North America has traditionally been fitted into the narrow time slot of 13,500 to 13,000 years ago. Recent data, however, reveal that Clovis occupations cluster at 13,200 to 12,900 years ago, so it now appears that Clovis people may have knapped their stone points for only 300 years (Hoffecker et al. 1993; Jones et al. 2008).

At the glacial maximum, North America south of the paired ice sheets hosted a fabulous array of big mammals (Kurten 1976; Krech 1999; Thomas 1999; Plew 2000; Gugliotta 2013). Herbivores included the woolly mammoth, mastodon, and tapir. Bigger than today's bison, the long-horned bison had enormous straight horns extending 8.3 feet (2.5 m). The giant beaver, large-headed llama, three species of horse, and western camel were contemporaries. The flat-headed peccary was possibly the most common large mammal. And then there were mule, white-tailed, and mountain deer; and caribou, four-horned pronghorn, yak, tundra and woodland muskox, and shrub-ox. The stag-moose was about the size of our moose. Several species of giant ground sloth grew up to 20 feet (6.1 m) in length. With their body plates, the pampathere and giant armadillo seemed well protected. Most of these large herbivores were long legged. The Pleistocene bighorn sheep, probably the ancestor of today's bighorn, was not only larger than the modern bighorn sheep but had long legs adapted for the steppes.

All of these herbivores were hunted by carnivores (Kurten 1976; Plew 2000). The Pleistocene's large mammals featured long-legged pursuit predators, like the gray wolf, American lion, and American cheetah. The dire wolf was larger than today's gray wolf. The short-faced bear, a pursuit predator weighing twice as much as the grizzly, was one of Earth's largest carnivorous mammals. Black and grizzly bears continue as modern species. The American lion was one of the globe's biggest lions ever. The New World's cheetah stalked the American pronghorn. To those big cats add the jaguar, margay, saber-toothed tiger and scimitar cat, cougar, and bobcat, and the result was the most spectacular array of cats ever assembled on Earth.

In North America an ecological revolution marked the end of the Pleistocene epoch—humans arrived and many of these large-bodied mammals disappeared (Thomas 1999; Mann 2005). In three millennia, from 12,000 to 9,000 years ago, more than 100 species of large mammals disappeared, a mass extinction that now stands as nothing less than one of our continent's most significant ecological events. Mammoths, mastodons, giant ground sloths, glyptodonts, giant armadillos, giant beavers, capybaras, native horses, camels, saber-toothed tigers, giant lions, dire wolves, cave bears—all these and more vanished. Only five small-bodied species disappeared, a contrast that could hint at a possible cause of these extinctions.

Two main competing hypotheses have arisen to explain these extinctions (Flannery 1994; Krech 1999; Thomas 1999). The changing environment idea holds that many megafauna species were unable to adapt to swift warming and drought and to associated changes in vegetation (Fagan 2000). In contrast, the overkill hypothesis posits that large-bodied mammals were exterminated by humans (Martin 2007). As I said earlier, the end of the last glaciation opened an ice-free corridor through which human hunters presumably dispersed southward. The continent's resident animals were evolutionarily unprepared for the sudden appearance of efficient, weapon-bearing people. In addition, secondary hypotheses about disease and extraterrestrial impacts have also been offered.

In the spirit of inclusiveness I'll offer a pluralistic view: the climate was changing, populations of large-bodied mammals were more stressed, they became more vulnerable to human hunters, their numbers were reduced, and their populations became less stable and entered a downward spiral. Such a multistressor scenario seems to have caused the extinction of the woolly mammoth in Beringia (MacDonald et al. 2012).

With the disappearance of large-bodied mammals, humans were forced to adapt. For example, a shorter projectile point with a longer groove in the center appeared (Gugliotta 2013). A Folsom point is characterized by a lanceolate outline, parallel or slightly convex sides, a concave base with earlike projections, often a small nipple at the base, and a flute on each side that extends the length of the point (Plew 1986; Cassells 1997). The Folsom period persisted from 11,000 to 10,200 years ago.

This change in stone point type indicates that human hunters shifted to smaller game. One of the most important Folsom digs, the Lindenmeier site, located in the shortgrass prairie in the eastern foothills of the Southern Rockies (Soapstone Prairie Natural Area, 30 miles [48 km] north of Fort Collins, north-central Colorado), has yielded hundreds of obsidian scrapers and spear points (Cassells 1997). Much of this obsidian came from Obsidian Cliff (eight miles [13 km] north of Norris), off the northern flank of Roaring Mountain (Yellowstone National Park, northwestern Wyoming) (Davis 1995), at least 390 miles (624 km) to the northwest.

The transition from Clovis to Folsom witnessed greater differentiation among regions. For example, by 10,000 years ago the people of Yellowstone had become separated into two cultural groups. The foothill-mountain people hunted bighorn sheep, mule deer, and bison; plains and basin groups used communal methods to kill dozens of bison. As you might expect, these two Yellowstone groups used different styles of projectile points.

By 10,000 years ago the Folsom-style point was no longer being widely used (Cassells 1997). A new weapon, the Plano point, was long and narrow and as finely worked as the Folsom point but without the central flutes (Plew 2000). The Plano cultural tradition featured greater social organization, like the coordination of more hunters and more complex kills. Their drive-hunt was so efficient that Plano people sometimes wasted food (Krech 1999). At the Olsen-Chubbuck site (16 miles [26 km] southeast of Kit Carson, east-central Colorado), 19 (10 percent) of the 193 bison that had been killed were not even touched, and 30 (15 percent) were only partially butchered (Fagan 2000). By Plano times wild plant foods were an increasing part of a community's subsistence. In addition to its diagnostic point, the Plano artifact assemblage included drills, scrapers, and sandstone metates. The Plano culture lasted from 10,000 to 8,000 years ago.

In a general way we can think of the Clovis period as the initial colonization, the Folsom as regional differentiation, and the Plano as local adaptation.

About 7,000 years ago people began to hunt smaller game and to gather more wild plants than they had in Paleoindian times (Cassells 1997; Plew 2000). They now speared or trapped deer, wolves, squirrels, birds, snakes, and lizards. They still used the atlatl, though. This culture, with its emphasis on hunting and gathering a wide variety of plants and animals, was called Archaic, which simply means "old" (Janetski 1987). Archaic people descended directly from Paleoindians. During the Archaic period the climate changed from cool and wet to warm and dry. Innovations included pottery, the bow and arrow, constructed dwellings, and increased seasonal sedentism.

The Archaic was a time of increasing technological and probably social complexity (Cassells 1997). Toolkits became larger. One technological improvement was perfecting the use of plant fibers for constructing coiled baskets, which were used to gather seeds and nuts. Cordage was also woven into lines for fishing and netting for snaring animals. Grinding tools, such as a handstone, called a mano, and a grinding slab, a metate, indicate that the diet was also evolving (Cannon 1995; Cassells 1997). Projectile points changed stylistically: instead of hafting a smoothed lanceolate point onto a stem, Archaic peoples began notching points, perhaps to provide more security when the point met a solid object like a rib cage.

As I mentioned earlier, in some places Archaic people migrated annually. The rotary engine model describes their annual cyclical movements (Cassells 1997). For example, after wintering in relatively mild foothills native Coloradans moved northward along the foothills in the spring, crossed west or south over the low snow-free passes, and then hunted in the high basins of North Park and Middle Park (both in north-central

Colorado) through the summer. In the fall, as bighorn sheep congregated along the Continental Divide for the rut, hunters completed this counterclockwise annual cycle by moving east out of Middle Park to the Divide area for a final hunt. They established winter base camps in river basins and parklands, areas that minimized problems with cold air drainage while offering sunshine, winter-ranging animals, and outcrops of lithic raw material.

By the time Columbus arrived in the New World, the Americas supported 75 million people that spoke 2,000 languages, each a reflection of a rich, distinct culture (Thomas 1999).

Trails facilitated the exchange of tools, information, and, of course, genes. (How can a backpacker not mention trails?) Most prehistoric human trails have been erased by nature's actions, but a few traces remain. During the last 8,000 years Indians used the Old Ute Trail to travel from Estes Park to Grand Lake (Rocky Mountain National Park, north-central Colorado). Its most recent prehistoric travelers, bands of Ute and Arapaho, owned dogs that dragged travois. They gouged parallel ruts that still scar this alpine landscape.

I've previously mentioned the 2,000- to 3,000-mile-long (3200–4800 km) trail that runs north to south along the eastern base of the Rockies (Stark 1997). Running Wolf said, "There is a well known trail we call the Old North Trail. It runs north and south along the Rocky Mountains. No one knows how long it has been used by the Indians. My father told me it originated in the migration of a great tribe of Indians from the distant north to the south, and all the tribes have, ever since, continued to follow in their tracks" (McClintock 1910). Native Americans used it for 10,000 years, initially on foot, then with travois-pulling dogs, and finally with horses. If, as Running Wolf implied, the original Paleoindians dispersed southward through the ice-free corridor, then the Old North Trail carried one of the most significant human dispersals of all time.

The trails that ran through the Rockies were part of a broader regional, even continental, network. Evidence of such vast interconnectedness has been uncovered in the eastern deciduous forest, specifically in the burial mounds of the Adena/Hopewell culture (Janetski 1987; Davis 1995). Within these cemeteries grave goods included foreign items. Obsidian of the tools from 30 Hopewellian sites in the Midwest (Ohio,

Illinois, Indiana, Michigan, and Ontario) had been quarried over 1,500 miles (2400 km) to the west—from the columnar formation of Yellowstone's Obsidian Cliff.

In some places along the Rockies people practiced communal game driving (Janetski 1987; Cassells 1997; Krech 1999). Some of the best documented are the post-Archaic high-altitude game drives along the Continental Divide in the Southern Rockies (22 miles [35 km] west of Boulder, north-central Colorado). The remnants of at least 50 such sites of varying ages persist between the southernmost Medicine Bow Mountains (Rocky Mountain National Park) and Berthoud Pass, a distance of about 50 miles (80 km). At the Murray site, located in the alpine zone on Mount Albion in the Front Range (17 miles [29 km] west of Boulder), there are 13 stone walls, 16 pits used as blinds, and 483 cairns. The drive walls and cairn lines funneled wild game, like bighorn sheep, up the slope from the grassy saddle between Albion and Kiowa Peaks to the crest of Albion Ridge. Many of the rock cairns along the margins of the drive lanes were decorated with sticks or hides, giving the illusion of humans. These human-mimics would have contained the quarry. One consistency of all drive systems is that the game animals were hustled downwind. At the end of a drive, at the kill site, the hunters hunkered in pit blinds.

A buffalo jump, known to some Indians as *piskun*, which translates as "deep-blood-kettle," was a cliff-type hunting site (Krech 1999; Cassells 1997; Thomas 1999; Fagan 2000; Plew 2000). In the Porcupine Hills, the Head-Smashed-In Buffalo Jump (11 miles [18 km] northwest of Fort Macleod, southwestern Alberta) was used off and on by people of the northern plains for 5,700 years ("Head-Smashed-In Buffalo Jump" 2002). As Nancy and I stood on the edge of this buffalo jump my imagination brought up images of shaking ground, the taut muscles of waiting ambushers—and the flared nostrils of one panicked bison bull being shoved to the edge by the inexorable pressure of his herdmates.

The oldest form of art is rock art. There are several major regions of rock art in the world: Australia, Africa, Europe, and western North America. Portrayals of masculine activities and exaggerated male genitalia suggest that men painted many of the images. (See, not much has changed over the millennia!) In the Central Rockies (southern Idaho), petroglyphs and pictographs appear to date from the Late Archaic (Plew 1986, 2000). A pictograph is a figure painted with a finger, stick, or reed by applying natural pigments like iron oxide and red ocher (Thomas 1999). The pictures may have marked trails or hunting facilities but they do not represent writing. My Big Creek figures seem to fit here. According to various hypotheses, rock art sites are found near suitable media, like pigments, and serve the practical function of marking resource areas like game trails. In some places, the figures in rock art are characteristic of specific places and times and thus have been used as diagnostic indicators of cultures that stretched across sacred landscapes (Simms 2010).

Western landscapes hold many sacred spots (Thomas 1999). Many tribes, for instance, regarded Yellowstone as sacred (Weixelman 2001). The Nez Perce went to Yellowstone to purify their bodies and souls. Other holy places include Chief Mountain (northeastern Glacier National Park, northwestern Montana), Devils Tower (Crook County, northeastern Wyoming), and Old Man Mountain (Estes Park, north-central Colorado).

The vision quest, a retreat in which a person receives insights through dreams and visions, has served as the spiritual focus of many Native Americans (B. Moore 1996). Several writers have identified Yellowstone as an area the Shoshone and Bannock used for vision questing (Weixelman 2001). Visions provide access to the supernatural forces underlying life. During a solitary journey of four to six days the person fasts and prays in hopes of receiving spiritual guidance in a powerful dream. In some tribes the vision quest marks a boy's passage into manhood. When a vision comes, usually in the form of an animal, natural phenomenon, or legendary creature, it reveals the dreamer's guardian.

Anthropologists have been of two minds about the relationship between Native Americans and their environment (Krech 1999; Penn 2003; Mann 2005). On one hand there's the image of the Noble Indian, also called the Ecological Indian, who felt sympathy with all living things, understood the systemic consequences of his actions, and worked to conserve Earth's harmonies. But we also know that before European contact the populations of some native peoples were checked by high densities and resource depletion (Thomas 1999). Further, Native Americans had three powerful, environment-changing technologies—fire, wooden tools, and the bow and arrow.

Clovis people did not use all the meat they butchered. When they killed a mammoth they took the choicest parts (Fagan 2000). Prehistoric sites reveal that Native Americans killed prime-aged and female animals, a habit that runs contrary to sustainable harvesting (Kay 1995). This suggests that Native Americans may have impacted pre-Columbian ungulate populations in some places (Krech 1999). Perhaps overkill was a foreign concept based in Western practice. My hunch is that most prehistoric human hunters were usually opportunistic—regardless of the odds of causing an ecological impact.

Lewis and Clark witnessed many fires in the prairies and forests (Mann 2005). Native Americans used fire to improve access to, and stimulate forage for, prey animals and to drive and encircle the animals (Krech 1999). In the Bitterroot Valley (west-central Montana), for several centuries before Euro-American settlement, Indian-ignited fires caused a near doubling of the fire frequency in montane and lower subalpine zones.

After we stumbled upon the rock art in Big Creek Canyon my mind wouldn't let go of several questions. Who drew the pictures? How did they live? What did the pictures mean? The homework of trying to understand the Big Creek pictographs led me to Lawrence A. Kingsbury, forest archaeologist of the Payette National Forest (Kingsbury 2012). Responding to my concern that the pictures might have been drawn recently, Larry asserted, "Europeans had nothing to do with the red pictographs!" He added that during both pre- and post-Columbian times, members of the Tukudeka used iron to create the red pigment. Although rock art is notoriously difficult to date, pictographs in the Salmon River Mountains have been estimated to be 800 to 1,000 years old (Reddy 1996). According to some anthropological hypotheses some of the rock art sites in southeastern Idaho are located in sacred places and were essential in religious beliefs.

What was the rock artists' lifestyle? Sheepeaters once lived throughout the mountains of the Northern and Central Rockies (central Idaho, southwestern Montana, and northwestern Wyoming) (Dominick, n.d.). This vast region includes the Salmon River Mountains. "Tukudeka" means "eaters of mountain sheep." They are classified in the Sheepeater branch of the Northern Shoshone (Reddy 1995b). Think of Sheepeaters as a group of extinct, mountain-living Shoshone with a characteristic culture. The Tukudeka migrated annually, that is, followed a pattern of seasonal rounds, which included hunting bighorn sheep at altitude and fishing for salmon in the summer, eating cached dried meats and roots in semisubterranean pit houses along major rivers in the winter, and gathering camas and other roots in mountain meadows in the spring (Janetski 1987; Reddy 1995b, 2002). They also drove bighorn sheep into game traps, which consisted of rock walls and a trap that used a natural wall like a cliff. At least at some times and places, their society consisted of small, isolated, economically independent groups composed of one or two nuclear families.

What do the red-brown figures on the cliff along Big Creek say about the artist? About me? Once the shock subsided, my overwhelming emotional reaction was one of comforting sameness, that the artist may not have been all that different from me. He also may have touched me where I was most insecure—my fear of dying anonymously. Perhaps I was attracted—jealous, actually—because the artist had successfully transcended his own bodily death. That rock artist now shares his immortality with Michelangelo, Darwin, and the Beatles.

CHAPTER 22

Themes

Like astronomers, evolutionary ecologists rely
heavily on a careful comparative approach.

Eric Pianka, *Evolutionary Ecology*

WE HAD SET UP the tent, inflated our pads, and raised the loft of our down bags; supped on hot pea soup and wolfed down freeze-dried lasagna; hung our stinky socks to air out and brushed our teeth. It had been a day with a common rhythm—strike camp and hike up along a stream through a canyon, work for several hours up switchbacks with brief detours to biologize or shoot a picture, snack briefly on nuts and dried fruit while appreciating the panorama from a pass, and then descend into an adjacent valley and seek out the next campsite. During this typical day Nancy and I saw charred boles, aspen clones, an elk herd, two rufous hummingbirds, several pikas, a variety of cushion plants, ground-hugging butterflies, a covey of white-tailed ptarmigan, two flocks of Clark's nutcrackers, six yellow-bellied marmots, stands of lodgepole pine, patches of scarlet gilia, and three dippers on midstream rocks. At various times during the course of this single day I was reminded of the remarkable adaptations that enable a variety of plants and animals to persist, even to thrive, in the extreme environment of the Rockies. Are there adaptations that set these organisms apart from the plants and animals of other regions? That is, do Rocky Mountain organisms offer recurring ecological and evolutionary themes? My answer to both is an assertive "yes."

I'll start with an observation that struck me during every Rockies walk. Many of the plants and animals we encountered along the trail—ponderosa pine, quaking aspen, Mormon cricket, tiger salamander, garter snake, white pelican, sandhill crane, spotted sandpiper, red-tailed hawk, cliff swallow, common raven, American robin, white-crowned sparrow, water shrew, snowshoe hare, red squirrel, coyote, gray wolf, black and grizzly bears, moose—are, or were until recently, geographically widespread. Sometimes it seemed like the trail was leading us through a subset of North America's generalist species, plants and animals with vast ranges and broad niches. Compared to the Sonoran Desert (southern Arizona), Appalachian Highlands (West Virginia, North Carolina), Caribbean islands (Dominica, Saba), coral reefs (Red Sea at Eilat, Israel; Kauai), lowland rainforest of Central America (Corcovado National Park, Costa Rica), and other places I've studied, the Rockies seem to host few habitat specialists. The Eastern Cordillera, for instance, hosts more endemic species, in part because of the Appalachians' antiquity and topographic diversity (Constantz 2004). This anecdotal observation begs for a quantitative test. And if the hypothesis is confirmed, what causes underlie the pattern?

Among the plants of the Rockies, a recurring theme is the presence of secondary compounds. Plants of all kinds—lupines, paintbrushes, lodgepole pines, spruces, quaking aspens—seem to synthesize, translocate, and sequester poisonous chemicals that deter herbivores. Although some secondary compounds may always be present, many seem to be induced by fresh damage. The kinds and amounts of secondary compounds vary at many spatial scales: various parts within a single plant, individuals within populations, among populations within species, and between species. These toxic chemicals also vary through time. Within such a heterogeneous chemical universe, a sulphur butterfly caterpillar, a haying pika, or a browsing elk needs to eat selectively, minimizing its ingestion of toxic chemicals while maximizing its intake of nutrients and energy. Herbivorous animals are picky—for good chemical reasons. Herbivores may live in a green world, but it's foraging by pointillism.

A third theme is habitat patchiness. Elevation and latitude jointly influence a place's thermal year, which determines its life zone. And elevation covaries with the intensity of wind, insolation and ultraviolet radiation, and soil depth and moisture, as well as with the length of the growing season. Aspect also contributes to site-specific environmental variation. These variables, in turn, covary with disturbance regimes, like the kind, amount, and timing of fire, drought, and irruptions of herbivorous insects. Finally, all of these environmental variables, both abiotic and biotic, interact with each other to create, maintain, and change patches of habitat that are scattered throughout the mountains. As we'll see in a bit, habitat patchiness has potential consequences for population sustainability and social behavior.

If we continue with the broad theme of spatially variable environments, several subthemes emerge. First, many Rocky Mountain ecosystems are disturbance dependent. Because wet, productive seasons can alternate with dry, dormant ones, fuels sometimes accumulate and dry out, and lightning can then ignite them. Burned environments, so regularly available, offer exploitable resources to which natural selection has tailored adaptations. Plants—such as lodgepole and whitebark pines, fireweed, and aspen—have evolved adaptations that resist cool fires; disperse seeds after fire; resprout and germinate in fertile, competitor-cleared burned zones; and, in some cases, even encourage their own immolation by growing and dropping flammable leaves and woody parts. Appalachian plant species are less fire dependent. A take-home lesson is that for many species of Rocky Mountain plants, fire is not a catastrophe; rather, it offers ecological opportunities. In addition to fire, other kinds of disturbances, like avalanches and floods, repeatedly create fresh habitat and reduce competitors.

And that leads directly to the fifth theme. Because montane habitats often occur as isolated high-elevation islands, some plant and animal species persist as sets of clusters, not as populations that are continuously distributed across the landscape. Species that persist as metapopulations feature adaptations for moderate levels of dispersing and colonizing. Many plants—such as whitebark pine, quaking aspen, and willows—were able to reestablish soon after the last glaciers retreated because of efficient seed dispersal adaptations. Although some animals—such as the spotted sandpiper, Clark's nutcracker, sandhill crane, calliope hummingbird, white-crowned sparrow, mountain bluebird, gray wolf, and moose—can cover a lot of ground in a day, thereby expanding into new habitat patches, other animals—such as butterflies, white-tailed ptarmigan, hoary marmot, pika, mountain goat, and bighorn sheep—live in small populations that are only weakly connected and persist as metapopulations.

Several recurring adaptations allow survival through winter. Reptiles like the garter snake, birds such as the rufous hummingbird, and mammals like the yellow-bellied marmot, moose, bighorn sheep, black and grizzly bears, and elk undergo an annual cycle in their amount of body fat. Others with more site fidelity store food in their environment during abundance and use it under scarcity. Caching comes in two forms, scatter hoarding—as in the Clark's nutcracker—and larder hoarding—as in bumblebees and the pika. One animal—the red squirrel—even does both in some places. Further, it is curious that several animals—the nutcracker, pika, and red squirrel—store much more food than they need to survive a winter. Why they do this is yet another mystery.

Another set of recurring themes deals with where animals spend the winter. Some highly mobile animals—such as the cliff swallow, white-crowned sparrow, sandhill crane, bighorn sheep, and prehistoric Native Americans—migrate(d) to warmer sites. Others stay in a warm hole—such as the garter snake, western rattlesnake, hoary marmot, and grizzly bear. Hibernation seems to have evolved to the highest degree in mid-sized mammals—hoary and yellow-bellied marmots—of midlatitudes. And still others continue to be active through the bitter season—the white-tailed ptarmigan, dipper, pika, red squirrel, gray wolf, and mountain goat.

Here's theme number eight. Because of adaptations that reduce their loss of heat, several montane organisms retain only a vestigial ability to cool themselves—moss campion, bumblebees, butterflies, ptarmigan, pika, and mountain goat. It seems that body design has been constrained by a trade-off between heat-retaining and heat-dissipating adaptations. This vulnerability to overheating, by the way, may limit these organisms' adaptation to global warming.

Of all the adaptations I've observed in Rocky Mountain organisms, one strikes me as fundamentally different from those characteristic of living things in other areas of North America—living in a group. Look at them all: patches of glacier lilies, clusters of whitebark pine, clones of aspen, colonies of bumblebees, schools of toad tadpoles, balls of garter snakes and rattlesnakes, flocks of sandhill cranes, gangs of ravens, colonies of cliff swallows, mountain bluebird helpers, crèches of batlets, families of hoary marmots, packs of gray wolves, adopted grizzly bear cubs, bands of mountain goats, herds of elk, bands of Native Americans. And more. It seems to me that compared to other parts of North America, the Rocky Mountains have a greater proportion of native species that live in cooperative groups.

Let's examine this hypothesis by breaking it into two questions: (1) Is it true? (2) If so, what causes it? This is one of the ideas I chewed on as

I trekked along Rocky Mountain trails, all the while reflecting it against my experiences in other places.

In thinking of why this hypothesis might be true, I'm impressed with the obvious need of Rocky Mountain organisms to prepare for winter and to avoid predators. A long energy-demanding winter places a premium on adaptations that facilitate the efficient accumulation and management of food for later use. And, I suggest, one of the best ways to do that is to cooperate with other individuals with like needs. Groups of individuals have more eyes to look for patches of food.

Groups also provide protection from predators. They do this in two ways, by enhancing vigilance and offering cover. In several stories I reported how individuals in groups can feed more because there are more vigilant eyes. Further, through the selfish herd effect, individuals can hide inside their group.

In contrast to life cycles in the Rockies, those of living things in many other places do not seem to be as dominated by the stresses of winter. With their lower elevations, shorter and milder winters, and longer growing seasons, the Ozark and Appalachian Highlands, for example, feature warmer and shorter winters, more even precipitation among seasons, and fewer wildfires. Appalachian plants and animals invest less in storing food for winter consumption.

Living in a group can also set the stage for the evolution of cooperation, nepotism, and other behaviors that characterize eusocial, or truly social, animals (Wilson 2012). It seems that Rocky Mountain animals have adaptations for meeting environmental constraints, thereby favoring the evolution of cooperative social behavior. I can think of no Appalachian counterpart to food finding in a cliff swallow colony, fishing by encircling American white pelicans, antipredator calls within a hoary marmot colony, or cooperative pup rearing in a wolf pack.

The prevalence of patchy habitats and the commonness of group living lead me to consider the roles of evolution by kin and group selection. I'm suggesting that the plants and animals of the Rocky Mountains may reflect the action of kin and group selection more than organisms elsewhere in North America. If this is true, so what? Not only should these forms of evolution produce more interactions, higher tolerance, and broader cooperation, but they should also yield more altruism. This is a testable hypothesis: Rocky Mountain organisms should be more selfless and less selfish than living things in other parts of our continent.

Now the challenge: I don't have the data to test this proposal. I haven't estimated the percentages of group-living reptiles, birds, and mammals in the Rockies and in other, similar-sized coastal, Appalachian, and Great Plains biomes. Nor have I quantified the level of altruistic behavior displayed by Rocky Mountain animals versus those in other places. So, aiming for objectivity, I'm obliged to ask, Is this seeming prevalence of group living just an artifact of what biologists have chosen to study? Of what caught my eye along the trail and what I've chosen to write about? Or is the pattern real? I hope another ecologist will find it worthy of a quantitative test.

In summary, I propose that, compared to living things in other North American regions, Rocky Mountain organisms have converged on several ecological and evolutionary themes. Many plant and animal species are widely distributed habitat generalists. Plants feature secondary compounds. Many ecosystems and their constituent species are disturbance dependent. Many species persist as metapopulations among archipelagos of high-altitude habitat islands. Overwintering adaptations include caching nonperishable foods in the environment and storing fat in bodies, as well as migration, hibernation, or maintaining winter activity. Some heat-retaining adaptations are so efficient that they render some organisms vulnerable to overheating. Finally, many animals live in cooperative groups. Many of these trends seem to be ultimately traceable to the Rockies' extreme environment and predation pressures.

I close this overview by admitting that another biologist could land on a different suite of generalizations. After all, I based my generalizations on a specific kind of immersion—walking on mountain trails during the summer. Another naturalist, kayaking down Rocky Mountain rivers, car camping in developed campgrounds at lower elevations, or cross-country skiing in the winter, could come away with different conclusions.

CHAPTER 23

Land Lines

An imaginary line, they say…
What line is not?
What line is more
Than a signal to the mind
To end an established illusion
And begin another,
Or simply to suggest that something
Abruptly stops, as if it would
Anywhere on this round earth.

George Franklin Halterman, "The Line"

IT TOOK US 12 days to backpack across the Greater Yellowstone Ecosystem (Yellowstone National Park and environs, northwestern Wyoming). Hiking westward, Nancy and I climbed up and over the Absaroka Range, skirted the northern foothills of the Two Ocean Plateau and Red Mountains, and rambled across the Madison Plateau. We grunted our way up to Eagle Pass; grappled with existential questions while enveloped by the solitude of the Thorofare; peered into Heart Lake's crystalline waters to witness a shoal of parallel, sculpted twigs; tried to peer through the steam veil rising off the Firehole River.

Along the way we also reveled in the place's living diversity. Thermophilic bacteria colored hot springs. Many wildflowers graced our trails, listed here in order of their placement along the visible light spectrum: red—scarlet paintbrush; pink—short-styled onion, bitterroot, Wood's rose, elephant's head, long-plumed avens; orange—orange mountain-dandelion; yellow—lance-leaved stonecrop, sulphur buckwheat, yellow columbine, yellow monkeyflower, globeflower, glacier lily, arrowleaf balsamroot; blue—lupine, many-flowered stickseed; purple—sticky geranium, harebell. White flowers included white geraniums, water hemlock, cow parsnip, field chickweed, and white bog orchid. The trail wound through forests of Engelmann spruce and Douglas-fir, doghair stands of lodgepole pine, and patches of quaking aspen.

Animals further punctuated our days—boreal toads in amplexus assembled their egg strings in a quiet backwater, the call of a sandhill crane woke us before dawn, parental dippers tried to keep up with voracious chicks in a nest overhanging a roaring stream, pastel bluebirds stood out amid fire-blackened boles, a bank swallow colony networked the air above a languid creek, Uinta ground squirrels inspected our gear at campsites, a family of river otters materialized in the morning mist, gray wolves howled at night, herds of elk grazed in river floodplains, bison chewed their cud in the shade of a tree.

Such a rich diversity of landscapes, plants, and animals! Then, suddenly, without psychological buffer, we felt the assault of an open, dry and dusty, orderly and sterile tree farm—the Targhee National Forest (western end of the Summit Lake Trail). This harsh insult serves as the synecdoche for what I nominate as the Rockies' most significant environmental issue—the antagonistic management of natural resources across property boundaries.

The West has been populated for almost two centuries, yet some folks still cling to a mind-set—the frontier mentality—that assumes that the supply of natural resources is endless (Turner 1921). Consequently, in some places environmental degradation grinds away. Threats to montane ecosystems include the construction and maintenance of certain kinds of roads, subdivisions, power lines, and buildings; certain practices in ranching, logging, and mining; and all dams (Ellis 1976; Alden et al. 1998). I twice used the word "certain" because within most activities I acknowledge a continuum from good to bad practices. Further, in some areas excess dewatering is degrading ecosystems. The deposition of atmospheric pollutants like nitrogen and mercury is impacting even the most remote watersheds. As the climate warms, perhaps with the desiccation of the lower and middle life zones, some species will disperse up mountains and northward along the Rockies while others will run out of cold places (Root et al. 2005; Tolme 2005/2006; Holtcamp 2010; Turlure et al. 2010; Beaubien and Hamann 2011).

Here's my general point. Toxins are carried by breezes over fences, and by streams across survey lines. The northern Yellowstone elk herd is managed by natural regulation within the park, but outside the park other agencies limit elk numbers through hunting. Property lines are permeable to stressors but environmental issues transcend boundaries.

Let's apply this idea of stressors moving across borders to a specific issue. The loss of whitebark pine, a keystone species, has the far-reaching consequences of changing the time frame of ecological succession, altering the distribution of subalpine vegetation, and eroding local plant and animal biodiversity (Mattson et al. 1992; Tomback et al. 2001; Hatch 2012). It saddened me to hike through too many places highlighted by whitebark skeletons.

The environmental stressors responsible for the death of whitebark pine are the unintended consequences of several human actions (Tomback et al. 2001). The introduced white pine blister rust, with its telltale sign of red-brown foliage on dying upper branches, has spread through whitebark pines. Old lodgepole forests that are protected from fire are subject to severe outbreaks of the mountain pine beetle, which then spread up mountains into the whitebark pine zone. Ironically, putting out low-intensity fires has increased the whitebark's risk from both destructive fires and pine bark beetles. Fire suppression has also allowed succession to favor other tree species. Reductions of habitat due to global warming are acting in synergy with other stressors to kill whitebark pine trees and are thereby reducing high-altitude habitat for subalpine fir and Engelmann spruce, Clark's nutcracker and grizzly bear.

So what? Why do we need the whitebark pine and the biodiversity it supports? And even more broadly, what is the value of biodiversity (Norton 1987; Cairns 1988)? We humans need a variety of plant and animal species for many reasons, including their contributions to:

1. understanding history—the plant dyes used in rock art, the beaver pelts that catalyzed exploration, and the woody materials that facilitated early European settlement;

2. outdoor recreation—such as trout fishing, landscape photography, and the introspection offered by backpacking;

3. education—learning about nature and ourselves;

4. commerce—guided elk hunting, harvesting mushrooms for sale, and using thermophilic bacteria for DNA fingerprinting;

5. applied science—improving foods and medicines;

6. environmental health—ecological goods and services, the domino effect of extinctions, and measurable ecological indicators;
7. aesthetics—landscape beauty and personal inspiration; and
8. needs yet unknown—Which species could potentially help us in the future?

So, for a whole host of reasons, it's in our own self-interest to protect native biodiversity.

What can be done to save this keystone mutualist, the whitebark pine, and its dependent organisms (Tomback et al. 2001)? Short-term Band-Aids could include the pruning of blister-rust-infected branches and the planting of whitebark seedlings. Over the long term we could work on a couple of fronts. We could accelerate the tree's evolution by breeding resistant strains of whitebark pine. Currently, about 5 percent of the trees in devastated populations are showing resistance. Perhaps, in the long run, the whitebark pine has enough genetic variation to adapt to global warming. We could also return the downslope lodgepole forests to a natural fire regime. Allow the burning of light fires to exclude firs and favor the pines. Foster a natural resistance to white pine blister rust by restoring native fire regimes so suitable caching conditions are available for Clark's nutcrackers and optimal growing conditions are created for whitebark pine seedlings. Regardless of which mix of short- and long-term conservation tactics we consider, saving the whitebark pine will involve rolling up our sleeves and working across land lines.

Great outcomes often start with a picture of where we want to go, so let me suggest a vision worthy of the place: the Rocky Mountains will forever host the ongoing evolution of native life.

This statement may seem simple, but it includes several important ideas. The traditional image of the so-called balance of nature has given way to an understanding of ecosystems comprising fluctuating energy flows and nutrient cycles, recurring and unpredictable ecological disturbances, and chaotically shifting landscape mosaics.

Here's another way to think of it. The phrase "balance of nature" implies equilibrium. Think of an equilibrium as a stable condition that is maintained by equal, opposing forces. In a dynamic equilibrium the stable point shifts slowly over the long term as a function of climatic or other slow changes in the environment (Boyce 1991). In contrast to ecosystems persisting at equilibrium, other ecosystems are characterized by outright chaos. Our thinking about ecosystems has changed from the idea that they're mainly at equilibrium to a view with more emphasis on chaotic change.

Traditional management of natural resources has focused on single species, specific sites, and short periods. However, an alternative environmental management goal is to sustain a place's constituents and processes. It is now established that the ecosystems of the Rocky Mountains are dynamic (Boyce 1991). These high places do not remain stable for long because of trophic-level interactions, such as those between plants and their irrupting herbivores; recurring disturbances, such as fire and avalanches; and random fluctuations imposed by environmental vagaries, such as unusually severe winters and unpredictable drought. I am suggesting that a desirable management goal is to maintain or restore the ecological processes—in all their fluctuating and unpredictable forms—that shape the dynamic landscape mosaic. And this will require us to cooperate across borders (Leopold 1991).

The increasing fragmentation of natural landscapes that were originally more continuous is one of the most important factors contributing to the loss of biodiversity (Harris 1984; Burkey 1988; Rolstad 1991; Robinson et al. 1992; Quammen 1996; Reed et al. 1996). The Greater Yellowstone Ecosystem is one of the few places along the Rockies that retain enough contiguous habitat to allow gene flow among some of the populations of some carnivore species (Craighead et al. 1999). Some large-bodied carnivores like the grizzly bear, gray wolf, and wolverine probably need more habitat than what is currently protected; the lynx, fisher, and river otter, all medium-sized predators, the so-called mesocarnivores, may get by with less. The genetic exchange between subpopulations, which function as parts of metapopulations, should be a management priority. To support metapopulations a practical component of reserve design would be to maintain or restore habitat connections among wilderness ecosystems.

Large nature reserves are needed to conserve native biological diversity (Newmark 1987). Take the Greater San Juan Mountain Area. Covering 26,400 square miles (66,000 km^2) (southwestern Colorado and north-central New Mexico), this area, which hosts a broad representation of the native species and ecological communities of the Southern Rockies, would qualify, like Yellowstone, as one such large nature reserve (Povilitis 1993).

On an even larger scale, the Yellowstone to Yukon (Y2Y) Conservation Initiative is a project to promote the beauty, environmental health, and natural diversity of a large part of the Western Cordillera (Chadwick 2000). Y2Y aims to conserve the biological communities at altitude from the Selwyn Mountains (eastern Yukon Territory) southward across the Liard River; continuing southward through the Canadian Rockies (Jasper and Banff National Parks, western Alberta), Northern Rockies (Waterton-Glacier International Peace Park, Alberta and Montana), and the Yellowstone area; and ending at the southern end of the Wind River Range (Bridger Wilderness, west-central Wyoming) (Heuer 2000). The total length of Y2Y would be 1,900 miles (3040 km). The intent of Y2Y's advocates is not to exclude land development but to proceed with human activities that do not overwhelm natural ecosystem processes.

As I've said several times in this book, many species will not remain viable over the long term without genetic exchange among their populations (O'Brien et al. 1985; Wilcox 1986; Burkey 1988). From a natural resource manager's point of view, a primary value of dispersal is its role in maintaining and extending the presence of a species through space by founding, refounding, and supplementing local populations (Templeton et al. 1990). Spreading the risk of extinction throughout a metapopulation can yield the almost unlimited survival of a species (Quinn and Hastings 1987).

Fragments of habitat have often been managed as islands (Wiens 1995). But a habitat patch is not isolated; it exists within a landscape mosaic (Margules et al. 1982; Rolstad 1991). The dynamics within a fragment are affected by external factors that vary as the mosaic structure changes (Quinn and Harrison 1988). This is why the simple analogy of a habitat fragment to an isolated oceanic island, as has been advocated by some conservationists, is only partly correct (Simberloff and Abele 1976). Management should be directed toward the mosaic, not just a delineated, stand-alone reserve (Saunders et al. 1991).

A key to saving some species is providing safe passage between reserves through hostile human territory (Stolzenburg 1991). Conservation strategies should include habitat strips that connect the sanctuaries (Hobbs et al. 1990; Claridge and Lindenmayer 1994; Haas 1995). Examples of dispersal corridors include fencerows, wooded streambanks, and wetlands. Riparia, which host a diverse array of species and ecological processes, are also high-priority habitat corridors. Their ecological diversity reflects the actions of variable flood regimes, shifting channels, and upland influences (Naiman et al. 1993). Effective riparian management could mitigate many of the threats created by habitat fragmentation.

The environmental issues and their solutions as sketched above lead to several practical recommendations (Wilson and Willis 1975). Because the number of species declines as one goes out along a narrow strip of land, a natural phenomenon called the peninsula effect, nature preserves of fixed area should be as round and continuous as possible (Murcia 1995). Individual preserves should also be made as large as possible (Blake and Karr 1987; Woodroffe and Ginsberg 1998). If we estimate the extinction rates of the most vulnerable taxon, then the minimum areas desired for protection should be those in which the initial and highest extinction rates will be reasonably low.

In the spirit of balanced reporting, though, I'll note that reconnecting habitat patches can also have negative consequences. Pathogens can spread via corridors (Stolzenburg 1991). So-called pathogen pollution has been detected with brucellosis in elk and bison, and chronic wasting disease in elk and deer. To evaluate the likelihood of pathogen pollution we need to better understand the ecology of wildlife diseases. Factors within a corridor that affect disease transmission include the numbers and density of livestock and humans, the quality of the habitat, and the amount of public versus private lands. The challenge is to see the unintended consequences ahead of time so as to ensure that human-engineered reconnections do the most good.

According to population biology theory, the odds that a population will go extinct depend on the number of individuals that the habitat can support, its per capita birth rate, the pace and variation of its growth rate, and its effective population size (Brussard 1987). These and other factors affect the risk of extinction in small isolated populations (Pimm et al. 1988; Williamson 1989). To address this issue, some conservation biologists have proposed three interim targets: (1) try to maintain a minimum viable population for any given species in any given habitat; this is the smallest isolated population that has a 99 percent chance of persisting for 1,000 years despite the foreseeable effects of demographic, environmental, and genetic fluctuations (Shaffer 1981). To meet that 99 percent/1,000-year goal, genetic analyses suggest the other two interim targets: (2) 5,000 individuals are needed to maintain sufficient genetic variation; and (3) one successful immigrant per generation is necessary to maintain an allele in a distant population (Craighead et al. 1999). These criteria will surely be adjusted as conservation biology continues to mature.

The approximate outer limits of the Greater Yellowstone Ecosystem include, in a clockwise direction, the towns of Bozeman and Red Lodge, Montana; Cody, Dubois, and Pinedale, Wyoming; and Ashton, Idaho (Eversman and Carr 1992). About 90 percent of the Ecosystem is on federal lands. Of these public lands, 44 percent are open to grazing, 40 percent are available for mineral exploration, and 19 percent have been identified as suitable for commercial timber harvesting. Also, interspersed among these public lands are privately owned parcels. No wonder disagreements arise among the Ecosystem's stakeholders about how to manage some species, like the gray wolf, and certain ecosystem processes, like fire (Leopold 1991).

When we step back and look at the big picture, we can better appreciate that differences in fundamental values lie at the root of many of the region's natural resource controversies (Barbee and Varley 1984; Elias 1996). And the heart of those policy differences is the philosophical question about the appropriate relationship between people and nature (Keiter and Boyce 1991). Should humans leave a place alone, so it develops and evolves on its own? Or should we be able to alter every square foot for our needs? A question between these extremes would be, What degree of use or exploitation should be allowed? How we answer these questions reflects different values, which, in turn, shape the policies of government agencies and constituency groups about how public lands should be used (Leopold 1991; Varley 1993).

We are witnessing in the Greater Yellowstone Ecosystem tentative forays into a new kind of public land management, one that reflects different values regarding our relationship with nature (Leopold et al. 1963). Its defining characteristic is a commitment to ecosystem management, a policy that reflects the ecological fact that natural processes do not stop at property lines (Keiter and Boyce 1991). This emerging policy includes several dimensions: it is committed to preserving and restoring biological diversity within a regional fauna and flora; it draws heavily on scientific principles and research; and it reflects broadly shared public values. And, most relevant to this essay, it is nurtured by interagency cooperation (Leopold 1991; Varley 1993).

As the rigor of jurisdictional lines softens, one of the big pregnant questions is whether consumptive uses can coexist with preservation (J. Craighead 1991; Keiter and Boyce 1991). Throughout the Greater Yellowstone Ecosystem, there is a lack of consensus on oil and gas exploration in surrounding national forests. As I shared in this chapter's opening story, there are stark differences in the level of logging allowed on various public parcels. Other than killing bison leaving the park, there is not yet an effective means of eradicating brucellosis from wild ungulates (Keiter 1997). These and other issues have traditionally been resolved piecemeal, by each jurisdiction or by each government agency, not comprehensively across boundaries on the basis of scientific data (Barbee and Varley 1984).

The Greater Yellowstone Coordinating Committee (GYCC) has started espousing a process-based approach to ecosystem management (Barbee et al. 1991). Locally formulated policies give people the opportunity to participate in decisions, so they are more likely to own the results (Keiter and Boyce 1991). Other multiagency initiatives include the Interagency Grizzly Bear Committee; the Jackson Hole Cooperative Elk Studies Group; a Northern Range group; interagency committees for the peregrine falcon, bald eagle, trumpeter swan, and gray wolf; and an interagency fire management program (Varley 1993). These initiatives bear witness to the spreading realization that the Greater Yellowstone Ecosystem is best managed by dissolving the jurisdictional lines that run across its landscape.

However, we are still far from having a holistic ecosystem management program for the Yellowstone region. As I write, the GYCC is composed of representatives from four federal agencies—the National Park Service, Forest Service, Fish and Wildlife Service, and Bureau of Land Management—but does not include staff from state and local governments, representatives of relevant nonprofit organizations, and private landowners (Keiter and Boyce 1991; GYCC 2013). This incomplete roster undermines the GYCC's ability to garner broad local support and forge a mutually shared vision.

Critical scientific questions remain to be answered before officials operating within the Ecosystem can fully implement ecosystem management (Keiter and Boyce 1991). For example, we need to know more about fire ecology, ungulate-range interactions, and natural long-term ecological change (Chadde and Kay 1988; Chadde and Kay 1991; Kay and Chadde 1992; Kay and Wagner 1994; Wagner 1994; Budiansky 1996; Kay 1997b). We also need more data about the relationships between various human activities and the natural environment, like the effects of global climate change, of clear-cutting on grizzly bears, and of winter recreation on wildlife (Stockwell et al. 1991; Cassirer et al. 1992; Romme and Turner 1992; Van Dyke and Klein 1996; Bartlein et al. 1997; Cole et al. 1997; Thompson and Henderson 1998; Gunther et al. 1998; Rowland et al. 2000).

Here is an example of an ecosystem-management approach for the entire Yellowstone ecosystem. Exurban development has been changing habitat in Yellowstone to the point that it may impact the long-term sustainability of the grizzly bear. To assess the potential impacts of alternative land-use scenarios, wildlife biologists linked two models, one that predicts rural development and another that predicts bear survival (Schwartz et al. 2012). They found that extremely low densities of residential development created population sinks, areas that absorb individual plants and animals from overproducing source areas. The research team saw that this source-sink system requires a landscape-scale approach. They recommended that land conservation efforts focus on retaining open space, educating the public to minimize human-bear conflicts, and minimizing management-related bear deaths. If it is to be implemented successfully, this strategy would involve multiple federal and state agencies, NGOs, and private landowners working seamlessly across the landscape.

The forays into ecosystem management currently playing out in Yellowstone reflect nothing less than a revolution in the management of public lands (Barbee et al. 1991; Keiter and Boyce 1991; Huff and Varley 1999). With Yellowstone's global prominence, I expect these developments to influence land management policies throughout the National Park Service, in other federal and state agencies, and ultimately around the world.

The concept of ecosystem management implies that natural resource officials will embrace all of the biotic and abiotic components of an ecosystem, and on a scale large enough to ensure a buffer against disturbances arising outside the ecosystem. An early step in effective ecosystem management is identifying a set of goals—measurable ecological conditions—

that will enable managers to decide when to intervene (Krausman 1998). I acknowledge that such management goals will have to be altered via adaptive management as conditions change and knowledge grows (Mattson et al. 1996).

In sum, the broad goal of ecosystem management is to allow natural ecological processes—nutrient cycling and energy flow, plant succession, fire and decomposition, competition and predation, symbiosis, and birth and death, in all their variation and unpredictability—to proceed unimpeded by overbearing human actions (Schaffer 1985). If ecosystem management is to yield healthy ecosystems, all of these natural processes need to transcend the arbitrary lines we've drawn across the mountains.

It is said that animals sometimes commit the Concorde Fallacy, the behavior of allocating resources according to past investment even though ideally the focus should be on expected future returns (Curio 1987; Arkes and Ayton 1999). That we humans are not always rational was shown by the builders of the Concorde supersonic passenger jet. During its design, even though the builders discovered it would run into economic disaster, they continued to build it anyway, arguing that otherwise the huge up-front investment would be wasted. Just because we've done something in a certain way in the past—invested a lot in it—doesn't mean we can't change how we implement a program, or even halt it altogether. Let's retain the right to change our minds. For example, could part of the Targhee tree farm, at least a buffer adjacent to the park, be allowed to undergo natural succession into a diverse forest that sustains a timber harvest?

Whether we're talking about protecting stands of whitebark pine, maintaining viable populations of charismatic megafauna, maximizing native biodiversity, or allowing natural chaos, all these issues point to the need for ecosystem management that transcends land lines. Only then will the Rocky Mountains host the ongoing evolution of native living things.

Epilogue

Remembrance and reflection how allied!

Alexander Pope, *The Complete Poetical Works*
of Alexander Pope

ALPENGLOW, from the German *alpen* for "mountain" and *glute* for "fire," is that brilliant rosy light that shines off a peak at the moment of sunrise or sunset (Sides 2001). Above a dark valley it creates a stunning effect. For example, at sunset, after direct sunshine has abandoned the valley, the west-facing peaks can be ablaze with reds and pinks. In two smashing pictures, *Winter Sunset, Gates of the Valley, Yosemite National Park, California, 1990* and *Self-Portrait at Dawn, Torres del Paine, Patagonia, Chile, 1985* (SCB 2006), the landscape photographer Galen Rowell captured what I consider to be some of the best images of this elusive phenomenon.

My concluding reflection—my personal alpenglow—returns me to the Clark's nutcracker. Its impressive adaptations—bulging throat pouch, efficient seed caching and retrieving, prodigious spatial memory, peaceful society, and seed-eating chicks—plus its impacts on other species—whitebark pine, red squirrel, grizzly bear—have taught us much about how life endures extreme montane environments, about ecosystem management...even about our own brains.

And, in turn, the future of the Clark's nutcracker depends on how well we implement ecosystem management. The codependence of nutcracker and whitebark pine cries for managing ecosystem processes, like fire regimes, and environmental issues, like exotic species, across the patchwork of public and private land parcels. For the sake of these inspiring mountain places, I beseech us: Let's please continue our embryonic entrées into ecosystem management. If we listen, the nutcracker will teach us how.

Thank Yous

Thank the people who help you along the way.

Mom and Dad

Many generous folks helped Nancy and me along the trail. Esther Coffin (Parks Canada [PC]) and Heidi Fengler (Jasper, Alberta) helped us plan and complete our backpacking trips through Jasper and Banff National Parks. Mike Philley introduced me to backpacking in Glacier National Park. During our through-hike of the Waterton-Glacier International Peace Park, Diane Rossetti (PC), Katie Cardston (Glacier National Park), and Sterling Schildt (East Glacier, Montana) were a huge help. Steve Opp (Montana Department of Environmental Quality) helped us plan a trek through the Bob Marshall Wilderness. Michael Boyce (REI, Missoula) and Debra Gale (USDA Forest Service [USFS]) generously shared their knowledge about the Selway-Bitterroot Wilderness. Jim Lee (Augusta, Montana) and Ian Bardwell (USFS) oriented us to the Scapegoat Wilderness. Ken Wotring (USFS) and Steve Hollenhorst (University of Idaho [UI]) helped us plan the Frank Church–River of No Return hike. In this huge wilderness area we were befriended by Linda at the Diamond Ranch, Aaron of Sun Valley Adventures, Buck at Simplot, Bob of Stanley Air Taxi, Linda and George of the Flying B Ranch, Scott Phillips and the River Monkeys, and Zach Lifton (UI) at Taylor Ranch. During our two treks across Yellowstone National Park (YNP) we were well served by Ivan Kowski and Anita Varley of the Backcountry Office; backcountry rangers Mike Ross, Gerald Mernin, Mark Marschall, and Paul Houston; Joel Nelson and Ann Rodman of the Spatial Analysis Center; and Ray and Darlene Rathmell at the Pebble Creek campground. Mike Clark of the Greater Yellowstone Coalition also advised us. Rex and Linda Poulson and Josh Hatten (all of Pinedale, Wyoming), Meredith Malek (USFS), and Stephen and Tamara Vook (Elkhart Guard Station) abetted our journey through the Wind River Range. Steve Brown (West Virginia Department of Natural Resources), Leslie McFadden (USFS), and Casey Clapsaddle (Rivers Unlimited) helped plan walks in the Rawah and Mount Zirkel Wilderness areas. John Hott (Gunnison, Colorado) helped us plan treks through the Collegiate and Indian Peaks Wilderness areas. For our backpack through the Weminuche Wilderness, Nancy Berry and Brian Parker (both USFS) advised and encouraged us. Michelle Brashears (The Sweat Shop, Capon Bridge, West Virginia) helped me strengthen my back and legs.

Many people helped me with the literature: Ken Armitage (University of Kansas); Rob Bleiweiss (University of Wisconsin); Carol Boggs (Stanford University); Diane Campbell (University of California–Irvine); Ken Cullings (NASA Ames Research Center); Mark Ford (USFS Fernow Experimental Forest, Parsons, West Virginia); Hilary Fredette (library) and Joe McNeel (Division of Forestry) (both at West Virginia University [WVU]); Steve French (Jackson, Wyoming); Ben Gadd (Jasper, Alberta); Steve Halterman (Massachusetts Department of Environmental Protection); Paul Hendricks (Montana Natural Heritage Program); Mark Jones (Capon Bridge, West Virginia); Terry Jones (West Virginia Division of Forestry); Larry Kingsbury (USFS Payette National Forest); Jens-Peter Kopelke (Forschungsinstitut Senckenberg, Frankfurt, Germany); Craig McClure (YNP); David Malakoff (National Public Radio); Ron Mumme (Allegheny College); Jenny Newland (Canaan Valley Institute [CVI]); Shirley Parsons (Augusta, West Virginia); Ron Preston (CVI); Anne Post Roy (US Fish and Wildlife Service [USFWS]); Paul Schullery (YNP); Hanne Small (Blacksburg, Virginia); Chris Vogel (CVI); Jim Waggy (Charleston, West Virginia); Nickolas Waser (University of California–Riverside); Ed Watson (CVI); Denise Webb (CVI); Andy White (USFWS); Paul Wilson (Fish and Wildlife Reference Service); and Emily Yost (YNP).

I received helpful data from Ken Aho (Montana State University); Myron (Mike) Baker (Colorado State University); Steve Brooks (CVI); Stan Boutin (University of Alberta); Ted and Betsy Campen (Billings, Montana); Mike Clark (Greater Yellowstone Coalition, Bozeman, Montana); Dorothy Dunning (WVU); Marco Festa-Bianchet (University of Sherbrooke); Bernd Heinrich (University of Vermont); Stephen Herrero (University of Calgary); Scott Hodges (University of California–Santa Barbara); Rebecca Irwin (Dartmouth College); Steve Kite (WVU); Korie Klink, Betsy Didrickson, and Jeb Barzen (all of the International Crane Foundation); William Morris (Duke University); Wayne Myers (Penn State University); Dan Otte (Academy of Natural Sciences); Therese Poland (USFS); Harry Power (Rutgers University); Beverly Rathcke (University of Michigan); Chris Sacchi (Kutztown University), James Thomson (University of Toronto); and Nick Waser (University of California–Riverside).

Several people criticized parts of the manuscript: Nancy Ailes, Betsy and Ted Campen, and David Malakoff. Friends at CVI created maps, solved computer problems, and helped in many other ways. Ellen Deroberts (Veterans Administration, Winchester, Virginia) preserved my writing. Reba Rauch, editor, and Laurel Anderton, copyeditor, helped me wrangle the manuscript into final form. My wife, Nancy Ailes, was trip planner, backpacking partner, and wilderness podiatrist.

Thanks to all.

Names of Plants and Animals

The name we give to something shapes our attitude to it.

Katherine Paterson, *Bridge to Terabithia*

Below is a list of the common names of plants and animals mentioned in the text, followed by their scientific name. Note that many of these taxa are not native to the Rocky Mountains.

PLANTS

alfalfa (*Medicago sativa*)
alpine avens (*Acomastylis rossii*)
alpine clover (*Trifolium dasyphyllum*)
alpine kittentail (*Besseya alpina*)
alpine paintbrush (*Castilleja rhexiifolia*)
Arctic willow (*Salix anglorum*)
arrowleaf balsamroot (*Balsamorhiza sagittata*)
aspens (*Populus*)
asters (Asteraceae)
Baker's lupine (*Lupinus amplus*)
balsam fir (*Abies balsamea*)
balsam poplar (*Populus balsamifera*)
beargrass (*Xerophyllum tenax*)
big bluestem (*Andropogon gerardii*)
bigleaf lupine (*Lupinus polyphyllus*)
big sagebrush (*Artemisia tridentata*)
birches (*Betula*)
biscuitroots (*Lomatium*)
bitterroot (*Lewisia rediviva*)
blazing star (*Mentzelia laevicaulis*)
blueberry (*Vaccinium myrtillus*)
blue columbine (*Aquilegia coerulea*)

bluegrasses (*Poa*)
boreal willow (*Salix borealis*)
bristlecone pine (*Pinus aristata*)
broad bean (*Vicia faba*)
buffaloberries (*Shepherdia*)
bush lupine (*Lupinus arboreus*)
cabbage (*Brassica oleracea*)
camas (*Camassia quamash*)
cedars (*Thuja*)
chestnut oak (*Quercus prinus*)
chilis (*Capsicum*)
choke cherry (*Prunus virginiana*)
clovers (*Trifolium*)
coastal larkspur (*Delphinium decorum*)
coca (*Erythroxylum*)
columbines (*Aquilegia*)
comfreys (*Symphytum*)
common juniper (*Juniperus communis*)
conifers (Gymnospermae)
cotton grasses (*Eriophorum*)
cow parsnip (*Heracleum lanatum*)
cowpea (*Vigna unguiculata*)
currants (*Ribes*)
Douglas-fir (*Pseudotsuga menziesii*)

early paintbrush (*Castilleja chromosa*)
elephant's head (*Pedicularis groenlandica*)
elk thistle (*Cirsium foliosum*)
Engelmann spruce (*Picea engelmannii*)
field chickweed (*Cerastium arvense*)
field gentian (*Gentianella campestris*)
figworts (Scrophulariaceae)
fireweed (*Epilobium angustifolium*)
firs (*Abies*)
foxglove (*Digitalis purpurea*)
Fremont cottonwood (*Populus fremontii*)
fuchsias (*Fuchsia*)
Gambel oak (*Quercus gambelii*)
giant red paintbrush (*Castilleja miniata*)
glacier lily (*Erythronium grandiflorum*)
globeflower (*Trollius albiflorus*)
goldenglow (*Rudbeckia ampla*)
gooseberries (*Ribes*)
grasses (Poaceae)
green algae (Chlorophyta)
harebell (*Campanula rotundifolia*)
heaths (Ericaceae)
hemlocks (*Tsuga*)
huckleberries (*Vaccinium*)
jack pine (*Pinus banksiana*)
Jeffrey pine (*Pinus jeffreyi*)
jewel lichens (*Xanthoria, Caloplaca*)
jewelweeds (*Impatiens*)
junipers (*Juniperus*)
Kincaid's lupine (*Lupinus sulphureus*)
lance-leaved stonecrop (*Sedum lanceolatum*)
larkspurs (*Delphinium*)
legumes (Fabaceae)
Lewis's monkeyflower (*Mimulus lewisii*)
lima bean (*Phaseolus lunatus*)
limber pine (*Pinus flexilis*)
lizard tail (*Eriophyllum staechadifolium*)

lodgepole lupine (*Lupinus parviflorus*)
lodgepole pine (*Pinus contorta*)
long-plumed avens (*Geum triflorum*)
lupines (*Lupinus*)
many-flowered stickseed (*Hackelia floribunda*)
maples (*Acer*)
marijuana (*Cannabis sativa*)
meadow bistort (*Polygonum bistorta*)
milkweeds (*Asclepias*)
monkeyflowers (*Mimulus*)
monkshood (*Aconitum columbianum*)
morning glory (*Ipomoea purpurea*)
moss campion (*Silene acaulis*)
mosses (Bryophyta)
mountain kittentail (*Besseya plantaginea*)
mountain snowberry (*Symphoricarpos oreophilus*)
mountain sorrel (*Oxyria digyna*)
mule-ears (*Wyethia amplexicaulis*)
mustards (Brassicaceae)
myrtle pachistima (*Paxistima myrsinites*)
narrowleaf cottonwood (*Populus angustifolia*)
narrowleaf lupine (*Lupinus angustifolius*)
narrowleaf plantain (*Plantago lanceolata*)
needle-and-thread grass (*Stipa comata*)
needlegrasses (*Stipa*)
Nelson's larkspur (*Delphinium nelsonii*)
northern red oak (*Quercus rubra*)
oaks (*Quercus*)
opium poppy (*Papaver somniferum*)
orange mountain dandelion (*Agoseris aurantiaca*)
Oregon grape (*Mahonia aquifolium*)
paintbrushes (*Castilleja*)
paper birch (*Betula papyrifera*)

penstemons (*Penstemon*)

phloxes (Polemoniaceae)

pines (*Pinus*)

pinyon pine (*Pinus edulis*)

ponderosa pine (*Pinus ponderosa*)

prairie lupine (*Lupinus lepidus*)

pussy paws (*Calyptridium umbellatum*)

pussytoes (*Antennaria*)

quaking aspen (*Populus tremuloides*)

red alder (*Alnus rubra*)

redberry elder (*Sambucus racemosa*)

red cedar (*Thuja plicata*)

red larkspur (*Delphinium nudicaule*)

reeds (Poaceae)

rushes (*Juncus*)

ryegrass (*Lolium perenne*)

sagebrushes (*Artemisia*)

saguaro cactus (*Carnegiea gigantea*)

scarlet gilia (*Ipomopsis aggregata*)

scarlet paintbrush (*Castilleja miniata*)

sedges (*Carex*)

sego lily (*Calochortus nuttallii*)

shooting star (*Dodecatheon meadia*)

short-styled onion (*Allium brevistylum*)

silky lupine (*Lupinus sericeus*)

silvery lupine (*Lupinus argenteus*)

sky pilot, skunkweed, Jacob's ladder (*Polemonium viscosum*)

snapdragons (*Antirrhinum*)

snowbed willow (*Salix herbacea*)

soopolallie (*Shepherdia canadensis*)

spiked speedwell (*Veronica spicata*)

spruces (*Picea*)

stemless lupine (*Lupinus lepidus*)

sticky geranium (*Geranium viscosissimum*)

stone pines (Cembrae)

subalpine fir (*Abies lasiocarpa*)

subalpine larkspur (*Delphinium barbeyi*)

sulphur buckwheat, sulphur flower (*Eriogonum*)

sulphur paintbrush (*Castilleja sulphurea*)

sundial lupine (*Lupinus perennis*)

tall mountain larkspur (*Delphinium occidentale*)

tealeaf willow (*Salix pulchra*)

Texas bluebonnet (*Lupinus texensis*)

Texas paintbrush (*Castilleja indivisa*)

timothy (*Phleum pratense*)

tree lupine (*Lupinus arboreus*)

velvet lupine (*Lupinus leucophyllus*)

water hemlock (*Cicuta*)

western serviceberry (*Amelanchier alnifolia*)

whitebark pine (*Pinus albicaulis*)

white birch (*Betula papyrifera*)

white bog orchid (*Platanthera dilatata*)

white geranium (*Geranium richardsonii*)

white lupine (*Lupinus albus*)

white phlox (*Phlox multiflora*)

white pine blister rust (a fungus; *Cronartium ribicola*)

white spruce (*Picea glauca*)

wholeleaf paintbrush (*Castilleja integra*)

Wight's paintbrush (*Castilleja wightii*)

wild parsnip (*Pastinaca sativa*)

willows (*Salix*)

Wood's rose (*Rosa woodsii*)

Wyoming paintbrush (*Castilleja linariaefolia*)

yellow bush lupine (*Lupinus arboreus*)

yellow columbine (*Aquilegia flavescens*)

yellow monkeyflower (*Mimulus guttatus*)

yellow paintbrush (*Castilleja flava*)

yellow sweet clover (*Melilotus officinalis*)

ANIMALS

African wild dog (*Lycaon pictus*)

Allen's hummingbird (*Selasphorus sasin*)

Alpine marmot (*Marmota marmota*)

American cheetah (*Miracinonyx trumani*)

American crow (*Corvus brachyrhynchos*)

American dipper (*Cinclus mexicanus*)

American lion (*Panthera leo atrox*)

American pipit (*Anthus rubescens*)

American redstart (*Setophaga ruticilla*)

American robin (*Turdus migratorius*)

American toad (*Bufo americanus*)

amphibians (Amphibia)

ancient bison (*Bison antiquus*)

anicia checkerspot butterfly (*Euphydryas anicia*)

Anna's hummingbird (*Calypte anna*)

antelopes (Bovidae)

ants (Formicidae)

anurans (Anura)

apes (Hominoidea)

aphids (Aphididae)

Apollo butterfly (*Parnassius apollo*)

Arctic blue butterfly (*Agriades glandon*)

Arctic ground squirrel (*Spermophilus parryii*)

Arctic wolf (*Canis lupus arctos*)

army cutworm moth (*Euxoa auxiliaris*)

Auvergne bear (*Ursus minimus*)

backswimmers (*Notonecta*)

badger (*Taxidea taxus*)

bald eagle (*Haliaeetus leucocephalus*)

bank swallow (*Riparia riparia*)

barn swallow (*Hirundo rustica*)

barred tiger salamander (*Ambystoma tigrinum mavortium*)

bats (Chiroptera)

bears (*Ursus*)

beaver (*Castor canadensis*)

bees (Apoidea)

beetles (Coleoptera)

Belding's ground squirrel (*Spermophilus beldingi*)

bighorn sheep (*Ovis canadensis*)

birds (Aves)

bison (*Bison bison*)

black bear (*Ursus americanus*)

black-billed magpie (*Pica hudsonia*)

black-capped chickadee (*Poecile atricapillus*)

black-tailed jackrabbit (*Lepus californicus*)

bluebirds (*Sialia*)

blue grouse (*Dendragapus obscurus*)

bobcat (*Felis rufus*)

bog fritillary (*Boloria eunomia*)

boreal toad (*Bufo boreas*)

Botta's pocket gopher (*Thomomys bottae*)

broad-tailed hummingbird (*Selasphorus platycercus*)

brook trout (*Salvelinus fontinalis*)

buff-tailed bumblebee (*Bombus terrestris*)

bumblebees (*Bombus*)

butterflies (Lepidoptera)

cabbage butterflies (Pierinae)

cabbage white butterfly (*Pieris rapae*)

California ground squirrel (*Spermophilus beecheyi*)

California grunion (*Leuresthes tenuis*)

California gull (*Larus californicus*)

calliope hummingbird (*Stellula calliope*)

camels (Camelidae)

Canada goose (*Branta canadensis*)

capybaras (*Hydrochoerus*)

caribou (*Rangifer tarandus*)

Cascades frog (*Rana cascadae*)
cats (Felidae)
cattle, domestic cow (*Bos primigenius*)
cave bear (*Ursus spelaeus*)
centipedes (Chilopoda)
cerambycid beetles (Cerambycidae)
chachalaca (*Ortalis*)
checkerspot butterflies (*Euphydryas*)
chestnut-sided warbler (*Setophaga pensylvanica*)
chickadees (*Poecile*)
chicken (*Gallus gallus*)
chimpanzee (*Pan troglodytes*)
chipmunks (*Tamias*)
chordates (Chordata)
chrysomelid beetles (Chrysomelidae)
Clark's nutcracker (*Nucifraga columbiana*)
cliff swallow (*Hirundo pyrrhonota*)
clouded sulphur butterfly (*Colias philodice*)
coho salmon (*Oncorhynchus kisutch*)
collared pika (*Ochotona collaris*)
Columbian ground squirrel (*Spermophilus columbianus*)
common carder bumblebee (*Bombus pascuorum*)
common eastern bumblebee (*Bombus impatiens*)
common raven (*Corvus corax*)
consobrinus bumblebee (*Bombus consobrinus*)
Cooper's hawk (*Accipiter cooperii*)
Costa's hummingbird (*Calypte costae*)
cougar, mountain lion, puma (*Felis concolor*)
coyote (*Canis latrans*)
crayfishes (Crustacea)
crickets (Gryllinae)
crows, jays, magpies, and ravens (Corvidae)
cuckoo bumblebees (*Psithyrus*)

curassow (*Crax rubra*)
cutthroat trout (*Salmo clarki*)
dance flies (Empididae)
darters and perches (Percidae)
decorated cricket (*Gryllodes supplicans*)
deer (*Odocoileus*)
deer mouse (*Peromyscus maniculatus*)
dippers (*Cinclus*)
dire wolf (*Canis dirus*)
dogs (Canidae)
doves (Columbidae)
dung fly (*Scatophaga stercoraria*)
earthworms (Oligochaeta)
Edith's checkerspot butterfly (*Euphydryas editha*)
Edwards bumblebee (*Bombus edwardsii*)
eels (Anguillidae)
elk, red deer (*Cervus canadensis*)
ermine (*Mustela erminea*)
Etruscan bear (*Ursus etruscus*)
Eurasian nutcracker (*Nucifraga caryocatactes*)
European chamois (*Rupicapra rupicapra*)
European common shrew (*Sorex araneus*)
European earwig (*Forficula auricularia*)
European hare (*Lepus europaeus*)
fairy shrimps (Anostraca)
falcons (*Falco*)
Fender's blue butterfly (*Icaricia icarioides fenderi*)
field cricket (*Gryllus integer*)
finches (Fringillidae)
fisher (*Martes pennanti*)
fishes (Osteichthyes)
flat-headed peccary (*Platygonus compressus*)
flies (Diptera)

forest tent caterpillar (*Malacosoma disstria*)
four-horned pronghorn (*Breameryx*)
foxes, wolves, and dogs (Canidae)
frogs and toads (Anura)
gall aphids (*Pemphigus*)
garter snakes (*Thamnophis*)
giant armadillo (*Priodontes giganteus*)
giant beaver (*Castoroides ohioensis*)
giant ground sloths (*Megatherium*)
giant short-faced bear (*Arctodus simus*)
giant waterbug (*Lethocerus americanus*)
Gila topminnow (*Poeciliopsis occidentalis*)
Gillette's checkerspot butterfly (*Euphydryas gillettii*)
Glanville fritillary butterfly (*Melitaea cinxia*)
glyptodonts (Glyptodontidae)
gnats (Nematocera)
goats (Bovidae)
gobies (Gobiidae)
golden eagle (*Aquila chrysaetos*)
golden-mantled ground squirrel (*Spermophilus lateralis*)
gopher snake (*Pituophis melanoleucus*)
grasshoppers (Orthoptera)
gray flycatcher (*Empidonax wrightii*)
gray jay (*Perisoreus canadensis*)
gray tiger salamander (*Ambystoma tigrinum diaboli*)
gray wolf (*Canis lupus*)
Great Basin gopher snake (*Pituophis catenifer deserticola*)
Great Basin rattlesnake (*Crotalus oreganus lutosus*)
great blue heron (*Ardea herodias*)
great eggfly butterfly (*Hypolimnas bolina*)
great tit (*Parus major*)

green-veined white butterfly (*Pieris napi*)
grizzly bear (*Ursus arctos*)
groundhog (*Marmota monax*)
ground squirrels (Sciuridae)
grouses (Tetraoninae)
guinea pig (*Cavia cobaya*)
guppy (*Poecilia reticulata*)
hairy woodpecker (*Picoides villosus*)
hamadryas baboon (*Papio hamadryas*)
hares (*Lepus*)
hawk moths (Sphingidae)
hawks (Accipitridae)
hoary marmot (*Marmota caligata*)
honeybees (*Apis mellifera*)
horned lark (*Eremophila alpestris*)
horses (*Equus*)
housefly (*Musca domestica*)
house mouse (*Mus domesticus*)
humans (*Homo sapiens*)
hummingbirds (Trochilidae)
hymenopterans (Hymenoptera)
icarioid blue butterfly (*Plebejus icarioides*)
Icelandic ptarmigan (*Lagopus muta*)
insects (Insecta)
jacanas (Jacanidae)
jaguar (*Felis onca*)
jays (Corvidae)
Karner blue butterfly (*Lycaeides melissa samuelis*)
katydids (Tettigoniidae)
ladybird beetles (Coccinellidae)
lagomorphs (Lagomorpha)
large-headed llama (*Hemiauchenia macrocephala*)
lazuli bunting (*Passerina amoena*)
leaf-miner flies (Agromyzidae)
leeches (Hirudinea)
leopard frog (*Rana pipiens*)
Lewis's woodpecker (*Melanerpes lewis*)

lice (Mallophaga)
lions (*Felis*)
little brown bat (*Myotis lucifugus*)
lizards (Lacertilia)
llama (*Lama glama*)
long-horned bison (*Bison antiquus*)
long-horned grasshoppers
    (Tettigoniidae)
long-tailed vole (*Microtus
    longicaudus*)
long-tailed weasel (*Mustela frenata*)
long-toed salamander (*Ambystoma
    macrodactylum*)
lynx (*Felis lynx*)
mammals (Mammalia)
mammoths (*Mammuthus*)
margay (*Felis wiedii*)
marmots (*Marmota*)
marsupials (Marsupialia)
marten (*Martes americana*)
masked shrew (*Sorex cinereus*)
mastodon (*Mammut americanum*)
Mead's sulphur butterfly (*Colias
    meadii*)
Mexican axolotl (*Ambystoma
    mexicanum*)
Mexican free-tailed bat (*Tadarida
    mexicana*)
mice (Cricetidae)
millipedes (Diplopoda)
minnows (Cyprinidae)
monkeys (Simiiformes)
montane shrew (*Sorex monticolus*)
montane vole (*Microtus montanus*)
moose (*Alces alces*)
Mormon cricket (*Anabrus simplex*)
moths (Lepidoptera)
mountain bluebird (*Sialia currucoides*)
mountain chickadee (*Poecile gambeli*)
mountain deer (*Navahoceros fricki*)
mountain goat (*Oreamnos americanus*)
mountain lion (*Felis concolor*)

mountain pine beetle (*Dendroctonus
    ponderosae*)
mule deer (*Odocoileus hemionus*)
muskox (*Ovibos moschatus*)
muskrat (*Ondatra zibethicus*)
nartee bushcricket (*Kawanaphila
    nartee*)
nighthawks (Chordeilinae)
northern flicker (*Colaptes auratus*)
northern goshawk (*Accipiter gentilis*)
Norway rat (*Rattus norvegicus*)
nutcrackers (*Nucifraga*)
nuthatches (*Sitta*)
Olympic marmot (*Marmota olympus*)
Oregon junco (*Junco hyemalis
    oreganus*)
Pacific rattlesnake (*Crotalus viridis
    oreganus*)
Pacific tree frog (*Hyla regilla*)
pampatheres (Pampatheriidae)
parsnip webworm (*Depressaria
    pastinacella*)
perching birds (Passeriformes)
peregrine falcon (*Falco peregrinus*)
phalaropes (*Phalaropus*)
pika (*Ochotona princeps*)
pine bark beetles (Scolytidae)
pine siskin (*Carduelis pinus*)
pipefishes (Syngnathidae)
Pleistocene bighorn sheep (*Ovis
    catclawensis*)
plorans grasshopper (*Eyprepocnemis
    plorans*)
plume moths (Pterophoridae)
pocket gophers (Geomyidae)
poison-arrow frogs (*Dendrobates*)
polar bear (*Ursus maritimus*)
porcupine (*Erethizon dorsatum*)
potato leaf beetle (*Epitrix cucumeris*)
prairie dogs (*Cynomys*)
prairie rattlesnake (*Crotalus viridis*)
primates (Primates)

pronghorn (*Antilocapra americana*)
ptarmigans (*Lagopus*)
quails (Odontophoridae)
Queen Alexandra's sulphur butterfly
    (*Colias alexandra*)
rabbits and hares (Lagomorpha)
rainbow trout (*Oncorhynchus mykiss*)
rattlesnakes (*Crotalus*)
red-backed vole (*Clethrionomys
    gapperi*)
red deer (*Cervus elaphus*)
red-legged frog (*Rana aurora*)
red-shafted flicker (*Colaptes auratus*)
red squirrel (*Tamiasciurus hudsonicus*)
red-tailed hawk (*Buteo jamaicensis*)
reptiles (Reptilia)
river otter (*Lutra canadensis*)
rock ptarmigan (*Lagopus muta*)
rock squirrel (*Spermophilus variegatus*)
Rocky Mountain elk (*Cervus
    canadensis nelsoni*)
Rocky Mountain locust (*Melanoplus
    spretus*)
rodents (Rodentia)
Roosevelt wapiti (*Cervus canadensis
    roosevelti*)
rosy-finches (*Leucosticte*)
rough-skinned newt (*Taricha
    granulosa*)
round-tailed ground squirrel
    (*Spermophilus tereticaudus*)
ruby-throated hummingbird
    (*Archilochus colubris*)
ruff (*Philomachus pugnax*)
ruffed grouse (*Bonasa umbellus*)
rufous hummingbird (*Selasphorus
    rufus*)
rupicaprids (Rupicaprini)
saber-toothed tiger (*Smilodon fatalis*)
sagebrush lizard (*Sceloporus graciosus*)
sage grouse (*Centrocercus
    urophasianus*)

salamanders (Caudata)
salmon (*Oncorhynchus*)
sandhill crane (*Grus canadensis*)
sandpipers (Scolopacidae)
scimitar cat (*Homotherium serum*)
Scudder's sulphur butterfly (*Colias
    scudderi*)
seahorses (Syngnathidae)
shadow darner dragonfly (*Aeshna
    umbrosa*)
sharp-tailed grouse (*Tympanuchus
    phasianellus*)
short-faced bear (*Arctodus simus*)
shrews (Soricidae)
shrub-ox (*Eucheratherium collinum*)
silver-spotted skipper butterfly
    (*Hesperia comma*)
silver-studded blue butterfly (*Plebejus
    argus*)
silvery blue butterfly (*Glaucopsyche
    lygdamus*)
smooth newt (*Lissotriton vulgaris*)
snails (Pulmonata)
snakes, serpents (Serpentes)
snowshoe hare (*Lepus americanus*)
songbirds (Oscines)
southern spadefoot toad (*Scaphiopus
    multiplicatus*)
sparrows (Emberizidae)
speckled wood butterfly (*Pararge
    aegeria*)
spiders (Araneae)
spotted frog (*Rana pretiosa*)
spotted sandpiper (*Actitis macularia*)
spring peeper (*Pseudacris crucifer*)
springtails (Collembola)
spruce budworms (*Choristoneura*)
spruce grouse (*Falcipennis canadensis*)
squirrels (Sciuridae)
stag-moose (*Cervalces scotti*)
Steller's jay (*Cyanocitta stelleri*)
sulphur butterflies (*Colias*)

swallowtail butterflies (Papilionidae)
swifts (Apodidae)
tapirs (*Tapirus*)
Tasmanian native-hen (*Tribonyx mortierii*)
teiid lizards (Teiidae)
termites (Isoptera)
three-spined stickleback (*Gasterosteus aculeatus*)
ticks (Ixodidae)
tiger salamander (*Ambystoma tigrinum*)
tiger swallowtail (*Papilio canadensis*)
timber rattlesnake (*Crotalus horridus*)
tits (*Parus*)
toads (Bufonidae)
Townsend's ground squirrel (*Spermophilus townsendii*)
Townsend's solitaire (*Myadestes townsendi*)
tree bumblebee (*Bombus hypnorum*)
tree lizard (*Urosaurus ornatus*)
tropical fowl mite (*Ornithonyssus bursa*)
trouts (*Salmo*)
true bugs (Hemiptera)
trumpeter swan (*Cygnus buccinator*)
tundra muskox (*Ovibos moschatus*)
tunicate (Urochordata)
tussock moths (Lymantriidae)
Uinta ground squirrel (*Urocitellus armatus*)
ungulates (Ungulata)
vagrant (wandering) shrew (*Sorex vagrans*)
Vancouver Island marmot (*Marmota vancouverensis*)
velvet bean moth (*Anticarsia gemmatalis*)
vertebrates (Vertebrata)
vertical bushcricket (*Requena verticalis*)

vipers (Viperidae)
warblers (Parulidae)
wasps (Hymenoptera)
water boatmen (*Corixa*)
water shrew (*Sorex palustris*)
weasels (*Mustela*)
western bumblebee (*Bombus occidentalis*)
western camel (*Camelops hesternus*)
western meadowlark (*Sturnella neglecta*)
western prairie rattlesnake (*Crotalus viridis viridis*)
western rattlesnake (*Crotalus viridis*)
western sulphur butterfly (*Pieris occidentalis*)
white-crowned sparrow (*Zonotrichia leucophrys*)
white-lined sphinx (*Celerio lineata*)
white pelican (*Pelecanus erythrorhynchos*)
white-tailed deer (*Odocoileus virginianus*)
white-tailed ptarmigan (*Lagopus leucurus*)
white-throated swift (*Aeronautes saxatalis*)
willow ptarmigan (*Lagopus lagopus*)
wolverine (*Gulo gulo*)
wolves (*Canis*)
wood frog (*Rana sylvatica*)
woodland muskox (*Symbos cavifrons*)
woodpeckers (Picidae)
woolly mammoth (*Mammuthus primigenius*)
worms (Annelida)
wrasses (Labridae)
yak (*Bos grunniens*)
yellow-bellied marmot (*Marmota flaviventris*)
yellow jackets (*Vespula*)

Glossary

Words are the coinage of thought...

John Hodges and Mary Whitten, *Harbrace College Handbook*

abdomen: the hindmost of the three major parts of an insect's body; belly

abiotic: refers to parts of an ecosystem that are not living, e.g., air, water, rock

accessory gland: small mass of tissue near the reproductive system of a male insect that secretes molecules that are transferred to the female during mating

acid: substance that liberates hydrogen ions; solution with a pH of less than 7

acorn: fruit of an oak

adaptation: inherited trait that has contributed to the reproductive success of an individual's ancestors and is expected to contribute similarly to the current generation

adaptive significance: the way a trait contributes to individual reproductive success

adipose: refers to animal fat; tissue composed of fat cells

age class: cohort of individuals of similar age

age distribution: number of individuals in each age category

aggregation: group of individuals

aggression: behavior in which one individual potentially harms another

agonistic: refers to combative behavior

airfoil: flat structure that creates lift when in motion relative to air, e.g., wing

alarm call: vocalization that warns others of predators and other threats

alarm substance: chemical released by an animal that alerts others of a predator

alcohol: organic compound with waterlike properties made of one or more alkyl (derived from CH_3) and hydroxyl (-OH) groups

alga: pl. algae; an often single-celled plant that is not differentiated into tissues

alien: not native; exotic

alkali: soluble salt in some soils of arid regions that can inhibit plant growth

alkalinity: buffer capacity; capacity of a solution to neutralize acid

alkaloid: bitter organic base found in seed plants that deters herbivores

allele: one of several possible forms of a given gene occupying the same relative position (locus) on homologous chromosomes, e.g., the alleles for brown and blue eyes

allogrooming: social behavior in which one individual cleans another

allomaternal care: female animals nursing and protecting unrelated young

alpenglow: series of colors that shift from orange to pink to purple that may be
    seen on mountains exposed to direct sunlight in the east as the sun sets in the
    west. The same color series in reverse reflects off peaks in the west at sunrise.

alpha: individual animal at the top of a dominance hierarchy

alpine: life zone above the upper treeline; pertaining to mountains

alternative reproductive behaviors: different mating acts by members of a sex

altruism: selflessness; foregoing reproduction while helping another reproduce

ambient: refers to surrounding conditions

amino acid: organic compound with acidic carboxyl (COOH) and basic amino
    (NH_2) groups that serves as the basic building unit of protein molecules

amphibian: vertebrate of the class Amphibia that normally metamorphoses from
    aquatic larva to terrestrial adult, e.g., frog

amplexus: clasping of a female amphibian by a male during mating

ampulla: sperm-containing part of a spermatophore

anal gland: cluster of secretory cells near the anus that release pheromones

anatomy: study of the structure of organisms' bodies

ancestral: refers to a trait or organism from which other features or taxa evolved

angiosperms: flowering plants

angle of repose: maximum angle (e.g., 32–36°) at which unconsolidated material
    stands without sliding

animal behavior: scientific study of the movements of animals

annual: one year's duration; organism that completes its life cycle within a year

antenna: long, thin, stringlike sensory organ on an invertebrate's head

anterior: refers to the head end of an animal

anther: pollen-bearing part of a flower's stamen

antiestrogenic: refers to a substance that opposes the actions of estrogen

antipredator behavior: acts that reduce the odds of being caught by a predator

antler: hornlike, deciduous, bony outgrowth of an ungulate's frontal bone

Anura: order of amphibians without tails; anurans, i.e., frogs and toads

anus: hole at the posterior end of a digestive tube

aposematic: refers to colors and actions that advertise an animal's unpalatability

archaeology: scientific study of the remains of past human life

Archaic: second major prehistoric human cultural tradition in North America

archipelago: cluster of islands

area effect: relationship in which small areas support fewer species than large
    areas

arteriosclerosis: chronic disease characterized by abnormal thickening and
    hardening of arterial walls

asexual reproduction: production of new individuals without union of gametes

aspect: cardinal direction that a site faces

assemblage: set of species found in a particular place

assimilation: incorporation of nutrients into tissues
association: set of species that are typically found together
asymmetry: condition in which an object's left and right sides are not mirror images of each other
atlatl: spear-flinging tool with a handle at one end and a hook at the other
atomic number: number of protons in an atom
aucubin: toxic iridoid glycoside ($C_{15}H_{22}O_9$) found widely in the plant kingdom that functions as an herbivore-deterring secondary compound
avalanche chute: trough with recurring slippages of large masses of snow
axolotl: sexually functional tiger salamander that still has a larval body form
bacteria: sing. bacterium; single-celled organisms without organelles
balance of nature: notion that organisms of an ecosystem occur in equilibrium
band: group of individuals of a large-bodied mammal, e.g., mountain goat
bar: vertical stripe on the side of an animal
bark stripping: the scraping of bark off a tree by an herbivorous animal
basal: refers to the base, e.g., a plant's basal leaves
basal metabolism: rate at which a resting organism expends energy
Basin and Range: physiographic province of western North America between the Colorado Plateau and Sierra Nevada
basking: behavior in which an organism positions its body so as to be warmed by sunshine
behavioral plasticity: ability of an animal to respond in different ways to the same stimulus, e.g., alternative feeding behaviors
belly plant: informal name for a cushion plant
benthic invertebrates: animals without backbones that live in streambeds
benzenoid: refers to a volatile hydrocarbon (C_6H_6) that acts as an herbivore-deterring secondary compound
Beringia: land bridge between Siberia and Alaska during the Pleistocene epoch
berry: fruit that is soft and pulpy throughout
best management practice: broadly accepted action intended to minimize environmental impacts
bet hedging: behavior that minimizes the odds of failure
biennial: of two years' duration; a plant that completes its life cycle in two years
bifurcation: a splitting in two
bigamy: mating system in which one male breeds with two females, or vice versa
bilateral: refers to two sides
bilateral asymmetry: extent to which two sides of an animal are not identical
bilateral symmetry: condition in which the two halves of an object are mirror images of each other
bioassay: measure of the magnitude of a stimulus, like a chemical, that causes a specific response in an organism
biodiversity: all the different kinds of living things, e.g., genetic diversity
biomass: weight of a particular kind of organism in a delineated area

biome: broad ecological unit, like a desert, characterized by distinct life forms

biota: set of species in a certain region or at a particular time

biotope: region of uniform environmental conditions

bog: wetland of saturated acidic soil and partially decayed sphagnum moss

bole: central trunk of a tree

bond: attraction between two individual animals

boreal: refers to the cool spruce-fir zone ranging from Alaska to Newfoundland

botany: scientific study of plants

boulder: piece of rock larger than 10 inches (0.26 m) across

boundary layer: zone of slow-moving air caused by friction with a solid object

bract: small, scalelike leaf growing at the base of a flower

broadleaf: type of plant with wide leaves, as distinct from conifers

brood: n., young animals that hatch from a single clutch of eggs; vb., to warm
    and protect babies

broody: refers to a parent warming and protecting its offspring

brown adipose: group of cells with many small fat droplets that generate heat

browniine: alkaloid $(C_{25}H_{41}NO_7)$ that acts as a plant secondary compound

browser: animal that eats woody twigs or shoots

brucellosis: disease thought to be transmitted between bison and cattle in the wild

bud: embryonic, rapidly growing tip of a plant

buffalo jump: cliff from which bison were driven over the edge

bugling: screech emitted by a bull elk during the rut

bulb: underground plant storage organ derived from a shoot

cache: n., food storage site; vb., to store

caecum: pouch in digestive system that serves as site of cellulose digestion

cairn: pile of stones built by humans to indicate a route

calcium: metallic element of the alkaline-earth group with atomic number 20

call: short, simple sound uttered by an animal

calorie: unit of energy that raises the temperature of 1 g of water by 1°C

cambium: layer of growing tissue between the bark and inner wood of trees

camouflage: patterns and colors that disguise an animal

canine: adj., refers to dogs; n., long, pointed tooth that penetrates meat

cannibalism: practice of eating members of one's own species

cannon bone: skeletal element in hoofed animals from hock to fetlock

canopy: uppermost layer of leaves in a plant community

carbohydrate: major class of organic compound made of carbon, hydrogen, and
    oxygen, e.g., sugar

carbon: nonmetallic element with atomic number 6 that is found in organic
    compounds

carbon dioxide: gas (CO_2) exhaled by animals and assimilated by plants

carnivore: meat-eating organism; member of the mammalian order Carnivora

carrion: dead and decaying animal

caste: specialized form of adult individuals in a eusocial insect colony catabolism: metabolic processes that break down molecules

catalpol: toxic iridoid glycoside ($C_{22}H_{26}O_{12}$) in plants that deters herbivores

catechol: benzenediol molecule [$C_6H_4(OH)_2$] that acts as secondary compound

caterpillar: immature lepidopteran that will undergo complete metamorphosis

catkin: tassel-like cluster of small flowers on alders and certain other trees

cellulose: glucose polymer that serves as structural support in plant cell walls

central-place foraging: food gathering that optimizes the time and/or energy invested in assembling foods in a central place

cerci: pair of appendages at the posterior end of an insect

chalk hills: rolling landscape underlain by porous limestone that supports a fragile grassland

chaparral: community of low, thick, scrubby evergreen shrubs in a semiarid climate

cheater: individual animal that circumvents another's adaptation to further its own reproductive success, e.g., nectar-robbing bee, false alarm–calling chickadee

cheek gland: tissues in the side of an animal's face that secrete pheromones

cheek marking: act of rubbing secretions from a cheek onto an object

chemical alarm signaling: releasing a chemical that communicates danger

chemical labeling: acquiring a unique chemical signature

chemistry: scientific study of matter and its changes

chemosensor: system that detects specific molecules in the environment

chert: rock resembling flint that is composed of quartz or chalcedony

chitin: hard, nitrogen-containing carbohydrate that forms an invertebrate's exoskeleton

chlorophyll: green pigment in plants that converts kinetic light energy to the chemical bonds of carbohydrates

cholesterol: steroid alcohol ($C_{27}H_{45}OH$) in animal body fluids

chorus howling: loud, sustained, doleful sound produced by a wolf pack

chromosome: threadlike structure bearing genes in the nucleus of a cell

chronic wasting disease: spontaneous, laterally transmitted spongiform encephalopathy in ungulates that leads to changed behavior, weight loss, and death

circumboreal: refers to something found around the Earth's northern latitudes

circumpolar: refers to something found around a polar region

cirque: steep-walled mountain basin excavated by a glacier

clay: earthy material made of particles up to 0.00008 inch (0.002 mm) in diameter

clear-cutting: method of timber harvesting in which all trees are cut

climate: long-term atmospheric conditions in a region

climax: community of plants that persists indefinitely because it replaces itself

cloaca: chamber in certain vertebrates (e.g., reptiles) through which products of the digestive, excretory, and reproductive systems pass to the outside

clone: group of genetically identical individuals

Clovis: oldest Native American culture, existed 11,500 to 10,500 years ago

clutch: group of eggs laid by a female

coevolution: process in which the adaptations of two species have been shaped by the species' mutual interactions

cohort: group of similar-aged individuals in one place

coiled basket: storage receptacle made of woven strands

cold drainage: the settling of cold air in low places

collecting time: amount of time it takes an animal to gather a unit of food

colonization: establishment of a new population in a formerly unoccupied place

colony: group of conspecific individuals living in a tight social group

combat dance: form of sexual competition in which two male rattlesnakes rise and attempt to throw each other to the ground

communication: two-way exchange of information between individuals

community: set of interacting species in a particular area

community structure: the kinds, numbers, and spatial relationships of the members of an ecological community

compensation: in a population, a high reproductive rate that makes up for a high death rate; when a plant regrows the mass it lost to herbivores

competition: struggle between living things for common limiting resources

compound: chemical resulting from the bonding of different elements

Concorde fallacy: committing resources as a function of past investments rather than expected returns; sunk cost fallacy

conduction: movement of heat from a hotter object to a cooler one

cone: reproductive organ of pines, spruces, and other conifers that bears ovules, pollen, and/or seeds within bracts

conifer: tree or shrub that bears seeds in cones; needle-leaved tree like pine

coniferous forest: biome in which the dominant vegetation is coniferous trees

coniferyl benzoate: secondary metabolite ($C_{11}H_{13}O_4$) in plants that deters herbivores

conservation biology: science that combines ecology, genetics, behavior, and evolution to manage rare species

conspecific: refers to an individual of the same species

consumptive uses: uses of natural resources that remove them, e.g., hunting

Continental Divide: line that runs north to south through the highest points of the Rocky Mountains and divides waters flowing eastward from those flowing westward

convection: mass movement of a warmed fluid to or from an object

convergent evolution: process of long-term change that yields similar features (e.g., wings in birds and bats) in unrelated organisms

cool fire: light fire; combustion of surface fuels at relatively low temperatures

cooperation: individual behavior that benefits other members of a group

coprophagy: practice of eating one's own feces

copulation: insertion of a male's penis into a female's vagina

copulation plug: mating plug; material deposited by a male in a female's reproductive tract that may inhibit subsequent insemination by other males
copulatory lock: prolonged intercourse caused by contraction of the female's
   vaginal sphincter and swelling of the male's penis
cordillera: long, narrow system of mountain ranges
Cordilleran Ice Sheet: Wisconsin continental glacier that covered most of
   western Canada and parts of Washington, Idaho, and Montana
core: central part of an animal's body; the bony central rod of a horn
corm: underground plant stem that stores food
corolla: all of the petals on a flower
correlation: reciprocal relation, or association, in the occurrence of two traits
corridor: a long, narrow habitat
cost-benefit: theory that organisms trade off allocations to competing tissues
countercurrent heat exchanger: system of juxtaposed arteries and veins that
   reduces the loss of heat from limbs
courtship: behaviors that lead to mating
courtship feeding: male's provision of food to a female prior to mating
covey: small, tight flock of a gallinaceous bird
cranium: skull; bone that encloses the brain
crepuscular: refers to the dim lighting of dawn and dusk or to behaviors that take
   place during these times
critical period: phase in which an animal is predisposed to learn a specific action
crop: food storage chamber in the neck of a bird
cross-pollination: fertilization of ovules by pollen from a different plant
crown fire: wildfire that burns treetops
crypsis: camouflage; pattern and colors that imitate the background
cuckold: male whose female mate has copulated with another male
cushion plant: herbaceous perennial alpine plant with a dense, plump, rounded
   mass of short stems and leaves
cutin: waxy polymer that is a main ingredient of the surface cuticle of plants
cytoplasm: jellylike substance in a cell
dagger point: fourth tine of a bull elk's antler
DDT: acronym for a colorless, odorless, crystalline insecticide
dear-enemy effect: recognition of a resident neighbor
deciduous: refers to tissue that is shed periodically, or to a species that does so
decomposer: organism that gains nutrients from nonliving organic matter
defecation: act of voiding feces
delayed implantation: mammalian reproduction in which the blastocyst does
   not implant in the uterine endometrium for several days or months, e.g., in
   bats and bears
delayed induced resistance: development of antiherbivory traits after a time lag
   following an assault by an herbivore
demography: statistical study of populations

den: n., secluded enclosure where an animal passes an inactive phase; hibernaculum; vb., to enter a den

density: crowdedness; weight per unit of volume

density dependence: response that varies with the degree of crowding

departure rule: factors that set the point at which an animal leaves a feeding patch

dermal shield: patch of thick skin on the rump of a mountain goat

desert: biome characterized by little precipitation and sparse plants

detoxication: neutralization of an ingested poison

detraline: alkaloid that acts as a plant secondary compound

detritus: pieces of dead organic matter

development: growth and differentiation of the tissues in a young organism; human-caused changes in land

diapause: period of inactivity induced by stressful environmental factors

dictyocarpine: alkaloid that serves as an herbivore-deterring secondary metabolite

differential reproductive success: differences in the number of successful offspring among individuals or kin groups

dimorphism: occurrence of two distinct kinds of individuals within a species

directional selection: natural selection for an extreme phenotype

disaccharide: sugar molecule made of two simple sugars bonded together

dispersal: one-way movement of organisms

disruptive camouflage: blending in due to a jumbled pattern that breaks an animal's outline

distal: refers to a body part that is relatively far from the body's core

distribution: geographic area inhabited by a particular group of living things

disturbance: ecological or environmental perturbation; an external factor that causes a change in an ecosystem

disturbance dependent: refers to an ecosystem maintained by recurring ecological changes

disturbance regime: long-term magnitude, sequence, and recurrence interval of environmental changes at a particular place

diurnal: refers to an animal that is active during the day

division of labor: social system in which different types of individuals do different kinds of work

DNA: deoxyribose nucleic acid, the molecule that encodes genetic information

DNA fingerprint: unique nucleotide sequence of an individual

doghair stand: crowded, even-aged group of lodgepole pines

dominance hierarchy: social system in which the top animal aggressively dominates all others, the second highest individual dominates all except the highest, and so on down to the most subordinate member that dominates none

dominant: refers to the species that is most abundant or exerts the greatest influence in a particular environment; an individual that wins fights

dormancy: state of being inactive

dorsal basking: behavior in which a butterfly catches sunshine by resting with its wings held out horizontally

drive-hunt: to hunt big game by herding the animals into a confined or fatal spot

dry nurse: female that cares for but does not suckle an infant

dynamic equilibrium: series of different steady states

ecdysone: insect hormone that causes molting

ecological chemistry: chemical interactions among living members of an ecosystem

ecological disturbance: environmental change that causes a population response

ecological niche: a species' place or role in an ecosystem or community

ecological succession: progressive, somewhat predictable changes in a region's plant community

ecology: study of interactions between living things and their environment

economic defendability: theory that animals aggressively fend off others if the net energy gain exceeds that of not being territorial

ecoregion: area characterized by a particular set of plant species

ecosystem: the set of living and nonliving things that interact in a specific area

ecosystem engineer: animal that physically alters the environment and determines community structure

ecosystem management: manipulation of the environment to achieve a certain ecological structure and function, e.g., setting fires to stimulate tree reseeding

edge detector: system that discerns a steep gradient of an aerial chemical

effective population size: the number of reproducing individuals in a population

ejaculate: mass of semen released by a male during a mating event

embryo: young animal at any stage of development prior to birth

emigrate: to leave an area in large numbers

endemic: refers to an organism that evolved in and remains restricted to a particular place

endocrine: refers to hormones and their actions

endotherm: organism whose body heat is derived from its own metabolism

energetic currency hypothesis: proposal that the amount of energy acquired by a foraging animal reflects its colony's energy status

energy budget: amount of energy that an organism allocates to various tissues or functions

energy flow: one-way movement of energy along trophic levels

energy maximizer: animal foraging so as to maximize its net energy intake

entomology: scientific study of insects

enzyme: protein molecule that catalyzes chemical reactions

ephemeral: temporary; herb that grows aboveground only in a certain season

epidemic: sudden spread of a disease through many individuals

epidermis: outer layer of cells of an animal's body

epithelium: surface layer of cells

equilibrium: condition that reflects the balance between opposing forces establishment: process whereby germinating seeds become independent plants; immigrants founding a new population

estrogenic: refers to a substance with properties similar to those of the hormone estrogen

estrus: state of a female mammal when she is fertile

eusocial: refers to a true social insect species, e.g., honeybee

evapotranspiration: sum of evaporation and plant transpiration

evergreen: plant that bears green leaves throughout the year, e.g., conifer

evolution: change in inherited features of organisms over generations

evolutionary ecology: scientific study of how ecological interactions shape the evolution of adaptations

exclosure: area fenced to keep out certain animals

excretion: elimination of a harmful substance from the body

exotic species: organism not native to a certain area, e.g., salt cedar, feral cat

explosive breeding: mating of many individuals in a brief period

extinct: refers to a volcano that is not expected to erupt again; a taxon that has disappeared

extinction: elimination of a species

extirpated: refers to a taxon that has disappeared from part of its range

extralimital migration: seasonal movement beyond normal limits

exudate: fluid that oozes out of an organism

facilitative relationship: mutualism between plant species that supports pollinator populations

facultative: optional

false alarm call: alarm sound issued by an animal when a predator is not present that mimics the sound made when a predator is present

family: level of biological classification, listed below order and above genus, that groups similar genera

fang: long, hollow, erectile tooth of a venomous snake

fat: organic compound that serves as a stored energy source in animals

fatty acid: organic acid that occurs naturally in fats and fatty oils

fauna: collective term for all the kinds of animals in a region

fecal glucocorticoid assay: noninvasive test of an organism's level of physiologic stress

feces: solid waste voided through the anus; scat

fecundity: number of offspring produced by a female

fertilization: union of male and female gametes

fiber: plant matter made of slender filaments

fire dependent: refers to organisms that need fire to complete their life cycle

fire management: use of fire to achieve specific environmental goals

fire regime: pattern of magnitudes and timing of wildfires in a particular area

fire return interval: fire recurrence interval; long-term average length of time between wildfires in a given place fire suppression: practice of putting out forest fires

fission: splitting in two

fitness: reproductive success of an individual, lineage, or kin group relative to others in the population

flavonoid: ketone $(C_{15}H_{10}O_2)$ that acts as a plant secondary compound

fledge: the act of a young bird beginning to fly

flint: hard quartz

flora: all the plant species of a given area

flowering plant: a species of the class Angiospermae; an angiosperm

fluctuating asymmetry: population trait in which individuals do not have identical left and right halves and in which the abnormal side varies randomly among individuals

flute: large flake scar on the basal face of Clovis and Folsom projectile points

follicle: small cavity in an animal's ovary that holds an egg

Folsom: second major Paleoindian culture, spanning from 11,000 to 10,200 years ago

foothills: small mountains along the edge of a big range

forage: n., plant material eaten by animals; vb., to gather food

forb: a broadleaf plant that dies back at the end of the growing season

fossil: preserved remains and signs of a once-living organism

founder effect: process in which a new population starting from a few pioneering individuals causes the derived population to differ from the source population

foundress: female wasp that starts a new colony

fragmentation: the breaking up of a large expanse of habitat into small isolated patches

fragmented: refers to scattered habitat patches

free fatty acid: organic molecule that circulates in the blood and is made of a long chain of carbon atoms with an acidic group at one end

frontal bone: part of the skull that forms the forehead

frontier mentality: attitude that a resource can be exploited without limits

front range: linear zone of mountains between bigger mountains and the plains

fructose: monosaccharide sugar $(C_6H_{12}O_6)$ found in plants

fruit: ripened seed-bearing ovary of a plant

fuels: cumulative amount of plant material available to sustain a fire

full siblings: brothers and sisters

fungus: plantlike organism that lacks chlorophyll and reproduces by spores, e.g., mushroom

G: unit of the force exerted by gravity on an object at rest; used to indicate the force exerted on an accelerating body

game driving: communal hunting practice of prehistoric humans that consisted of scaring game toward waiting hunters

gene: unit of heredity; section of DNA that codes for a specific protein molecule

gene flow: movement of genes among the individuals of a population

generalist: refers to an organism that is relatively unspecialized

genetic diversity: genetic variation; the number of different kinds of genes

genetic drift: random change in the proportions of alleles within a population

genetic heterozygosity: level of diversity in the alleles of a particular population

genetics: scientific study of inheritance

genitalia: external organs of the reproductive system, e.g., vagina, penis

genome: complete genetic makeup of an individual

genotype: genetic constitution of an organism

geophyte: land plant that endures stressful seasons as a subterranean organ

germination: process by which a young plant sprouts from a seed

gestation: process within a female animal by which a zygote develops into a neonate

gill: external organ of an aquatic animal that exchanges gases

glacial maximum: period in which continental ice sheets were most expansive

glaciations: episodes in which a landscape is covered by an expanding ice sheet

glacier: large mass of flowing ice

gland: organ that synthesizes a substance for release to other body parts

glossa: insect's tongue

glucose: simple sugar $(C_6H_{12}O_6)$ formed by plants during photosynthesis

glycoside: nitrogen-containing ring compound that functions as a toxic herbivore-deterring secondary substance in plants, e.g., calactin in milkweed

gonad: organ in an animal that produces gametes

gorget: patch of iridescent feathers on the throat of a male hummingbird

gradient: gradual change in a variable along a line

granite: coarse-grained igneous rock composed mostly of quartz and feldspar

grassland: semiarid biome dominated by grasses

gravid: refers to a female animal carrying ripe eggs or embryos

grazer: animal that feeds on grasses and forbs, e.g., pronghorn, bison

grazophile: plant that benefits from being grazed

ground fire: wildfire confined to short plants

grove: small bunch of trees

growing season: phase of the year that is warm enough to support plant growth

grub: insect larva

guard hairs: long, coarse hairs that form a protective coating over underfur

gymnosperm: plant with seeds that are not enclosed in an ovary, e.g., conifer

gypsum: soft mineral $(CaSO_4 \cdot 2H_2O)$ commonly found in sedimentary rocks

habitat: specific place where an organism lives

habitat island: habitat fragment, a patch of a particular kind of plant community

habitat selection: choosing to live in a certain environment

half siblings: half sibs; brothers and sisters that share only one parent

handicap model: hypothesis that female choice exaggerates male traits so much that they reduce male survival

handling time: amount of time it takes an animal to manipulate its food

harem: group of females defended by a male

hawk: to catch a prey animal in midair

haystack: haypile; a pile of plant clippings assembled by a pika

heartworm: parasitic roundworm (*Dirofilaria immitis*) that can cause congestive heart failure in some mammals

heat avoidance: movements that position an animal to reduce its heat gain

heathland: place where the plant community is dominated by heaths

hemolymph: bloodlike fluid in invertebrates that transports nutrients and gases

herb: plant with no persistent aboveground woody parts, e.g., grasses, forbs

herbaceous: refers to an herb

herbivore: animal that eats plants, e.g., grasshopper, elk

hermaphroditism: condition of featuring the traits of both sexes

herpetology: scientific study of amphibians and reptiles

heterozygous: refers to an organism that carries different alleles at a given chromosomal locus

hibernaculum: den; a warm protective site used by overwintering animals

hibernation: prolonged dormancy during winter

hierarchy: group of animals in which each individual is subordinate to the one above it

hippocampus: part of the vertebrate brain that functions in spatial memory

Holarctic: refers to something that occurs in the Earth's northern temperate regions

homeostasis: relative stability of a living thing despite ambient changes

homeotherm: animal that maintains unchanging internal body temperature

home range: area normally covered by an animal during its daily activities

homozygous: refers to an individual living thing that has identical alleles at a given chromosomal locus

honest advertisement: offered cues that correctly represent the signaler's condition

honey stomach: pouch of a bee's esophagus that stores nectar

hormone: circulating cellular product that causes specific effects in other cells

horn: pinnacle carved by glacial erosion on all sides of a mountain; permanent outgrowth of the frontal bone of some ungulates

host plant: food plant of a larval insect or of a parasite

hot fire: high-temperature combustion that burns all plants and soil organic matter

humerus: long bone between the shoulder and elbow

hummel: mature, antlerless male elk

humus: dark, partially decomposed matter that forms the soil's upper layer

hybrid: refers to an offspring from parents with different genes

hydrolyze: to break a molecule's bond and bind hydrogen and oxygen in place

hyperparasite: a parasite of parasites

hyperphagia: period of heavy feeding

hypophagia: period of little or no feeding

hypothermia: depression of metabolism and body temperature

hypothesis: educated scientific guess that can be tested

hypsithermal interval: the warmest time of our current interglacial

ice-free corridor: long, thin zone that was not covered by glacial ice

ice sheet: glacier that covers a large part of a continent

immigrant: individual that arrives at a place from somewhere else

immigration: movement of an organism into a place where it was previously absent

implantation: insertion of a blastocyst into a uterine wall

imprinting: type of learning in which a young animal develops a close association with an early stimulus (e.g., a chemical or a moving thing)

inbreeding: mating of closely related individuals

inbreeding depression: maladaptive symptoms in offspring that issue from closely related parents

incisor: a cutting tooth anterior to a canine tooth in mammals

inclusive fitness: relative reproductive success of a kin group within a population of competing kin groups

incubation: warming of eggs by a parent bird

incubation patch: hot naked spot on the belly of a nesting bird

indicator: variable measured to evaluate the condition of a system

indigenous: refers to an organism that lives naturally in a particular place

individual recognition: ability to discriminate among individuals

individual reproductive success: fitness; number of offspring that successfully reproduce

inducible defense: change in an organism (e.g., spines, secondary compounds) caused by exposure to a harmful agent (e.g., herbivore, predator) that reduces the effectiveness of subsequent attacks

infanticide: the killing of young animals

inflorescence: cluster of flowers on a plant

infrared radiation: wavelengths beyond the red end of the electromagnetic spectrum that are invisible to humans

infrasound: sound frequencies that are too low for the human ear to hear

insectivore: organism that eats insects; mammal in the order Insectivora

insolation: amount of incoming solar radiation

instinct: genetically encoded, relatively unvarying behavior elicited the first time a particular stimulus is experienced

insulation: material that slows the movement of heat

interbreeding: mating of individuals from different groups

intersexual conflict: behaviors resulting from differences in the direction of natural selection on members of the two sexes

interspecific competition: interactions with negative consequences between individuals of different species

intraspecific competition: interactions with negative consequences between individuals of the same species

intrinsic: refers to an internal cause

invasion: entry and establishment of an organism in a new place

invertebrate: animal without a backbone, e.g., insect, snail

iridescence: shiny metallic colors that result from the diffraction of light rays and not from pigmentation, e.g., a male hummingbird's red gorget

iridoid: class of bitter herbivore-deterring glycosides found in plants

iris: opaque contractile diaphragm perforated by a pupil in the vertebrate eye

iron oxide: ferric oxide; the red oxide of iron (Fe_2O_3); rust

irruption: sudden increase in the number of individuals of an animal population and their dispersal from the area of high density

island biogeography: study of kinds and numbers of organisms on habitat patches

island population: group of interbreeding individuals living on a habitat patch

isolate: a small parcel of habitat; a small population on such a parcel

Jacobson's organ: tissues in the roof of a vertebrate's mouth that detect odors

jasper: opaque quartz

juvabione: plant hormone that halts the development of herbivorous insects

juvenile hormone: secreted molecule that promotes insect larval growth but prevents metamorphosis

keel: anterior platelike bony extension of the bird sternum

keratin: fibrous proteins that make up the outer layer of horns

keystone species: type of organism whose actions determine significant structural and functional features of an ecosystem, e.g., lodgepole pine, gray wolf

kidney fat index: measure of an animal's physical condition based on its amount of perirenal fat

kieserite: mineral ($MgSO_4 \cdot H_2O$) that is a white hydrous magnesium sulfate

kin avoidance: repelling or being repelled by close genetic relatives

kinetic energy: force of movement

kin recognition: ability to identify closely related individuals and to behave differently toward them

kin selection: differential reproductive success among groups of genetically related individuals

knapping: shaping a rock with quick blows

krummholz: stunted, twisted trees growing at the treeline

lactation: the process of a female mammal producing milk and feeding it to a baby

land bridge: narrow piece of land connecting major continents, e.g., Beringia

landscape ecology: study of the interactions of adjacent ecological communities

landscape mosaic: pattern of habitat patches across the land

language: communication that includes symbols and rules for relating them

larder hoarding: storing food in one place

larva: pl. larvae; immature animal that will undergo complete metamorphosis

lateral basking: behavior in which a butterfly rests with its wings held above its
    body
Laurentide Ice Sheet: continental glacier that covered much of eastern North
    America during the Wisconsin glaciations of the Pleistocene epoch
lava: magma that has erupted onto Earth's surface
lava tube: channel that forms in cooling lava
layering: type of vegetative reproduction by trees in which the branches touch
    the ground, take root, and develop into a separate tree
learning: changing behavior in response to experiences
lee: downwind
lek: piece of ground where the males of a species gather to display to females
lichen: small plant made of an alga and a fungus living symbiotically
lick: site that offers minerals to mammals
life history: life cycle; sequence of stages from birth to death in one generation
life span: longevity; time from birth to death
lifetime reproductive success: number of offspring that in turn reproduce; fitness
life zones: horizontal bands of distinctive plant life associated with the gradual
    change in climate with increasing elevation
limiting factor: limited resource; scarce material that limits an organism's
    functions
linear hierarchy: society of individuals defined by who dominates whom
lipid: substance, like fat and wax, that serves as a structural chemical of cells
lithic: refers to stone
litter: set of offspring born to a female mammal at one time; surface layer of a
    forest floor consisting of partly decomposed organic matter
lodge: portable Indian dwelling made of poles and hides
lone wolf: individual gray wolf that is not a member of a pack
longevity: length of time an organism lives
loreal pit: infrared-sensing organ on the face of a pit viper
Lyme disease: infectious disease caused by a spirochete bacteria (*Borrelia*) and
    transmitted through the bite of a tick (*Ixodes*)
macfadienoside: iridoid glycoside that deters herbivores
macroinvertebrate: small but visible animal without a backbone
macroscopic: refers to small objects that are still visible to the naked eye
magnesium: silver-white metallic element with atomic number 12
major: plant species on which a bumblebee focuses its foraging attention
mammal: member of the class Mammalia, characterized by having body hair, giv-
    ing birth to living young, and being nursed on milk from the mother's breast
mammalogy: scientific study of mammals
mammoth: any of several extinct species of Pleistocene elephants
management: human actions that maintain or change an ecosystem
mandible: lower jaw that consists of two fused bones
mano: handstone used to grind plant foods

marginal habitat: a place less than ideal for sustaining a particular species

masseter: muscle that closes the jaws

mass extinction: sudden catastrophic loss of many species

mass march: sudden dispersal by many individuals; mass dispersal

mast: collective set of fruits that have fallen onto the forest floor

mastodon: any of several extinct elephant-like mammals in the genus *Mammut*

mating call: sound issuing from a male animal to induce a female to breed

mating plug: material excreted by a male animal during copulation that solidifies and presumably blocks the female's reproductive tract from insemination by subsequent males

mating system: social behavior in which individuals of one sex select members of the opposite sex for mating

matriline: multigenerational lineage of female animals

meadow: low-lying plant community with moist soils, few trees, and many grasses

megafauna: set of large-bodied mammal species

mercury: heavy, silver-white, poisonous metallic element with atomic number 80

metabolism: collective set of chemical processes that occur in an organism

metamorphosis: transformation; major change from immature to adult animal, e.g., tadpole to frog, caterpillar to butterfly

metapodial: refers to bones of the metacarpus or metatarsus in thoracic limbs

metapopulation: set of interacting populations

metate: rock slab on which vegetable matter is ground with a mano

microbe: microorganism; organism that requires a microscope to be seen

microclimate: site-specific atmospheric conditions, e.g., a canyon's coolness

microenvironment: ambient conditions of a small site

microfauna: community of microscopic animals

microhabitat: structure of a small, specific place where an organism lives

midden: cache of a valuable resource

migration: regular back-and-forth seasonally cued movements by large numbers of animals between one region and another

milk tooth: temporary deciduous tooth of a young mammal

mineral: solid crystalline compound created by inorganic processes

mineral soil: layer of underlying soil that is low in organic matter

minimum viable population: smallest number of interbreeding individuals likely to support a population's long-term survival

minor: plant species visited only occasionally by a foraging bumblebee

mitochondrial DNA: molecule in mitochondria that carries genetic information, abbreviated mDNA

mitochondrion: pl. mitochondria; organelle in eukaryotic cells that stores and regulates energy and contains genetic material

molecular weight: sum of all atomic weights in a molecular formula

molt: shedding and replacing an exterior covering, e.g., shedding feathers molting hormone: chemical that causes molting in invertebrates, e.g., ecdysone

Mongoloid: refers to a major human race native to Asia

monogamy: mating system in which an animal has one mate at a time

monosaccharide: molecule made of one simple sugar unit, e.g., glucose

montane life zone: plant community between the transition zone, which is open woodland that lies between the shrub and fir forest zones, and the boreal zone

morph: type; external form

morphology: an organism's obvious structure

mosaic: patchwork pattern of vegetation types across a landscape

mossland: place where the plant community is dominated by mosses

multigenet tree cluster: clump of unrelated conspecific trees

multitree cluster: clump of individuals of a single tree species

mushroom: enlarged aerial fruiting body of some fungi

mutation: spontaneous genetic change

mutualism: type of symbiosis in which both partners benefit

mycorrhiza: pl. mycorrhizae; symbiosis between fungi and plant roots

naiad: aquatic young of a mayfly, dragonfly, or stonefly

nares: nostrils

natal: refers to the place of birth

Native American: member of the first group of humans to colonize North America; a descendant of this group; First People; First Nation

natural burn policy: management that allows naturally ignited fires to burn

natural regulation: policy of allowing an ecosystem to alter itself

natural selection: process of differential survival and reproduction among individuals that causes the frequencies of genetically determined traits to change over generations

nature preserve: land parcel managed to maintain certain species

Nearctic: refers to the northern temperate and Arctic regions of the New World

nectar: sugary solution in a flower that attracts pollinating animals

nectar robbing: harvesting nectar by sucking it through a hole cut in a flower

nectar spur: long, thin extension of a flower that contains a nectary

nectary: part of a flower that holds nectar

needle: long, thin leaf of a conifer

neonate: newly born animal

neotene: animal that is sexually mature but features immature body traits

neoteny: state of being sexually mature while still in larval form

nepotism: the favoring of genetic relatives

nestling: young bird living in a nest

net energy intake: profit in energy left after subtracting the costs of obtaining it

neurogenesis: the growing of new nerve cells

neurology: study of the nervous system

neuron: nerve cell

neuroplasticity: ability of a brain to develop new neurons and functions neurotoxin: substance that is poisonous to nerve tissue

niche: ecological role of an organism; specific part of a habitat occupied by an organism

nitrogen: gaseous element that makes up 78 percent of the atmosphere and serves as a plant nutrient

nitrogen fixer: plant that takes in atmospheric nitrogen and stores it in its roots

Noble Indian: Ecological Indian; Native Americans who pursue environmental sustainability

nocturnal hypothermia: torpor at night

nomadic: refers to an animal that wanders from place to place without a pattern

nonequilibrial: refers to a system that is not stable

noxious: refers to material that is distasteful

nuptial feeding: the act of a male offering food to a female during courtship

nuptial gift: food offered by a male to elicit sexual receptivity in a female

nuptial pad: roughened swelling on the inner finger of a male toad

nurse plant: plant that aids establishment of young members of a different species

nursery band: a group of young mammals and their mothers

nut: nonsplitting one-seeded fruit with a hard outer wall

nutrient: substance needed for growth and maintenance, e.g., nitrogen

nutrient cycle: path of an essential substance through an ecosystem

nymph: immature insect that looks somewhat like the adult and does not undergo complete metamorphosis

obligate: refers to something that is unfailing; restricted to a specific mode of life

obsidian: dark-colored volcanic glass

ocher: earthy red or yellow impure iron ore used as a pigment

olfaction: sense of smell

omega: lowest-ranking individual in the social hierarchy of a group-living animal

omnivore: animal that eats a variety of plant and animal foods, e.g., raven

operational sex ratio: numbers of sexually active individuals of each sex

opportunistic: refers to a living thing that exploits new circumstances

optimal: refers to a combination of traits that maximizes reproductive success

optimal foraging theory: set of hypotheses predicting food choice, time spent at each food patch, foraging direction, and other actions of a foraging animal

optimality theory: idea that the traits of living things reflect trade-offs that collectively maximize certain outcomes like reproductive success or heat retention

organic: refers to molecules that contain carbon; matter that is or was alive

ornithology: scientific study of birds

osmotic: refers to the water and ionic relations of a living thing

osteoporosis: chronic disease characterized by the weakening of bones

outbreeding: mating of individuals with different traits

outcrop: bedrock exposed at the surface

outcrossing: mating of individuals of different strains; outbreeding

ovary: part of a plant's pistil that produces seeds; in female animals, the organ
    that produces eggs
overcompensation: plant response in which it regrows more than was removed
    by an herbivore
overkill hypothesis: idea that humans exterminated the Pleistocene megafauna
oviduct: tube that conveys eggs from an ovary
oviposition: egg laying
ovipositor: organ on the posterior end of a female animal that deposits eggs
ovulation: release of eggs by an animal's ovary
ovum: pl. ova; a female animal's egg cell
oxidation: chemical process of combining with oxygen
oxygen: colorless, odorless gaseous element with atomic number 8
pack: group of predators operating as a unit, e.g., wolf pack
pair bond: relationship in which an animal stays close to and cooperates with a
    member of the opposite sex
palate: roof of the mouth
paleoecology: science of reconstructing the interactions between prehistoric
    organisms and their environments
Paleoindian: oldest human cultural tradition in North America
paleontology: branch of geology that deals with plant and animal remains
paniculate: refers to a pyramidal, loosely branched flower cluster
papilla: fleshy hair
paradigm: ideas that define a scientific field during a particular period of time
parasite: organism living in or on another plant or animal and deriving its
    nutrition from the host organism to the detriment of the host, e.g., flea
parasitoid: small-bodied insect that parasitizes another insect
parental care: behavior by an adult animal that enhances the offspring's survival
parental effort: parental investment; resources allocated to one's offspring
park: large meadow or mountain grassland surrounded by forest
parotoid gland: structure on the neck of toads that secretes a poison
parsimony: preference for the least complex explanation for an observation
parturition: giving birth
parvovirus: single-stranded, host-specific DNA virus that causes disease in some
    animals
passive dispersal: process of organisms being carried away by wind or flowing
    water
patch: small, circumscribed area of habitat
paternal care: parental care provided by a father
paternity: state of being a father
pathogen: organism that causes disease
pattern camouflage: method of blending in by looking like the background
peck order: hierarchy of social dominance
pectoralis muscles: major flight muscles in a bird's chest

peninsula effect: decrease in species richness outward along a peninsula

penis: external genitalium that conveys sperm from male to female

perennial: refers to something that lasts several years; plant that lives three or more years

periglacial: refers to the area around a glacier influenced by the ice's coldness

perioral: refers to something around the mouth

permafrost: permanently frozen ground

petal: modified leaf of the corolla of a flower

petiole: leaf stem; thin connector between an insect's thorax and its abdomen

petroglyph: image or symbol carved in stone

pH: measure of hydrogen ion concentration of a material

pharmacology: scientific study of chemical effects on living systems

phenolic: refers to a caustic organic compound (C_6H_5OH) that acts as an herbivore-deterring secondary compound in plants

phenotype: outward characteristics of an organism

phenotypic marker: outwardly detectable indicator of an individual's kinship

phenotypic matching: assessing genetic relationship by comparing one's outwardly observable traits to another's

pheromone: volatile chemical that communicates between animals

philopatry: behavior of returning to one's place of birth

phosphorus: nonmetallic element of the nitrogen group with atomic number 15

photosynthesis: process by which green plants synthesize carbohydrates from carbon dioxide and water by using light as an energy source

physiology: scientific study of the functions of tissues and organs

pictograph: picture painted on a rock

pinivore: animal that eats pines or parts of pines

pioneer species: plant or animal adapted to barren substrate

piperidine: organic six-membered ring compound ($C_5H_{11}N$) that acts as an herbivore-deterring secondary metabolite in some plants

pitch: semihardened tree sap

pituitary: small endocrine gland in the brain that secretes hormones that affect several functions in other body parts

plains: extensive area of gently rolling semiarid country dominated by grasses

plankton: organisms of limited swimming ability that drift with the currents

Plano: third major culture within the Paleoindian tradition, spanning from 10,000 to 8,000 years ago

plant community: association of interacting plant species

plant hormone: molecule synthesized by plants that affects insect growth

plantigrade: refers to walking on the sole with the heel touching the ground

plateau: extensive high-elevation flatland dissected by steep valleys

play behavior: lively actions by young animals that function to practice life skills

play fighting: rudimentary aggression exhibited by young animals

poikilotherm: animal whose body temperature roughly follows ambient, e.g., fish pollen: tiny, often powdery, male reproductive cells formed in a flower's stamens

pollination: process in which pollen moves to and fertilizes ovules in plants

pollinator: animal that transports pollen from a stamen to a stigma

pollutant: human-created matter or energy that degrades an ecosystem

polygyny: mating system in which a male mates with more than one female

polymorphism: presence of several distinct forms of individuals within a population

population: group of individuals of the same species that interbreed

population biology: study of the characteristics (e.g., density) and changes (e.g., growth) of populations

population density: number of conspecific individuals within a given area

population dynamics: temporal changes in measures of population status

potassium: silver-white element of the alkali metal group with atomic number 19

prairie: gently rolling landscape with fertile soil, grass cover, and few trees

pre-Columbian condition: status before the year 1492

predator: living thing that eats animals

primary feather: one of the main quills of a bird's wing that creates lift

primary metabolite: compound that is essential to a basic cellular reaction

primary succession: changes in a plant community that begin on bare soil

primiparity: status of a female that has had a first offspring

probe time: amount of time a bee spends with its glossa in a flower

proboscis: pl. proboscises; an elongate tubular process of an animal's oral region

producer: autotroph; organism that uses the sun's energy to make organic substances from inorganic material through photosynthesis

production: storage of energy in the form of plant organic matter

projectile point: stone tool with a pointed end for penetrating an animal

prolactin: hormone that stimulates milk production in female mammals

prominent perch: high, frequently used vantage point

promiscuous: refers to an organism that mates with multiple partners

protease: enzyme that hydrolyzes protein

protein: organic molecule made of amino acids that provides structure to cells

proteolytic: refers to an enzyme that hydrolyzes protein molecules

proximal: refers to a part that is relatively near the body's core

proximate factor: proximal cue; immediate environmental stimulus of an individual's response

pseudoestrus: female condition of exhibiting the outward signs of estrus yet not undergoing physiological estrus

pseudopregnancy: condition of a female mammal that is not pregnant yet exhibits the outward manifestations of being pregnant

pupa: inactive stage of an insect during which a larva transforms into an adult

pyridine: nitrogen-containing molecule that acts as a plant secondary compound

pyrollidine: nitrogen-containing molecule that acts as a plant secondary compound quadruped: four-legged animal

queen: breeding female in a colony of a social insect

quinone: pungent cyclic compound $(C_6H_4O_2)$ that acts as a plant secondary compound

rabies: acute viral disease of the nervous system of endothermic animals

racemose: refers to inflorescence with a long axis bearing flowers on short stems, e.g., fireweed

radiation: swift evolution of several new species from one ancestral species

rain shadow: leeward side of a mountain that receives little rainfall

range: geographic distribution of a type of living thing; land with plants suitable for grazing; a separate mountain unit

rank: individual's position in a social hierarchy

raptor: bird of prey, e.g., hawk, eagle, owl

rattle: sound-emitting shaker at the posterior end of a rattlesnake

recessive: refers to an allele that causes a visible phenotype only in homozygous individuals

reciprocal grooming: behavior in which two individuals alternately manipulate each other's hair

recognition allele: gene that creates an obvious indicator of kinship

recolonization: establishment of a species in a place it previously occupied

recombination: genetic shuffling between generations that yields new kinds of individuals

recruit: n., new individual in a population; vb., process of joining a population

recruitment: addition of individuals to a population

recurrence interval: average time between repeating events

reflectance basking: behavior in which a butterfly rests with its wings in a *V*

reforestation: the re-covering of an area by trees

refugium: pl. refugia; relatively stable place during climate change

regeneration: replacement; regrowth of plants

regulatory gene: section of DNA that controls the action of other genes

relict: organism that has survived while related ones have gone extinct

rendezvous site: aboveground activity area for wolf pups

repeat photography: method for detecting temporal trends by comparing pictures of a given place over a span of time

repertoire: variety of sounds issuing from an individual animal

reproductive effort: proportion of total resources invested in reproduction

reproductive strategy: suite of adaptations that maximizes the reproductive success of a particular population or species

reproductive success: relative number of offspring that in turn have offspring

resident: animal that lives in a place year-round

resin: sticky, clearish sap of a plant

resource: environmental component used by a living thing, e.g., minerals

respiration: gas exchange; chemical reactions in cells that transform energy resprouting: form of vegetative growth in which a plant sends up new stems

resting coil: circular shape assumed by a snake while resting or sit-and-wait hunting

resting metabolism: rate of physiological processes of an inactive organism

restoration, ecological: the returning of original species and ecological functions

retina: light-sensitive layer of cells along the posterior surface of an eye

rhyolite: fine-grained volcanic rock, often with large crystals of quartz and alkali feldspar and with a chemical composition similar to that of granite

riparium: pl. riparia; ecosystem alongside a water body

ritualized behavior: nonvarying, presumably genetically programmed action

rock art: imaginative aesthetic images on stone

rookery: place where many conspecifics breed and rear their young

roosting: resting with a group repeatedly at a site

rootlet: small plant root

root nodule: swelling on a plant root inhabited by nitrogen-fixing bacteria

rotary engine model: hypothesis concerning the movement of people in an annual cycle through a series of places that offered seasonally abundant resources

rotational grazing: cycling a livestock herd through a series of fields

ruminant: even-toed ungulate in the suborder Ruminantia that lacks upper incisor teeth, has a multichambered stomach, and chews its cud, e.g., bighorn sheep

runaway selection: hypothesis that female choice exaggerates male traits to the male bearer's detriment

runout zone: lower reach of an avalanche chute

rut: autumnal state of sexual excitement in male ungulates

sagittal: refers to the medial plane of an animal's body

salicortin: phenolic glycoside that acts as a plant secondary metabolite

saliva: secretion of water, mucin, and starch-splitting enzyme in the mouth that lubricates and predigests food

sandstone: sedimentary rock composed of cemented sand grains

sap: juice within a plant

saponin: glucoside that acts as a plant secondary compound

savanna: open woodland habitat characterized by scattered trees

scale: repeating helically arranged unit of a gymnosperm's cone; tiny colored platelike covering of a butterfly wing; small platelike unit covering reptiles

scat marking: using fecal smells to communicate with conspecifics

scatter hoarding: caching food in many sites

scavenger: animal that eats the dead remains and wastes of other organisms

scent gland: tissues that secrete substances that give individuals their unique smells

scent-marking: leaving a body secretion on an object to communicate one's condition school: cluster of swimming animals

scrub: stunted vegetation growing on infertile soil

search image: distinguishing prey from background by detecting key cues

secondary compound: molecule in plant tissues that does not participate in basic metabolism and is toxic to herbivores

secondary herbivory: eating plant parts that have regrown after prior herbivory

secondary nectar robbing: removing nectar from a flower through a hole previously cut by a nectar robber

secondary succession: changes in a plant community after part of its vegetation is destroyed, e.g., revegetation after a cool fire

sedentism: habit of being settled and relatively unmoving

seed: fertilized ripened ovule of a flowering plant that contains an embryo

seedling: young plant growing from a seed

seedpod: dry seed vessel

seed set: development of mature seeds from ovules

selection: short for natural selection

self-incompatible: refers to a plant in which self-pollination yields less viable offspring

selfing: breeding system in which a plant's pollen fertilizes its own ovules

semiparasite: organism that extracts part of its food from another living thing

sensitive period: phase in which a particular tissue responds to a specific stimulus

sepal: a usually green unit of the outer whorl of a flower

sequential mutualism: interaction in which early-flowering plant species support pollinators that then visit late-flowering species

sequester: to concentrate something in a small place

serotiny: adaptation in which pine cones remain closed until after a fire

settling velocity: speed at which an object falls through a fluid

sex ratio: proportions of male and female individuals in a population

sex reversal: mating system in which the members of one sex feature behaviors more typical of those of the opposite sex

sexual dimorphism: external differences (other than genitalia) between members of the opposite sex, e.g., antlered bull elk versus nonantlered cow

sexual reproduction: producing new individuals by the union of gametes

sexual selection: differential ability of members of one sex to acquire mates

shade tolerant: refers to a plant that grows well under a canopy

shaft: wooden handle of a tool

shaker muscles: tissues that oscillate a snake's tail

shale: fine-grained sedimentary rock characterized by thin, easily fractured layers whose original constituents were clays and muds

shield: part of a cricket's exoskeleton that extends posteriorly over the abdomen

shifting mosaic metapopulation: network of small populations that undergo ongoing extinction and colonization

shivering: simultaneous contraction of antagonistic muscles to generate heat

shoot: small stem bud rising from an established root
shrub: small woody plant that branches at ground level
siblings: sibs; a sibship; a sibling group; a bunch of brothers and sisters
Sinodont: Chinese
sit-and-wait predator: carnivore that rests until prey gets close enough to strike
site fidelity: degree to which an organism stays at or returns to a specific place
slow-wave sleep: stage of rest featuring deep breathing and slow heart rate
sneak male: subordinate male that attempts to circumvent female choice
snout-vent length: distance from the tip of an animal's nose to its anus
snowbank: pile of persistent snow
snow crater: hole in a snowfield dug by an animal to expose plant food
snowfield: level expanse of snow
snowpack: mass of snow that has accumulated in a particular place
snow regime: amount and timing of a place's snowfall
social behavior: interactions between two or more individuals
social hierarchy: order of who dominates whom in a local animal group
social insect: insect species that features division of labor and altruistic workers
social rank: individual animal's position in its group's dominance hierarchy
social structure: kinds of individuals and their interactions within a group
sodium: silvery soft element in the alkali metal group with atomic number 11
soil: unconsolidated mineral and organic material occurring above bedrock
soma: all of the cells in an individual except gametes
somatic: refers to nonreproductive tissues
somatic mutation: spontaneous genetic change in nonreproductive tissue
songbird: oscine; bird in the suborder Passeri that issues sound notes
specialist: organism with a comparatively narrow niche
species: group of organisms with similar anatomy that interbreed and produce
    fertile offspring
species richness: number of species in a place
sperm: mobile male gamete
spermatheca: saclike organ in female animals that stores sperm
spermatophore: packet containing many sperm cells
spermatophylax: protein-rich part of a spermatophore
sperm competition: evolutionary consequences of the ejaculates from two or
    more males simultaneously occurring in a female's reproductive tract
sphincter: circular muscles that constrict a tube
stamen: male part of a flower that produces pollen
staminate flower: flower with stamens and pollen; a male flower
stand: patch of trees that is comparatively uniform in composition
standard metabolism: pace of a body's chemical reactions when at rest
stem: aerial upright part of a woody plant
sternum: breastbone
stigma: part of a flower's pistil that receives the pollen

stimulus: pl. stimuli; environmental change that triggers a response
stressor: human-created matter or energy that degrades an ecosystem
strike: swift motion by which a snake bites prey or a threatening animal
style: part of a flower's pistil between the stigma and ovary
subalpine: life zone below the alpine, characterized by spruce and fir forests
subarctic: refers to the region north of the northern temperate zone
subclimax: penultimate community of a successional sequence
sublimation: transition of a substance directly from a solid to a vapor phase
sublingual pouch: throat pouch; storage chamber under the floor of the mouth
submissive posture: behavior signaling inferiority
subnivean: refers to the zone under the snow
subordinate: individual animal that is dominated by another
subshrub: low, ground-hugging woody plant
subsistence: obtaining food by hunting and gathering
subspecies: group of individuals within a species with distinguishing features
substrate: underlying solid material that an organism lives on
subtoxic: refers to a poisonous chemical that injures but does not kill
succession: ecological succession, the more or less predictable replacement of one
    plant community by another
sucker: vertical shoot produced by the roots of certain woody plants
sucrose: disaccharide sugar ($C_{12}H_{22}O_{11}$) common in land plants
sugar: simple carbohydrate made of a monosaccharide (e.g., glucose) or a
    disaccharide (e.g., sucrose)
sulfate: salt (SO_4) of sulfuric acid
surface fire: relatively cool combustion of a site's short vegetation
surface-to-volume ratio: relationship of surface area to inner body volume
sustainable use: exploiting a resource so it can be used by future generations
switchback: zigzag of a trail on a steep mountainside
symbiosis: intimate biological relationship between members of two species
symmetrical: refers to an object that can be divided into self-similar parts
sympathetic nervous system: part of the autonomic nervous system that affects
    secretion and the contraction of smooth muscles and blood vessels
synthesis: production of a new molecule by the union of elements or simpler
    compounds or by the breakdown of a complex compound
tadpole: aquatic larval amphibian with external gills and a long tail
tallgrass prairie: plant community of grasses and forbs growing in the Midwest
    on fertile soil and maintained by periodic fire
talus: angled pile of coarse rock fragments at the base of a steep slope
tannin: astringent phenolic molecule that acts as a plant secondary compound
taxon: pl. taxa; a unit of related living things, e.g., genus
temperate: refers to the midlatitude region between the Arctic and the tropics
temperate climate: long-term atmospheric conditions of Earth's midlatitudes
temperature inversion: lid imposed on a lower air mass by stable upper air

terpenoid: organic molecule $(C_{10}H_{16})$ in conifers that deters herbivores

territoriality: behavior in which an organism defends a particular area

territory: defended area

theory: hypothesis that is broadly accepted because it has been repeatedly supported by empirical findings

thermogenesis: production of heat

thermophilic: refers to an organism that lives in a hot place

thermoregulation: control of body temperature within a narrow range

thorax: middle section of an insect's body

three-migration model: hypothesis that First People colonized North America in three episodes

thyroid: endocrine gland that secretes thyroxin

thyroxin: thyroid-secreted hormone that controls development and metabolism

tibia: inner bone of the vertebrate hind limb between the knee and ankle

time budget: amount of time an animal spends in various activities

time minimizer: animal that spends little time foraging and much in other activities

tine: pointed branch of an antler; fork of a snake's tongue

toolkit: set of implements used by a prehistoric human society

torpor: state in which an individual's metabolism drops to a low level

toxic: refers to a poisonous substance

trade-off: principle that increased allocation of resources to one function causes a decreased investment in others

trailhead: start of a trail, where you leave the car

transient: animal that is passing through; a nomad, drifter

translocation: movement of a substance from one part of a plant to another

translucent: refers to an object that allows the passage of some light

transpiration: loss of water by evaporation from leaves and other plant parts

traplining: pattern of foraging in which an animal repeatedly visits the same sequence of sites

travel time: time spent moving while gathering food

travois: primitive Indian vehicle made of a platform on two trailing poles

treeline: elevation or latitude beyond which trees do not grow

tremulacin: phenolic glycoside that acts as a plant secondary compound

triangulation: method of finding one's position by using bearings from three fixed points

Trickster: character in Indian stories that represents ambiguous categories

triglyceride: glycerol with three fatty acids that is a main constituent of animal fat

trophic: refers to feeding

trophic level: feeding level; e.g., producer, herbivore, carnivore

tropolone: secondary compound that deters herbivores, e.g., colchicine

tropotaxis: navigating toward an object by simultaneously comparing the intensity of a stimulus on two sides of the sensor's body

truth in advertising: hypothesis that sexual selection in male traits accurately indicates genetic fitness

tundra: biome found north of the treeline that often has boggy or frozen soil

turnover: changes in individuals or species at a given place

ultimate factor: long-term evolutionary cause of an adaptation

ultraviolet radiation: light beyond the violet end of the visible spectrum

undercompensation: response of a plant injured by an herbivore in which it does not replace its lost mass

underfur: soft, thick, woolly layer of short hairs that acts as insulation

understory: middle layer of foliage in a forest that includes shrubs

ungulate: mammal with hooves, e.g., bighorn sheep, elk, cow

updraft: warm, rising mass of air

uptake: absorption of a nutrient by plant tissues

urea: weak base $[CO(NH_2)_2]$ that is the main component of mammalian urine

urine: excretory product of animal kidneys

uterus: organ in female mammals that holds and nourishes developing offspring

vagina: opening to a female's reproductive system

vascular plant: plant with specialized conductive tissues, e.g., seed plants

vas deferens: sperm duct in a male animal

vegetative growth: increase of a plant's somatic tissues

venom: poisonous fluid produced by an animal

vent: cloacal opening

ventral: refers to the belly side of an animal

ventriloquistic: refers to sound whose origin is difficult to locate

vertebrate: animal with a backbone, e.g., fish, reptile, mammal

vigilance: alertness for predators

virus: microscopic entity, possibly living, that reproduces in living cells

vision quest: personal retreat in which a Native American seeks his identity

vitamin B: complex of water-soluble organic molecules that is essential in minute quantities and has various metabolic functions

vitellogenesis: production and storage of yolk in a developing egg

viviparity: giving birth to active young that have developed within the mother

volatile: refers to a substance that readily changes from a solid or liquid to a gas

volcano: opening in Earth's crust from which gas, ash, and lava erupt

vomer: bone of the vertebrate skull that forms the mouth's vault

vomeronasal fenestrae: tiny holes that connect a mouth to Jacobson's organs

vulva: lips of the vagina

warning call: sound produced by an animal that alerts others to danger

warning coloration: aposematic colors; obvious colors that signal unpalatability

weaning: process by which a female mammal stops nursing her offspring

weather: daily atmospheric conditions at a site

weed species: plant that exploits newly disturbed habitat; organism in an unwanted place

Western Cordillera: mountain chain that runs north-south through North,
    Central, and South America
wetland: type of ecosystem characterized by hydric soils and plants adapted to
    these conditions
wet nurse: female mammal that suckles another female's offspring
wilderness: remote tract of land where natural communities are relatively little
    altered by modern civilization
wildfire: combustion of plants started and maintained by natural forces
winter burn: death of conifer needles from wind and frozen ground
winter dormancy: lowered metabolism during winter
winter range: area where a herding animal overwinters
winter-sleep: long-term, somewhat depressed metabolic state typical of bears
within-patch foraging: movements by a foraging animal within a cluster of food
woodland: patch of low-density trees
woody: refers to a firm-stemmed plant that persists aboveground over winter
worker: caste of a eusocial insect specialized for nonbreeding tasks
yearling: animal that is one year old
young-of-the-year: new offspring born that year

References

Abbot, P., et al. 2011. Inclusive fitness theory and eusociality. *Nature* 471 (March 24): E1–E4.

Adam, M. D., and J. R. Des Lauriers. 1998. Observations of hummingbirds ingesting mineral-rich compounds. *Journal of Field Ornithology* 69: 257–261.

Adams, L. G., and J. A. Bailey. 1983. Winter forages of mountain goats in central Colorado. *Journal of Wildlife Management* 47: 1237–1243.

Adler, F. R., and C. D. Harvell. 1990. Inducible defenses, phenotypic variability and biotic environments. *Trends in Ecology and Evolution* 5: 407–410.

Adler, L. S. 2000. Alkaloid uptake increases fitness in a hemiparasitic plant via reduced herbivory and increased pollination. *American Naturalist* 156: 92–99.

———. 2002. Host effects on herbivory and pollination in a hemiparasitic plant. *Ecology* 83: 2700–2710.

———. 2003. Host species affects herbivory, pollination, and reproduction in experiments with parasitic *Castilleja*. *Ecology* 84: 2083–2091.

Adovasio, J. M., and J. Page. 2002. *The first Americans: In pursuit of archaeology's greatest mystery*. New York: Modern Library.

Agrawal, A. A., and R. Karban. 1999. Why induced defenses may be favored over constitutive strategies in plants. In *The ecology and evolution of inducible defenses*, edited by R. Tollrian and C. D. Harvell, 45–61. Princeton, NJ: Princeton University Press.

Aho, K., N. Huntly, J. Moen, and T. Oksanen. 1998. Pikas (*Ochotona princeps*: Lagomorpha) as allogenic engineers in an alpine ecosystem. *Oecologia* 114: 405–409.

Alcock, J. 1984. *Animal behavior: An evolutionary approach*. 3rd ed. Sunderland, MA: Sinauer Associates.

Alcock, J., and T. F. Houston. 1987. Resource defense and alternative mating tactics in the banksia bee, *Hylaeus alcyoneus* (Erichson). *Ethology* 76: 177–188.

Alden, P., B. Cassie, J. Grassy, J. D. W. Kahl, A. Leventer, D. Mathews, and W. B. Zomlefer. 1998. *National Audubon Society field guide to the Rocky Mountain states*. New York: Alfred A. Knopf.

Alexander, A. J., and M. van Staaden. 1989. Alternative sexual tactics in male bladder grasshoppers (Orthoptera, Pneumoridae). In *Alternative life-history styles in animals*, edited by M. N. Bruton, 261–277. Dordrecht, Netherlands: Kluwer Academic Publishers.

Allen, T., and J. A. Clarke. 2005. Social learning of food preferences by white-tailed ptarmigan chicks. *Animal Behaviour* 70: 305–310.

Ally, D., K. Ritland, and S. P. Otto. 2010. Aging in a long-lived clonal tree. *PLOS Biology* 8: 1–8.

Alt, G. L. 1984. Cub adoption in the black bear. *Journal of Mammalogy* 65: 511–512.

Altshuler, D. L., and R. Dudley. 2002. The ecological and evolutionary interface of hummingbird flight physiology. *Journal of Experimental Biology* 205: 2325–2336.

———. 2006. The physiology and biomechanics of avian flight at high altitude. *Integrative and Comparative Biology* 46: 62–71.

Altshuler, D. L., R. Dudley, and J. A. McGuire. 2004a. Resolution of a paradox: Hummingbird flight at high elevation does not come without a cost. *Proceedings of the National Academy of Sciences of the United States of America* 101: 17731–17736.

Altshuler, D. L., F. G. Stiles, and R. Dudley. 2004b. Of hummingbirds and helicopters: Hovering costs, competitive ability, and foraging strategies. *American Naturalist* 163: 16–25.

Ames, L. J., J. D. Felley, and M. H. Smith. 1979. Amounts of asymmetry in centrarchid fish inhabiting heated and nonheated reservoirs. *Transactions of the American Fisheries Society* 108: 489–495.

Andersen, D. C., and D. W. Johns. 1977. Predation by badger on yellow-bellied marmot in Colorado. *Southwestern Naturalist* 22: 283–284.

Anderson, A. V. R., and R. J. Taylor. 1983. Patterns of morphological variation in a population of mixed species of *Castilleja* (Scrophulariaceae). *Systematic Botany* 8: 225–232.

Anderson, J. E., and W. H. Romme. 1991. Initial floristics in lodgepole pine (*Pinus contorta*) forests following the 1988 Yellowstone fires. *International Journal of Wildland Fire* 1: 119–124.

Arkes, H. R., and P. Ayton. 1999. The sunk cost and Concorde effects: Are humans less rational than lower animals? *Psychological Bulletin* 125: 591–600.

Armitage, K. B. 1977. Social variety in the yellow-bellied marmot: A population-behavioural system. *Animal Behaviour* 25: 585–593.

———. 1982. Marmots and coyotes: Behavior of prey and predator. *Journal of Mammalogy* 63: 503–505.

———. 1984. Recruitment in yellow-bellied marmot populations: Kinship, philopatry, and individual variability. In *The biology of ground-dwelling squirrels: Annual cycles, behavioral ecology and sociality*, edited by J. O. Murie and G. R. Michener, 377–403. Symposium on sociability in ground squirrels, prairie dogs, and marmots, Banff, Canada, September 29–October 3, 1982.

———. 1998. Reproductive strategies of yellow-bellied marmots: Energy conservation and differences between the sexes. *Journal of Mammalogy* 79: 385–393.

————. 2004. Badger predation on yellow-bellied marmots. *American Midland Naturalist* 151: 378–387.

Armitage, K. B., and J. F. Downhower. 1970. Interment behavior in the yellow-bellied marmot (*Marmota flaviventris*). *Journal of Mammalogy* 51: 177–178.

Armitage, K. B., and G. E. Gurri-Glass. 1994. Communal nesting in yellow-bellied marmots. In *Actual problems of marmots investigation*, edited by V. Rumiantsev, 14–26. Moscow: ABF Publishing.

Armitage, K. B., J. C. Melcher, and J. M. Ward Jr. 1990. Oxygen consumption and body temperature in yellow-bellied marmot populations from montane-mesic and lowland-xeric environments. *Journal of Comparative Physiology B* 160: 491–502.

Armitage, K. B., and O. A. Schwartz. 2000. Social enhancement of fitness in yellow-bellied marmots. *Proceedings of the National Academy of Sciences of the United States of America* 97: 12149–12152.

Armitage, K. B., D. H. Van Vuren, A. Ozgul, and M. K. Oli. 2011. Proximate causes of natal dispersal in female yellow-bellied marmots, *Marmota flaviventris*. *Ecology* 92: 218–227.

Arms, K., P. Feeny, and R. C. Lederhouse. 1974. Sodium: Stimulus for puddling behavior by tiger swallowtail butterflies, *Papilio glaucus*. *Science* 185: 372–374.

Armstrong, D. P. 1987. Economics of breeding territoriality in male calliope hummingbirds. *Auk* 104: 242–253.

Armstrong, E. A. 1942. *Bird display and behaviour: An introduction to the study of bird psychology*. New York: Oxford University Press.

Artiss, T., W. M. Hochachka, and K. Martin. 1999. Female foraging and male vigilance in white-tailed ptarmigan (*Lagopus leucurus*): Opportunism or behavioural coordination? *Behavioral Ecology and Sociobiology* 46: 429–434.

Artiss, T., and K. Martin. 1995. Male vigilance in white-tailed ptarmigan, *Lagopus leucurus*: Mate guarding or predator detection? *Animal Behaviour* 49: 1249–1258.

Asa, C. S., and C. Valdespino. 1998. Canid reproductive biology: An integration of proximate mechanisms and ultimate causes. *American Zoologist* 38: 251–259.

Ashton, S., D. Gutierrez, and R. J. Wilson. 2009. Effects of temperature and elevation on habitat use by a rare mountain butterfly: Implications for species responses to climate change. *Ecological Entomology* 34: 437–446.

As the wolf's world turns. 2009. *Defenders* 84 (1) (Winter): 6–7.

Attenborough, D. 1998. *The life of birds*. Princeton, NJ: Princeton University Press.

Austad, S. N. 1984. A classification of alternative reproductive behaviors and methods for field-testing ESS models. *American Zoologist* 24: 309–319.

Ayisi, K. K., D. H. Putnam, C. P. Vance, and P. H. Graham. 1992. Dinitrogen fixation, nitrogen and dry matter accumulation, and nodulation in white lupine. *Crop Science* 32: 1197–1202.

Ayotte, J. B., K. L. Parker, J. M. Arocena, and M. P. Gillingham. 2006. Chemical composition of lick soils: Functions of soil ingestion by four ungulate species. *Journal of Mammalogy* 87: 878–888.

Badyaev, A. V. 1998. Environmental stress and developmental stability in dentition of the Yellowstone grizzly bears. *Behavioral Ecology* 9: 339–344.

Badyaev, A. V., K. R. Foresman, and M. V. Fernandes. 2000. Stress and developmental stability: Vegetation removal causes increased fluctuating asymmetry in shrews. *Ecology* 81: 336–345.

Baguette, M., J. Clobert, and N. Schtickzelle. 2011. Metapopulation dynamics of the bog fritillary butterfly: Experimental changes in habitat quality induced negative density-dependent dispersal. *Ecography* 34: 170–176.

Bailey, J. K., J. A. Schweitzer, B. J. Rehill, D. J. Irschick, T. G. Whitham, and R. L. Lindroth. 2007. Rapid shifts in the chemical composition of aspen forests: An introduced herbivore as an agent of natural selection. *Biological Invasions* 9: 715–722.

Bailey, N. W., D. T. Gwynne, and M. G. Ritchie. 2005. Are solitary and gregarious Mormon crickets (*Anabrus simplex*, Orthoptera, Tettigoniidae) genetically distinct? *Heredity* 95: 166–173.

Baker, H. G., and I. Baker. 1975. Studies of nectar-constitution and pollinator-plant coevolution. In *Coevolution of animals and plants*, edited by L. E. Gilbert and P. H. Raven, 100–140. Austin: University of Texas Press.

Baker, W. L., J. A. Munroe, and A. E. Hessl. 1997. The effects of elk on aspen in the winter range in Rocky Mountain National Park. *Ecography* 20: 155–165.

Balda, R. P. 1980. Recovery of cached seeds by a captive *Nucifraga caryocatactes*. *Zeitschrift für Tierpsychologie* 52: 331–346.

Balda, R. P., and A. C. Kamil. 1989. A comparative study of cache recovery by three corvid species. *Animal Behaviour* 38: 486–495.

———. 1992. Long-term spatial memory in Clark's nutcracker, *Nucifraga columbiana*. *Animal Behaviour* 44: 761–769.

Baldwin, I. T., and J. C. Schultz. 1983. Rapid changes in tree leaf chemistry induced by damage: Evidence for communication between plants. *Science* 221: 277–279.

Ballard, W. B., J. S. Whitman, and C. L. Gardner. 1987. Ecology of an exploited wolf population in south-central Alaska. *Wildlife Monographs*, no. 98 (July): 3–54.

Balter, M. 2011. Tracing the paths of the First Americans. *Science* 333: 1692.

Barash, D. P. 1974. The evolution of marmot societies: A general theory. *Science* 185: 415–420.

Barbee, R. D., P. Schullery, and J. D. Varley. 1991. The Yellowstone vision: An experiment that failed or a vote for posterity? 80–85. *Proceedings of the Partnerships in Parks and Preservation Conference*, Albany, NY, September 9–12.

Barbee, R. D., and J. D. Varley. 1984. The paradox of repeating error: Yellowstone National Park from 1872 to biosphere reserve and beyond, 125–130. *Proceed-*

ings of the Conference on the Management of Biosphere Reserves, Great Smoky Mountains National Park, Gatlinburg, TN, November 27–29.

Barclay, R. M. R., C. L. Lausen, and L. Hollis. 2001. What's hot and what's not: Defining torpor in free-ranging birds and mammals. *Canadian Journal of Zoology* 79: 1885–1890.

Barja, I., F. J. de Miguel, and F. Barcena. 2004. The importance of crossroads in faecal marking behaviour of the wolves (*Canis lupus*). *Naturwissenschaften* 91: 489–492.

Barnes, V. G., Jr., and R. B. Smith. 1993. Cub adoption by brown bears, *Ursus arctos middendorffi*, on Kodiak Island, Alaska. *Canadian Field-Naturalist* 107: 365–367.

Bartlein, P. J., C. Whitlock, and S. L. Shafer. 1997. Future climate in the Yellowstone National Park region and its potential impact on vegetation. *Conservation Biology* 11: 782–792.

Bartos, D. L., and W. F. Mueggler. 1981. Early succession in aspen communities following fire in western Wyoming. *Journal of Range Management* 34: 315–318.

Bazazi, S., C. C. Ioannou, S. J. Simpson, G. A. Sword, C. J. Torney, P. D. Lorch, and I. D. Couzin. 2010. The social context of cannibalism in migratory bands of the Mormon cricket. *PLOS One* 5(12), e15118.doi:10.1371/journal.pone.0015118.

Beani, L., and S. Turillazzi. 1988. Alternative mating tactics in males of *Polistes dominulus* (Hymenoptera: Vespidae). *Behavioral Ecology and Sociobiology* 22: 257–264.

Beaubien, E., and A. Hamann. 2011. Spring flowering response to climate change between 1936 and 2006 in Alberta, Canada. *BioScience* 61: 514–524.

Becklin, K. M., and H. E. Kirkpatrick. 2006. Compensation through rosette formation: The response of scarlet gilia (*Ipomopsis aggregata*: Polemoniaceae) to mammalian herbivory. *Canadian Journal of Botany* 84: 1298–1303.

Bednekoff, P. A., and R. P. Balda. 1997. Clark's nutcracker spatial memory: Many errors might not be due to forgetting. *Animal Behaviour* 54: 691–698.

Beekman, M., G. A. Sword, and S. J. Simpson. 2008. Biological foundations of swarm intelligence. In *Swarm intelligence: Introduction and applications*, edited by C. Blum and D. Merkle, 3–41. Berlin: Springer.

Beever, E. A. 2002. Persistence of pikas in two low-elevation national monuments in the western United States. *Park Science* 21: 23–29.

———. 2009. Ecological silence of the grasslands, forests, wetlands, mountains, and seas. *Conservation Biology* 23: 1320–1322.

Behler, J. L., and F. W. King. 1979. *National Audubon Society field guide to North American reptiles and amphibians*. New York: Alfred A. Knopf.

Beidelman, L. H., R. G. Beidelman, and B. E. Willard. 2000. *Plants of Rocky Mountain National Park*. Helena, MT: Rocky Mountain Nature Association and Falcon Publishing.

Belden, L. K., E. L. Wildy, A. C. Hatch, and A. R. Blaustein. 2000. Juvenile western toads, *Bufo boreas*, avoid chemical cues of snakes fed juvenile, but not larval, conspecifics. *Animal Behaviour* 59: 871–875.

Bell, G. 1978. The handicap principle in sexual selection. *Evolution* 32: 872–885.

Bellemain, E. J., E. Swenson, and P. Taberlet. 2006a. Mating strategies in relation to sexually selected infanticide in a non-social carnivore: The brown bear. *Ethology* 112: 238–246.

Bellemain, E., A. Zedrosser, S. Manel, L. P. Waits, P. Taberlet, and J. E. Swenson. 2006b. The dilemma of female mate selection in the brown bear, a species with sexually selected infanticide. *Proceedings of the Royal Society B: Biological Sciences* 273: 283–291.

Belsky, A. J. 1986. Does herbivory benefit plants? A review of the evidence. *American Naturalist* 127: 870–892.

Bender, L. C. 1996. Harem sizes and adult sex ratios in elk (*Cervus elaphus*). *American Midland Naturalist* 136: 199–202.

Benson, D. P. 2002. Low extra-pair paternity in white-tailed ptarmigan. *Condor* 104: 192–197.

Bentley, M. D., D. E. Leonard, E. K. Reynolds, S. Leach, A. B. Beck, and I. Muraskoshi. 1984. Lupine alkaloids as larval feeding deterrents for spruce budworm, *Choristoneura fumiferana* (Lepidoptera: Tortricidae). *Annals of the Entomological Society of America* 77: 398–400.

Berenbaum, M. R., and A. R. Zangerl. 1994. Costs of inducible defense: Protein limitation, growth, and detoxification in parsnip webworms. *Ecology* 75: 2311–2317.

Bergelson, J., and M. J. Crawley. 1992. The effects of grazers on the performance of individuals and populations of scarlet gilia, *Ipomopsis aggregata*. *Oecologia* 90: 435–444.

Bergelson, J., T. Juenger, and M. J. Crawley. 1996. Regrowth following herbivory in *Ipomopsis aggregata*: Compensation but not overcompensation. *American Naturalist* 148: 744–755.

Bernays, E. A., G. C. Driver, and M. Bilgener. 1989. Herbivores and plant tannins. *Advances in Ecological Research* 19: 263–302.

Beuchat, C. A., W. A. Calder III, E. J. Braun. 1990. The integration of osmoregulation and energy balance in hummingbirds. *Physiological Zoology* 63: 1059–1081.

Bezener, A., and L. Kershaw. 1999. *Rocky Mountain nature guide*. Edmonton, AB: Lone Pine Publishing.

Biardi, J. E., and R. G. Coss. 2011. Rock squirrel (*Spermophilus variegatus*) blood sera affects proteolytic and hemolytic activities of rattlesnake venoms. *Toxicon* 57: 323–331.

Biel, M. J. 1996. Denning and hibernation behavior of bears in Yellowstone National Park. Information Paper No. BMO-10, Bear Management Office, Yellowstone National Park, WY.

Bildstein, K. L. 1983. Why white-tailed deer flag their tails. *American Naturalist* 121: 709–715.

Blake, J. G., and J. R. Karr. 1987. Breeding birds of isolated woodlots: Area and habitat relationships. *Ecology* 68: 1724–1734.

Blaustein, A. R. 1983. Kin recognition mechanisms: Phenotypic matching or recognition alleles? *American Naturalist* 121: 749–754.

Blaustein, A. R., M. Bekoff, J. A. Byers, and T. J. Daniels. 1991. Kin recognition in vertebrates: What do we really know about adaptive value? *Animal Behaviour* 41: 1079–1083.

Blaustein, A. R., K. S. Chang, H. G. Lefcort, and R. K. O'Hara. 1990. Toad tadpole kin recognition: Recognition of half siblings and the role of maternal cues. *Ethology, Ecology and Evolution* 2: 215–226.

Blaustein, A. R., and R. K. O'Hara. 1986. Kin recognition in tadpoles. *Scientific American*, January, 108–116.

Blaustein, A. R., and B. Waldman. 1992. Kin recognition in anuran amphibians. *Animal Behaviour* 44: 207–221.

Bleiweiss, R. 1998. Origin of hummingbird faunas. *Biological Journal of the Linnean Society* 65: 77–97.

Blouin, S. F., and M. Blouin. 1988. Inbreeding avoidance behaviors. *Trends in Ecology and Evolution* 3: 230–233.

Blumstein, D. T. 1999. Alarm calling in three species of marmots. *Behaviour* 136: 731–757.

Blumstein, D. T., and K. B. Armitage. 1997. Alarm calling in yellow-bellied marmots: I. The meaning of situationally variable alarm calls. *Animal Behaviour* 53: 143–171.

———. 1998. Why do yellow-bellied marmots call? *Animal Behaviour* 56: 1053–1055.

Blumstein, D. T., and J. C. Daniel. 2004. Yellow-bellied marmots discriminate between the alarm calls of individuals and are more responsive to calls from juveniles. *Animal Behaviour* 68: 1257–1265.

Blumstein, D. T., and O. Munos. 2005. Individual, age and sex-specific information is contained in yellow-bellied marmot alarm calls. *Animal Behaviour* 69: 353–361.

Blumstein, D. T., A. Ozgul, V. Yovovich, D. H. Van Vuren, and K. B. Armitage. 2006. Effect of predation risk on the presence and persistence of yellow-bellied marmot (*Marmota flaviventris*) colonies. *Journal of Zoology* 270: 132–138.

Blumstein, D. T., J. Steinmetz, K. B. Armitage, and J. C. Daniel. 1997. Alarm calling in yellow-bellied marmots: II. The importance of direct fitness. *Animal Behaviour* 53: 173–184.

Bock, W. J., R. P. Balda, and S. B. Vander Wall. 1973. Morphology of the sublingual pouch and tongue musculature in Clark's nutcracker. *Auk* 90: 491–519.

Bortolotti, G. R., and J. R. Garielson. 1995. Fluctuating asymmetry in the skeleton of the American kestrel, *Falco sparverius*: A test of the consequences of sexual size dimorphism. *Canadian Journal of Zoology* 73: 141–145.

Bonatto, S. L., and F. M. Salzano. 1997. A single and early migration for the peopling of the Americas supported by mitochondrial DNA sequence data. *Proceedings of the National Academy of Sciences of the United States of America* 94: 1866–1871.

Boomsma, J. J., et al. 2011. Only full-sibling families evolved eusociality. *Nature* 471 (March 24): E4–E5.

Borrell, B. 2009. What's so hot about chili peppers? Smithsonian. http://www .smithsonianmag.com/science-nature/whats-so-hot-about-chili-peppers -116907465/.

Borror, D. J., D. M. DeLong, and C. A. Triplehorn. 1981. *An introduction to the study of insects*. Philadelphia: Saunders College Publishing.

Borror, D. J., and R. E. White. 1970. *A field guide to the insects of America north of Mexico*. Boston: Houghton Mifflin.

Botkin, D. B. 2004. *Our natural history: The lessons of Lewis and Clark*. Oxford: Oxford University Press.

Bourgaud, F., A. Gravot, S. Milesi, and E. Gontier. 2001. Production of plant secondary metabolites: A historical perspective. *Plant Science* 161: 839–851.

Boyce, M. S. 1991. Natural regulation or the control of nature? In *The Greater Yellowstone Ecosystem: Redefining America's wilderness heritage*, edited by R. B. Keiter and M. S. Boyce, 183–208. New Haven, CT: Yale University Press.

Bradbury, S. M., R. M. Danielson, and S. Visser. 1998. Ectomycorrhizas of regenerating stands of lodgepole pine (*Pinus contorta*). *Canadian Journal of Botany* 76: 218–227.

Brady, K. M., and K. B. Armitage. 1999. Scent-marking in the yellow-bellied marmot (*Marmota flaviventris*). *Ethology, Ecology and Evolution* 11: 35–47.

Brady, K. S., and D. Hamer. 1992. Use of a summit mating area by a pair of courting grizzly bears, *Ursus arctos*, in Waterton Lakes National Park, Alberta. *Canadian Field-Naturalist* 106: 519–520.

Brandt, C. A. 1985. The evolution of sexual differences in natal dispersal: A test of Greenwood's hypothesis. *Contributions in Marine Science* 68: 386–396.

Breedlove, D. E., and P. R. Ehrlich. 1968. Plant-herbivore coevolution: Lupines and lycaenids. *Science* 162: 671–672.

Brodin, A., and K. Lundborg. 2003. Is hippocampal volume affected by specialization for food hoarding in birds? *Proceedings of the Royal Society of London B: Biological Sciences* 270: 1555–1563.

Brody, A. K., and J. Melcher. 1985. Infanticide in yellow-bellied marmots. *Animal Behaviour* 33: 673–674.

Brooks, M. 1967. *The life of the mountains*. New York: McGraw-Hill.

Brown, J. K., and N. V. DeByle. 1987. Fire damage, mortality, and suckering in aspen. *Canadian Journal of Forest Research* 17: 1100–1109.

Bruin, J., M. Dicke, and M. W. Sabelis. 1992. Plants are better protected against spider-mites after exposure to volatiles from infested conspecifics. *Experientia* 48: 525–529.

Bruin, J., M. W. Sabelis, and M. Dicke. 1995. Do plants tap SOS signals from their infested neighbors? *Trends in Ecology and Evolution* 10: 167–170.

Brussard, P. F. 1987. The likelihood of persistence of small populations of large animals. *Proceedings of the Desert Fishes Council* 16–18: 221–234.

Budiansky, S. 1996. Yellowstone's unraveling. *US News & World Report*, September 16, 80–83.

Burkey, T. V. 1988. Extinction in nature reserves: The effect of fragmentation and the importance of migration between reserve fragments. *Oikos* 55: 75–81.

Cade, W. H. 1981. Alternative male strategies: Genetic differences in crickets. *Science* 212: 563–564.

Cairns, J., Jr. 1988. Can the global loss of species be stopped? *Speculations in Science and Technology* 11: 189–196.

Calder, W. A., III. 1987. Southbound through Colorado: Migration of rufous hummingbirds. *National Geographic Research* 3 (1): 40–51.

———. 1994. When do hummingbirds use torpor in nature? *Physiological Zoology* 67: 1051–1076.

———. 1998. Red-hot hummers. *Nature Conservancy*, March–April, 12–16.

Calder, W. J., K. J. Horn, and S. B. St. Clair. 2011. Conifer expansion reduces the competitive ability and herbivore defense of aspen by modifying light environment and soil chemistry. *Tree Physiology* 31: 582–591.

Canals, R. M., V. R. Eviner, D. J. Herman, and F. S. Chapin III. 2005. Plant colonizers shape early N-dynamics in gopher mounds. *Plant and Soil* 276: 327–334.

Cannon, K. P. 1995. Blood residue analyses of ancient stone tools reveal clues to prehistoric subsistence patterns in Yellowstone. *Cultural Resource Management* (National Park Service, US Department of the Interior) 18: 14–16.

Cantor, L. F., and T. G. Whitham. 1989. Importance of belowground herbivory: Pocket gophers may limit aspen to rock outcrop refugia. *Ecology* 70: 962–970.

Carey, D. B., and M. Wink. 1994. Elevational variation of quinolizidine alkaloid contents in a lupine (*Lupinus argenteus*) of the Rocky Mountains. *Journal of Chemical Ecology* 20: 849–858.

Carey, H. V. 1985. Nutritional ecology of yellow-bellied marmots in the White Mountains of California. *Holarctic Ecology* 8: 259–264.

Carleton, S. A., B. H. Bakken, and C. M. del Rio. 2006. Metabolic substrate use and the turnover of endogenous energy reserves in broad-tailed hummingbirds (*Selasphorus platycercus*). *Journal of Experimental Biology* 209: 2622–2627.

Carmichael, C. n.d. The formula for faster climbing. *Bicycling*. http://www.bicycling.com/training-nutrition/training-fitness/formula-faster-climbing.

Carrera, R., and W. B. Ballard. 2003. Elk distribution in Mexico: A critical review. *Wildlife Society Bulletin* 31: 1272–1276.

Cassells, E. S. 1997. *The archaeology of Colorado.* Rev. ed. Boulder, CO: Johnson Books.

Cassirer, E. F., D. J. Freddy, and E. D. Ables. 1992. Elk responses to disturbance by cross-country skiers in Yellowstone National Park. *Wildlife Society Bulletin* 20: 375–381.

Cazares, E., and J. M. Trappe. 1994. Spore dispersal of ectomycorrhizal fungi on a glacier forefront by mammal mycophagy. *Mycologia* 86: 507–510.

Chadde, S., and C. Kay. 1988. Willows and moose: A study of grazing pressure, Slough Creek exclosure, Montana, 1961–1986. Montana Forest and Conservation Experiment Station, Research Note 24, University of Montana, Missoula.

———. 1991. Tall-willow communities on Yellowstone's northern range: A test of the "natural-regulation" paradigm. In: *The Greater Yellowstone Ecosystem: Redefining America's wilderness heritage,* edited by R. B. Keiter and M. S. Boyce, 231–262. New Haven, CT: Yale University Press.

Chadwick, D. H. 1983. *A beast the color of winter: The mountain goat observed.* Lincoln: University of Nebraska Press.

———. 1997. King of the mountain. *National Wildlife,* August–September. http://www.nwf.org/News-and-Magazines/National-Wildlife/Animals /Archives/1997/King-of-the-Mountain.aspx.

———. 2000. *Yellowstone to Yukon.* Washington, DC: National Geographic Society.

Chai, P., A. C. Chang, and R. Dudley. 1998. Flight thermogenesis and energy conservation in hovering hummingbirds. *Journal of Experimental Biology* 201: 963–968.

Charland, M. B., and P. T. Gregory. 1989. Feeding rate and weight gain in postpartum rattlesnakes: Do animals that eat more always grow more? *Copeia* 1989: 211–214.

Charnov, E. L., and J. R. Krebs. 1975. The evolution of alarm calls: Altruism or manipulation? *American Naturalist* 109: 107–112.

Chen, P.-Y., A. G. Stokes, and J. McKittrick. 2009. Comparison of the structure and mechanical properties of bovine bone and antler of the North American elk. *Acta Biomaterialia* 5: 693–706.

Chessin, M., and A. E. Zipf. 1990. Alarm systems in higher plants. *Botanical Review* 56: 193–235.

Chiszar, D., W. Lukas, and H. M. Smith. 1997. Response to rodent saliva by two species of rodentiophagous snakes. *Journal of Chemical Ecology* 23: 829–836.

Chiszar, D., T. Melcer, R. Lee, C. W. Radcliffe, and D. Duvall. 1990. Chemical cues used by prairie rattlesnakes (*Crotalus viridis*) to follow trails of rodent prey. *Journal of Chemical Ecology* 16: 79–86.

Chiszar, D., K. Stimac, and T. Boyer. 1983. Effects of mouse odors on visually-induced and strike-induced chemosensory searching in prairie rattlesnakes (*Crotalus viridis*). *Chemical Senses* 7: 301–308.

Chiszar, D., A. Walters, and H. M. Smith. 2008. Rattlesnake preference for envenomated prey: Species specificity. *Journal of Herpetology* 42: 764–767.

Chivers, D. P., J. M. Kiesecker, A. Marco, E. L. Wildy, and A. R. Blaustein. 1999a. Shifts in life history as a response to predation in western toads (*Bufo boreas*). *Journal of Chemical Ecology* 25: 2455–2464.

Chivers, D. P., J. M. Kiesecker, E. L. Wildy, L. K. Belden, L. B. Kats, and A. R. Blaustein. 1999b. Avoidance response of post-metamorphic anurans to cues of injured conspecifics and predators. *Journal of Herpetology* 33: 472–476.

Claridge, A. W., and D. B. Lindenmayer. 1994. The need for a more sophisticated approach toward wildlife corridor design in the multiple-use forests of southeastern Australia: The case for mammals. *Pacific Conservation Biology* 1: 301–307.

Clark, R. W. 2004. Feeding experience modifies the assessment of ambush sites by the timber rattlesnake, a sit-and-wait predator. *Ethology* 110: 471–483.

———. 2006. Post-strike behavior of timber rattlesnakes (*Crotalus horridus*) during natural predation events. *Ethology* 112: 1089–1094.

Clark, T. W., and M. R. Stromberg 1987. *Mammals in Wyoming*. Lawrence: Museum of Natural History, University of Kansas.

Clark, W. 1805. Journal entry, Thursday, August 22, 1805. *Journals of the Lewis and Clark Expedition Online*. University of Nebraska, Lincoln. http://lewisandclarkjournals.unl.edu/read/?_xmlsrc=1805-08-22.xml&_xslsrc=LCstyles.xsl.

Clarke, G. M. 1995. Relationships between developmental stability and fitness: Application for conservation biology. *Conservation Biology* 9: 18–24.

Clarke, J. A. 2010. White-tailed ptarmigan food calls enhance chick diet choice: Learning nutritional wisdom? *Animal Behaviour* 79: 25–30.

Clarke, J. A., and R. E. Johnson. 1992. The influence of spring snow depth on white-tailed ptarmigan breeding success in the Sierra Nevada. *Condor* 94: 622–627.

Clary, D., and D. M. Kelly. 2011. Cache protection strategies of a non-social food-caching corvid, Clark's nutcracker (*Nucifraga columbiana*). *Animal Cognition* 14: 735–744.

Clausen, T. P., P. B. Reichardt, J. P. Bryant, R. A. Werner, K. Post, and K. Frisby. 1989. Chemical model for short-term induction in quaking aspen (*Populus tremuloides*) foliage against herbivores. *Journal of Chemical Ecology* 15: 2335–2346.

Clayton, N. S. 1998. Memory and the hippocampus in food-storing birds: A comparative approach. *Neuropharmacology* 37: 441–452.

Clayton, N. S., and D. W. Lee. 1998. Memory and the hippocampus in food-storing birds. In *Animal cognition in nature: The convergence of psychology and biology in laboratory and field*, edited by R. P. Balda, I. M. Pepperberg, and A. C. Kamil, 99–118. San Diego: Academic Press.

Climate change and the pika. 2009. Interpretive Resource Bulletin Series, Crown of the Continent Research Learning Center, Glacier National Park, West Glacier, MT.

Coffey, G. 2004. Indian paintbrush: The sunset shades of *Castilleja*. *Bay Nature* (Berkeley, CA), April–June, 15.

Cole, E. K., M. D. Pope, and R. G. Anthony. 1997. Effects of road management on movement and survival of Roosevelt elk. *Journal of Wildlife Management* 61: 1115–1126.

Collins, J. P. 1981. Distribution, habitats and life history variation in the tiger salamander, *Ambystoma tigrinum*, in east-cental and southeast Arizona. *Copeia* 1981: 666–675.

Collins, J. P., J. L. Brunner, V. Miera, M. J. Parris, D. M. Schock, and A. Storfer. 2003. Ecology and evolution of infectious disease. In *Amphibian conservation*, edited by R. D. Semlitsch, 137–151. Washington, DC: Smithsonian Institution Press.

Collins, J. P., and J. E. Cheek. 1983. Effect of food and density on development of typical and cannibalistic salamander larvae in *Ambystoma tigrinum nebulosum*. *American Zoologist* 23: 77–84.

Collins, J. P., and J. R. Holomuzki. 1984. Intraspecific variation in diet within and between trophic morphs in larval tiger salamanders (*Ambystoma tigrinum nebulosum*). *Canadian Journal of Zoology* 62: 168–174.

Collins, J. P., J. B. Mitton, and B. A. Pierce. 1980. *Ambystoma tigrinum*: A multispecies conglomerate? *Copeia* 1980: 938–941.

Collins, J. P., K. E. Zerba, and M. J. Sredl. 1993. Shaping intraspecific variation: Development, ecology and the evolution of morphology and life history variation in tiger salamanders. *Genetica* 89: 167–183.

Conant, R. 1958. *A field guide to reptiles and amphibians*. Boston: Houghton Mifflin.

Conner, D. A. 1982a. Dialects versus geographic variation in mammalian vocalizations. *Animal Behaviour* 30: 297–298.

———. 1982b. Geographic variation in short calls of pikas (*Ochotona princeps*). *Journal of Mammalogy* 63: 48–52.

———. 1984. The role of acoustic display in territorial maintenance in the pika. *Canadian Journal of Zoology* 62: 1906–1909.

———. 1985a. Analysis of the vocal repertoire of adult pikas: Ecological and evolutionary perspectives. *Animal Behaviour* 33: 124–134.

———. 1985b. The function of the pika short call in individual recognition. *Zeitschrift für Tierpsychologie 67: 131–143.*

Constantz, G. 1968a. Some observations on hummingbirds of Flathead Lake, Montana. Unpublished term paper, University of Montana Biological Station, Flathead Lake, MT.

———. 1968b. Territoriality in male calliope hummingbirds. Unpublished term paper. University of Montana Biological Station, Flathead Lake, MT.

———. 1975. Behavioral ecology of mating in the male Gila topminnow, *Poeciliopsis occidentalis* (Cyprinodontiformes: Poeciliidae). *Ecology* 56: 966–973.

———. 1980. Growth of nestling rufous hummingbirds. *Auk* 97: 622–624.

———. 2004. *Hollows, peepers, and highlanders: An Appalachian Mountain ecology.* 2nd ed. Morgantown: West Virginia University Press.

Cook, P. M., M. P. Rowe, and R. W. Van Devender. 1994. Allometric scaling and interspecific differences in the rattling sounds of rattlesnakes. *Herpetologica* 50: 358–368.

Cordoba-Aguilar, A. 1995. Fluctuating asymmetry in paired and unpaired damselfly males *Ischnura denticollis* (Burmeister) (Odonata: Coenagrionidae). *Journal of Ethology* 13: 129–132.

Cote, S. D. 2000a. Determining social rank in ungulates: A comparison of aggressive interactions recorded at a bait site and under natural conditions. *Ethology* 106: 945–955.

———. 2000b. Dominance hierarchies in female mountain goats: Stability, aggressiveness and determinants of rank. *Behaviour* 137: 1541–1566.

Cote, S. D., and M. Festa-Bianchet. 2001a. Birthdate, mass and survival in mountain goat kids: Effects of maternal characteristics and forage quality. *Oecologia* 127: 230–238.

———. 2001b. Life-history correlates of horn asymmetry in mountain goats. *Journal of Mammalogy* 82: 389–400.

Cote, S. D., M. Festa-Bianchet, and K. G. Smith. 1998. Horn growth in mountain goats (*Oreamnos americanus*). *Journal of Mammalogy* 79: 406–414.

Craighead, F., Jr. 1973. The great divide: Ramparts of the Rockies. In *Wilderness U.S.A.*, edited by S. L. Fishbein, 132–161. Washington, DC: National Geographic Society.

———. 1979. *Track of the grizzly.* San Francisco: Sierra Club Books.

Craighead, F. L., M. E. Gilpin, and E. R. Vyse. 1999. Genetic considerations for carnivore conservation in the Greater Yellowstone Ecosystem. In *Carnivores in ecosystems: The Yellowstone experience*, edited by T. W. Clark, A. P. Curlee, S. C. Minta, and P. M. Kareiva, 284–321. New Haven, CT: Yale University Press.

Craighead, J. J. 1991. Yellowstone in transition. In: *The Greater Yellowstone Ecosystem: Redefining America's wilderness heritage*, edited by R. B. Keiter and M. S. Boyce, 27–39. New Haven, CT: Yale University Press.

Craighead, J. J., F. C. Craighead, and R. J. Davis. 1963. *A field guide to Rocky Mountain wildflowers: Northern Arizona and New Mexico to British Columbia.* Boston: Houghton Mifflin.

Craighead, L., D. Paetkau, H. V. Reynolds, E. R. Vyse, and C. Strobeck. 1995. Microsatellite analysis of paternity and reproduction in Arctic grizzly bears. *Journal of Heredity* 86: 255–261.

Crawford, J. L., S. P. McNulty, J. B. Sowell, and M. D. Morgan. 1998. Changes in aspen communities over 30 years in Gunnison County, Colorado. *American Midland Naturalist* 140: 197–205.

Creel, S. 2005. Dominance, aggression, and glucocorticoid levels in social carnivores. *Journal of Mammalogy* 86: 255–264.

Creel, S., J. E. Fox, A. Hardy, J. Sands, B. Garrott, and R. O. Peterson. 2002. Snowmobile activity and glucocorticoid stress responses in wolves and elk. *Conservation Biology* 16: 809–814.

Crespi, B. J. 1988. Alternative male mating tactics in a thrips: Effects of sex ratio variation and body size. *American Midland Naturalist* 119: 83–92.

Crump, M. L. 1983. Opportunistic cannibalism by amphibian larvae in temporary aquatic environments. *American Naturalist* 121: 281–289.

Curio, E. 1987. Animal decision-making and the "Concorde Fallacy." *Trends in Ecology and Evolution* 2: 148–152.

Dane, B. 2002. Retention of offspring in a wild population of ungulates. *Behaviour* 139: 1–21.

Darimont, C. T., T. E. Reimchen, and P. C. Paquet. 2003. Foraging behaviour by gray wolves on salmon in coastal British Columbia. *Canadian Journal of Zoology* 81: 349–353.

Darling, F. F. 1937. *A herd of red deer: A study of animal behavior*. Oxford: Oxford University Press.

Darwin, C. 1859. *The origin of species by means of natural selection or by the preservation of favored races in the struggle for life*. Reprint, New York: Modern Library, Random House.

Davis, L. B. 1995. National historical landmark considerations. In *The obsidian cliff plateau prehistoric lithic source, Yellowstone National Park, Wyoming*, edited by L. B. Davis, S. A. Aaberg, and J. G. Schmitt, 59–67. Selections Series No. 6. Denver, CO: Division of Cultural Research, Rocky Mountain Region, National Park Service, US Department of the Interior.

Dawkins, R. 1976. *The selfish gene*. New York: Oxford University Press.

Dearing, M. D. 1996. Disparate determinants of summer and winter diet selection of a generalist herbivore, *Ochotona princeps*. *Oecologia* 108: 467–478.

———. 1997a. Effects of *Acomastylis rossii* tannins on a mammalian herbivore, the North American pika, *Ochotona princeps*. *Oecologia* 109: 122–131.

———. 1997b. The function of haypiles of pikas (*Ochotona princeps*). *Journal of Mammalogy* 78: 1156–1163.

———. 1997c. The manipulation of plant toxins by a food-hoarding herbivore, *Ochotona princeps*. *Ecology* 78: 774–781.

Degani, G., S. Goldenberg, and M. R. Warburg. 1980. Cannibalistic phenomena in *Salamandra salamandra* larvae in certain water bodies and under experimental conditions. *Hydrobiologia* 75: 123–128.

Delgiudice, G. D., F. J. Singer, and U. S. Seal. 1991. Physiological assessment of winter nutritional deprivation in elk of Yellowstone National Park. *Journal of Wildlife Management* 55: 653–664.

del Pilar Vilarino, M., G. Maregianni, M. Y. Grass, S. R. Leicach, and D. A. Ravetta. 2005. Post-damage alkaloid concentration in sweet and bitter lupin varieties and its effect on subsequent herbivory. *Journal of Applied Entomology* 129: 233–238.

del Rio, C. M., J. E. Schondube, T. J. McWhorter, and L. G. Herrera. 2001. Intake responses in nectar feeding birds: Digestive and metabolic causes, osmoregulatory consequences, and coevolutionary effects. *American Zoologist* 41: 902–915.

Demarchi, M. W., S. R. Johnson, and G. F. Searing. 2000. Distribution and abundance of mountain goats, *Oreamnos americanus*, in westcentral British Columbia. *Canadian Field-Naturalist* 114: 301–306.

de Saint-Exupéry, A. 1943. *The little prince*. New York: Harcourt Brace Jovanovich.

Devito, J., D. P. Chivers, J. M. Kiesecker, A. Marco, E. L. Wildy, and A. R. Blaustein. 1998. The effects of snake predation on metamorphosis of western toads, *Bufo boreas* (Amphibia, Bufonidae). *Ethology* 104: 185–193.

DeVoto, B., ed. 1953. *The journals of Lewis and Clark*. Boston: Houghton Mifflin.

DeWoody, J., C. A. Rowe, V. D. Hipkins, and K. E. Mock. 2008. "Pando" lives: Molecular genetic evidence of a giant aspen clone in central Utah. *Western North American Naturalist* 68: 493–497.

Dewsbury, D. A. 1982. Ejaculate cost and male choice. *American Naturalist* 119: 601–610.

Dicke, M. 1999. Evolution of induced indirect defense of plants. In *The ecology and evolution of inducible defenses*, edited by R. Tollrian and C. D. Harvell, 62–88. Princeton, NJ: Princeton University Press.

Diller, L. V., and R. L. Wallace. 1984. Reproductive biology of the northern Pacific rattlesnake (*Crotalus viridis oreganus*) in northern Idaho. *Herpetologica* 40: 182–193.

———. 1996. Comparative ecology of two snake species (*Crotalus viridis* and *Pituophis melanoleucus*) in southwestern Idaho. *Herpetologica* 52: 343–360.

Dimmick, C. R. 1993. Life history and the development of cache-recovery behaviors in Clark's nutcracker. PhD diss., Northern Arizona University.

Diner, B., D. Berteaux, J. Fyles, and R. L. Lindroth. 2009. Behavioral archives link the chemistry and clonal structure of trembling aspen to the food choice of North American porcupine. *Oecologia* 160: 687–695.

Dissecting rattlesnake damage. 1978. *Science News*, August 19, 121.

Dominick, D. n.d. The Sheepeaters. http://windriverhistory.org/exhibits/sheep eaters/Resources/Dominick.pdf.

Dorfman, A. 2000. Archaeology: New ways to the New World. *Time*, April 17, 70. http://content.time.com/time/magazine/article/0,9171,996633,00.html

Downey, J. C., and W. C. Fuller. 1961. Variation in *Plebejus icarioides* (Lycaenidae). I. Food plant specificity. *Journal of the Lepidopterists' Society* 15: 34–42.

Downhower, J. F., and K. B. Armitage. 1971. The yellow-bellied marmot and the evolution of polygamy. *American Naturalist* 105: 355–370.

Drummond, C. S. 2008. Diversification of *Lupinus* (Leguminosae) in the western New World: Derived evolution of perennial life history and colonization of montane habitats. *Molecular Phylogenetics and Evolution* 48: 408–421.

Dugatkin, L. A. 1997. *Cooperation among animals: An evolutionary perspective.* Oxford: Oxford University Press.

Dunford, C. 1977. Kin selection for ground squirrel alarm calls. *American Naturalist* 111: 782–785.

Durrell, G. 1988. *The amateur naturalist.* New York: Alfred A. Knopf.

Duvall, D., M. B. King, and K. J. Gutzwiller. 1985. Behavioral ecology and ethology of the prairie rattlesnake. *National Geographic Research* 1: 80–111.

Duvall, D., and G. W. Schuett. 1997. Straight-line movement and competitive mate searching in prairie rattlesnakes, *Crotalus viridis viridis. Animal Behaviour* 54: 329–334.

Dyer, A. G., H. M. Whitney, S. E. J. Arnold, B. J. Glover, and L. Chittka. 2006. Bees associate warmth with floral colour. *Nature* 442: 525.

Eberhard, W. G. 1993. Evaluating models of sexual selection: Genitalia as a test case. *American Naturalist* 142: 564–571.

Edwards, P. J., and S. D. Wratten. 1982. Wound-induced changes in palatability in birch (*Betula pubescens* Ehrh. ssp. *pubescens*). *American Naturalist* 120: 816–818.

Eggert, A.-K., and S. K. Sakaluk. 1994. Fluctuating asymmetry and variation in the size of courtship gifts in decorated crickets. *American Naturalist* 144: 708–716.

Ehrlich, P. R., and P. H. Raven. 1964. Butterflies and plants: A study in coevolution. *Evolution* 18: 586–608.

Ehrlich, P. R., and R. R. White. 1980. Colorado checkerspot butterflies: Isolation, neutrality, and the biospecies. *American Naturalist* 115: 328–341.

Elias, S. A. 1996. *The Ice-Age history of national parks in the Rocky Mountains.* Washington, DC: Smithsonian Institution Press.

Eliot, J. L. 2004. Warming to each other. *National Geographic,* August.

Ellers, J., and C. L. Boggs. 2004. Evolutionary genetics of dorsal wing colour in *Colias* butterflies. *Journal of Evolutionary Biology* 17: 752–758.

Elliott, G. P., and W. L. Baker. 2004. Quaking aspen (*Populus tremuloides* Michx.) at treeline: A century of change in the San Juan Mountains, Colorado, USA. *Journal of Biogeography* 31: 733–745.

Ellis, W. S. 1976. *The majestic Rocky Mountains.* Washington, DC: National Geographic Society.

El Sayed, G. 1999. Evaluation of food consumption, haemolymph protein content and survival of the grasshopper *Euprepocnemis plorans* fed on clover, lupine or horsebean. *Insect Science and its Application* 18: 333–339.

Emlen, J. M., D. C. Freeman, and J. H. Graham. 1993. Nonlinear growth dynamics and the origin of fluctuating asymmetry. *Genetica* 89: 77–96.

Emmel, T. C. 1976. *Population biology*. New York: Harper and Row.

Endler, J. A. 1988. Frequency-dependent predation, crypsis and aposematic coloration. *Philosophical Transactions of the Royal Society of London B* 319: 505–523.

Enquist, M., and A. Arak. 1993. Selection of exaggerated male traits by female aesthetic senses. *Nature* 361: 446–448.

Estep, K., T. Poole, C. W. Radcliffe, B. O'Connell, and D. Chiszar. 1981. Distance traveled by mice after envenomation by a rattlesnake (*C. viridis*). *Bulletin of the Psychonomic Society* 18: 108–110.

Evans, H. E. 1997. *The natural history of the Long Expedition to the Rocky Mountains, 1819–1820*. New York: Oxford University Press.

Eversman, S., and M. Carr. 1992. *Yellowstone ecology: A road guide*. Missoula, MT: Mountain Press.

Fagan, B. M. 2000. *Ancient North America: The archaeology of a continent*. 3rd ed. New York: Thames and Hudson.

Fagerstrom, T. 1989. Anti-herbivory chemical defense in plants: A note on the concept of cost. *American Naturalist* 133: 281–287.

Fedy, B., and K. Martin. 2011. The influence of fine-scale habitat features on regional variation in population performance of alpine white-tailed ptarmigan. *Condor* 113: 306–315.

Fedy, B. C., K. Martin, C. Ritland, and J. Young. 2008. Genetic and ecological data provide incongruent interpretations of population structure and dispersal in naturally subdivided populations of white-tailed ptarmigan (*Lagopus leucura*). *Molecular Ecology* 17: 1905–1917.

Feeny, P. 1975. Biochemical coevolution between plants and their insect herbivores. In *Coevolution of animals and plants*, edited by L. E. Gilbert and P. H. Raven, 3–19. Austin: University of Texas Press.

Fenton, M. B., and L. E. Licht. 1990. Why rattle snake? *Journal of Herpetology* 24: 274–279.

Ferriere, R., and R. E. Michod. 2011. Inclusive fitness in evolution. *Nature* 471 (March 24): E6–E7.

Festa-Bianchet, M., and S. D. Cote. 2008. *Mountain goats: Ecology, behavior, and conservation of an alpine ungulate*. Washington, DC: Island Press.

Festa-Bianchet, M., M. Urquhart, and K. G. Smith. 1993. Mountain goat recruitment: Kid production and survival to breeding age. *Canadian Journal of Zoology* 72: 22–27.

FitzGerald, G. J. 1991. The role of cannibalism in the reproductive ecology of the threespine stickleback. *Ethology* 89: 177–194.

FitzGerald, G. J., and J. Morrissette. 1992. Kin recognition and choice of shoal mates by threespine sticklebacks. *Ethology, Ecology and Evolution* 4: 273–283.

FitzGerald, G. J., and N. van Havre. 1987. The adaptive significance of cannibalism in sticklebacks (Gasterosteidae: Pisces). *Behavioral Ecology and Sociobiology* 20: 125–128.

Fladmark, K. R. 1986. Getting one's Berings. *Natural History*, November, 8–19.

Flannery, T. 1994. *The future eaters: An ecological history of the Australasian lands and people*. New York: Grove Press.

———. 2002. *The eternal frontier: An ecological history of North America and its peoples*. New York: Atlantic Monthly Press.

Fletcher, C. 1976. *The new complete walker*. Rev. ed. New York: Alfred A. Knopf.

Fletcher, R. 1985. Regenerating aspen. *Forestry Research West* (August): 16–19.

Flora and fauna. 1999. *Yellowstone National Park Magazine*, 72–79. San Francisco: American Park Network.

Fontaine, J. 1999. Wolf recovery. Oral presentation at US Fish and Wildlife Service's National Conservation Training Center, Shepherdstown, WV.

Forristal, V. E., S. Creel, M. L. Taper, B. M. Scurlock, and P. C. Cross. 2012. Effects of supplemental feeding and aggregation on fecal glucocorticoid metabolite concentrations in elk. *Journal of Wildlife Management* 76: 694–702.

Forsyth, A., and R. D. Montgomerie. 1987. Alternative reproductive tactics in the territorial damselfly *Calopteryx maculata*: Sneaking by older males. *Behavioral Ecology and Sociobiology* 21: 73–81.

Fournier, F., and M. Festa-Bianchet. 1995. Social dominance in adult female mountain goats. *Animal Behaviour* 49: 1449–1459.

Fowells, H. A. 1965. Silvics of forest trees of the United States. Agriculture Handbook No. 271. Washington, DC: Forest Service, US Department of Agriculture.

Fowler, S. V., and J. H. Lawton. 1985. Rapidly induced defenses and talking trees: The devil's advocate position. *American Naturalist* 126: 181–195.

Fox, L. R. 1975. Cannibalism in natural populations. *Annual Review of Ecology and Systematics* 6: 87–106.

Frank, D. A., and S. J. McNaughton. 1993. Evidence for the promotion of aboveground grassland production by native large herbivores in Yellowstone National Park. *Oecologia* 96: 157–161.

Fraser, E. C., V. J. Lieffers, and S. M. Landhausser. 2004. Wounding of aspen roots promotes suckering. *Canadian Journal of Botany* 82: 310–315.

Freeland, W. J., and D. H. Janzen. 1974. Strategies in herbivory by mammals: The role of plant secondary compounds. *American Naturalist* 108: 269–289.

Friederici, P. 2008. Real movers and shakers. *National Wildlife*, February–March, 14–15.

Futuyma, D. J. 1979. *Evolutionary biology*. Sunderland, MA: Sinauer Associates.

Gadd, B. 1995. *Handbook of the Canadian Rockies*. 2nd ed. Jasper, AB: Corax Press.

Gadgil, M. 1972. Male dimorphism as a consequence of sexual selection. *American Naturalist* 106: 574–580.

Gaines, M. S., and L. R. McClenaghan Jr. 1980. Dispersal in small mammals. *Annual Review of Ecology and Systematics* 11: 163–196.

Gamboa, G. J., H. K. Reeve, and W. G. Holmes. 1991. Conceptual issues and methodology in kin-recognition research: A critical discussion. *Ethology* 88: 109–127.

Gangestad, S. W., R. Thornhill, and R. A. Yeo. 1994. Facial attractiveness, developmental stability, and fluctuating asymmetry. *Ethology and Sociobiology* 15: 73–85.

Gannon, V. P. J., and D. M. Secoy. 1984. Growth and reproductive rates of a northern population of the prairie rattlesnake, *Crotalus v. viridis*. *Journal of Herpetology* 18: 13–19.

Gardarsson, A., and R. Moss. 1970. Selection of food by Icelandic ptarmigan in relation to its availability and nutritive value. In *Animal populations in relation to their food resources*, edited by A. Watson, 47–71. British Ecological Society, Symposium No. 10. Oxford: Blackwell Scientific Publications.

Gass, C. L., M. T. Romich, and R. K. Suarez. 1999. Energetics of hummingbird foraging at low ambient temperature. *Canadian Journal of Zoology* 77: 314–320.

Gegear, R. J., and T. M. Laverty. 1995. Effect of flower complexity on relearning flower-handling skills in bumble bees. *Canadian Journal of Zoology* 73: 2052–2058.

Geist, V. 1986. The paradox of the great Irish stags. *Natural History*, March, 54–65.

Gendron, R. P., and O. J. Reichman. 1995. Food perishability and inventory management: A comparison of three caching strategies. *American Naturalist* 145: 948–968.

Gerson, E. A., and R. G. Kelsey. 1998. Variation of piperidine alkaloids in ponderosa (*Pinus ponderosa*) and lodgepole pine (*P. contorta*) foliage from central Oregon. *Journal of Chemical Ecology* 24: 815–827.

Gibson, B. M., and A. C. Kamil. 2001. Tests for cognitive mapping in Clark's nutcrackers (*Nucifraga columbiana*). *Journal of Comparative Psychology* 115: 403–417.

Giesen, K. M. 1993. Natal dispersal and recruitment of juvenile white-tailed ptarmigan in Colorado. *Journal of Wildlife Management* 57: 72–77.

Giesen, K. M., C. E. Braun, and T. A. May. 1980. Reproduction and nest-site selection by white-tailed ptarmigan in Colorado. *Wilson Bulletin* 92: 188–199.

Gill, F. B. 1990. *Ornithology*. New York: W. H. Freeman.

Glaudas, X., T. Jezkova, and J. A. Rodriguez-Robles. 2008. Feeding ecology of the Great Basin rattlesnake (*Crotalus lutosus*, Viperidae). *Canadian Journal of Zoology* 86: 723–734.

Goat Lick Overlook. n.d. Glacier National Park, National Park Service, US Department of the Interior.

Godbout, C., and J. A. Fortin. 1985. Synthesized ectomycorrhizae of aspen: Fungal genus level of structural characterization. *Canadian Journal of Botany* 63: 252–262.

Golan, L., C. Radcliffe, T. Miller, B. O'Connell, and D. Chiszar. 1982. Trailing behavior in prairie rattlesnakes (*Crotalus viridis*). *Journal of Herpetology* 16: 287–293.

Goldsmith, S. K. 1987. The mating system and alternative reproductive behaviors of *Dendrobias mandibularis* (Coleoptera: Cerambycidae). *Behavioral Ecology and Sociobiology* 20: 111–115.

Goodyear, A. J., and A. C. Kamil. 2004. Clark's nutcrackers (*Nucifraga columbiana*) and the effects of goal-landmark distance on overshadowing. *Journal of Comparative Psychology* 118: 258–264.

Gordon, M. S. 1972. *Animal physiology: Principles and adaptations*. 2nd ed. New York: Macmillan.

Gould-Beierle, K. L., and A. C. Kamil. 1996. The use of local and global cues by Clark's nutcrackers, *Nucifraga columbiana*. *Animal Behaviour* 52: 519–528.

———. 1998. Use of landmarks in three species of food-storing corvids. *Ethology* 104: 361–378.

———. 1999. The effect of proximity on landmark use in Clark's nutcrackers. *Animal Behaviour* 58: 477–488.

Grahame, K. 1980. *The wind in the willows*. New York: Henry Holt.

Grant, M. C. 1993. The trembling giant. *Discover*, October. http://discover magazine.com/1993/oct/thetremblinggian285.

Graves, B. M., and D. Duvall. 1985. Avomic prairie rattlesnakes (*Crotalus viridis*) fail to attack rodent prey. *Zeitschrift für Tierpsychologie* 67: 161–166.

———. 1990. Spring emergence patterns of wandering garter snakes and prairie rattlesnakes in Wyoming. *Journal of Herpetology* 24: 351–356.

———. 1993. Reproduction, rookery use, and thermoregulation in free-ranging, pregnant *Crotalus v. viridis*. *Journal of Herpetology* 27: 33–41.

Grayson, D. K. 2005. A brief history of Great Basin pikas. *Journal of Biogeography* 32: 2103–2111.

Green, G. I., D. J. Mattson, and J. M. Peek. 1997. Spring feeding on ungulate carcasses by grizzly bears in Yellowstone National Park. *Journal of Wildlife Management* 61: 1040–1055.

Greene, H. W. 1997. *Snakes: The evolution of mystery in nature*. Berkeley: University of California Press.

Grenard, S. 2000. Is rattlesnake venom evolving? *Natural History*, July–August, 44–49.

Griffin, D. H., M. Schaedle, M. J. DeVit, and P. D. Manion. 1991. Clonal variation of *Populus tremuloides* responses to diurnal drought stress. *Tree Physiology* 8: 297–304.

Grigore, M. T., and E. J. Tramer. 1996. The short-term effect of fire on *Lupinus perennis* (L.). *Natural Areas Journal* 16: 41–48.

Gronemeyer, P. A., B. J. Dilger, J. L. Bouzat, and K. N. Paige. 1997. The effects of herbivory on paternal fitness in scarlet gilia: Better moms also make better pops. *American Naturalist* 150: 592–602.

Grundel, R., N. B. Pavlovic, and C. L. Sulzman. 1998. Habitat use by the endangered Karner blue butterfly in oak woodlands: The influence of canopy cover. *Biological Conservation* 85: 47–53.

Guglielmo, C. G., W. H. Karasov, and W. J. Jakubas. 1996. Nutritional costs of a plant secondary metabolite explain selective foraging by ruffed grouse. *Ecology* 77: 1103–1115.

Gugliotta, G. 2013. The first Americans. *Smithsonian*, February, 38–47.

Gullion, G. W., and A. A. Alm. 1983. Forest management and ruffed grouse populations in a Minnesota coniferous forest. *Journal of Forestry* 81: 529–532.

Gummer, D. L., and R. M. Brigham. 1995. Does fluctuating asymmetry reflect the importance of traits in little brown bats (*Myotis lucifugus*)? *Canadian Journal of Zoology* 73: 990–992.

Gunther, K. 1994. Food habits of grizzly bears and black bears in Yellowstone National Park. Information Paper No. BMO-3, Bear Management Office, Yellowstone National Park, WY.

———. 1998. Characteristics of black bears and grizzly bears in Yellowstone National Park. Information Paper No. BMO-2, Bear Management Office, Yellowstone National Park, WY.

Gunther, K. A., M. J. Biel, and H. L. Robison. 1998. Factors influencing the frequency of road-killed wildlife in Yellowstone National Park, 32–42. In *International Conference on Wildlife Ecology and Transport (ICOWET)*, Fort Myers, FL, February 9–12.

Gwynne, D. T. 1981. Sexual difference theory: Mormon crickets show role reversal in mate choice. *Science* 213: 779–780.

———. 1983. Coy conquistadors of the sagebrush. *Natural History*, October, 69–75.

———. 1984. Sexual selection and sexual differences in Mormon crickets (Orthoptera: Tettigoniidae, *Anabrus simplex*). *Evolution* 38: 1011–1022.

———. 1986. Courtship feeding in katydids (Orthoptera: Tettigoniidae): Investment in offspring or in obtaining fertilizations? *American Naturalist* 128: 342–352.

———. 1988a. Courtship feeding and the fitness of female katydids (Orthoptera: Tettigoniidae). *Evolution* 42: 545–555.

———. 1988b. Courtship feeding in katydids benefits the mating male's offspring. *Behavioral Ecology and Sociobiology* 23: 373–377.

———. 1990. Testing parental investment and the control of sexual selection in katydids: The operational sex ratio. *American Naturalist* 136: 474–484.

GYCC. 2013. Greater Yellowstone Coordinating Committee. http://fedgycc.org/index.html.

Gyger, M., S. J. Karakashian, and P. Marler. 1986. Avian alarm calling: Is there an audience effect? *Animal Behaviour* 34: 1570–1572.

Haas, C. A. 1995. Dispersal and use of corridors by birds in wooded patches on an agricultural landscape. *Conservation Biology* 9: 845–854.

Hafner, D. J., and R. M. Sullivan. 1995. Historical and ecological biogeography of nearctic pikas (Lagomorpha: Ochotonidae). *Journal of Mammalogy* 76: 302–321.

Haines, A. L. 1955. *Osborne Russell's journal of a trapper*. Oregon Historical Society. http://user.xmission.com/~drudy/mtman/html/ruslintr.html.

Hairston, N. G., F. E. Smith, and L. B. Slobodkin. 1960. Community structure, population control, and competition. *American Naturalist* 94: 421–425.

Halfpenny, J. C. 2001. *Scats and tracks of the Rocky Mountains: A field guide to the signs of seventy wildlife species*. 2nd ed. Guilford, CT: Globe Pequot Press.

Halterman, G. F. 1981. The Line. Originally published in *Poet Lore* 60 (1); reprinted in *Paper Boat*, no address, unpaginated.

Halvorson, J. J., J. L. Smith, and E. H. Franz. 1991. Lupine influence on soil carbon, nitrogen and microbial activity in developing ecosystems at Mount St. Helens. *Oecologia* 87: 162–170.

Hamel, S., and S. D. Cote. 2007. Habitat use patterns in relation to escape terrain: Are alpine ungulate females trading-off better foraging sites for safety? *Canadian Journal of Zoology* 85: 933–943.

Hamel, S., S. D. Cote, and M. Festa-Bianchet. 2010. Maternal characteristics and environment affect the costs of reproduction in female mountain goats. *Ecology* 91: 2034–2043.

———. 2011. Tradeoff between offspring mass and subsequent reproduction in a highly iteroparous mammal. *Oikos* 120: 690–695.

Hamel, S., S. D. Cote, J.-M. Gaillard, and M. Festa-Bianchet. 2009a. Individual variation in reproductive costs of reproduction: High-quality females always do better. *Journal of Animal Ecology* 78: 143–151.

Hamel, S., J.-M. Gaillard, and M. Festa-Bianchet. 2009b. Individual quality, early-life conditions, and reproductive success in contrasted populations of large herbivores. *Ecology* 90: 1981–1995.

Hamer, D., and S. Herrero. 1990. Courtship and use of mating areas by grizzly bears in the Front Ranges of Banff National Park, Alberta. *Canadian Journal of Zoology* 68: 2695–2697.

Hamer, D., S. Herrero, and K. Brady. 1991. Food and habitat used by grizzly bears, *Ursus arctos*, along the Continental Divide in Waterton Lakes National Park, Alberta. *Canadian Field-Naturalist* 105: 325–329.

Hanski, I., M. Kuussaari, and M. Nieminen. 1994. Metapopulation structure and migration in the butterfly *Melitaea cinxia*. *Ecology* 75: 747–762.

Hanski, I., T. Pakkala, M. Kuussaari, and L. Guangchun. 1995. Metapopulation persistence of an endangered butterfly in a fragmented landscape. *Oikos* 72: 21–28.

Haroldson, M. A., K. A. Gunther, and T. Wyman. 2008. Possible grizzly cub adoption in Yellowstone National Park. *Yellowstone Science* 16 (2): 42–44.

Harrington, F. H., and C. S. Asa. 2003. Wolf communication. In *Wolves: Behavior, ecology, and conservation*, edited by L. D. Mech and L. Boitani, 66–103. Chicago: University of Chicago Press.

Harris, L. D. 1984. *The fragmented forest: Island biogeography theory and the preservation of biotic diversity.* Chicago: University of Chicago Press.

Harrison, S. 1995. Lack of strong induced or maternal effects in tussock moths (*Orgyia vetusta*) on bush lupine (*Lupinus arboreus*). *Oecologia* 103: 343–348.

Harrison, S., and J. L. Maron. 1995. Impacts of defoliation by tussock moths (*Orgyia vetusta*) on the growth and reproduction of bush lupine (*Lupinus arboreus*). *Ecological Entomology* 20: 223–229.

Harrison, S., D. D. Murphy, and P. R. Ehrlich. 1988. Distribution of the bay checkerspot butterfly, *Euphydryas editha bayensis*: Evidence for a metapopulation model. *American Naturalist* 132: 360–382.

Hartman, F. A. 1961. Locomotor mechanisms of birds. *Smithsonian Miscellaneous Collections* 143: 1–91.

Haruta, M., J. A. Pedersen, and C. P. Constabel. 2001. Polyphenol oxidase and herbivore defense in trembling aspen (*Populus tremuloides*): cDNA cloning, expression, and potential substrates. *Physiologia Plantarum* 112: 552–558.

Harvell, C. D. 1990. The ecology and evolution of inducible defenses. *Quarterly Review of Biology* 65: 323–340.

Hatch, C. 2012. Saving a species. *American Forests*, Fall: 32–39.

Haukioja, E. 1982. Inducible defences of white birch to a geometrid defoliator, *Epirrita autumnata*. In *Proceedings of the Fifth International Symposium on Insect-Plant Relationships*, March 1–4, edited by J. H. Visser and A. K. Minks, 199–203. Wageningen, Netherlands: Pudoc Press.

Haukioja, E., and S. Neuvonen. 1985. Induced long-term resistance of birch foliage against defoliators: Defensive or incidental? *Ecology* 66: 1303–1308.

Haverly, J. E., and K. V. Kardong. 1996. Sensory deprivation effects on the predatory behavior of the rattlesnake, *Crotalus viridis oreganus*. *Copeia* 1996: 419–428.

Hayes, W. K. 1991. Ontogeny of striking, prey-handling and envenomation behavior of prairie rattlesnakes (*Crotalus v. viridis*). *Toxicon* 29: 867–875.

Hayes, W. K., P. Lavin-Murcio, and K. V. Kardong. 1995. Northern Pacific rattlesnakes (*Crotalus viridis oreganus*) meter venom when feeding on prey of different sizes. *Copeia* 1995: 337–343.

Head-Smashed-In Buffalo Jump. 2002. Information guide. http://history.alberta.ca/headsmashedin/docs/hsibj_infoguide_vs3.pdf.

Healy, S. D., and J. R. Krebs. 1992. Food storing and the hippocampus in corvids: Amount and volume are correlated. *Proceedings of the Royal Society of London B: Biological Sciences* 248: 241–245.

———. 1993. Development and hippocampal specialization in a food-storing bird. *Behavioural Brain Research* 53: 127–131.

Hebblewhite, M. 2005. Predation by wolves interacts with the North Pacific Oscillation (NPO) on a western North American elk population. *Journal of Animal Ecology* 74: 226–233.

Hebblewhite, M., P. C. Paquet, D. H. Pletscher, R. B. Lessard, and C. J. Callaghan. 2003. Development and application of a ratio estimator to estimate wolf kill rates and variance in a multiple-prey system. *Wildlife Society Bulletin* 31: 933–946.

Hecht, J. 2006. March of the Mormon cricket cannibals. NewScientist.com, February 27. http://www.newscientist.com/article/dn8781-march-of-the -mormon-cricket-cannibals.html.

Heinen, J. T., and J. A. Abdella. 2005. On the advantages of putative cannibalism in American toad tadpoles (*Bufo a. americanus*): Is it active or passive and why? *American Midland Naturalist* 153: 338–347.

Heinrich, B. 1972. Patterns of endothermy in bumblebee queens, drones and workers. *Journal of Comparative Physiology* 77: 65–79.

———. 1975a. Energetics of pollination. *Annual Review of Ecology and Systematics* 6: 139–170.

———. 1975b. Thermoregulation in bumblebees. II. Energetics of warm-up and free flight. *Journal of Comparative Physiology* 96: 155–166.

———. 1976a. Bumblebee foraging and the economics of sociality. *American Scientist* 64: 384–395.

———. 1976b. The foraging specializations of individual bumblebees. *Ecological Monographs* 46: 105–128.

———. 1979a. *Bumblebee economics*. Cambridge, MA: Harvard University Press.

———. 1979b. "Majoring" and "minoring" by foraging bumblebees, *Bombus vagans*: An experimental analysis. *Ecology* 60: 245–255.

———. 1986. Comparative thermoregulation of four montane butterflies of different mass. *Physiological Zoology* 59: 616–626.

———. 1990. The antifreeze of bees. *Natural History*, July, 52–59.

Herre, E. A., and W. T. Wcislo. 2011. In defence of inclusive fitness theory. *Nature* 471 (March 24): E8–E9.

Hersch, E. I., and B. A. Roy. 2007. Context-dependent pollinator behavior: An explanation for patterns of hybridization among three species of Indian paintbrush. *Evolution* 61: 111–124.

Hersch-Green, E. I., and R. Cronn. 2009. Tangled trios? Characterizing a hybrid zone in *Castilleja* (Orobanchaceae). *American Journal of Botany* 96: 1519–1531.

Hersek, M. J., D. H. Owings, and R. F. Hennessy. 1992. Combat between rattlesnakes (*Crotalus viridis oreganus*) in the field. *Journal of Herpetology* 26: 105–107.

Heschel, M. S., and K. N. Paige. 1995. Inbreeding depression, environmental stress, and population size variation in scarlet gilia (*Ipomopsis aggregata*). *Conservation Biology* 9: 126–133.

Hessl, A. E., and L. J. Graumlich. 2002. Interactive effects of human activities, herbivory and fire on quaking aspen (*Populus tremuloides*) age structures in western Wyoming. *Journal of Biogeography* 29: 889–902.

Heuer, K. 2000. A grizzly a day. *Backpacker*, April, 66–72, 114.

Heuschen, B., A. Gumbert, and K. Lunau. 2005. A generalized mimicry system involving angiosperm flower colour, pollen and bumblebees' innate colour preferences. *Plant Systematics and Evolution* 252: 121–137.

Hewitt, D. G., and T. A. Messmer. 2000. Ruffed grouse (*Bonasa umbellus*) foraging in aspen stands during winter in northern Utah. *Western North American Naturalist* 60: 211–215.

Hews, D. K. 1988. Alarm response in larval western toads, *Bufo boreas*: Release of larval chemicals by a natural predator and its effect on predator capture efficiency. *Animal Behaviour* 36: 125–133.

Hiebert, S. M. 1990. Energy costs and temporal organization of torpor in the rufous hummingbird (*Selasphorus rufus*). *Physiological Zoology* 63: 1082–1097.

Hildebrand, G. V., S. D. Farley, C. T. Robbins, T. A. Hanley, K. Titus, and C. Servheen. 1996. Use of stable isotopes to determine diets of living and extinct bears. *Canadian Journal of Zoology* 74: 2080–2088.

Hill, J. K., C. D. Thomas, and O. T. Lewis. 1996. Effects of habitat patch size and isolation on dispersal by *Hesperia comma* butterflies: Implications for metapopulation structure. *Journal of Animal Ecology* 65: 725–735.

Hill, S. R., Jr. 1995. Migratory chronology of adult tiger salamanders and survey of larvae in Ice Lake Reservoir in the Northern Range of Yellowstone National Park. In *Greater Yellowstone predators: Ecology and conservation in a changing landscape*, edited by A. P. Curlee, A.-M. Gillesberg, and D. Casey, 131–136. Jackson, WY: Northern Rockies Conservation Cooperative.

Hirth, D. H., and D. R. McCullough. 1977. Evolution of alarm signals in ungulates with special reference to white-tailed deer. *American Naturalist* 111: 31–42.

Hobbie, S. E., and F. S. Chapin III. 1998. An experimental test of limits to tree establishment in Arctic tundra. *Journal of Ecology* 86: 449–461.

Hobbs, R. J., B. M. J. Hussey, and D. A. Saunders. 1990. Nature conservation: The role of corridors. *Journal of Environmental Management* 31: 93–94.

Hobson, K. A. 2000. Breeding bird communities in boreal forest of western Canada: Consequences of "unmixing" the mixedwoods. *Condor* 102: 759–769.

Hodges, J. C., and M. E. Whitten. 1962. *Harbrace college handbook*. 5th ed. New York: Harcourt, Brace and World.

Hoffecker, J. F., W. R. Powers, and T. Goebel. 1993. The colonization of Beringia and the peopling of the New World. *Science* 259: 46–53.

Hoffman, R. E., and C. E. Braun. 1977. Characteristics of a wintering population of white-tailed ptarmigan in Colorado. *Wilson Bulletin* 89: 107–115.

Holomuzki, J. R., and J. P. Collins. 1987. Trophic dynamics of a top predator, *Ambystoma tigrinum nebulosum* (Caudata: Ambystomatidae), in a lentic community. *Copeia* 1987: 949–957.

Holomuzki, J. R., J. P. Collins, and P. E. Brunkow. 1994. Trophic control of fishless ponds by tiger salamander larvae. *Oikos* 71: 55–64.

Holtcamp, W. 2010. Silence of the pikas. *BioScience*, January, 8–12.

Howard, J. L. 1996. *Populus tremuloides*. In *Fire Effects Information System*, USDA Forest Service, Rocky Mountain Research Station, Fire Sciences Laboratory. http://www.fs.fed.us/database/feis/.

Huff, D. E., and J. D. Varley 1999. Natural regulation in Yellowstone National Park's northern range. *Ecological Applications* 9: 17–29.

Hughes, C., and R. Eastwood. 2006. Island radiation on a continental scale: Exceptional rates of plant diversification after uplift of the Andes. *Proceedings of the National Academy of Sciences of the United States of America* 103: 10334–10339.

Hunt, C. B. 1976. The soaring young Rockies. In *Our continent: A natural history of North America*, edited by S. L. Fishbein, 264–295. Washington, DC: National Geographic Society.

Hunter, M. D., and J. C. Schultz. 1995. Fertilization mitigates chemical induction and herbivore responses within damaged oak trees. *Ecology* 76: 1226–1232.

Huntly, N. J., A. T. Smith, and B. L. Ivins. 1986. Foraging behavior of the pika (*Ochotona princeps*), with comparisons of grazing versus haying. *Journal of Mammalogy* 67: 139–148.

Hurly, T. A., and R. J. Robertson. 1987. Scatterhoarding by territorial red squirrels: A test of the optimal density model. *Canadian Journal of Zoology* 65: 1247–1252.

Hurly, T. A., R. D. Scott, and S. D. Healy. 2001. The function of displays of male rufous hummingbirds. *Condor* 103: 647–651.

Husseman, J. S., D. L. Murray, G. Power, C. Mack, C. R. Wenger, and H. Quigley. 2003. Assessing differential prey selection patterns between two sympatric large carnivores. *Oikos* 101: 591–601.

Hutchings, J. A., and R. A. Myers. 1988. Mating success of alternative maturation phenotypes in male Atlantic salmon, *Salmo salar*. *Oecologia* 75: 169–174.

Hutchins, H. E., and R. M. Lanner. 1982. The central role of Clark's nutcracker in the dispersal and establishment of whitebark pine. *Oecologia* 55: 192–201.

Hwang, S.-Y., and R. L. Lindroth. 1997. Clonal variation in foliar chemistry of aspen: Effects on gypsy moths and forest tent caterpillars. *Oecologia* 111: 99–108.

———. 1998. Consequences of clonal variation in aspen phytochemistry for late season folivores. *Ecoscience* 5: 508–516.

Ibekwe, A. M., A. C. Kennedy, J. J. Halvorson, and C.-H. Yang. 2007. Characterization of developing microbial communities in Mount St. Helens pyroclastic substrate. *Soil Biology and Biochemistry* 39: 2496–2507.

Inouye, D. W., B. Barr, K. B. Armitage, and B. D. Inouye. 2000. Climate change is affecting altitudinal migrants and hibernating species. *Proceedings of the National Academy of Sciences of the United States of America* 97: 1630–1633.

Irwin, R. E. 2000. Hummingbird avoidance of nectar-robbed plants: Spatial location or visual cues. *Oikos* 91: 499–506.

Irwin, R. E., and A. K. Brody. 1998. Nectar robbing in *Ipomopsis aggregata*: Effects on pollinator behavior and plant fitness. *Oecologia* 116: 519–527.

———. 1999. Nectar-robbing bumble bees reduce the fitness of *Ipomopsis aggregata* (Polemoniaceae). *Ecology* 80: 1703–1712.

———. 2000. Consequences of nectar robbing for realized male function in a hummingbird-pollinated plant. *Ecology* 81: 2637–2643.

Jakubas, W. J., and G. W. Gullion. 1990. Coniferyl benzoate in quaking aspen: A ruffed grouse feeding deterrent. *Journal of Chemical Ecology* 16: 1077–1088.

———. 1991. Use of quaking aspen flower buds by ruffed grouse: Its relationship to grouse densities and bud chemical composition. *Condor* 93: 473–485.

Jancovich, J. K., E. W. Davidson, J. F. Morado, B. L. Jacobs, and J. P. Collins. 1997. Isolation of a lethal virus from the endangered tiger salamander *Ambystoma tigrinum stebbinsi*. *Diseases of Aquatic Organisms* 31: 161–167.

Jandt, J. M., and A. Dornhaus. 2009. Spatial organization and division of labour in the bumblebee *Bombus impatiens*. *Animal Behaviour* 77: 641–651.

Janetski, J. C. 1987. *The Indians of Yellowstone Park*. Salt Lake City: University of Utah Press.

Jansen, G., H.-U. Jurgens, and F. Ordon. 2009. Effects of temperature on the alkaloid content of seeds of *Lupinus angustifolius* cultivars. *Journal of Agronomy and Crop Science* 195: 172–177.

Janzen, D. H. 1985. A host plant is more than its chemistry. In *125 years of biological research 1858–1983: A symposium. Illinois Natural History Survey Bulletin* 33: 141–174.

Jaremo, J., J. Tuomi, and P. Nilsson. 1999. Adaptive status of localized and systemic defense responses in plants. In *The ecology and evolution of inducible defenses*, edited by R. Tollrian and C. D. Harvell, 33–44. Princeton, NJ: Princeton University Press.

Jelinski, D. E., and L. J. Fisher. 1991. Spatial variability in the nutrient composition of *Populus tremuloides*: Clone-to-clone differences and implications for cervids. *Oecologia* 88: 116–124.

Jenkins, D. L., et al. 2012. Clovis Age western stemmed projectile points and human coprolites at the Paisley Caves. *Science* 337: 223–228.

Jensen, M. N. 2000. Breeze keeps trees apart. *Science Now*, August 9. http://news.sciencemag.org/environment/2000/08/breeze-keeps-trees-apart.

Johnsgard, P. A. 1973. *Grouse and quails of North America*. Lincoln: University of Nebraska Press.

Johnson, K. A., and R. L. Crabtree. 1999. Small prey of carnivores in the Greater Yellowstone Ecosystem. In: *Carnivores in ecosystems: The Yellowstone experience*, edited by T. W. Clark, A. P. Curlee, S. C. Minta, and P. M. Kareiva, 238–263. New Haven, CT: Yale University Press.

Johnstone, J. F., and F. S. Chapin. 2003. Non-equilibrium succession dynamics indicate northern migration of lodgepole pine. *Global Change Biology* 9: 1401–1409.

Jones, J. E., E. Antoniadis, S. J. Shettleworth, and A. C. Kamil. 2002. A comparative study of geometric rule learning by nutcrackers (*Nucifraga columbiana*), pigeons (*Columba livia*), and jackdaws (*Corvus monedula*). *Journal of Comparative Psychology* 116: 350–356.

Jones, J. R., and N. V. DeByle. 1985. Climates. In: *Aspen: Ecology and management in the United States*, edited by N. V. DeByle and R. P. Winokur, 57–64. USDA Forest Service, Rocky Mountain Forest and Range Experiment Station, Fort Collins, CO. General Technical Report No. RM-119.

Jones, T. L., J. F. Porcasi, J. M. Eriandson, H. Dallas Jr., T. A. Wake, and R. Schwaderer. 2008. The protracted Holocene extinction of California's flightless sea duck (*Chendytes law*) and its implications for the Pleistocene overkill hypothesis. *Proceedings of the National Academy of Sciences of the United States of America* 105: 4105–4108.

Juenger, T., and J. Bergelson. 1997. Pollen and resource limitation of compensation to herbivory in scarlet gilia, *Ipomopsis aggregata*. *Ecology* 78: 1684–1695.

———. 2000a. Does early season browsing influence the effect of self-pollination in scarlet gilia? *Ecology* 8: 41–48.

———. 2000b. The evolution of compensation to herbivory in scarlet gilia, *Ipomopsis aggregata*: Herbivore-imposed natural selection and the quantitative genetics of tolerance. *Evolution* 54: 764–777.

Kamil, A. C., and R. P. Balda. 1985. Cache recovery and spatial memory in Clark's nutcracker (*Nucifraga columbiana*). *Journal of Experimental Psychology* 11: 95–111.

Kamil, A. C., R. P. Balda, and S. Good. 1999. Patterns of movement and orientation during caching and recovery by Clark's nutcrackers, *Nucifraga columbiana*. *Animal Behaviour* 57: 1327–1335.

Kamil, A. C., and J. E. Jones. 1997. The seed-storing corvid Clark's nutcracker learns geometric relationships among landmarks. *Nature* 390: 276–279.

———. 2000. Geometric rule learning by Clark's nutcrackers (*Nucifraga columbiana*). *Journal of Experimental Psychology* 26: 439–453.

Kanoh, Y. 1996. Pre-oviposition ejaculation in externally fertilizing fish: How sneaker male rose bitterlings contrive to mate. *Ethology* 102: 883–899.

Karban, R., and I. T. Baldwin. 1997. *Induced responses to herbivory*. Chicago: University of Chicago Press.

Karban, R., and J. H. Myers. 1989. Induced plant responses to herbivory. *Annual Review of Ecology and Systematics* 20: 331–348.

Karels, T. J., and R. Boonstra. 2003. Reducing solar heat gain during winter: The role of white bark in northern deciduous trees. *Arctic* 56: 168–174.

Kashian, D. M., D. B. Tinker, M. G. Turner, and F. L. Scarpace. 2004. Spatial heterogeneity of lodgepole pine sapling densities following the 1988 fires in Yellowstone National Park, Wyoming, USA. *Canadian Journal of Forest Research* 34: 2263–2276.

Kay, C. E. 1993. Aspen seedlings in recently burned areas of Grand Teton and Yellowstone National Parks. *Northwest Science* 67: 94–104.

———. 1995. Aboriginal overkill and native burning: Implications for modern ecosystem management. *Western Journal of Applied Forestry* 10: 121–126.

———. 1997a. The condition and trend of aspen, *Populus tremuloides*, in Kootenay and Yoho National Parks: Implications for ecological integrity. *Canadian Field-Naturalist* 111: 607–616.

———. 1997b. Yellowstone: Ecological malpractice. *PERC Reports* 15 (2): 5–39.

Kay, C. E., and S. Chadde. 1992. Reduction of willow seed production by ungulate browsing in Yellowstone National Park. In *Proceedings: Symposium on ecology and management of riparian shrub communities*, Sun Valley, ID, May 29–31, compiled by W. P. Clary, E. D. McArthur, D. Bedunah, and C. L. Wambolt, 92–99. Ogden, UT: Intermountain Research Station, USDA Forest Service.

Kay, C. E., and F. H. Wagner. 1994. Historical condition of woody vegetation on Yellowstone's northern range: A critical evaluation of the "natural regulation" paradigm. In *Plants and their environments: Proceedings of the first biennial scientific conference on the Greater Yellowstone Ecosystem*, September 16–18, Yellowstone National Park, WY, edited by D. G. Despain, 151–169. Denver, CO: Natural Resources Publication Office, National Park Service, US Department of the Interior.

Kaye, T. N. 1999. Obligate insect pollination of a rare plant, *Lupinus sulphureus* ssp. *kincaidii*. *Northwest Science* 73: 50–52.

Keiter, R. B. 1997. Greater Yellowstone's bison: Unraveling of an early American conservation achievement. *Journal of Wildlife Management* 61: 1–11.

Keiter, R. B., and M. S. Boyce. 1991. Greater Yellowstone's future: Ecosystem management in a wilderness environment. In *The Greater Yellowstone Ecosystem: Redefining America's wilderness heritage*, edited by R. B. Keiter and M. S. Boyce, 379–415. New Haven, CT: Yale University Press.

Kelly, D. M., A. C. Kamil, and K. Cheng. 2010. Landmark use by Clark's nutcrackers (*Nucifraga columbiana*): Influence of disorientation and cue rotation on distance and direction estimates. *Animal Cognition* 13: 175–188.

Kemp, D. J., and A. K. Krockenberger. 2002. A novel method of behavioural thermoregulation in butterflies. *Journal of Evolutionary Biology* 15: 922–929.

Kevan, P. G., S. D. St. Helens, and I. Baker. 1983. Hummingbirds feeding from exudates on diseased scrub oak. *Condor* 85: 251–252.

Kiesecker, J. M., D. P. Chivers, and A. R. Blaustein. 1996. The use of chemical cues in predator recognition by western toad tadpoles. *Animal Behaviour* 52: 1237–1245.

Kieser, J. A., and H. T. Groeneveld. 1991. Fluctuating odontometric asymmetry, morphological variability, and genetic monomorphism in the cheetah *Acinonyx jubatus. Evolution* 45: 1175–1183.

King, M. B., and D. Duvall. 1990. Prairie rattlesnake seasonal migrations: Episodes of movement, vernal foraging and sex differences. *Animal Behaviour* 39: 924–935.

King, M., D. McCarron, D. Duvall, G. Baxter, and W. Gern. 1983. Group avoidance of conspecific but not heterospecific chemical cues by prairie rattlesnakes (*Crotalus viridis*). *Journal of Herpetology* 17: 196–198.

Kingsbury, L. A. 2012. Personal communication, February 21. Forest archaeologist, Payette National Forest, McCall, ID.

Kingsolver, J. G. 1985. Butterfly engineering. *Scientific American*, August, 106–113.

Kingsolver, J. G., and W. B. Watt. 1983. Thermoregulatory strategies in *Colias* butterflies: Thermal stress and the limits to adaptation in temporally varying environments. *American Naturalist* 121: 32–55.

Kissner, K. J., M. R. Forbes, and D. M. Secoy. 1997. Rattling behavior of prairie rattlesnakes (*Crotalus viridis viridis*, Viperidae) in relation to sex, reproductive status, body size, and body temperature. *Ethology* 103: 1042–1050.

Klaver, R. W., J. J. Claar, D. B. Rockwell, H. R. Mays, and F. Acevedo. 1986. Grizzly bears, insects, and people: Bear management in the McDonald Peak region, Montana. In *Proceedings of the grizzly bear habitat symposium*, compiled by G. P. Contreras and K. E. Evans, 204–211. General Technical Report INT-207. Ogden, UT: Intermountain Research Station, USDA Forest Service.

Kleiman, D. G. 1977. Monogamy in mammals. *Quarterly Review of Biology* 52: 39–69.

———. 2011. Canid mating systems, social behavior, parental care and ontogeny: Are they flexible? *Behavior Genetics* 41: 803–809.

Knight, R. R., and L. L. Eberhardt. 1984. Projected future abundance of the Yellowstone grizzly bear. *Journal of Wildlife Management* 48: 1434–1438.

Koch, E. D., and C. R. Peterson. 1995. *Amphibians and reptiles of Yellowstone and Grand Teton National Parks*. Salt Lake City: University of Utah Press.

Kodric-Brown, A., and J. H. Brown. 1984. Truth in advertising: The kinds of traits favored by sexual selection. *American Naturalist* 124: 309–323.

Krausman, P. R. 1998. Conflicting views of ungulate management in North America's western national parks. *Wildlife Society Bulletin* 26: 369–371.

Krebs, J. R. 1990. Food-storing birds: Adaptive specialization in brain and behavior? *Philosophical Transactions of the Royal Society of London B: Biological Sciences* 329: 153–160.

Krech, S., III. 1999. *The ecological Indian: Myth and history*. New York: W. W. Norton.

Krushinskaya, N. L. 1966. Some complex forms of feeding behavior of the nutcracker *Nucifraga caryocatactes* after removal of the archeocortex. *Zhurnal Evoliutsionnoi Biokhimii i Fiziologii* [Journal of Evolutionary Biochemistry and Physiology] (Moscow) 2: 563–568.

Kulin, R. M., P.-Y. Chen, F. Jiang, and K. S. Vecchio. 2011. A study of the dynamic compressive behavior of elk antler. *Materials Science and Engineering* 31: 1030–1041.

Kunkel, K., and D. H. Pletscher. 2001. Winter hunting patterns of wolves in and near Glacier National Park, Montana. *Journal of Wildlife Management* 65: 520–530.

Kunkel, K. E., T. K. Ruth, D. H. Pletscher, and M. G. Hornocker. 1999. Winter prey selection by wolves and cougars in and near Glacier National Park, Montana. *Journal of Wildlife Management* 63: 901–910.

Kurten, B. 1976. Life in the Ice Age: Prelude to today. In: *Our continent: A natural history of North America,* edited by S. L. Fishbein, 142–162. Washington, DC: National Geographic Society.

Kuussaari, M., I. Hanski, and M. Singer. 2000. Local specialization and landscape-level influence on host use in an herbivorous insect. *Ecology* 81: 2177–2187.

Kuwamura, T. 1987. Male mating territory and sneaking in a maternal mouth-brooder, *Pseudosimochromis curvifrons* (Pisces; Cichlidae). *Journal of Ethology* 5: 203–206.

Kyle, C. J., T. J. Karels, C. S. Davis, S. Mebs, B. Clark, C. Strobeck, and D. S. Hik. 2007. Social structure and facultative mating systems of hoary marmots (*Marmota caligata*). *Molecular Ecology* 16: 1245–1255.

Lack, D. 1968. *Ecological adaptations for breeding in birds.* London: Chapman and Hall.

Lacy, R. C., and P. W. Sherman. 1983. Kin recognition by phenotype matching. *American Naturalist* 121: 489–512.

LaGory, K. E. 1987. The influence of habitat and group characteristics on the alarm and flight response of white-tailed deer. *Animal Behaviour* 35: 20–25.

Lair, H. 1990. The calls of the red squirrel: A contextual analysis of function. *Behaviour* 115: 254–282.

Landhausser, S. M., D. Deshaies, and V. J. Lieffers. 2010. Disturbance facilitates rapid range expansion of aspen into higher elevations of the Rocky Mountains under a warming climate. *Journal of Biogeography* 37: 68–76.

Lank, D. B., C. M. Smith, O. Hanotte, T. Burke, and F. Cooke. 1995. Genetic polymorphism for alternative mating behaviour in lekking male ruff *Philomachus pugnax. Nature* 378: 59–62.

Lanner, R. M. 1996. *Made for each other: A symbiosis of birds and pines.* New York: Oxford University Press.

Lanner, R. M., and B. K. Gilbert. 1994. Nutritive value of whitebark pine seeds, and the question of their variable dormancy. In *Proceedings—International Workshop on Subalpine Stone Pines and Their Environment: The Status of our Knowledge,* compiled by W. C. Schmidt and F.-K. Holtmeier, 206–211. General Technical Report INT-GTR-309. Ogden, UT: Intermountain Research Station, USDA Forest Service.

Lantz, G. 2002. Stalwart species. *American Forests*, Summer: 30–33.

Larison, J. R. 2003. Rebuttal to Reynolds (2003). *Auk* 120: 229–230.

Larison, J. R., J. G. Crock, and C. M. Snow. 2001. Timing of mineral sequestration in leg bones of white-tailed ptarmigan. *Auk* 118: 1057–1062.

Larom, D., M. Garstang, K. Payne, R. Raspet, and M. Lindeque. 1997. The influence of surface atmospheric conditions on the range and area reached by animal vocalizations. *Journal of Experimental Biology* 200: 421–431.

Launey, M. E., P.-Y. Chen, J. McKittrick, and R. O. Ritchie. 2010. Mechanistic aspects of the fracture toughness of elk antler bone. *Acta Biomaterialia* 6: 1505–1514.

Laverty, T. M. 1994. Costs to foraging bumble bees of switching plant species. *Canadian Journal of Zoology* 72: 43–47.

Laverty, T. M., and R. C. Plowright. 1988. Flower handling by bumblebees: A comparison of specialists and generalists. *Animal Behaviour* 36: 733–740.

Lavin-Murcio, P., B. G. Robinson, and K. V. Kardong. 1993. Cues involved in relocation of struck prey by rattlesnakes, *Crotalus viridis oreganus*. *Herpetologica* 49: 463–469.

Leadbeater, E., and L. Chittka. 2011. Do inexperienced bumblebee foragers use scent marks as social information? *Animal Cognition* 14: 915–919.

Leary, R. F., F. W. Allendorf, and K. L. Knudsen. 1983. Developmental stability and enzyme heterozygosity in rainbow trout. *Nature* 301: 71–72.

———. 1984. Superior developmental stability of heterozygotes at emzyme loci in salmonid fishes. *American Naturalist* 124: 540–551.

LeBoeuf, B. J. 1978. Social behavior in some marine and terrestrial carnivores. In *Contrasts in behavior*, edited by E. S. Reese and F. J. Lighter, 251–279. New York: John Wiley and Sons.

Lee, R. K. K., D. A. Chiszar, and H. M. Smith. 1988. Post-strike orientation of the prairie rattlesnake facilitates location of envenomated prey. *Journal of Ethology* 6: 129–134.

Lee, S., M. Ralphs, K. Panter, D. Cook, and D. Gardner. 2007. Alkaloid profiles, concentration, and pools in velvet lupine (*Lupinus leucophyllus*) over the growing season. *Journal of Chemical Ecology* 33: 75–84.

Leonard, A. S., and D. R. Papaj. 2011. "X" marks the spot: The possible benefits of nectar guides to bees and plants. *Functional Ecology* 25: 1293–1301.

Leopold, A. S., S. A. Cain, C. M. Cottam, I. N. Gabrielson, and T. L. Kimball. 1963. Wildlife management in the national parks. *Transactions of the North American and Natural Resource Conference* 28: 29–44.

Leopold, L. B. 1991. Foreword to *The Greater Yellowstone Ecosystem: Redefining America's wilderness heritage*, edited by R. B. Keiter and M. S. Boyce, ix–xii. New Haven, CT: Yale University Press.

Levin, D. A. 1976a. Alkaloid-bearing plants: An ecogeographic perspective. *American Naturalist* 110: 261–284.

———. 1976b. The chemical defenses of plants to pathogens and herbivores. *Annual Review of Ecology and Systematics* 7: 121–159.

Levine, M. T., and K. N. Paige. 2004. Direct and indirect effects of drought on compensation following herbivory in scarlet gilia. *Ecology* 85: 3185–3191.

Lewin, R. 1982. *Thread of life: The Smithsonian looks at evolution.* Washington, DC: Smithsonian Institution.

———. 1984a. Is sexual selection a burden? *Science* 226: 526–527.

———. 1984b. Practice catches theory in kin recognition. *Science* 223: 1049–1051.

Lewis, J. L., and A. C. Kamil. 2006. Interference effects in the memory for serially presented locations in Clark's nutcrackers, *Nucifraga columbiana. Journal of Experimental Psychology* 32: 407–418.

Lewis, K. C., J. Alers-Garcia, and L. J. Wright. 2010. Green tea catechins applied to susceptible hosts inhibit parasitic plant attachment success. *Crop Science* 50: 253–264.

Lewis, M. A., and J. D. Murray. 1993. Modeling territoriality and wolf-deer interactions. *Nature* 366: 738–740.

Li, H. L., and J. J. Willaman. 1972. Recent trends in alkaloid hunting. *Economic Botany* 26: 61–67.

Liggett, A. C., I. F. Harvey, and J. T. Manning. 1993. Fluctuating asymmetry in *Scatophaga stercoraria* L.: Successful males are more symmetrical. *Animal Behaviour* 45: 1041–1043.

Lihoreau, M., L. Chittka, and N. E. Raine. 2010. Travel optimization by foraging bumblebees through readjustments of traplines after discovery of new feeding locations. *American Naturalist* 176: 744–757.

———. 2011. Trade-off between travel distance and prioritization of high-reward sites in traplining bumblebees. *Functional Ecology* 25: 1284–1292.

Lindroth, R. L., and K. K. Kinney. 1998. Consequences of enriched CO_2 and defoliation for foliar chemistry and gypsy moth performance. *Journal of Chemical Ecology* 24: 1677–1696.

Lindroth, R. L., and S. B. St. Clair. Adaptations of quaking aspen (*Populus tremuloides* Michx.) for defense against herbivores. *Forest Ecology and Management* (forthcoming).

Lockwood, J. A. 2004. *Locust: The devastating rise and mysterious disappearance of the insect that shaped the American frontier.* New York: Basic Books.

Loeb, M. L. G., J. P. Collins, and T. J. Maret. 1994. The role of prey in controlling expression of a trophic polymorphism in *Ambystoma tigrinum nebulosum. Functional Ecology* 8: 151–158.

Loehle, C. 1988. Philosophical tools: Potential contributions to ecology. *Oikos* 51: 97–104.

Lopez, B. H. 1978. *Of wolves and men.* New York: Simon and Schuster.

Lorch, P. D., G. A. Sword, D. T. Gwynne, and G. L. Anderson. 2005. Radiotelemetry reveals differences in individual movement patterns between outbreak and non-outbeak Mormon cricket populations. *Ecological Entomology* 30: 548–555.

Lucas, J. R., A. Brodin, S. R. de Kort, and N. S. Clayton. 2004. Does hippocampal size correlate with degree of caching specialization? *Proceedings of the Royal Society B: Biological Sciences* 271: 2423–2429.

Lucas, J. R., and R. D. Howard. 1995. On alternative reproductive tactics in anurans: Dynamic games with density and frequency dependence. *American Naturalist* 146: 365–397.

Lucchini, V., J. Hoglund, S. Klaus, J. Swenson, and E. Randi. 2001. Historical biogeography and a mitochondrial DNA phylogeny of grouse and ptarmigan. *Molecular Phylogenetics and Evolution* 20: 149–162.

Lundberg, H. 1980. Effects of weather on foraging-flights of bumblebees (Hymenoptera, Apidae) in a subalpine/alpine area. *Holarctic Ecology* 3: 104–110.

Lung, M. A., and M. J. Childress. 2007. The influence of conspecifics and predation risk on the vigilance of elk (*Cervus elaphus*) in Yellowstone National Park. *Behavioral Ecology* 18: 12–20.

Lutterschmidt, W. I., G. A. Marvin, and V. H. Hutchison. 1994. Alarm response by a plethodontid salamander (*Desmognathus ochrophaeus*): Conspecific and heterospecific "schreckstoff." *Journal of Chemical Ecology* 20: 2751–2759.

Macartney, J. M., and P. T. Gregory. 1988. Reproductive biology of female rattlesnakes (*Crotalus viridis*) in British Columbia. *Copeia* 1988: 47–57.

Macartney, J. M., K. W. Larsen, and P. T. Gregory. 1989. Body temperatures and movements of hibernating snakes (*Crotalus* and *Thamnophis*) and thermal gradients of natural hibernacula. *Canadian Journal of Zoology* 67: 108–114.

MacDonald, G. M., D. W. Beilman, Y. V. Kuzmin, L. A. Orlova, K. V. Kremenetski, B. Shapiro, R. K. Wayne, and B. Van Valkenburgh. 2012. Pattern of extinction of the woolly mammoth in Beringia. *Nature Communications*, June 12, doi:10.1038/ncomms1881.

Mace, R. D., and J. B. Waller. 1997. Spatial and temporal interaction of male and female grizzly bears in northwestern Montana. *Journal of Wildlife Management* 61: 39–52.

Mackessy, S. P. 1988. Venom ontogeny in the Pacific rattlesnakes *Crotalus viridis helleri* and *C. v. oreganus*. *Copeia* 1988: 92–101.

———. 2010. Evolutionary trends in venom composition in the western rattlesnakes (*Crotalus viridis* sensu lato): Toxicity vs. tenderizers. *Toxicon* 55: 1463–1474.

MacNulty, D. R., D. W. Smith, J. A. Vucetich, L. D. Mech, D. R. Stahler, and C. Packer. 2009. Predatory senescence in ageing wolves. *Ecology Letters* 12: 1347–1356.

Maekawa, K., and H. Onozato. 1986. Reproductive tactics and fertilization success of mature male Miyabe charr, *Salvelinus malma miyabai*. *Environmental Biology of Fishes* 15: 119–129.

Magnhagen, C. 1992. Alternative reproductive behavior in the common goby, *Pomatoschistus microps*: An ontogenetic gradient? *Animal Behaviour* 44: 182–184.

Mainguy, J., S. D. Cote, E. Cardinal, and M. Houle. 2008. Mating tactics and mate choice in relation to age and social rank in male mountain goats. *Journal of Mammalogy* 89: 626–635.

Mainguy, J., S. D. Cote, and D. W. Coltman. 2009. Multilocus heterozygosity, parental relatedness and individual fitness components in a wild mountain goat, *Oreamnos americanus*, population. *Molecular Ecology* 18: 2297–2306.

Maloof, J. E., and D. W. Inouye. 2000. Are nectar robbers cheaters or mutualists? *Ecology* 81: 2651–2661.

Mann, C. C. 2005. *1491: New revelations of the Americas before Columbus*. New York: Vintage Books.

Marchand, P. J. 1987. *Life in the cold: An introduction to winter ecology*. Hanover, NH: University Press of New England.

Maret, T. J., and J. P. Collins. 1994. Individual responses to population size structure: The role of size variation in controlling expression of a trophic polyphenism. *Oecologia* 100: 279–285.

Margules, C., A. J. Higgs, and R. W. Rafe. 1982. Modern biogeographic theory: Are there any lessons for nature reserve design? *Biological Conservation* 24: 115–128.

Marko, M. D., and F. R. Stermitz. 1997. Transfer of alkaloids from *Delphinium* to *Castilleja* via root parasitism: Nonditerpenoid alkaloid analysis by electrospray mass spectrometry. *Biochemical Systematics and Ecology* 25: 279–285.

Maron, J. L. 1997. Interspecific competition and insect herbivory reduce bush lupine (*Lupinus arboreus*) seedling survival. *Oecologia* 110: 284–290.

———. 1998. Insect herivivory above- and below-ground: Individual and joint effects on plant fitness. *Ecology* 79: 1281–1293.

———. 2001. Intraspecific competition and subterranean herbivory: Individual and interactive effects on bush lupine. *Oikos* 92: 178–186.

Maron, J. L., and P. G. Connors. 1996. A native nitrogen-fixing shrub facilitates weed invasion. *Oecologia* 105: 302–312.

Maron, J. L., and R. L. Jefferies. 1999. Bush lupine mortality, altered resource availability, and alternative vegetation states. *Ecology* 80: 443–454.

Maron, J. L., and E. L. Simms. 1997. Effect of seed predation on seed bank size and seedling recruitment of bush lupine (*Lupinus arboreus*). *Oecologia* 111: 76–83.

Marquis, R. J. 1991. Evolution of resistance to herbivores. *Evolutionary Trends in Plants* 5: 23–29.

Martin, K., P. B. Stacey, and C. E. Braun. 2000. Recruitment, dispersal, and demographic rescue in spatially-structured white-tailed ptarmigan populations. *Condor* 102: 503–516.

Martin, K., and K. L. Wiebe. 2004. Coping mechanisms of alpine and Arctic breeding birds: Extreme weather and limitations to reproductive resilience. *Integrative and Comparative Biology* 44: 177–185.

Martin, P. S. 2007. *Twilight of the mammoths: Ice Age extinctions and the rewilding of America.* Berkeley: University of California Press.

Marvier, M. A. 1995. Parasitic plant-host interactions: Plant performance and indirect effects on parasite-feeding herbivores. *Ecology* 77: 1398–1409.

———. 1998. A mixed diet improves performance and herbivore resistance of a parasitic plant. *Ecology* 79: 1272–1280.

Maschinski, J., and T. G. Whitham. 1989. The continuum of plant responses to herbivory: The influence of plant association, nutrient availability, and timing. *American Naturalist* 134: 1–19.

Mathews, D. 2003. *Rocky Mountain natural history.* Portland, OR: Raven Editions.

Matthies, D. 1997. Parasite-host interactions in *Castilleja* and *Orthocarpus*. *Canadian Journal of Botany* 75: 1252–1260.

Mattson, D. J. 1997a. Selection of microsites by grizzly bears to excavate biscuitroots. *Journal of Mammalogy* 78: 228–238.

———. 1997b. Use of lodgepole pine cover types by Yellowstone grizzly bears. *Journal of Wildlife Management* 61: 480–496.

———. 1997c. Use of ungulates by Yellowstone grizzly bears *Ursus arctos*. *Biological Conservation* 81: 161–177.

Mattson, D. J., B. M. Blanchard, and R. R. Knight. 1992. Yellowstone grizzly bear mortality, human habituation, and whitebark pine seed crops. *Journal of Wildlife Management* 56: 432–442.

Mattson, D. J., C. M. Gillin, S. A. Benson, and R. R. Knight. 1991. Bear feeding activity at alpine insect aggregation sites in the Yellowstone ecosystem. *Canadian Journal of Zoology* 69: 2430–2435.

Mattson, D. J., S. Herrero, R. G. Wright, and C. M. Pease. 1996. Science and management of Rocky Mountain grizzly bears. *Conservation Biology* 10: 1013–1025.

Mattson, D. J., and C. Jonkel. 1990. Stone pines and bears. In *Proceedings of the Symposium on Whitebark Pine Ecosystems: Ecology and management of a high-mountain resource*, March 29–31, Bozeman, MT, compiled by W. C. Schmidt and K. J. MacDonald, 223–236. General Technical Report INT-270, USDA Forest Service.

Mattson, D. J., and D. P. Reinhart. 1995. Influences of cutthroat trout (*Oncorhynchus clarki*) on behaviour and reproduction of Yellowstone grizzly bears (*Ursus arctos*), 1975–1989. *Canadian Journal of Zoology* 73: 2072–2079.

———. 1997. Excavation of red squirrel middens by Yellowstone grizzly bears in the whitebark pine zone. *Journal of Applied Ecology* 34: 926–940.

Maynard Smith, J. 1965. The evolution of alarm calls. *American Naturalist* 94: 59–63.

Mayr, G. 2004. Old World fossil record of modern-type hummingbirds. *Science* 304: 861–864.

McArthur, C., C. T. Robbins, A. E. Hagerman, and T. A. Hanley. 1993. Diet selection by a ruminant generalist browser in relation to plant chemistry. *Canadian Journal of Zoology* 71: 2236–2243.

McClintock, W. 1910. *The Old North Trail, or life, legends and religion of the Blackfeet Indians*. Reprint, Lincoln: University of Nebraska Press, 1999.

McCracken, G. F. 1984. Communal nursing in Mexican free-tailed bat maternity colonies. *Science* 223: 1090–1091.

McKechnie, A. E., and B. G. Lovegrove. 2002. Avian facultative hypothermic responses: A review. *Condor* 104: 705–724.

McKechnie, A. M., A. T. Smith, and M. M. Peacock. 1994. Kleptoparasitism in pikas (*Ochotona princeps*): Theft of hay. *Journal of Mammalogy* 75: 488–491.

McKittrick, J., P.-Y. Chen, L. Tombolato, E. E. Novitskaya, M. W. Trim, G. A. Hirata, E. A. Olevsky, M. F. Horstemeyer, and M. A. Meyers. 2010. Energy absorbent natural materials and bioinspired design strategies: A review. *Materials Science and Engineering C* 30: 331–342.

McLellan, B. N., and F. W. Hovey. 1995. The diet of grizzly bears in the Flathead River drainage of southeastern British Columbia. *Canadian Journal of Zoology* 73: 704–712.

M'Closkey, R. T., R. J. Deslippe, C. P. Szpak, and K. A. Baia. 1990. Ecological correlates of the variable mating system of an iguanid lizard. *Oikos* 59: 63–69.

McNaughton, S. 2008. A cautionary tail. *National Geographic*, June.

Mead, J. I. 1987. Quaternary records of pika, *Ochotona*, in North America. *Boreas* 16: 165–172.

Meadows, R. 2010. We all gotta go sometime. *PLOS Biology* 8 (8), e1000455. doi:10.1371/journal.pbio.1000455.

Mech, L. D. 1970. *The wolf: The ecology and behavior of an endangered species*. Minneapolis: University of Minnesota Press.

———. 1991. *The way of the wolf*. Stillwater, MN: Voyageur Press.

———. 2007. Possible use of foresight, understanding, and planning by wolves hunting muskoxen. *Arctic* 60: 145–149.

Mech, L. D., and L. D. Frenzel Jr. 1971. An analysis of the age, sex, and condition of deer killed by wolves in northeastern Minnesota. In *Ecological studies of the timber wolf in northeastern Minnesota*, edited by L. D. Mech and L. D. Frenzel, 35–51. Research Paper NC-52. Saint Paul, MN: North Central Forest Experiment Station, USDA Forest Service.

Mech, L. D., L. D. Frenzel Jr., R. R. Ream, and J. W. Winship. 1971. Movements, behavior, and ecology of timber wolves in northeastern Minnesota. In *Ecological studies of the timber wolf in northeastern Minnesota*, edited by L. D. Mech and L. D. Frenzel, 1–35. Research Paper NC-52. Saint Paul, MN: North Central Forest Experiment Station, USDA Forest Service.

Meffe, G. K., and M. L. Crump. 1987. Possible growth and reproductive benefits of cannibalism in the mosquitofish. *American Naturalist* 129: 203–212.

Melcer, T., and D. Chiszar. 1989. Striking prey creates a specific chemical search image in rattlesnakes. *Animal Behaviour* 37: 477–486.

Melcher, J. C., K. B. Armitage, and W. P. Porter. 1990. Thermal influences on the activity and energetics of yellow-bellied marmots (*Marmota flaviventris*). *Physiological Zoology* 63: 803–820.

Meng, S. X., M. Rudnicki, V. J. Lieffers, D. E. B. Reid, and U. Silins. 2006. Preventing crown collisions increases the crown cover and leaf area of maturing lodgepole pine. *Journal of Ecology* 94: 681–686.

Merila, J., and M. Bjorklund. 1995. Fluctuating asymmetry and measurement error. *Systematic Biology* 44: 97–101.

Michaelian, M., E. H. Hogg, R. J. Hall, and E. Arsenault. 2011. Massive mortality of aspen following severe drought along the southern edge of the Canadian boreal forest. *Global Change Biology* 17: 2084–2094.

Michaels, H. J., X. J. Shi, R. J. Mitchell, and B. Schmid. 2007. Effects of population size on performance and inbreeding depression in *Lupinus perennis*. *Oecologia* 154: 651–661.

Millspaugh, J. J., R. J. Woods, K. E. Hunt, K. J. Raedeke, G. C. Brundige, B. E. Washburn, and S. K. Wasser. 2001. Fecal glucocorticoid assays and the physiological stress response in elk. *Wildlife Society Bulletin* 29: 899–907.

Milne, L. J., and M. Milne. 1962. *The mountains*. New York: Time.

———. 1980. *The Audubon Society field guide to North American insects and spiders*. New York: Alfred A. Knopf.

Minckley, T. A., R. K. Shriver, and B. Shuman. 2012. Resilience and regime change in a southern Rocky Mountain ecosystem during the past 17,000 years. *Ecological Monographs* 82: 49–68.

Minton, S. A. 1987. Poisonous snakes and snakebite in the U.S.: A brief review. *Northwest Science* 61: 130–137.

Mitton, J. B., and M. C. Grant. 1996. Genetic variation and the natural history of quaking aspen. *BioScience* 46: 25–31.

Moilanen, A., A. T. Smith, and I. Hanski. 1998. Long-term dynamics in a metapopulation of the American pika. *American Naturalist* 152: 530–542.

Moller, A. P. 1988. False alarm calls as a means of resource usurpation in the great tit *Parus major*. *Ethology* 79: 25–30.

———. 1992. Parasites differentially increase the degree of fluctuating asymmetry in secondary sexual characters. *Journal of Evolutionary Biology* 5: 691–699.

———. 1994. Symmetrical male sexual ornaments, paternal care, and offspring quality. *Behavioral Ecology* 5: 188–194.

Moller, A., B. Pavlick, A. G. Hile, and R. P. Balda. 2001. Clark's nutcrackers *Nucifraga columbiana* remember the size of their cached seeds. *Ethology* 107: 451–461.

Molyneux, R. J., S. T. Lee, D. R. Gardner, K. E. Panter, and L. F. James. 2007. Phytochemicals: The good, the bad and the ugly? *Phytochemistry* 68: 2973–2985.

Moore, B. 1996. *The Lochsa story: Land ethics in the Bitterroot Mountains*. Missoula, MT: Mountain Press.

Moore, T. 1817. *Lalla Rookh: An oriental romance.* New York: Thomas Y. Crowell. Reprinted in *The poetical works of Thomas Moore,* edited by C. Kent, 1883. London: George Routledge and Sons.

Moran, N., and W. D. Hamilton. 1980. Low nutritive quality as defense against herbivores. *Journal of Theoretical Biology* 86: 247–254.

Morrison, S. F., G. Pelchat, A. Donahue, and D. S. Hik. 2009. Influence of food hoarding behavior on the overwinter survival of pikas in strongly seasonal environments. *Oecologia* 159: 107–116.

Morse, D. H. 1980. *Behavioral mechanisms in ecology.* Cambridge, MA: Harvard University Press.

Moss, R. 1974. Winter diets, gut lengths, and interspecific competition in Alaskan ptarmigan. *Auk* 91: 737–746.

Muir, J. 1901. Among the animals of Yosemite. Reprinted in *The grizzly bear: Portraits from life,* edited by B. D. Haynes and E. Haynes, 141–151. Norman: University of Oklahoma Press.

Murcia, C. 1995. Edge effects in fragmented forests: Implications for conservation. *Trends in Ecology and Evolution* 10: 58–62.

Naiman, R. J., H. Decamps, and M. Pollock. 1993. The role of riparian corridors in maintaining regional biodiversity. *Ecological Applications* 3: 209–212.

Naumann, K., L. J. Rankin, and M. B. Isman. 1994. Systemic action of neem seed extract on mountain pine beetle (Coleoptera: Scolytidae) in lodgepole pine. *Journal of Economic Entomology* 87: 1580–1585.

Nebeker, T. E., R. A. Tisdale, and R. F. Schmitz. 1995. Comparison of oleoresin flow in relation to wound size, growth rates, and disease status of lodgepole pine. *Canadian Journal of Botany* 73: 370–375.

Neuvonen, S., E. Haukioja, and A. Molarius. 1987. Delayed inducible resistance against a leaf-chewing insect in four deciduous tree species. *Oecologia* 74: 363–369.

Newman, D. A., and J. D. Thomson. 2005. Effects of nectar robbing on nectar dynamics and bumblebee foraging strategies in *Linaria vulgaris* (Scrophulariaceae). *Oikos* 110: 309–320.

Newmark, W. D. 1987. A land-bridge island perspective on mammalian extinctions in western North American parks. *Nature* 325: 430–432.

NGS (National Geographic Society). 1972. Indians of North America. Map supplement to *National Geograhic,* December, 739A.

Nieminen, M., M. C. Singer, W. Fortelius, K. Schops, and I. Hanski. 2001. Experimental confirmation that inbreeding depression increases extinction risk in butterfly populations. *American Naturalist* 157: 237–244.

Niklas, K. J. 1994. Plant allometry: The scaling of form and process. Chicago: University of Chicago Press.

Niko'skii, A. A., and N. A. Formozov. 1983. Effects of biotope on the rhythmic pattern of the alarm signal of pikas. *Moscow University Biological Sciences Bulletin* 38: 1–7.

Nilsson, J.-A. 1994. Energetic stress and the degree of fluctuating asymmetry: Implications for a long-lasting, honest signal. *Evolutionary Ecology* 8: 248–255.

Norton, B. G. 1987. *Why preserve natural variety?* Princeton, NJ: Princeton University Press.

Nowak, M. A., C. E. Tarnita, and E. O. Wilson. 2010. The evolution of eusociality. *Nature* 466 (August 26): 1057–1062.

O'Brien, S. J., M. E. Roelke, L. Marker, A. Newman, C. A. Winkler, D. Meltzer, L. Colly, J. F. Evermann, M. Bush, and D. E. Wildt. 1985. Genetic basis for species vulnerability in the cheetah. *Science* 227: 1428–1434.

O'Connell, B. 1983. Strike-induced chemosensory searching in prairie rattle-snakes (*Crotalus viridis*) during daytime and at night. *Journal of Herpetology* 17: 193–196.

O'Hara, R. K., and A. R. Blaustein. 1982. Kin preference behavior in *Bufo boreas* tadpoles. *Behavioral Ecology and Sociobiology* 11: 43–49.

———. 1985. *Rana cascadae* tadpoles aggregate with siblings: An experimental field study. *Oecologia* 67: 44–51.

Oksman-Caldentey, K.-M., and D. Inze. 2004. Plant cell factories in the post-genomic era: New ways to produce designer secondary metabolites. *Trends in Plant Science* 9: 433–440.

Olson, D. H. 1989. Predation on breeding western toads (*Bufo boreas*). *Copeia* 1989: 391–397.

Olson, D. H., A. R. Blaustein, and R. K. O'Hara. 1986. Mating pattern variability among western toad (*Bufo boreas*) populations. *Oecologia* 70: 351–356.

Ornelas, J. F. 1994. Serrate tomia: An adaptation for nectar robbing in hummingbirds. *Auk* 111: 703–710.

Osborne, J. 1998. *The ruby-throated hummingbird.* Austin: University of Texas Press.

Osier, T. L., and R. L. Lindroth. 2004. Long-term effects of defoliation on quaking aspen in relation to genotype and nutrient availability: Plant growth, phytochemistry and insect performance. *Oecologia* 139: 55–65.

Oster, G., and B. Heinrich. 1976. Why do bumblebees major? A mathematical model. *Ecological Monographs* 46: 129–133.

Owen, D. F., and R. G. Wiegert. 1976. Do consumers maximize plant fitness? *Oikos* 27: 488–492.

———. 1981. Mutualism between grasses and grazers: An evolutionary hypothesis. *Oikos* 36: 376–378.

Packer, C., and A. E. Pusey. 1983. Adaptations of female lions to infanticide by incoming males. *American Naturalist* 121: 716–728.

Paige, K. N. 1992. Overcompensation in response to mammalian herbivory: From mutualistic to antagonistic interactions. *Ecology* 73: 2076–2085.

———. 1999. Regrowth following ungulate herbivory in *Ipomopsis aggregata*: Geographic evidence for overcompensation. *Oecologia* 118: 316–323.

Paige, K. N., and M. D. Rausher. 1994. Herbivory and *Ipomopsis aggregata*: Differences in response, differences in experimental protocol: A reply to Bergelson and Crawley. *American Naturalist* 143: 739–749.

Paige, K. N., and T. G. Whitham. 1985. Individual and population shifts in flower color by scarlet gilia: A mechanism for pollinator tracking. *Science* 227: 315–317.

———. 1987. Overcompensation in response to mammalian herbivory: The advantage of being eaten. *American Naturalist* 129: 407–416.

Palmer, A. R., and C. Strobeck. 1986. Fluctuating asymmetry: Measurement, analysis, patterns. *Annual Review of Ecology and Systematics* 17: 391–421.

Panter, K. E., D. R. Gardner, and R. J. Molyneux. 1998. Teratogenic and fetotoxic effects of two piperidine alkaloid-containing lupines (*L. formosus* and *L. arbustus*) in cows. *Journal of Natural Toxins* 7: 131–140.

Panter, K. E., L. F. James, and D. R. Gardner. 1999. Lupines, poison-hemlock and *Nicotiana* spp.: Toxicity and teratogenicity in livestock. *Journal of Natural Toxins* 8: 117–134.

Parchman, T. L., C. W. Benkman, B. Jenkins, and C. A. Buerkle. 2011. Low levels of population genetic structure in *Pinus contorta* (Pinaceae) across a geographic mosaic of co-evolution. *American Journal of Botany* 98: 669–679.

Parker, A. J., and K. C. Parker. 1983. Comparative successional roles of trembling aspen and lodgepole pine in the southern Rocky Mountains. *Great Basin Naturalist* 43: 447–455.

Parker, M. R., B. A. Young, and K. V. Kardong. 2008. The forked tongue and edge detection in snakes (*Crotalus oreganus*): An experimental test. *Journal of Comparative Psychology* 122: 35–40.

Pasteels, J. M., and M. Rowell-Rahier. 1992. The chemical ecology of herbivory on willows. *Proceedings of the Royal Society of Edinburgh* 96B: 63–73.

Paterson, K. 1977. *Bridge to Terabithia*. New York: Thomas Crowell.

Patterson, B. D., and J. L. Patton. 1990. Fluctuating asymmetry and allozymic heterozygosity among natural populations of pocket gophers (*Thomomys bottae*). *Biological Journal of the Linnean Society* 40: 21–36.

Peacock, M. M. 1997. Determining natal dispersal patterns in a population of North American pikas (*Ochotona princeps*) using direct mark-resight and indirect genetic methods. *Behavioral Ecology* 8: 340–350.

Peacock, M. M., and A. T. Smith. 1997a. The effect of habitat fragmentation on dispersal patterns, mating behavior, and genetic variation in a pika (*Ochotona princeps*) metapopulation. *Oecologia* 112: 524–533.

———. 1997b. Nonrandom mating in pikas *Ochotona princeps*: Evidence for inbreeding between individuals of intermediate relatedness. *Molecular Ecology* 6: 801–811.

Pearson, T. G. 1917. *Birds of America, Part II*. Garden City, NY: Garden City Books.

Pease, C. M., and D. J. Mattson. 1999. Demography of the Yellowstone grizzly bears. *Ecology* 80: 957–975.

Peat, J., J. Tucker, and D. Goulson. 2005. Does interspecific size variation in bumblebees allow colonies to efficiently exploit different flowers? *Ecological Entomology* 30: 176–181.

Pelletier, F., J. Mainguy, and S. D. Cote. 2009. Rut-induced hypophagia in male bighorn sheep and mountain goats: Foraging under time budget constraints. *Ethology* 115: 141–151.

Penn, D. J. 2003. The evolutionary roots of our environmental problems: Toward a Darwinian ecology. *Quarterly Review of Biology* 78: 275–301.

Peters, J. 2001. The frustrated engineer. Poem in L. F. Baptista, Feathered gems: The song and dance of hummingbirds. *California Wild* 54 (4): 14–20.

Peters, R. H. 1983. *The ecological implications of body size*. Cambridge: Cambridge University Press.

Peterson, R. O., A. K. Jacobs, T. D. Drummer, L. D. Mech, and D. W. Smith. 2002. Leadership behavior in relation to dominance and reproductive status in gray wolves, *Canis lupus*. *Canadian Journal of Zoology* 80: 1405–1412.

Peterson, R. T. 1990. *A field guide to western birds*. 3rd ed. Boston: Houghton Mifflin.

Petranka, J. W. 1998. *Salamanders of the United States and Canada*. Washington, DC: Smithsonian Institution Press.

Petterson, J. R. 1992. Yellow-bellied marmot, *Marmota flaviventris*, predation on pikas, *Ochotona princeps*. *Canadian Field-Naturalist* 106: 130–131.

Pfennig, D. W. 1997. Kinship and cannibalism. *BioScience* 47: 667–675.

Pfennig, D. W., and J. P. Collins. 1993. Kinship affects morphogenesis in cannibalistic salamanders. *Nature* 362: 836–838.

Pfennig, D. W., J. P. Collins, and R. E. Ziemba. 1999. A test of alternative hypotheses for kin recognition in cannibalistic tiger salamanders. *Behavioral Ecology* 10: 436–443.

Pfennig, D. W., M. L. G. Loeb, and J. P. Collins. 1991. Pathogens as a factor limiting the spread of cannibalism in tiger salamanders. *Oecologia* 88: 161–166.

Pfennig, D. W., P. W. Sherman, and J. P. Collins. 1994. Kin recognition and cannibalism in polyphenic salamanders. *Behavioral Ecology* 5: 225–232.

Phillips, H. W. 1999. *Central Rocky Mountain wildflowers*. Helena, MT: Falcon Publishing.

———. 2001. *Northern Rocky Mountain wildflowers*. Helena, MT: Falcon Publishing.

Pianka, E. R. 1994. *Evolutionary ecology*. 5th ed. New York: HarperCollins College Publishers.

Pimm, S. L., H. L. Jones, and J. Diamond. 1988. On the risk of extinction. *American Naturalist* 132: 757–785.

Plew, M. G. 1986. *An introduction to the archaeology of southern Idaho*. Boise, ID: Boise State University.

———. 2000. *The archaeology of the Snake River Plain*. Boise, ID: Department of Anthropology, Boise State University.

Polziehn, R. O., J. Hamr, F. F. Mallory, and C. Strobeck. 2000. Microsatellite analysis of North American wapiti (*Cervus elaphus*) populations. *Molecular Ecology* 9: 1561–1576.

Pomiankowski, A. 1987. The "handicap principle" works without Fisher. *Trends in Ecology and Evolution* 2: 2–3.

Pope, A. 1732. Essay on man: Epistle I: VII. Reprinted in *The complete poetical works of Alexander Pope*, edited by H. W. Boynton, 1903. Boston: Houghton Mifflin.

Povilitis, T. 1993. Applying the biosphere reserve concept to a greater ecosystem: The San Juan Mountain area of Colorado and New Mexico. *Natural Areas Journal* 13: 18–28.

Powers, D. R. 1987. Effects of variation in food quality on the breeding territoriality of the male Anna's hummingbird. *Condor* 89: 103–111.

Pureswaran, D. S., R. Gries, and J. H. Borden. 2004. Quantitative variation in monoterpenes in four species of conifers. *Biochemical Systematics and Ecology* 32: 1109–1136.

Quammen, D. 1996. *The song of the dodo: Island biogeography in an age of extinctions*. New York: Simon and Schuster.

Quinn, J. F., and S. P. Harrison. 1988. Effects of habitat fragmentation and isolation on species richness: Evidence from biogeographic patterns. *Oecologia* 75: 132–140.

Quinn, J. F., and A. Hastings. 1987. Extinction in subdivided habitats. *Conservation Biology* 1: 198–208.

Radesater, T., and H. Halldorsdottir. 1993. Fluctuating asymmetry and forceps size in earwigs, *Forficula auricularia*. *Animal Behaviour* 45: 626–628.

Ramsay, M. A., and R. L. Dunbrack. 1986. Physiological constraints on life history phenomena: The example of small bear cubs at birth. *American Naturalist* 127: 735–743.

Rapaport, L., and J. Haight. 1987. Some observations regarding allomaternal caretaking among captive Asian elephants (*Elephas maximus*). *Journal of Mammalogy* 68: 438–442.

Rathcke, B. 1983. Competition and facilitation among plants for pollination. In *Pollination biology*, edited by L. Real, 305–329. Orlando, FL: Academic Press.

Raven, P. H., and H. Curtis. 1970. *Biology of plants*. New York: Worth Publishers.

Rawlins, J. E. 1980. Thermoregulation by the black swallowtail butterfly, *Papilio polyxenes* (Lepidoptera: Papilionidae). *Ecology* 61: 345–357.

Reddy, S. D. 1995a. American Indians of Idaho, the Payette National Forest and the Frank Church–River of No Return Wilderness. Heritage Program, Payette National Forest, Intermountain Region, USDA Forest Service.

———. 1995b. Shadows in the Wilderness: The story of the Northern Shoshoni Band, the Tukudika, in the Frank Church–River of No Return Wilderness and the Payette National Forest. Heritage Program, Payette National Forest, Intermountain Region, USDA Forest Service.

———. 1996. The mountain wickiup. Frank Church–River of No Return Wilderness, Heritage Program, Regions 1 and 4, USDA Forest Service.

———. 2002. The Tukudika, Indians of the wilderness. Frank Church-River of No Return Wilderness, Heritage Program, Regions 1 and 4, USDA Forest Service.

Reed, R. A., J. Johnson-Barnard, and W. L. Baker. 1996. Fragmentation of a forested Rocky Mountain landscape, 1950–1993. *Biological Conservation* 75: 267–269.

Reynolds, S. J. 2003. Mineral retention, medullary bone formation, and reproduction in the white-tailed ptarmigan (*Lagopus leucurus*): A critique of Larison et al. (2001). *Auk* 120: 224–228.

Reznick, D. N. 2010. *The Origin then and now: An interpretive guide to the Origin of Species*. Princeton, NJ: Princeton University Press.

Rhoades, D. F., and J. C. Bergdahl. 1981. Adaptive significance of toxic nectar. *American Naturalist* 117: 798–803.

Richardson, S. C. 2004. Are nectar-robbers mutualists or antagonists? *Oecologia* 139: 246–254.

Ricklefs, R. E. 1990. *Ecology*. 3rd ed. New York: W. H. Freeman.

Rimbey, C. W. 1969. Crooked calf disease. *California Agriculture*, May, 7–8.

Ripple, W. J., and E. J. Larsen. 2000. Historic aspen recruitment, elk, and wolves in northern Yellowstone National Park, USA. *Biological Conservation* 95: 361–370.

Roach, W. J., N. Huntly, and R. Inouye. 2001. Talus fragmentation mitigates the effects of pikas, *Ochotona princeps*, on high alpine meadows. *Oikos* 92: 315–324.

Robinson, G. R., R. D. Holt, M. S. Gaines, S. P. Hamburg, M. L. Johnson, H. S. Fitch, and E. A. Maretinko. 1992. Diverse and contrasting effects of habitat fragmentation. *Science* 257: 524–526.

Roden, J. S., and R. W. Pearcy. 1993a. The effect of flutter on the temperature of poplar leaves and its implications for carbon gain. *Plant, Cell and Environment* 16: 571–577.

———. 1993b. The effect of leaf flutter on the flux of CO_2 in poplar leaves. *Functional Ecology* 7: 669–675.

———. 1993c. Effect of leaf flutter on the light environment of poplars. *Oecologia* 93: 201–207.

———. 1993d. Photosynthetic gas exchange response of poplars to steady-state and dynamic light environments. *Oecologia* 93: 208–214.

Rodhouse, T. J., E. A. Beever, L. K. Garrett, K. M. Irvine, M. R. Jeffress, M. Munts, and C. Ray. 2010. Distribution of American pikas in a low-elevation lava landscape: Conservation implications from the range periphery. *Journal of Mammalogy* 91: 1287–1299.

Rolstad, J. 1991. Consequences of forest fragmentation for the dynanics of bird populations: Conceptual issues and the evidence. *Biological Journal of the Linnean Society* 42: 149–163.

Romeo, G., S. Lovari, and M. Festa-Bianchet. 1997. Group leaving in mountain goats: Are young males ousted by adult females? *Behavioural Processes* 40: 243–246.

Romme, W. H., and M. G. Turner. 1992. Global climate change in the Greater Yellowstone Ecosystem. *Yellowstone Science*, Fall: 2–5.

Romme, W. H., M. G. Turner, R. H. Gardner, W. W. Hargrove, G. A. Tuskan, D. G. Despain, and R. A. Renkin. 1997. A rare episode of sexual reproduction in aspen (*Populus tremuloides* Michx.) following the 1988 Yellowstone fires. *Natural Areas Journal* 17: 17–25.

Romme, W. H., M. G. Turner, G. A. Tuskan, and R. A. Reed. 2005. Establishment, persistence, and growth of aspen (*Populus tremuloides*) seedlings in Yellowstone National Park. *Ecology* 86: 404–418.

Romme, W. H., M. G. Turner, L. L. Wallace, and J. S. Walker. 1995. Aspen, elk, and fire in northern Yellowstone National Park. *Ecology* 76: 2097–2106.

Root, T. L., D. P. MacMynowski, M. D. Mastrandrea, and S. H. Schneider. 2005. Human-modified temperatures induce species changes: Joint attribution. *Proceedings of the National Academy of Sciences of the United States of America* 102: 7465–7469.

Rose, S. M. 1960. A feedback mechanism of growth control in tadpoles. *Ecology* 41: 188–199.

Rosenkilde, P., and A. P. Ussing. 1996. What mechanisms control neoteny and regulate induced metamorphosis in urodeles? *International Journal of Developmental Biology* 40: 665–673.

Rosing, N. 1998. *Yellowstone*. Buffalo, NY: Firefly Books.

Roth, S., R. L. Lindroth, J. C. Volin, and E. L. Kruger. 1998. Enriched atmospheric CO_2 and defoliation: Effects on tree chemistry and insect performance. *Global Change Biology* 4: 419–430.

Rowe, M. P., and D. H. Owings. 1990. Probing, assessment, and management during interactions between ground squirrels and rattlesnakes. Part 1: Risks related to rattlesnake size and body temperature. *Ethology* 86: 237–249.

———. 1996. Probing, assessment and management during interactions between ground squirrels (Rodentia: Sciuridae) and rattlesnakes (Squamata: Viperidae). Part 2: Cues afforded by rattlesnake rattling. *Ethology* 102: 856–874.

Rowland, M. M., M. J. Wisdom, B. K. Johnson, and J. G. Kie. 2000. Elk distribution and modeling in relation to roads. *Journal of Wildlife Management* 64: 672–684.

Rumbaugh, M. D., and D. A. Johnson. 1991. Field acetylene reduction rates of *Lupinus argenteus* along an elevational gradient. *Great Basin Naturalist* 51: 192–197.

Rundus, A. S., D. H. Owings, S. S. Joshi, E. Chinn, and N. Giannini. 2007. Ground squirrels use an infrared signal to deter rattlesnake predation. *Proceedings of the National Academy of Sciences of the United States of America* 104: 14372–14376.

Rutowski, R. L. 1997. Sexual dimorphism, mating systems and ecology in butter-flies. In *The evolution of mating systems in insects and arachnids*, edited by J. C. Choe and B. J. Crespi, 257–272. Cambridge: Cambridge University Press.

Ryden, H. 1991. A red squirrel's life is more than just a tempest in a treetop. *Smithsonian*, November, 146–155.

Saastamoinen, M., and I. Hanski. 2008. Genotypic and environmental effects on flight activity and oviposition in the Glanville fritillary butterfly. *American Naturalist* 171: 701–712.

Sakaluk, S. K., and R. L. Smith. 1988. Inheritance of male parental investment in an insect. *American Naturalist* 132: 594–601.

Saleh, N., and L. Chittka. 2007. Traplining in bumblebees (*Bombus impatiens*): A foraging strategy's ontogeny and the importance of spatial reference memory in short-range foraging. *Oecologia* 151: 719–730.

Saleh, N., K. Ohashi, J. D. Thomson, and L. Chittka. 2006. Facultative use of the repellent scent mark in foraging bumblebees: Complex versus simple flowers. *Animal Behaviour* 71: 847–854.

Sands, J., and S. Creel. 2004. Social dominance, aggression and faecal glucocorti-coid levels in a wild population of wolves, *Canis lupus*. *Animal Behaviour* 67: 387–396.

Saunders, D. A., R. J. Hobbs, and C. R. Margules. 1991. Biological consequences of ecosystem fragmentation: A review. *Conservation Biology* 5: 18–32.

SCB (Sierra Club Books). 2006. *Galen Rowell: A retrospective*. San Francisco: Sierra Club Books.

Schaffer, W. M. 1985. Order and chaos in ecological systems. *Ecology* 66: 93–106.

Schleucher, E. 2004. Torpor in birds: Taxonomy, energetics, and ecology. *Physiological and Biochemical Zoology* 77: 942–949.

Schmidt, D. F., W. K. Hayes, and F. E. Hayes. 1993. Influence of prey movement on the aim of predatory strikes of the western rattlesnake (*Crotalus viridis*). *Great Basin Naturalist* 53: 203–206.

Schoennagel, T., M. G. Turner, and W. H. Romme. 2003. The influence of fire return interval and serotiny on postfire lodgepole pine density in Yellowstone National Park. *Ecology* 84: 2967–2978.

Schullery, P. 1992. *The bears of Yellowstone*. Worland, WY: High Plains Publishing.

Schultz, J. C. 1988. Plant responses induced by herbivores. *Trends in Ecology and Evolution* 3: 45–49.

Schwartz, C. C., P. H. Gude, L. Landenburger, M. A. Haroldson, and S. Pod-ruzny. 2012. Impacts of rural development on Yellowstone wildlife: Linking grizzly bear *Ursus arctos* demographics with projected residential growth. *Wildlife Biology* 18: 246–257.

Schwartz, C. C., M. A. Haroldson, G. C. White, R. B. Harris, S. Cherry, K. A. Keating, D. Moody, and C. Servheen. 2006. Temporal, spatial, and environ-mental influences on the demographics of grizzly bears in the Greater Yellow-stone Ecosystem. *Wildlife Monographs* 161 (1): 1–8.

Schwartz, C. C., S. D. Miller, and M. A. Haroldson. 2003. Grizzly bear. In *Wild mammals of North America: Biology, management, and conservation*, 2nd ed., edited by G. A. Feldhamer, B. C. Thompson, and J. A. Chapman, 556–586. Baltimore: Johns Hopkins University Press.

Schwartz, O. A., and K. B. Armitage. 1980. Genetic variation in social mammals: The marmot model. *Science* 207: 665–667.

Schwartz, O. A., K. B. Armitage, and D. Van Vuren. 1998. A 32-year demography of yellow-bellied marmots (*Marmota flaviventris*). *Journal of Zoology* 246: 337–346.

Schwenk, K. 1994. Why snakes have forked tongues. *Science* 263: 1573–1577.

Seigler, D., and P. W. Price. 1976. Secondary compounds in plants: Primary functions. *American Naturalist* 110: 101–105.

Semlitsch, R. D., and J. W. Gibbons. 1985. Phenotypic variation in metamorphosis and paedomorphosis in the salamander *Ambystoma talpoideum. Ecology* 66: 1123–1130.

Servheen, C. 1983. Grizzly bear food habits, movements, and habitat selection in the Mission Mountains, Montana. *Journal of Wildlife Management* 47: 1026–1035.

Sexton, O. J., and J. R. Bizer. 1978. Life history patterns of *Ambystoma tigrinum* in montane Colorado. *American Midland Naturalist* 99: 101–118.

Shafer, A. B. A., and J. C. Hall. 2010. Placing the mountain goat: A total evidence approach to testing alternative hypotheses. *Molecular Phylogenetics and Evolution* 55: 18–25.

Shaffer, M. L. 1981. Minimum population sizes for species conservation. *BioScience* 31: 131–134.

Shaw, R. J. 1992. *Wildflowers of Grand Teton and Yellowstone National Parks*. Salt Lake City: Wheelwright Press.

Shaw, R. J., and D. On. 1979. *Plants of Waterton-Glacier National Parks*. Missoula, MT: Mountain Press.

Sherman, P. W. 1977. Nepotism and the evolution of alarm calls. *Science* 197: 1246–1253.

Sherry, D. F. 1989. Food storing in the Paridae. *Wilson Bulletin* 101: 289–304.

Shooter. n.d. First People. http://www.firstpeople.us/FP-Html-Wisdom /Shooter.html.

Shriner, W. M. 1998. Yellow-bellied marmot and golden-mantled ground squirrel responses to heterospecific alarm calls. *Animal Behaviour* 55: 529–536.

Shuster, S. M., and M. J. Wade. 1991. Equal mating success among male reproductive strategies in a marine isopod. *Nature* 350: 608–610.

Sides, H., ed. 2001. What's alpenglow? In *Why moths hate Thomas Edison*, 126–127. New York: W. W. Norton.

Simberloff, D. S., and L. G. Abele. 1976. Island biogeography theory and conservation practice. *Science* 191: 285–286.

Simmons, L. W. 1995. Relative parental expenditure, potential reproductive rates, and the control of sexual selection in katydids. *American Naturalist* 145: 797–808.

Simms, E. L., and M. D. Rausher. 1987. Costs and benefits of plant resistance to herbivory. *American Naturalist* 130: 570–581.

Simms, S. R. 2010. *Traces of Fremont: Society and rock art in ancient Utah.* Salt Lake City: University of Utah Press.

Simpson, S. J., G. A. Sword, P. D. Lorch, and I. D. Couzin. 2006. Cannibal crickets on a forced march for protein and salt. *Proceedings of the National Academy of Sciences of the United States of America* 103: 4152–4156.

Singer, F. J., and J. L. Doherety. 1985. Movements and habitat use in an unhunted population of mountain goats, *Oreamnos americanus. Canadian Field-Naturalist* 99: 205–217.

Smith, A. 1997. The art of making hay. *National Wildlife*, April–May, 31–35.

Smith, A. T., and J. M. Foggin. 1999. The plateau pika (*Ochotona curzoniae*) is a keystone species for biodiversity on the Tibetan plateau. *Animal Conservation* 2: 235–240.

Smith, A. T., and B. L. Ivins. 1983. Colonization in a pika population: Dispersal vs. philopatry. *Behavioral Ecology and Sociobiology* 13: 37–47.

———. 1984. Spatial relationships and social organization in adult pikas: A facultatively monogamous mammal. *Zeitschrift für Tierpsychologie* 66: 289–308.

Smith, B. L. 1998. Antler size and winter mortality of elk: Effects of environment, birth year, and parasites. *Journal of Mammalogy* 79: 1038–1044.

Smith, C. C. 1968. The adaptive nature of social organization in the genus of tree squirrels *Tamiasciurus. Ecological Monographs* 38: 31–63.

Smith, D. W., T. D. Drummer, K. M. Murphy, D. S. Guernsey, and S. B. Evans. 2004. Winter prey selection and estimation of wolf kill rates in Yellowstone National Park, 1995–2000. *Journal of Wildlife Management* 68: 153–166.

Smith, D. W., L. D. Mech, M. Meagher, W. E. Clark, R. Jaffe, M. K. Phillips, and J. A. Mack. 2000. Wolf-bison interactions in Yellowstone National Park. *Journal of Mammalogy* 81: 1128–1135.

Smith, R. J. F. 1973. Testosterone eliminates alarm substance in male fathead minnows. *Canadian Journal of Zoology* 51: 875–876.

———. 1979. Alarm reaction of Iowa and johnny darters (*Etheostoma*, Percidae, Pisces) to chemicals from injured conspecifics. *Canadian Journal of Zoology* 57: 1278–1282.

———. 1986. Evolution of alarm signals: Role of benefits of retaining group members or territorial neighbors. *American Naturalist* 128: 604–610.

———. 1989. The response of *Asterropteryx semipunctatus* and *Gnatholepis anjerensis* (Pisces, Gobiidae) to chemical stimuli from injured conspecifics, an alarm response in gobies. *Ethology* 81: 279–290.

Smith, R. L. 1980. Daddy water bugs. *Natural History*, February, 56–63.

Smith, T. L., K. V. Kardong, and P. A. Lavin-Murcio. 2000. Persistence of trailing behavior: Cues involved in poststrike behavior by the rattlesnake (*Crotalus viridis oreganus*). *Behaviour* 137: 691–703.

Smulders, T. V., A. D. Sasson, and T. J. DeVoogd. 1995. Seasonal variation in hippocampal volume in a food-storing bird, the black-capped chickadee. *Journal of Neurobiology* 27: 15–25.

Solberg, E. J., and B.-E. Saether. 1993. Fluctuating asymmetry in the antlers of moose (*Alces alces*): Does it signal male quality? *Proceedings of the Royal Society B: Biological Sciences* 254: 251–255.

Spellenberg, R. 1998. *National Audubon Society field guide to North American wildflowers, western region*. New York: Alfred A. Knopf.

Spomer, R. 1996. *The rut: The spectacular fall ritual of North American horned and antlered animals*. Minocqua, WI: Willow Creek Press.

Stahler, D. R., D. W. Smith, and D. S. Guernsey. 2006. Foraging and feeding ecology of the gray wolf (*Canis lupus*): Lessons from Yellowstone National Park, Wyoming, USA. *Journal of Nutrition* 136: 1923S–1926S.

Stanley, S. M. 1986. *Earth and life through time*. New York: W. H. Freeman.

Stark, C. P., C. Tiernan, and D. Chiszar. 2011. Effects of deprivation of vomeronasal chemoreception on prey discrimination in rattlesnakes. *Psychological Record* 61: 363–370.

Stark, P. 1997. The Old North Trail. *Smithsonian*, July, 56–66.

Stauffer, D. F., and S. R. Peterson. 1985a. Ruffed and blue grouse habitat use in southeastern Idaho. *Journal of Wildlife Management* 49: 459–466.

———. 1985b. Seasonal micro-habitat relationships of ruffed grouse in southeastern Idaho. *Journal of Wildlife Management* 49: 605–610.

Stebbins, R. C., and N. W. Cohen. 1995. *A natural history of amphibians*. Princeton, NJ: Princeton University Press.

Stenglein, J. L., L. P. Waits, D. E. Ausband, P. Zager, and C. M. Mack. 2011. Estimating gray wolf pack size and family relationships using noninvasive genetic sampling at rendezvous sites. *Journal of Mammalogy* 92: 784–795.

Stevens, M. T., M. G. Turner, G. A. Tuskan, W. H. Romme, L. E. Gunter, and D. M. Waller. 1999. Genetic variation in postfire aspen seedlings in Yellowstone National Park. *Molecular Ecology* 8: 1769–1780.

Steyaert, S. M. G., J. A. Endrestol, K. Hacklander, J. E. Swenson, and A. Zedrosser. 2012. The mating system of the brown bear *Ursus arctos*. *Mammal Review* 42: 12–34.

Stockley, P., J. B. Searle, D. W. Macdonald, and C. S. Jones. 1996. Correlates of reproductive success within alternative mating tactics of the common shrew. *Behavioral Ecology* 7: 334–340.

Stockwell, C. A., G. C. Bateman, and J. Berger. 1991. Conflicts in national parks: A case study of helicopters and bighorn sheep time budgets at the Grand Canyon. *Biological Conservation* 56: 317–328.

Stoehr, A. M., and H. Goux. 2008. Seasonal phenotypic plasticity of wing melanisation in the cabbage white butterfly, *Pieris rapae* L. (Lepidoptera: Pieridae). *Ecological Entomology* 33: 137–143.

Stokkan, K.-A. 1992. Energetics and adaptations to cold in ptarmigan in winter. *Ornis Scandinavica* 23: 366–370.

Stolzenburg, W. 1991. The fragment connection. *Nature Conservancy*, July–August, 18–25.

Storer, T. I., and L. P. Tevis Jr. 1955. *California grizzly*. Berkeley: University of California Press.

Stout, J. C., and D. Goulson. 2001. The use of conspecific and interspecific scent marks by foraging bumblebees and honeybees. *Animal Behaviour* 62: 183–189.

Strassmann, J. E., et al. 2011. Kin selection and eusociality. *Nature* 471 (March 24): E5–E6.

Streubel, D. 1989. *Small mammals of the Yellowstone ecosystem*. Boulder, CO: Roberts Rinehart.

Strickberger, M. W. 1968. *Genetics*. New York: Macmillan.

Suarez, R. K., and C. L. Gass. 2002. Hummingbird foraging and the relation between bioenergetics and behavior. *Comparative Biochemistry and Physiology Part A: Molecular and Integrative Physiology* 133: 335–343.

Suzuki, K., H. Suzuki, D. Binkley, and T. J. Stohlgren. 1999. Aspen regeneration in the Colorado Front Range: Differences at local and landscape scales. *Landscape Ecology* 14: 231–237.

Swaddle, J. P. 1997. Developmental stability and predation success in an insect predator-prey system. *Behavioral Ecology* 8: 433–436.

Swaddle, J. P., M. S. Witter, and I. C. Cuthill. 1994. The analysis of fluctuating asymmetry. *Animal Behaviour* 48: 986–989.

Swaisgood, R. R., D. H. Owings, and M. P. Rowe. 1999a. Conflict and assessment in a predator-prey system: Ground squirrels versus rattlesnakes. *Animal Behaviour* 57: 1033–1044.

Swaisgood, R. R., M. P. Rowe, and D. H. Owings. 1999b. Assessment of rattlesnake dangerousness by California ground squirrels: Exploitation of cues from rattling sounds. *Animal Behaviour* 57: 1301–1310.

Sword, G. 2012. Mormon cricket ecology and evolution. University of Sydney School of Biological Sciences. http://sydney.edu.au/science/biology/molecular_ecology/research/crickets.shtml.

Sword, G. A., P. D. Lorch, and G. T. Gwynne. 2005. Migratory bands give crickets protection. *Nature* 433: 703 + supplement.

———. 2008. Radiotelemetric analysis of the effects of prevailing wind direction on Mormon cricket migratory band movement. *Environmental Entomology* 37: 889–896.

Taborsky, M., B. Hudde, and P. Wirtz. 1987. Reproductive behavior and ecology of *Symphodus* (*Crenilabrus*) *ocellatus*, a European wrasse with four types of male behavior. *Behaviour* 102: 82–118.

Tait, D. E. N. 1980. Abandonment as a reproductive tactic: The example of grizzly bears. *American Naturalist* 115: 800–808.

Talloen, W., H. Van Dyck, and L. Lens. 2004. The cost of melanization: Butter-fly wing coloration under environmental stress. *Evolution* 58: 360–366.

Tamm, S., D. P. Armstrong, and Z. J. Tooze. 1989. Display behavior of male calliope hummingbirds during the breeding season. *Condor* 91: 272–279.

Tardiff, S., and J. A. Stanford. 1998. Grizzly bear digging: Effects on subalpine meadow plants in relation to mineral nitrogen availability. *Ecology* 79: 2219–2228.

Templeton, A. R., K. Shaw, E. Routman, and S. D. Davis. 1990. The genetic consequences of habitat fragmentation. *Annals of the Missouri Botanical Garden* 77: 13–27.

Tennesen, M. 2009a. Snakebit. *Scientific American*, April, 27–29.

———. 2009b. Venom emergency! *National Wildlife* (World Edition), October–November, 20–22.

Thamarus, K. A., and G. R. Furnier. 1998. Temporal and genotypic variation of wound-induced gene expression in bark of *Populus tremuloides* and *P. gran-didentata*. *Canadian Journal of Forest Research* 28: 1611–1620.

Thomas, C. D., and S. Harrison. 1992. Spatial dynamics of a patchily distributed butterfly species. *Journal of Animal Ecology* 61: 437–446.

Thomas, D. H. 1999. *Exploring ancient native America: An archaeoloical guide.* New York: Routledge.

Thomas, V. G. 1987. Similar winter energy strategies of grouse, hares, and rabbits in northern biomes. *Oikos* 50: 206–212.

Thompson, C. W., I. T. Moore, and M. C. Moore. 1993. Social, environmental and genetic factors in the ontogeny of phenotypic differentiation in a lizard with alternative male reproductive strategies. *Behavioral Ecology and Socio-biology* 33: 137–146.

Thompson, J. N. 1988. Evolutionary genetics of oviposition preference in swallowtail butterflies. *Evolution* 42: 1223–1234.

Thompson, M. J., and R. E. Henderson. 1998. Elk habituation as a credibility challenge for wildlife professionals. *Wildlife Society Bulletin* 26: 477–483.

Thornhill, R. 1976. Sexual selection and paternal investment in insects. *American Naturalist* 110: 153–163.

———. 1993. The allure of symmetry. *Natural History* 102: 30–37.

Thornhill, R., and J. Alcock. 1983. *The evolution of insect mating systems.* Cambridge, MA: Harvard University Press.

Threatened species: Grizzly bear, *Ursus arctos horribilis*. 1995. Biologue Series, US Fish and Wildlife Service, US Department of the Interior.

Tinker, D. B., W. H. Romme, W. W. Hargrove, R. H. Gardner, and M. G. Turner. 1994. Landscape-scale heterogeneity in lodgepole pine serotiny. *Canadian Journal of Forestry Research* 24: 897–903.

Tobalske, B. W., D. R. Warrick, C. J. Clark, D. R. Powers, T. L. Hedrick, G. A. Hyder, and A. A. Biewener. 2007. Three-dimensional kinematics of hum-mingbird flight. *Journal of Experimental Biology* 210: 2368–2382.

Tollrian, R., and C. D. Harvell, eds. 1999. *The ecology and evolution of inducible defenses*. Princeton, NJ: Princeton University Press.

Tolme, P. 2005/2006. No room at the top. *National Wildlife*, December–January, 22–30.

Tomback, D. F. 1978. Foraging strategies of Clark's nutcracker. *Living Bird* 16: 123–161.

———. 1980. How nutcrackers find their food stores. *Condor* 82: 10–19.

———. 1982. Dispersal of whitebark pine seeds by Clark's nutcracker: A mutualism hypothesis. *Journal of Animal Ecology* 51: 451–467.

———. 1998. Clark's nutcracker. In *The Birds of North America*, edited by A. Poole and F. Gill. Cornell Laboratory of Ornithology and Academy of Natural Sciences. No. 331.

Tomback, D. F., S. F. Arno, and R. E. Keane, eds. 2001. *Whitebark pine communities: Ecology and restoration*. Washington, DC: Island Press.

Torick, L. L., D. F. Tomback, and R. Espinoza. 1996. Occurrence of multi-genet tree clusters in "wind-dispersed" pines. *American Midland Naturalist* 136: 262–266.

Toth, Z., H. Hoi, and A. Hettyey. 2011. Kin discrimination during egg-cannibalism in smooth newts: Does competition matter? *Journal of Zoology* 284: 46–52.

Tracy, B. F., and S. J. McNaughton. 1997. Elk grazing and vegetation responses following a late season fire in Yellowstone National Park. *Plant Ecology* 130: 111–119.

Travis, S. E., and K. B. Armitage. 1972. Some quantitative aspects of the behavior of marmots. *Transactions of the Kansas Academy of Science* 75: 308–321.

Trefry, S. A., and D. S. Hik. 2009. Eavesdropping on the neighbourhood: Collared pika (*Ochotona collaris*) responses to playback calls of conspecifics and heterospecifics. *Ethology* 115: 928–938.

———. 2010. Variation in pika (*Ochotona collaris, O. princeps*) vocalizations within and between populations. *Ecography* 33: 784–795.

Trewhella, K. E., S. R. Leather, and K. R. Day. 1997. Insect induced resistance in lodgepole pine: Effects on two pine feeding insects. *Journal of Applied Entomology* 121: 129–136.

Trivers, R. L. 1971. The evolution of reciprocal altruism. *Quarterly Review of Biology* 46: 35–57.

———. 1972. Parental investment and sexual selection. In *Sexual selection and the descent of man*, edited by B. Campbell, 136–179. Chicago: Aldine.

———. 1985. *Social evolution*. Menlo Park, CA: Benjamin/Cummings.

Trumble, J. T., D. M. Kolodny-Hirsch, and I. P. Ting. 1993. Plant compensation for arthropod herbivory. *Annual Review of Entomology* 38: 93–119.

Trut, L. N., I. Z. Plyusnina, and I. N. Oskina. 2004. An experiment on fox domestication and debatable issues of evolution of the dog. *Russian Journal of Genetics* 40: 644–655.

Turlure, C., J. Choutt, M. Baguette, and H. Van Dyck. 2010. Microclimatic buffering and resource-based habitat in a glacial relict butterfly: Significance for conservation under climate change. *Global Change Biology* 16: 1883–1893.

Turner, F. J. 1921. *The frontier in American history*. New York: Henry Holt.

Turner, M. G., W. H. Romme, R. H. Gardner, and W. W. Hargrove. 1997. Effects of fire size and pattern on early succession in Yellowstone National Park. *Ecological Monographs* 67: 411–433.

Ulrich, T. J. 1984. *Birds of the Northern Rockies*. Missoula, MT: Mountain Press.

Vail, S. G. 1992. Selection for overcompensatory plant responses to herbivory: A mechanism for the evolution of plant-herbivore mutualism. *American Naturalist* 139: 1–8.

Valentine, D. W., and M. Soule. 1973. Effects of p,p'-DDT on developmental stability of pectoral fin rays in the grunion, *Leuresthes tenuis*. *Fisheries Bulletin* 71: 921–926.

Van der Meijden, E., M. Wijn, and H. J. Verkaar. 1988. Defence and regrowth, alternative plant strategies in the struggle against herbivores. *Oikos* 51: 355–363.

van der Vaart, E., R. Verbrugge, and C. K. Hemelrijk. 2011. Corvid caching: Insights from a cognitive model. *Journal of Experimental Psychology, Animal Behavior Proceedings* 37: 330–340.

Vander Wall, S. B. 1982. An experimental analysis of cache recovery in Clark's nutcracker. *Animal Behaviour* 30: 84–94.

———. 1994. Removal of wind-dispersed pine seeds by ground-foraging vertebrates. *Oikos* 69: 125–132.

———. 2003. Effects of seed size of wind-dispersed pines (*Pinus*) on secondary seed dispersal and the caching behavior of rodents. *Oikos* 100: 25–34.

———. 2008. On the relative contributions of wind vs. animals to seed dispersal of four Sierra Nevada pines. *Ecology* 89: 1837–1849.

Vander Wall, S. B., and R .P. Balda. 1977. Coadaptations of the Clark's nutcracker and the pinon pine for efficient seed harvest and dispersal. *Ecological Monographs* 47: 89–111.

———. 1983. Remembrance of seeds stashed. *Natural History*, September, 60–65.

Vander Wall, S. B., and H. E. Hutchins. 1983. Dependence of Clark's nutcracker, *Nucifraga columbiana*, on conifer seeds during the postfledging period. *Canadian Field-Naturalist* 97: 208–214.

Van Dyke, F., and W. C. Klein. 1996. Response of elk to installation of oil wells. *Journal of Mammalogy* 77: 1028–1041.

Van Valen, L. 1962. A study of fluctuating asymmetry. *Evolution* 16: 125–142.

Van Vuren, D. H. 2001. Predation on yellow-bellied marmots (*Marmota flaviventris*). *American Midland Naturalist* 145: 94–100.

Van Vuren, D., and K. B. Armitage 1994. Survival of dispersing and philopatric yellow-bellied marmots: What is the cost of dispersal? *Oikos* 69: 179–181.

Varley, J. 1993. Research in Yellowstone. *BioScience* 43 (3): 3–4.

Varley, J. D., and P. Schullery. 1998. *Yellowstone fishes: Ecology, history, and angling in the park*. Mechanicsburg, PA: Stackpole Books.

Verpoorte, R. 1998. Exploration of nature's chemodiversity: The role of secondary metabolites as leads in drug development. *Drug Discovery Today* 3: 232–238.

Vogel, S. 2003. *Comparative biomechanics: Life's physical world*. Princeton, NJ: Princeton University Press.

von Elsner-Schack, I. 1986. Habitat use by mountain goats, *Oreamnos americanus*, on the eastern slopes region of the Rocky Mountains at Mount Hamell, Alberta. *Canadian Field-Naturalist* 100: 319–324.

Voss, S. R., and H. B. Shaffer. 1997. Adaptive evolution via a major gene effect: Paedomorphosis in the Mexican axolotl. *Proceedings of the National Academy of Sciences of the United States of America* 94: 14185–14189.

Waddington, K. D. 1983. Foraging behavior of pollinators. In *Pollination biology*, edited by L. Real, 213–239. Orlando, FL: Academic Press.

Wagner, D., P. Doak, and A. Watson. 2007. Variable extrafloral nectar expression and its consequences in quaking aspen. *Canadian Journal of Botany* 85: 1–9.

Wagner, F. H. 1994. Scientist says Yellowstone Park is being destroyed. *High Country News*, May 30, 14–15.

Waldman, B. 1982. Sibling association among schooling toad tadpoles: Field evidence and implications. *Animal Behaviour* 30: 700–713.

———. 1984. Kin recognition and sibling association among wood frog (*Rana sylvatica*) tadpoles. *Behavioral Ecology and Sociobiology* 14: 171–180.

———. 1986. Preference for unfamiliar siblings over familiar non-siblings in American toad (*Bufo americanus*) tadpoles. *Animal Behaviour* 34: 48–53.

———. 1987. Mechanisms of kin recognition. *Journal of Theoretical Biology* 128: 159–185.

———. 1988. The ecology of kin recognition. *Annual Review of Ecology and Systematics* 19: 543–571.

Waldman, B., and K. Adler. 1979. Toad tadpoles associate preferentially with siblings. *Nature* 282: 611–613.

Waldman, B., P. C. Frumhoff, and P. W. Sherman. 1988. Problems of kin recognition. *Trends in Ecology and Evolution* 3: 8–13.

Walker, B. S. 1973. *The great divide*. New York: American Wilderness/Time-Life Books.

Wallace, L. L., and S. A. Macko. 1993. Nutrient acquisition by clipped plants as a measure of competitive success: The effects of compensation. *Functional Ecology* 7: 326–331.

Wallace, R. L., and L. V. Diller. 1990. Feeding ecology of the rattlesnake, *Crotalus viridis oreganus*, in northern Idaho. *Journal of Herpetology* 24: 246–253.

Waller, J. S., and R. D. Mace. 1997. Grizzly bear habitat selection in the Swan Mountains, Montana. *Journal of Wildlife Management* 61: 1032–1039.

Wallis, C. M., R. W. Reich, K. J. Lewis, and D. P. W. Huber. 2010. Lodgepole pine provenances differ in chemical defense capacities against foliar and stem diseases. *Canadian Journal of Forest Research* 40: 2333–2344.

Waltz, E. C. 1982. Alternative mating tactics and the law of diminishing returns: The satellite threshold model. *Behavioral Ecology and Sociobiology* 10: 75–83.

Waltz, E. C., and L. L. Wolf. 1984. By jove!! Why do alternative mating tactics assume so many different forms? *American Zoologist* 24: 333–343.

———. 1998. Alternative mating tactics in male white-faced dragonflies (*Leucor-rhinia intacta*): Plasticity of tactical options and consequences for reproductive success. *Evolutionary Ecology* 2: 205–231.

Wan, X., V. J. Lieffers, and P. S. Chow. 2010. Nitrate stimulates root suckering in trembling aspen (*Populus tremuloides*). *Canadian Journal of Forest Research* 40: 1962–1969.

Wang, G. G. 2003. Early regeneration and growth dynamics of *Populus tremuloides* suckers in relation to fire severity. *Canadian Journal of Forest Research* 33: 1998–2006.

Warrick, D. R. 2009. Lift production in the hovering hummingbird. *Proceedings of the Royal Society B: Biological Sciences* 276: 3747–3752.

Wassink, J. 1991. *Birds of the Central Rockies*. Missoula, MT: Mountain Press.

Watson, P. J., and R. Thornhill. 1994. Fluctuating asymmetry and sexual selection. *Trends in Ecology and Evolution* 9: 21–25.

Watt, W. B., F. S. Chew, L. R. G. Snyder, A. G. Watt, and D. E. Rothschild. 1977. Population structure of pierid butterflies. I. Numbers and movements of some montane *Colias* species. *Oecologia* 27: 1–22.

Wayne, R. K., W. S. Modi, and S. J. O'Brien. 1986. Morphological variability and asymmetry in the cheetah (*Acinonyx jubatus*), a genetically uniform species. *Evolution* 40: 78–85.

Weeden, R. B. 1967. Seasonal and geographic variation in the foods of adult white-tailed ptarmigan. *Condor* 69: 303–309.

Weidenmuller, A., C. Kleineidam, and J. Tautz. 2002. Collective control of nest climate parameters in bumblebee colonies. *Animal Behaviour* 63: 1065–1071.

Weisz, P. B. 1963. *The science of biology*. 2nd ed. New York: McGraw-Hill.

Weixelman, J. O. 2001. Fear or reverence? Native Americans and the geysers of Yellowstone. *Yellowstone Science*, Fall, 2–11.

Welch, K. C. 2011. The power of feeder-mask respirometry as a method for examining hummingbird energetics. *Comparative Biochemistry and Physiology Part A: Molecular and Integrative Physiology* 158: 276–286.

Welch, K. C., Jr., D. L. Altshuler, and R. K. Suarez. 2007. Oxygen consumption rates in hovering hummingbirds reflect substrate-dependent differences in P/O ratios: Carbohydrate as a "premium fuel." *Journal of Experimental Biology* 210: 2146–2153.

Welch, K. C., Jr., B. H. Bakken, C. M. del Rio, and R. K. Suarez. 2006. Hummingbirds fuel hovering flight with newly ingested sugar. *Physiological and Biochemical Zoology* 79: 1082–1087.

Welch, K. C., Jr., and R. K. Suarez. 2007. Oxidation rate and turnover of ingested sugar in hovering Anna's (*Calypte anna*) and rufous (*Selasphorus rufus*) hummingbirds. *Journal of Experimental Biology* 210: 2154–2162.

Welty, J. C. 1962. *The life of birds.* Philadelphia: W. B. Saunders.

————. 1982. *The life of birds.* 3rd ed. Philadelphia: Saunders College Publishing.

West Eberhard, M. J. 1975. The evolution of social behavior by kin selection. *Quarterly Review of Biology* 50: 1–33.

Wetterer, J. K. 1989. Central place foraging theory: When load size affects travel time. *Theoretical Population Biology* 36: 267–280.

Whitaker, J. O., Jr. 1980. *The Audubon Society field guide to North American mammals.* New York: Alfred A. Knopf.

White, D., Jr., K. C. Kendall, and H. D. Picton. 1998. Grizzly bear feeding activity at alpine army cutworm moth aggregation sites in northwest Montana. *Canadian Journal of Zoology* 76: 221–227.

————. 1999. Potential energetic effects of mountain climbers on foraging grizzly bears. *Wildlife Society Bulletin* 27: 146–151.

White, K. S., G. W. Pendleton, D. Crowley, H. J. Griese, K. J. Hundertmark, T. McDonough, L. Nichols, M. Robus, C. A. Smith, and J. W. Schoen. 2011. Mountain goat survival in coastal Alaska: Effects of age, sex, and climate. *Journal of Wildlife Management* 75: 1731–1744.

Whitehead, D. R. 1983. Wind pollination: Some ecological and evolutionary perspectives. In *Pollination biology*, edited by L. Real, 97–108. Orlando, FL: Academic Press.

Whitney, H. M., L. Chittka, T. J. A. Bruce, and B. J. Glover. 2009. Conical epidermal cells allow bees to grip flowers and increase foraging efficiency. *Current Biology* 19: 948–953.

Whitney, S. 1998. *Western forests: A National Audubon Society nature guide.* New York: Alfred A. Knopf.

Whittaker, R. H., and P. P. Feeny. 1971. Allelochemics: Chemical interactions between species. *Science* 171: 757–770.

Wiegmann, D. D., D. A. Wiegmann, and F. A. Waldron. 2003. Effects of a reward downshift on the consummatory behavior and flower choices of bumblebee foragers. *Physiology and Behavior* 79: 561–566.

Wiens, J. A. 1995. Habitat fragmentation: Island v. landscape perspectives on bird conservation. *Ibis* 137 (Supplement S1): S97–S104.

Wilbur, H. M., and J. P. Collins. 1973. Ecological aspects of amphibian metamorphosis. *Science* 182: 1305–1314.

Wilcox, B. A. 1986. Extinction models and conservation. *Trends in Ecology and Evolution* 1: 46–48.

Wilkening, J. L., C. Ray, E. A. Beever, and P. F. Brussard. 2011. Modeling contemporary range retraction in Great Basin pikas (*Ochotona princeps*) using data on microclimate and microhabitat. *Quaternary International* 235: 77–88.

Williams, A. G., and T. G. Whitham. 1986. Premature leaf abscission: An induced plant defense against gall aphids. *Ecology* 67: 1619–1627.

Williams, E. H. 1995. Fire-burned habitat and reintroductions of the butterfly *Euphydryas gillettii* (Nymphalidae). *Journal of the Lepidopterists' Society* 49: 183–191.

Williams, G. C. 1966. *Adaptation and natural selection: A critique of some current evolutionary thought*. Princeton, NJ: Princeton University Press.

Williams, J. S. 1999. Compensatory reproduction and dispersal in an introduced mountain goat population in central Montana. *Wildlife Society Bulletin* 27: 1019–1024.

Williamson, M. 1989. Natural extinctions on islands. *Philosophical Transactions of the Royal Society of London B* 325: 457–468.

Wilson, E. O. 1975. *Sociobiology: The new synthesis*. Cambridge, MA: Harvard University Press.

———. 2012. *The social conquest of Earth*. New York: Liveright.

Wilson, E. O., and E. O. Willis. 1975. Applied biogeography. In *Ecology and evolution of communities*, edited by M. L. Cody and J. M. Diamond, 522–534. Cambridge, MA: Harvard University Press.

Winnie, J., Jr. 1996 *High life: Animals of the alpine world*. Flagstaff, AZ: Northland.

Wissinger, S. A., H. H. Whiteman, M. Denoel, M. L. Mumford, and C. B. Aubee. 2010. Consumptive and nonconsumptive effects of cannibalism in fluctuating age-structured populations. *Ecology* 91: 549–559.

Witjes, S., K. Witsch, and T. Eltz. 2011. Reconstructing the pollinator community and predicting seed set from hydrocarbon footprints on flowers. *Oecologia* 166: 161–174.

Wong, M. M. L., B. C. Fedy, S. Wilson, and K. M. Martin. 2009. Adoption in rock and white-tailed ptarmigan. *Wilson Journal of Ornithology* 121: 638–641.

Woodroffe, R., and J. R. Ginsberg. 1998. Edge effects and the extinction of populations inside protected areas. *Science* 280: 2126–2128.

Wooley, S. C., J. R. Donaldson, A. C. Gusse, R. L. Lindroth, and M. T. Stevens. 2007. Extrafloral nectaries in aspen (*Populus tremuloides*): Heritable genetic variation and herbivore-induced expression. *Annals of Botany* 100: 1337–1346.

Wooley, S. C., S. Walker, J. Vernon, and R. L. Lindroth. 2008. Aspen decline, aspen chemistry, and elk herbivory: Are they linked? Aspen chemical ecology can inform the discussion of aspen decline in the West. *Rangelands* 30: 17–21.

Young, B. A., and I. P. Brown. 1995. The physical basis of the rattling sound in the rattlesnake *Crotalus viridis oreganus*. *Journal of Herpetology* 29: 80–85.

Zahavi, A. 1975. Mate selection: A selection for a handicap. *Journal of Theoretical Biology* 53: 205–214.

Zahavi, A., and A. Zahavi. 1997. *The handicap principle: A missing piece of Darwin's puzzle*. New York: Oxford University Press.

Zedrosser, A., B. Dahle, O.-G. Stoen, and J. E. Swenson. 2009. The effects of
    primiparity on reproductive performance in the brown bear. *Oecologia* 160:
    847–854.
Ziemba, R. E., and J. P. Collins. 1999. Development of size structure in tiger
    salamanders: The role of intraspecific interference. *Oecologia* 120: 524–529.
Ziemba, R. E., M. T. Myers, and J. P. Collins. 2000. Foraging under the risk of
    cannibalism leads to divergence in body size among tiger salamander larvae.
    Oecologia 124: 225–231.
Zimma, B. O., M. Ayasse, J. Tengo, F. Ibarra, C. Schulz, and W. Francke. 2003.
    Do social parasitic bumblebees use chemical weapons? (Hymenoptera,
    Apidae). *Journal of Comparative Physiology A* 189: 769–775.
Zvereva, E. L., M. V. Kozlov, P. Niemela, and E. Haukioja. 1997. Delayed
    induced resistance and increase in leaf fluctuating asymmetry as responses of
    Salix borealis to insect herbivory. *Oecologia* 109: 368–373.

Index

abandonment, of grizzly bear cubs, 212
Absaroka Range (Wyoming), 258
adaptation: and antiherbivore strategies of plants, 24–34, 67; of mountain goats
  to extreme alpine environments, 214–26; for micromanagement of energy in
  hummingbirds, 148–60; overcompensation of plants in response to grazing
  as, 49; and predatory behaviors of western rattlesnake, 127–35; and recurring
  strategies for survival through winter, 254–55; and responses of plants to grazing, 49; and secondary compounds in modern plants, 32; and semiparasitism
  of paintbrush plants, 36–39; and significance of size of elk antlers, 227–38;
  synthesis of alkaloids by lupines as dynamic, 34; and theory of natural
  selection, 7; white-tailed ptarmigan as example of evolutionary convergence
  of metabolic, 136–47; winter environment of pika and morphological, 166.
  See also evolution and evolutionary biology; natural selection
Adena/Hopewell culture, 247
Admiralty Island (Alaska), 204
adoption: by grizzly bears, 200, 212–13; by white-tailed ptarmigans, 143
aerodynamics, of hummingbird flight, 154–55
aesthetics, and biodiversity, 261
African wild dog, 212
age: and aggression in mountain goats, 222; of aspen clones, 61, 64; of leaders of
  gray wolf packs, 197; and mating tactics of mountain goats, 218; and predatory
  skills of gray wolf, 191; and survival of mountain goats, 223
aggression: and dominance relationships of mountain goats, 222; by dominant
  male elk, 231; and falling injuries to mountain goats, 224; of pikas, 166; and
  social behavior of yellow-bellied marmots, 179, 180, 181
Ailes, Nancy, 4, 11, 21, 35, 50, 57, 82, 94, 123, 136, 161, 173, 199, 200, 227, 239, 252, 258
Åland Islands (Finland), 99, 102–3
alarm signals: and aggregations of boreal toad tadpoles, 117; of hoary marmots,
  163, 174; of pikas, 163; of yellow-bellied marmots, 182–86. *See also* communication
Alaska: diet of grizzly bears in, 204; and geographic range of aspen, 58; and
  willows as winter diet of ptarmigans, 145
Albion, Mount (Colorado), 248

About The Author

Born on the mid-Atlantic coastal plain (Washington, DC), George Constantz spent six years of his childhood among the iguanas of the Magdalena River's flooded forests (Barranquilla, Colombia) and chasing roadrunners through the Chihuahuan Desert (Chihuahua, Mexico). Since receiving a BA in biology in the northern foothills of the Ozark Highlands (University of Missouri–St. Louis, east-central Missouri) and a PhD in zoology in the Sonoran Desert (Arizona State University, Tempe, central Arizona), he has worked as a park naturalist, fish ecologist, and river conservationist. George's first book was *Hollows, Peepers, and Highlanders: An Appalachian Mountain Ecology*. He lives with his wife, Nancy Ailes, on a small farm in the Cacapon River watershed of the Ridge and Valley Province in the central Appalachians (northeastern West Virginia).